Wordsworthian Errancies

Wordsworthian Errancies

❧ The Poetics of Cultural Dismemberment

DAVID COLLINGS

The Johns Hopkins University Press · Baltimore and London

© 1994 The Johns Hopkins University Press
All rights reserved
Printed in the United States of America on acid-free paper

The Johns Hopkins University Press
2715 North Charles Street
Baltimore, Maryland 21218-4319
The Johns Hopkins University Press Ltd., London

ISBN 0-8018-4848-2

Library of Congress Cataloging-in-Publication Data will be found
at the end of this book.

A catalog record for this book is available from the British Library.

for Terri

No social project worthy of the name has ever really existed . . . in the end no group has ever really conceived itself as social, that is to say in solidarity with its own values and coherent in its collective project, in short, there has never been even the shadow nor the embryo of a responsible collective subject, nor even the possibility of an objective of this kind.

— JEAN BAUDRILLARD

Society is an ultimate impossibility, an impossible object.

— ERNESTO LACLAU

Human sexuality is constituted as a kind of psychic shattering, as a threat to the stability and integrity of the self—a threat which perhaps only the masochistic nature of sexual pleasure allows us to survive.

— LEO BERSANI

Contents

Acknowledgments

I owe a great debt to Jean-Pierre Mileur, who introduced me to Romantic poetry, challenged me with the insights of literary theory, inspired me with his own writing, directed my first project on Wordsworth, and has patiently supported me as my argument has taken a new and rather different form. Without his influence and encouragement, I would never have written this book. I owe an equal debt to Carole Fabricant, who exemplifies, both in her teaching and in her activism, the engaged intellectual and unceasingly reminds me of the political responsibilities of the critic. I hope this book begins to do justice to the powerful combination of concerns that is their shared legacy to me.

Many others have influenced this project over the years. Robert Essick and John Steadman read the dissertation and gave me many useful suggestions. Jerome Christensen's brilliant seminar on the careers of Coleridge and Byron at Johns Hopkins during the summer of 1989 introduced me to several modes of interpretation which, combined with the concerns I mentioned above, enabled me to get a new start on the book. Students in several seminars at Bowdoin College forced me to sharpen my arguments, playing a much larger role than they suspected. Chris Castiglia and Chris Reed made me far more aware than before of the intellectual and political reach of queer theory. Helen Robbins suggested possible revisions on an early draft of Chapter Three. Gordon Taylor and James Watson invited me to present a version of Chapter Three at the University of Tulsa, and several members of that audience, especially Holly Laird, challenged me with thoughtful responses. Lucinda Cole and Rick Swartz gave me valuable feedback during the project's later stages. Kidder Smith read the introduction from a refreshing perspective. And the anonymous reader at Johns Hopkins helped me immensely in the final stage of revision.

I can hardly begin to name all of the teachers, friends, and colleagues at Pacific Union College, the University of California, Riverside, the University of Tulsa, and Bowdoin College who have shaped my thinking, my teaching, and my life in countless ways. I am especially indebted to my colleagues Franklin Burroughs, Celeste Goodridge, Joseph Litvak, and Ann Kibbie, who encouraged me as this project neared completion.

The Junior Leave program at Bowdoin College gave me the opportunity to complete most of the manuscript during the 1990–1991 school year. Without such generous support, this project would never have borne fruit.

Finally, I thank Terri Nickel for her rigorous responses to the manuscript at every stage, for her constantly provocative intellectual presence, and most of all for the joy of her companionship throughout these years.

A portion of Chapter Five was published as "A Vocation of Error: Authorship as Deviance in the 1799 *Prelude*" in *Papers on Language and Literature* 29 (1993): 215–35. I presented a version of Chapter Six at the Modern Language Convention, December 1991, in San Francisco, and another version of that chapter has appeared as "Covenant in Hyperbole: The Disruption of Tradition in Michael," *Studies in Romanticism* 32 (1993).

Wordsworthian Errancies

Introduction

✦ Consider four of Wordsworth's texts, written around 1793, 1798–99, and 1804. A solitary traveler is compelled to leave all signs of humanity behind and journey into the absolute night of tempests, into the region of the unbearable violence of human sacrifice, and then seeks refuge in a lonely spital haunted by the ghost of a murdered man (*Salisbury Plain*). A wandering child stumbles off the beaten path onto the scene of murder and punishment, and in the following episode, pleasurably anticipating a similar scene of violence, takes refuge on a summit overlooking the crossroads (the spots of time of the 1799 *Prelude*). A tourist in the Alps takes the wrong path, witnesses the apocalyptic disfiguration of nature, and then spends a sleepless night in a hotel, stunned with the sounds of rivers that meet nearby (the Simplon Pass episode of *The Prelude* Book 6). A visitor in Paris, disturbed by the unreadable violence of the September Massacres he associates with the Square of the Carousel, retreats to a high room in a nearby hotel, where he imagines that the violence has forever disturbed the world's sleep (*Prelude* Book 10).[1]

The rich interpretive traditions that surround these episodes touch on a wide variety of concerns, including the history of antiwar poetry in England, the *mise en scène* of the autobiographical text, the oedipal dynamics of these renditions of childhood trauma, the sublime, and the generic shapelessness of Wordsworth's account of the French Revolution. Yet even this elliptical and tendentious recital of passages that Wordsworth wrote for very different purposes suggests that they rely upon the same underlying figural structure. Whether the poet deplores the violence (as in *Salisbury Plain* and the September Massacres episode) or celebrates its sublimity (as in the spots of time and the Simplon Pass episode), whether he describes the wandering solitary as himself or another, he consistently deploys an internally coherent set of terms: the turn onto the wrong path, unreadable or disfiguring violence, the crossroads, the uninhabitable shelter. Rather than inscribing eighteenth-century aesthetics, radical politics, or Enlightenment philosophy in poetic form, Wordsworth reworks them within his own terms; his discussions of the body politic, the mind, or art inevitably expand upon a tropological dynamic with a logic of its own.

These texts obey this logic not because they are founded upon a body of knowledge which supersedes all other discourses but rather because they emerge from the conviction that something has suspended the process whereby discourse constitutes itself in the first place. Certain readers might be tempted to argue, then, that these texts demonstrate how they are undone by a rhetorical or tropological instability characteristic of literary language. But for Wordsworth figuration is never entirely a matter of the commonplaces and tropes of the literary text, the interplay of terms on its rhetorical surface; he writes as if the primary figural structure is not language but culture. (Here and throughout the book *culture* refers not to the question of intellectual cultivation or Arnoldian refinement but rather to that of the institutional structure of human societies.)

This much is already clear in several passages I mentioned above. For example, Wordsworth renders the instability of the inside/outside opposition as the ruined building, the shelter that does not shelter, a product of culture which can no longer protect its inhabitants from the ravages of nature. In the absence of a clear boundary between itself and nature, the shelter begins to resemble the threshold, the indeterminate space where the inside and the outside, culture and nature, become interchangeable. For Wordsworth, to collapse language's originary oppositions is to profane the rites that give cultural structures a firm foundation. This link becomes explicit in some passages; Wordsworth describes the violence of the September Massacres as an unreadable text, suggesting that culture itself is a text that has been disfigured by violence. Here and elsewhere, Wordsworth does not clearly distinguish between the unraveling of language and the undoing of the cultural order.

Wordsworth's insistence that figuration is primarily cultural affiliates him with a certain tradition in twentieth-century cultural theory. Jacques Lacan, inheriting and adapting the work of Claude Levi-Strauss, argues that the structures of kinship operate like a language: "The marriage tie is governed by an order of preference whose law concerning the kinship names is, like language, imperative for the group in its forms, but unconscious in its structure." Kinship is a language in which people, rather than words, are exchanged for each other, become figures for each other. No longer located in a written text, language reappears as what Lacan calls the symbolic order, the "primordial Law" that structures identity, gender roles, and marriage alliances (*Écrits* 66). In this passage Lacan also builds upon the work of Marcel Mauss, who demonstrates that gift exchange operates as a system of obligations, whereby anyone who receives a gift incurs an obligation to give to a third party (Mauss 22). In this system, a gift is at once possession and debt; property, like the Lacanian name, is at once one's own and something received from, and owed to, another. Thus property relations are also structured like a language and belong to the symbolic order (cf. Goux 88–133). Finally, insofar as Lacan describes the incest taboo as a primordial Law imposed in the name of the "dead Father" (*Écrits* 66, 199), he evokes Freud's theory of the primordial murder of the father and evokes a theory of sacrifice which he never explicitly articulates. He thus indirectly brings into play the work of René Girard, who contests Freud and Lacan but nevertheless provides an account of sacrifice which converges with their theories on several points. According to Girard, on ritual occasions culture suspends the law, mimetically reenacts the primordial crisis, and then, via the symbolic violence of sacrifice, reestablishes the law and the entire system of social differentiation (*Violence* 89–103). Apparently culture cannot assert its official character without restaging the entire process of its origination, without mimetically destroying the symbolic order and constructing it anew.

Taken together, these authors provide a largely consistent theory of the figural dynamic of archaic culture. Such a theory is immensely useful for reading Wordsworth, for again and again he evokes an elemental model of culture. To borrow a phrase from Stephen Greenblatt, one could say that Wordsworth's is a "poetics of culture," a "study of the collective making of distinct cultural practices and inquiry into the relations among these practices" (5). But Wordsworth, taking for granted that an elementary poetics of culture has already been formulated, plays off its basic forms, disfigures its constitutive terms, and thus fashions what I will call a poetics of cultural dismemberment. Although such a poetics could remain frozen in the moment of disruption, in the shock of pure unintelligibility, Wordsworth instead attempts to make unreadability readable, to discern a practice in what violates practices, and to make a collective out of the undoing of the collective. In effect, he attempts to write a culture that survives in the form of its own destruction.

The exemplary figure of such a duplicitous poetics is the wandering male solitary who, in straying from the proper path, may or may not arrive at the goal of his quest. In rhetorical terms, this figure is errancy or hyperbole. As Jean-Pierre Mileur argues, "hyperbole is not just the language of heights aspired to and depths fallen to; it is also the language of detours, of exaggeration, errancy, extra-vagance. And just as . . . hyperbolic depths are perspectivally indistinguishable from hyperbolic heights, so are wanderings from the true path indistinguishable from true quests" (*Romance* 31–32). They are indistinguishable because one cannot know whether the wanderer strays beyond the law into the sublime or outside it into a world of violence—whether into transcendence or destruction. Once the wanderer goes beyond the familiar conceptual enclosure, its terms can no longer name or judge his quest; apparent opposites, such as heights and depths, become near-synonyms in a logic that confounds the system of differences (cf. *Romance* 32). (Here and throughout this book I make Wordsworth's ruthlessly androcentric practice explicit by using the masculine pronoun in reference to the figures in his work.)

At first, the trope of errancy or hyperbole seems to rework a familiar interpretation of the solitary who wanders through the landscape in search of the sublime. But in fact, this figure captures one of the most unsettling features of romance. As soon as the solitary errs from the proper path, he loses the ability to distinguish between the true and false path; accordingly, he no longer knows whether he strays or has returned to the true path, whether he is outside or inside culture. He cannot tell the difference between crime and the law, between hyperbole and the proper. No wonder it is so difficult to find an instance in Wordsworth's texts of a society where the law reigns, of a proper path from which to stray. In effect, then, errancy becomes the condition of the entire social order, which is at once beyond and outside the law, transcending and destroying itself, joining with the sublime and returning to the state of nature. What Mileur says of the wanderer applies just as well to culture; in its hyperbolic form, it cannot distinguish revolutionary transformation from dismemberment, new beginning from apocalyptic end.

In the texts I discuss in this book, Wordsworth consistently exploits the indeterminacy of hyperbole in order to rework the figures that constitute culture. The buildings meant to protect people from nature collapse into the earth; intended to defend their inhabitants from hostile strangers, they become the site of murder, the haunt of those made homeless by violence. The kinship system designed to provide each subject with a name and identity dissolves, leaving each little more than the darkness of a nameless subjectivity. As a result, society becomes a collective of solitaries who cannot distinguish themselves from each other. Deprived of any familiar mode of social relations, they encounter each other with extraordinary anxiety, regarding the other both as the rival and as a double of the self (e.g., the gibbet scene of *Adventures on Salisbury Plain;* "The Discharged Soldier"). The family fractures; the errant father strays from home, and the abandoned wife, like her cottage, gradually disappears into the speargrass

(*Ruined Cottage*). Whether an act of charity or a testament of the patrimonial lands, often the gift is not even accepted, much less passed on, and property, no longer possessed in the usual way, becomes uncanny ("The Discharged Soldier"; "Michael"). Refusing to accept the name of the father, the errant son takes a masochistic pleasure in the threat of castration, at times attempting to provoke the father to punish him violently (the 1799 *Prelude*, Part One). As sacred rituals cease to be efficacious, sacrifice devolves back into the literal, murderous violence it was supposed to prevent (*Salisbury Plain*). The memorials that were to honor the dead collapse into a straggling heap, marking instead the failure to remember or to bury the dead ("Michael"). Even nature, that final defense against the void, turns out to be indistinguishable from the deluge that has wrenched its surface and will do so again (the 1805 *Prelude*). In certain texts, Wordsworth achieves a radical negativity, reducing culture to a rupture in nature. Consciousness becomes sheer excess, something utterly out of place in the landscape ("Incipient Madness"; "The Thorn").

Such a relentless dismantling of culture has its effects upon the language of these texts. Neither a means of intelligibility nor of unintelligibility, at times (particularly in the Salisbury Plain poems, "Goody Blake," and "The Thorn") they become machines of syntax which run on the various possibilities of meter and rhyme, the abstract combination of sound with sound, speaking with silence. Theirs is a nonsignifying yet articulate language, hovering on the threshold between nonsense and meaning. Poems that begin with questions never quite answer them (*Prelude*); those that seem to promise a narrative resolution suspend closure in the endless repetition of a tale without beginning or end (*Adventures on Salisbury Plain; Borderers*).

Wordsworth refigures culture in such precise ways that one suspects he is working within a particular tradition of thinking about culture. Alan Bewell demonstrates that Wordsworth engages the thinking of the Enlightenment philosophers of the eighteenth century, those who speculated upon the origins and history of culture, mythology, language, death, and the earth. Like many poets before him, he intended to speculate in his own right in an encyclopedic poem, *The Recluse*, which was to set forth a comprehensive statement on the familiar subjects of moral philosophy— on man, nature, and human life. Although he never finished this vast project, it continued to be his "governing intention" as a poet and shaped the concerns of many of his shorter lyrics, which implicitly take up many problems in the history of culture (1–47). Similarly, many scholars (including Z. S. Fink, Kenneth MacLean, Leslie Chard, Raymond Williams, John Williams, J. G. A. Pocock, David Simpson, and Nigel Leask) demonstrate in various ways that Wordsworth inherits and reworks the political language of the neo-Harringtonian Real Whigs or Commonwealthmen of eighteenth-century England. The antiministerial rhetoric of rustic virtue informs Wordsworth's writing from "A Letter to the Bishop of Llandaff" through the Preface to *Lyrical Ballads* and the later prose tracts, from the Salisbury Plain poems through *The Prelude* and beyond. This way of reading of Wordsworth's career is allied with Bewell's, for over the course of the century certain British philosophers working in the Real Whig tradition—particularly those in the Scottish school—and Continental *philosophes* had considerable influence upon each other and adopted each other's characteristic concerns. Perhaps Wordsworth was both a recluse and a Real Whig, someone who intended his poetic *magnum opus* to be an encyclopedic defense of agrarian radicalism.

Despite his ambitions, Wordsworth resists this kind of pretension. Bewell argues that "Wordsworth's best poems had their genesis in his antagonism towards this philosophical model, in his attempt to write within and at the same time to displace, submerge, or repress the very paradigm that had initially authorized them" (5). If *The Recluse* is his intention, it is also his antiintention, the text against which he must write, the model of culture he must refuse. In much the same way, he sustains the Real Whig political tradition throughout his long career but also endlessly negates its idealizing vision of the rural community. Thus his poems as frequently deviate from philosophical and political as from generic norms. Unwilling to master the dissolution of culture or to recuperate it within a discourse of knowledge, he ends up suspending knowledge, dissolving even political and philosophical articulations of cultural dissolution.

Whence, then, does Wordsworth derive his poetics of culture? Does it stem from a historical experience, from a profoundly disorienting event? In *The Prelude*, Book 10, he writes that England's decision to go to war with revolutionary France meant "Change and subversion" not for his "single self alone" but for "the minds of all ingenuous Youth." Against his will, he was taken from his proper path and cast into "another region" (10.231–33, 238–41).[2] Yet no event could determine the way in which he registered that event in his writing. If it truly displaced him in the way he describes, it could have silenced him, confused him, or provoked him into an enraged response. Could it have begun, then, in an authorial crisis in which he lost the proper discourses in which to interpret contemporary events? Later in Book 10 Wordsworth describes how he pressed political and philosophical inquiry so far that they eventually discredited themselves and left him at a loss, without any legitimate discourse but mathematics (867–904). But by itself, such an authorial crisis would scarcely have prompted him to invent a viable poetics. The only plausible starting point for Wordsworth's career as a poet of hyperbole is neither a historical occasion (e.g., the war with France) nor a largely biographical response to it (a crisis) but an interpretive act, a decision to read culture as the scene of its own undoing.

This interpretation took shape over two stages. First, in texts such as *Salisbury Plain* he interprets the war as only one aspect of tyranny's generalized war upon the poor. Everything in culture, from the state and property relations to the law, conspired to uproot them, to deprive them of their livelihood, and eventually to kill them. This sort of culture, Wordsworth writes, is the same as its apparently barbaric opposite, human sacrifice. In this phase, he practices a hyperbolic politics, one that finds traces of oppression on every hand and effaces the specificity of complaint by generalizing the possible expressions of tyranny. Culture is so hopelessly cruel that one can only hope to eradicate it, to overturn it entirely with the discourses of Enlightenment. But in the second move, already implicit in the imagery of this poem, he recognizes the destabilizing force of such a hyperbolic stance, reading the rage with which he denounces tyranny as the mirror of the violence of tyranny itself; the discourses of opposition to the war are instances of what they would protest. Thus the site of disturbance is not war but rather errancy, a condition in which one cannot distinguish between one's total critique of a violent culture and one's longing to overturn it in total violence. Absolute tyranny and total Enlightenment are indistinguishable. Only with this gesture, which becomes clearer in the poem's revision as *Adventures on Salisbury Plain,* does Wordsworth equate true with false paths, the wanderer's innocence and his guilt, the shelter with the scene of crime, the exercise of law with a travesty of justice. Only in this move does poetry itself become a mode of reproducing trauma in the very discourse of protest against its causes. If this poet ever endured a crisis of total disorientation, he emerged from it by making it the basis of his poetics.

Thus the poetics of errancy, which apparently emerged in response to the outbreak of war, expands its concerns to include the disfigurement of British society as a whole. In fact, this interpretive act is so radical that it eclipses its occasion. Reading the war and crisis as aspects of an absolute threat to culture carries Wordsworth far beyond any political agenda toward a totalizing theory of culture identical with its undoing. War ceases to be a historically delimited product of politically interested decisions and becomes a total break, a sublime meta-event that takes place everywhere and nowhere, transforming culture into its opposite. As a result, one can no longer distinguish between the destruction and institution of culture, between the extraordinary violence of war and the ordinary functioning of the social order.

The poet's hyperbolic reading of cultural dislocation might seem to have cut him off from any familiar tradition and given him a poetics so errant that it was unreadable. Yet precisely in this apparent departure from discursive norms, this poetry joins the rather different tradition of Gothic excess. Although like most other discourses the Gothic finally emphasized the possible coherence of the social order, it nevertheless derived pleasure from those inexplicable events that effaced, for example, the difference between the living and the dead. On some level the literature of sensationalism had already begun to fashion a poetics of cultural dismemberment. Without its terms, Wordsworth could never have given culture's break from itself an intelligible form; with them, he can claim in *Salisbury Plain* that with the outbreak of war a demonic darkness engulfs the world, an absolute past invades the present, the dead assault the living, and the Druidical violence of human sacrifice dismembers the social body. More than a moral shock (*Prelude* 10.233–34), the war becomes the ultimate sensationalist moment, at once terrifying and pleasurable, of pure destruction.

By appropriating Gothic excess in this hyperbolic gesture, Wordsworth makes it into a crucial aspect of his poetics (cf. Swann "Transport"; "Suffering"). Over the years, he remains steeped in this tradition as he keeps up with popular fashions and reworks them freely for his own purposes. The Salisbury Plain poems play with the vogue of sentimental anti-war poetry, *The Borderers* with the new British interest in Continental sensationalist drama, and the *Lyrical Ballads* with several genres of magazine verse and translations of Bürger's supernaturalist ballads (Schulman 230–31; Thorslev; Parker "Spectacles"; Mayo; J. E. Jordan; Jacobus *Tradition* 184–261). In these and other texts, Wordsworth attempts to resist supernaturalism and to create an alternative poetics (Hartman *Unremarkable* 58–74; cf. Averill *Suffering*). Although resisting the Gothic, like certain of his contemporaries he transforms it into a subtle and perhaps even more uncanny discourse. Terry Castle argues that the ghosts that Ann Radcliffe explains away in *The Mysteries of Udolpho* (1794) reappear as the apparitions of loved ones who haunt the mind when they are dead or far away ("Spectralization"). Something similar happens in Wordsworth's texts, in which encounters with wandering apparitions or sightings of ghastly shapes in the landscape figure the mind's memory of its own actions or anticipations of its own fate. The supernatural becomes natural, the ghostly an aspect of the mind's invisible workings, and the uncanny a dimension of the canny or familiar. As a result, nature begins to seethe with the energies of the supernatural, the mind haunts itself like a ghost, and social relations be-come strange. This muted, pervasive ghostliness no longer threatens the symbolic order so openly that culture can respond to it with a narrative resolution or ritual expulsion; on the contrary, it poses an implicit threat from a place that remains perpetually out of reach. The disruption of the symbolic thus becomes a part of the ordinary functioning of culture, so thoroughly habitual that it can even provide the basis for the emergence of a new and uncanny social formation (as Wordsworth suggests in the Pref-ace to *Lyrical Ballads*). Culture begins to verge on the unnameable, as if it is founded not in the name of the dead father but in the experience of encountering his ghost. Once Wordsworth domesticates the supernatural and treats it as an aspect of ordinary experience, it becomes for him what psychoanalysis is for many modern readers: a way of interpreting what is alien in culture and in the self.

Wordsworth's Gothic, hyperbolic poetics has immense implications for his conception of masculine identity and sexuality. His totalizing inter-pretation of the war leads almost inevitably toward a conception of a radi-cally divided, masochistic subject. When he reads war as an absolute event, he makes it impossible for his hapless traveler to do anything but to submit to, and at least involuntarily to embrace, total violence. No longer given a name and identity by the symbolic order, the solitary wanderer can no longer tell himself apart from any other and, in the logic of the Lacanian imaginary, imagines the other as his own specular counterpart, at once his mirror image and rival. Much as culture survives in the mode of its own undoing, each male solitary embodies his own death; this wanderer is not so solitary after all, for he conceives of himself only through the image of his hostile counterpart, the corpse or ghost of the rival he killed. In a simi-lar way, the wanderer no longer lives according to the familiar paradigms of heterosexual desire. The vagrant will never make it back home to rejoin his abandoned wife, nor will he ever cease to be obsessed by trauma. Plea-sure and pain, mastery and subjection become indistinguishable. Words-worth explores several versions of this deviant sexuality in his texts: the ascetic renunciation of the body, the predatory haunting of another subjec-tivity (*Borderers*); the ascetic fantasy of suffering so greatly that one achieves a state beyond suffering (in several texts of 1797–98); the masochistic fan-tasy of revenge against the abandoning mother (*Ruined Cottage;* "The Thorn"); the homoerotic fantasy of taking pleasure in being punished by the father (the 1799 *Prelude*); and the nihilistic eroticism of taking pleasure in the world's loss (the 1805 *Prelude*). This dismembered culture, it turns out, is so spectacularly deviant that it takes pleasure in its traumatic con-dition.

The deviance of these male wanderers applies to Wordsworth the author as well. In the brilliantly outrageous 1799 *Prelude,* Part One, he suggests that he became a poet in those moments when he imagined that paternal presences in the landscape were about to wound him severely. Yet Wordsworth responds to his own deviant ecstasies with a certain ambivalence about errancy in general. If, as I have suggested, the self is indistinguishable from the other, then the poet fears that his poetic self may be alien to him, that he did not choose for hyperbole at all but was chosen by it in the moment when some unknown force invaded him. What results is a highly unstable rhetoric in which the poet at once claims a more than human privilege for himself and renounces hyperbolic poetics altogether. His attitude toward errancy is itself errant. At times he openly celebrates the pleasure of fearful visitations (Part One), the excitement of passionate repetition (the Note to "The Thorn"), and deviance from educational and philosophical discipline (*Prelude* Book 5); at others he lauches a political attack upon the profane violence of war (*Salisbury Plain*), attempts to domesticate errancy somewhat (the 1798 texts), and brings sublimity into the context of a philosophical and poetic closure (the ascent of Snowdon). All along, he works at cross-purposes both to sustain and dismantle culture; as a poet, he seems to be as self-divided and anxious as one of his solitaries.

This ambivalent Wordsworth is rather different from the one that usually emerges from studies of his poetry. Critics often agree that he writes a "humanizing" poetry or that his texts have very few sexual overtones. My emphases may arise from the fact that I base my readings upon the early manuscripts that the poet never published in that original form. By taking advantage of the scholarly industry that made those manuscripts available, I have contributed to the trend criticized by Jonathan Arac, who points out that such criticism inevitably constructs a private author who "has no relation to the 'Wordsworth' who figured in the arguments or perceptions of his contemporaries" (50–51). Although most of the texts I discuss did finally reach the light of day, whether in 1814, 1842, or 1850, Arac's point holds true; the poet I find here would have largely escaped the perceptions of his contemporaries. But literary history works both ways. If one reads the texts as they were written at a particular moment in cultural history, one can discern more powerfully how they are affiliated with the discourses ascendant at that moment than if one reads instead those versions published many decades later. One implicit goal of this study is to suggest that the poet's early work affiliates him far more than suspected with the Gothic discourses of the mid 1790s, with the excessive and sensationalist literature he ostensibly scorned.

To explore the poetics I have outlined here within the limits of a single book, I focus upon a rather narrow group of texts, written between 1793 and 1805, which deploys a consistent figural structure in ways that court, but ultimately resist, the logic of narrative. This means that I do not discuss a number of Wordsworth's lyrics, including most of the shorter poems in *Lyrical Ballads*, "Tintern Abbey," and the Intimations Ode, which unsettle discursive paradigms in somewhat different ways. Because of space limitations, I also do not discuss several texts of direct concern in my argument, including *Home at Grasmere*, "Resolution and Independence," Book 7 of *The Prelude*, and the Preface to *Lyrical Ballads*, Wordsworth's telling prose statement of his stance, which subtly fractures the political and social theories of such importance for the projected *Recluse*.[3] One of the key limits of this project is that it does not include readings of these texts, although the following chapters do take into account, albeit indirectly, the challenges that they pose.

To read Wordsworth in the way I have outlined here is to rethink several received interpretive traditions. For one thing, this study emerges from a loosely defined concern with errancy in writing about Wordsworth over the past two decades. Because of the variety of critical approaches to Wordsworth and the different terms that interpreters have used in evoking this quality, it has never been very clear that they have been writing about something remarkably similar, which appears in their work now as a theme, now as a rhetorical figure, now as an obsession or mood. Among the best discussions in this regard are Frances Ferguson's analysis of the errant passions (64–66) and the "noncoincidence of the subject with itself" in Wordsworthian memory (117, 122); Jerome Christensen's account of the way in which Wordsworth's texts, refusing final explanations, remain on the level of narrative or interpretive anxiety ("Sublime," "Misery"); Jonathan Wordsworth's emphasis upon the thematics of borders and of ghosts (*Borders*); Paul Jay's description of the interminable self-reflexiveness of Wordsworth's autobiography (38–91); Reeve Parker's treatment of "looseness" in "Michael" ("Finishing"); and Jean-Pierre Mileur's discussion of errancy throughout Wordsworth and in current antithetical theory (*Romance*). In the arguments that follow, I have attempted to bring such concerns together into an interpretive strategy that can move freely across various regions of Wordsworth's texts and trace within them the effects of a pervasive disfiguration.

This emphasis upon the vexatious dynamics of these texts might seem to place this book within the classical tradition of deconstruction. To a certain extent, this impression is correct, since this book owes a great deal to the de Manian tradition in Wordsworth criticism. One of de Man's projects, of course, was to carry out a critique of metaphor, of any figure that claims to substitute for its (referential) ground (*Allegories* 20–78, 135–59). Insofar as his *metaphor* resembles the founding trope of Lacan's symbolic order or what Girard describes as the ritual of sacred violence, this project implicates him in a critique of all such officializing rituals. This perspective on metaphor enables him and those he influenced less to deconstruct Wordsworth's texts than to describe how they already are instances of deconstruction. Such critics demonstrate, for example, that Wordsworth articulates the unreadability of the text and the ungrounded nature of trope; on this level, the work of de Manian critics (such as Isobel Armstrong, Timothy Bahti, Cathy Caruth, Cynthia Chase, Geraldine Friedman, J. Douglas Kneale, and Andrzej Warminski) are crucial for the readings below. Unfortunately, however, few of them discuss how their rhetorical analyses bear upon the figural strategies that constitute the social or cultural text. And since they tend to assume that Wordsworth's texts reveal the operation of rhetorical instability in general, few ask why or how Wordsworth became so invested in his own particular disfiguring project. To begin a historical reading of Wordsworth one has to point out the historical and social implications of de Manian deconstruction, to replace the "deconstructive abyss" with a "shocking and even painful" world, the fully anxious domain of a dangerous "cultural reality" (Litvak 145).

For the most part, then, in this book I subsume deconstruction into the enterprise of theorizing the dismemberment of culture. Surprisingly enough, there are ample resources for such an enterprise in the work of those theorists, often working in entire ignorance of each other, who discuss culture in the condition of war or total crisis. Lacan's theory of aggressivity in the imaginary order, Girard's account of the sacrificial crisis, and Elaine Scarry's discussion of the body in pain reinforce and supplement each other's work. Since Freud's discussion of war trauma in *Beyond the Pleasure Principle,* psychoanalysis has often explored the pleasures of violation, and accordingly this study calls upon the work of Jean Laplanche and Leo Bersani, theorists of masochistic sexuality.[4]

This shift from deconstruction to a theory of cultural trauma results in a surprisingly altered conception of the social order. Most analyses of the politics of literary texts quite rightly depend upon a stable series of oppositions between political stances or ideological positionings, distinguishing clearly between a given agenda and its opposition. Post-Derridean theory, of course, questions such a general practice, insofar as it challenges the sway of what it calls the binary opposition. Giving this critique a more precise and radical form, theorists of cultural dismemberment emphasize radical reversibility, demonstrating that any given term can readily metamorphose into its opposite. The self is another, the victor is the victim, and the hero is the criminal; to abandon is to be abandoned, to fear mutilation is to desire it, and (by extension) to dread disaster is to find it enchanting. The total refusal of culture is total complicity in its operation.

Although I use such theories, like de Man I tend to argue that a version of them already operates in Wordsworth's texts. This theoretical shift, then, in effect replaces the poet of figural sophistication with the impresario of enchanting disaster and makes it possible to demonstrate that he is far more outrageous than readers have generally recognized, that he not only champions deviance and a nearly overt homoeroticism but links them intimately with his status as a poet. It is time, I think, to admit that *imagination*—that deep, resonant innerness beloved of humanist criticism—is an alibi for the erotics of disorientation, the pleasures of the wound. Wordsworth derives his poetics not from the buoyant hopes of the French Revolution, as has often been claimed, but from the violence that shattered those hopes, experiencing the disfiguring event, no doubt, as a moral shock (*Prelude* 10.233–34) and also as a kind of unspeakable pleasure and the bestowal of an unnameable privilege. Much more than a war poet, then, he makes it difficult to distinguish between the destruction and the transfiguration of culture.

Yet the strong link between Wordsworth and those theorists whose work he anticipates suggests that one cannot read his poetry historically without beginning to question this entire theoretical tradition. It is not so far from certain moments in this poet to writers like Nietzsche, Artaud, Bataille, Foucault, and Derrida, to name one lineage, or to Freud, Lacan, Laplanche, and Bersani, to name another. If one chooses not to identify retrospectively with Wordsworth, to celebrate him as a prototype of the ideal avant-garde intellectual, then it may be better to interrogate the poetics of disaster and to ask whether a stance that repudiates all ideologies is not itself ideological. If in fact culture functions in the mode of its destruction, what kind of politics remains to us? What sort of hope can sustain a culture that has attained the knowledge of its constitutive violence, that sees even in its ordinary functioning the signs of trauma? The answer, I think, would be neither to reinstate the archaic symbolic order as a social practice nor to construct an even more radical refusal of culture, but rather to fashion a self-consciously fractured politics oriented by the partial and contingent conditions of the historical moment.

Although I cannot pursue this larger project here, I nevertheless intend this book to share the perspective of those theorists, such as Antonio

Gramsci, Mikhail Bakhtin, Ernesto Laclau, and Chantal Mouffe, who attack the totalizing, hyperbolic interpretations of culture in order to interpret it as the site of conflict among a host of different cultures, languages, discourses, and modes of power.[5] In their view, neither power nor transgression is ever absolute, for each is only a limited part of a wide array of competing forms of power or resistance. In my hopeful reading of their work, they demonstrate that a unanimous, unconscious consensus—through which our society has tended to conceive the social contract, the system of kinship exchange, the economy, and language—has never existed and that the primal crime, which supposedly led to the establishment of the symbolic order, never took place. Culture cannot be dismembered precisely because it never constituted a single body politic in the first place. It has always been the site of what Girard would call the routine violence of discursive conflict and battles for power; despite its endless appeal to ritual resolutions, it is never finally rid of profane contestation. Insisting that conflict is ineradicable, that culture takes shape in some way through profane violence, discredits power's claims to innocence without giving cause for a total critique of culture itself. Only from this perspective, I think, can one avoid either naturalizing culture or launching a potentially depoliticizing critique of all forms of social organization. And only in this way can one finally discern the limits of Wordsworth's hyperbolic stance and recognize, for example, that the outbreak of war with France did not threaten to undo culture but rather intensified the ordinary processes of political conflict.

Thus the critique of hyperbole applies just as well to Wordsworth's conception of deviant masculinity. To read the latter historically, of course, one would not interpret it according to psychoanalytic knowledge but rather place it within a genealogy of the perverse, one that at least potentially would link the Gothic, versions of Romanticism, and psychoanalysis. The focus of this study would not be to trace the history of any particular sexuality as it is normally understood but rather the eroticization of cultural crisis, the "decadence" whereby certain figures take pleasure in a real or imagined modernity. It may turn out that deviance, far from being a marginal discourse, is none other than the canonical tradition of British poetry for the last two centuries (cf. Donald 239) and that Wordsworth, who has long seemed the most decorous of poets in that tradition, is one of the most flaming deviants of them all.[6] If it is past time to celebrate what is unofficial or outrageous in his work, as I suggested above, it is also time to begin a critique of what may be a rather official tradition of disastrous sexuality.

The double movement of my argument—at once to celebrate and to interrogate a hyperbolic poetics—operates in regard to other concerns as well. Certain highly influential new historicist critics, for example, have generated a debate concerning the level of historical engagement in Wordsworth's poetry. Positing historical reality as the indisputable ground of meaning, they are tempted to read such literature as little more than a lie against history, a beautiful falsification of material conditions, a "Romantic ideology" (McGann 81–92). To resist this temptation and recognize that literature consists of more than a falsification, they argue that literature's denial of history creates the history it attempts to deny; Marjorie Levinson, for example, states that "the poets create *themselves* as creatures . . . of the age and they do so by *refusing* what is given to them as the age." This "manner of negating the given," however, "is the determined expression of an epochal spirit which, paradoxically, comes into being with and *only* with that repetition" (*Historicism* 3). Alan Liu accepts this position and reformulates it: "the literary text is not just the displacement but the overdetermined and agonic *denial* of historical reference," a denial which, in turn, is itself "overdetermined" by material and historical context (*Wordsworth* 47).

These critics formulate the important insight that the text comes about only by negating history and by distancing itself from other possible representations of history—in short, through some form of symbolic violence. But they do not consider the possibility that Wordsworth himself already shares something of their concern. His texts often articulate the sense that history is unreadable, that legitimate grounds for discourse have disappeared, and that representation is therefore impossible. As I argue in Chapter Eight, at some points he treats his own memories of the French Revolution as in some way unrepresentable, implying that if one gets too close to historical actuality it escapes the genres of history writing which attempt to capture it. Strangely enough, in his own way he exposes the very problematic that new historicism describes. To remain true to the inaccessible referential ground, he must fall silent or represent the impossibility of representation. Even more radically than McGann, for example, who tends to conceive of literature as "false consciousness" (8–10) and thereby to imply that there is, somewhere, a true consciousness, an accurate and sufficient representation, Wordsworth suggests that history is abandoned from the start to figuration, that it will always be alienated from the "real" event.

Of course, through this gambit Wordsworth does not escape history as such or the field of historically circumscribed discourses. Even the refusal of representation is a form of representation. Thus his subtle stance necessarily implicates him in what we might call, in this context, the history of the idea that history is unreadable. His effacement of the referent places him again in the tradition of hyperbolic reading. To read this poet in a truly historical way, then, one must begin to interrogate the tradition of the total critique of knowledge or utter erasure of referent and begin to imagine the possibility of partial and contingent knowledges.

Finally, the mode of this argument applies to the politics of gender in Wordsworth's poetry as well. In recent years critics have begun the task, long overdue, of exposing this poet's androcentrism, often doing so with subtlety and grace (e.g., Jacobus *Romanticism* 187–266; Heinzelman). But at times critics have focused upon his insufferably smug claim to phallo-cratic power and contrasted it with the stance of contemporary women writers, including Dorothy Wordsworth (Homans *Women Writers* 41–103; Mellor 144–69). However sympathetic I am with the latter project, I cannot join in its procedure, for it radically simplifies an entire oeuvre, reducing it to its most pompous passages and thus transforming it into little more than a monument of official culture. Yet much as Dorothy contests the sublime aesthetics of William's work, so does William himself, perpetually revising the most soaring passages with an eye to a very different effect (cf. Gal-perin). In a similar vein, Marlon Ross argues that Wordsworth depicts women as objects of "masculine desire," but he never attempts to explain why the male wanderer of his poetry derives more pleasure either from his *failure* to complete his odyssey and return home to woman or from her *absence* there (46–49, 72–86). Relying far too much upon an implicitly sexist and heterosexist binary contrast between patriarchy and femininity, these readings fail to do justice to the full complexity of Wordsworth's construc-tion of gender.

As I have already suggested, Wordsworth is anything but a typical patriarch. He persistently unburies the dead father, makes him uncanny, and deprives him of his official status. Refusing the name-of-the-father and disrupting the initiation ceremonies designed to bestow that name upon him ("Michael"), he in effect renounces traditional masculine author-ity. This does not make him an oedipal rebel, a revolutionary like Blake's Orc who inevitably participates in the patriarchal system he opposes. Rather, as I argue in Chapters Five and Eight, it skews the entire oedipal scenario by making the prospect of castration itself into a source of plea-sure. It subsumes oedipal rivalry within a homoerotic game of mutual viola-tion and revenge, dispensing with the usual oedipal resolution, complete with its rites of kinship and heterosexual coupling, in favor of masochistic pleasure enjoyed for its own sake. Similarly, Wordsworth undermines the normative conception of the pre-oedipal maternal body. Although in an ancient gesture he associates that body with nature, in *The Ruined Cottage* he implicitly concludes that the immediate bodily presence to which he wishes to return never existed. It was a figure, an element in a fantasy, from the start. Despite his own wishes, then, he ends up contesting the idealization of the prelinguistic mother.

Wordsworth's resistance to patriarchal notions of masculinity and to essentialist notions of femininity does not, however, make him an advocate for a new conception of gender. Although a certain kind of patriarchy collapses along with the symbolic order in his texts, he never goes on to imagine an alternative to that order. No matter how much he exposes or resists the paternal metaphor, the authority of the dead father, and the entire structure of kinship exchange, he cannot conceive of a society founded on any other basis. Here again he resembles Lacan; because he clings to an archaic model of culture, he cannot imagine a challenge to the dead father which would not also dismember culture as a whole.[7] As a result, when he imagines that cultural dismemberment produces a deviant, even queer masculinity, he also assumes that it abandons women to their precultural condition, or more precisely, as I have just argued, to their status as figures in a male fantasy of that condition. In *The Ruined Cottage,* for example, the pedlar's masochistic fantasy concerning Margaret culminates in the comforting image of her disappearance into nature. The same gesture that shatters traditional masculinity also produces searingly misogynistic fantasies.

Thus this book hopes to pose a set of questions that to my knowledge have not yet been asked in Wordsworth studies. In what way does the assault upon a traditional masculinity produce another kind of masculinity, perhaps more haunted and violent than before? Why is a traumatized masculinity dependent upon the neglect of women or, worse, the masochistic fantasy of their disappearance? In short, to what extent does the long tradition of hyperbolic masculinity not only discredit patriarchy but also embody another form of male dominance in which the writing of excess itself becomes an androcentric discourse?

These questions return us to the even larger issues from which they arise and which go far beyond the scope of this book. Why would culture wish to survive in the mode of its undoing? How does it profit from the mode of its own destruction? How does radical theory profit from its hyperbolic critique of knowledge? And what is the ultimate purpose of the radical political negation of the status quo? If contemporary literary criticism cannot help but write from within some aspect of the tradition of hyperbole, it can also begin to put that tradition in question.

ONE

All Track Quite Lost

Errancy in the Salisbury Plain Poems

In 1804, Wordsworth, remembering his response to England's going to war against France in 1793, wrote:

> And now the strength of Britain was put forth
> In league with the confederated Host;
> Not in my single self alone I found,
> But in the minds of all ingenuous Youth,
> Change and subversion from this hour. No shock
> Given to my moral nature had I known
> Down to that very moment; neither lapse
> Nor turn of sentiment that might be named
> A revolution, save at this one time;
> All else was progress on the self-same path
> On which with a diversity of pace
> I had been travelling; this a stride at once
> Into another region.   .   .   .
>
> . . . .
> .   .   .   .   .   . I, who with the breeze
> Had played, a green leaf on the blessed tree
> Of my beloved Country—nor had wished
> For happier fortune than to wither there—
> Now from my pleasant station was cut off,
> And tossed about in whirlwinds. (10.229–41, 253–58)

According to this passage, the onset of war profoundly dislocated Wordsworth, as if he had suddenly stepped off the "self-same" path, a path that never departed from itself, into "another region," or as if some external force had suddenly stripped him of his "station," his secure unmoving social identity, and tossed him about in whirlwinds, in a radically ungrounded space of nothing but movement. Clearly Wordsworth uses the word *revolution* here in what had become its old sense, a turn or revolving of the world; even more specifically, however, here he links this "turn of sentiment" with a "lapse," a fall, a wrong turn.[1] A turn, in fact, not into another region like this one, but into the opposite of a region: a whirlwind in which one does nothing but turn.

In this passage Wordsworth provides his own account of the relation between the French Revolution and his work. If, as readers have argued, the poet organizes *The Prelude* as a series of falls and recoveries while repeatedly denying that he fell at all (J. Wordsworth *Borders* 231–78), here at last he admits outright to a lapse, one so important that he reserves the term *revolution* for it rather than for that other Revolution in France (cf. Hodgson 45–48). But this moment of self-interpretation neither stabilizes his text nor makes it any easier for his readers to discern the hidden relations between history and his poetry. Because the revolution deprives him of his station, even one from which he could witness the whirlwind or interpret it, it is an event that cannot be interpreted in any terms, except as something that exceeds interpretation. Wordsworth no doubt locates the moment of his revolution here, but as the space of dislocation and unreadability, as the unmastered moment in his own text.

Late in the passage on the outbreak of war, Wordsworth describes a moment on the verge of this dislocation. Passing a month in the Isle of Wight, he saw the British fleet preparing for war:

> I beheld the Vessels lie,
> A brood of gallant creatures, on the Deep
> I saw them in their rest, a sojourner
> Through a whole month of calm and glassy days
> In that delightful Island which protects
> Their place of convocation; there I heard
> Each evening, walking by the still sea-shore,
> A monitory sound that never failed,
> The sunset cannon. While the Orb went down
> In the tranquillity of Nature, came
> That voice, ill requiem! seldom heard by me
> Without a spirit overcast, a deep
> Imagination, thought of woes to come,
> And sorrow for mankind, and pain of heart.   (10.293–306)

What Wordsworth described earlier as a spatial dislocation is temporal here; at each nightfall the sunset prefigured the coming of the world's night, as if the revolving of the planet images a darker turning. Moreover, he locates himself not in other regions but on their uncanny threshold, recounting how he walked on the verge of the sea at the edge of night. Even the landscape verged on a shattering event; the stillness of the sea was too still, nature too tranquil. Only a whirlwind could loom beneath such glassy surfaces (as Wordsworth suggests in the Peele Castle elegy). Each night without fail, so regularly that it seemed to express a more than human thought, the cannon marked the sunset with a "monitory sound," voicing pre-monitions of sorrow and woe for mankind. Wordsworth returned through an entire month to the same threshold and listened repeatedly to the same voice, hoping in part that his anxious repetition would keep the night from coming and the world from war, but in part falling under the spell of that strange sound. Obsessed by the sunset and its sound, he was drawn to the shore again and again, gradually falling prey to his untoward thoughts.

In this extended passage in *The Prelude* Wordsworth borrows the figure of dislocation from the poetry he wrote to protest that war, *Salisbury Plain* (1793–94) and its revision *Adventures on Salisbury Plain* (written mostly in 1795–96).[2] These poems depict a rather literal stride into another region, Salisbury Plain, a region of whirlwinds and tempests, of homeless wanderers and haunted ruins. The echo of these poems in *The Prelude* suggests that Wordsworth read them as allegories of the world's dislocation by war, a reading he made explicit in the Advertisement to yet another revision, *Guilt and Sorrow* (1842), in which once again he recounts how, having spent a month in 1793 "in the Isle of Wight, in view of the fleet which was then preparing for sea off Portsmouth at the commencement of the war, [he] left the place with melancholy forebodings," certain that the war "would be of long continuance, and productive of distress and misery beyond all possible calculation." He then journeyed across Salisbury Plain:

> The monuments and traces of antiquity, scattered in abundance over that region, led me unavoidably to compare what we know or guess of those remote times with certain aspects of modern society, and with calamities, principally those consequent upon war, to which, more than other classes of men, the poor are subject. (Gill *SPP* 217)

Although the Advertisement emphasizes the analogy between the human sacrifices of those remote times with the fate of the poor in wartime, it also implicitly links the journey across the plain with Wordsworth's forebodings. The analogy between ancient and modern, which stabilizes Wordsworth's language of political protest, becomes more than an analogy. To have "forebodings" of "distress beyond all possible calculation" is already to imagine the coming of war as the arrival of an incalculable future, as

Wordsworth does explicitly in the *Prelude* passages on the Isle of Wight to which the Advertisement alludes. Thus to make the journey onto the plain is to literalize the forebodings, to find the future in a geographical place, and to encounter the war's incalculable violence in the shape of human sacrifice. The journey ceases to be the setting solely for political meditations and becomes an allegory of the war's dislocation of the world.

In the final paragraph of the Advertisement, "to obviate some distraction" in readers who know Salisbury Plain well, Wordsworth explains that "of the features described as belonging to it, one or two are taken from other desolate parts of England" (Gill *SPP* 217). This scrupulous attention to fact seems to ground the poem all the more in actual landscapes and physical journeys through England. Yet the admission that the poem is made up of various landscapes of desolation removes it from particular geographical reference and implicitly refers it instead to a constructed, allegorical landscape of desolation. Here again the literal journey becomes a figure for the "stride . . . Into another region."

Wordsworth's revisitings of the Salisbury Plain poems show that they threaten the stability of a political rhetoric that would separate the poet of protest from the incalculable misery he wishes to describe. As long as the misery of the poor remains knowable by analogy, it is at least rhetorically calculable; it is still somewhere on the map, contained within the terms of protest, and thus almost as distant from the poet as the sacrifices of those remote times. But once the journey takes the poet into the domain of desolation and human sacrifice, the analogue of poverty becomes literal, the poet loses control over his own rhetoric, and instead of troping the war it tropes (turns) him, cutting him off from the "self-same" ground of the proper and the literal, tossing him about in the whirlwinds of an incalculable revolution. The sudden loss of ground, the moral shock, is thus the loss of a discursive station on the basis of which Wordsworth interpreted the world. Encountering an uncontainable, unreadable war, the protester finds himself read by what he wanted to read, mastered by an event that no discourse could master.

To be mastered by his own rhetoric, tossed about in the breeze with which he had played (10.253–54): this is the condition of hyperbole, of being carried away beyond the proper bounds. The revolution, it seems, is an exemplary hyperbole, cutting him off from the solid ground of meaning and taking him into the domain of tropic whirlwinds. But it is also a moment of hyperbolic wandering; this traveler, like the poet of what Binswanger calls "Extravagance," has wandered "too far out upon his precipice to go back" (Bloom *Anxiety* 105). Here Wordsworth accounts for his moral revolution so exhaustively in the language of hyperbole, "the language of detours, of exaggeration, errancy, extra-vagance" (*Romance* 31), that the two terms become synonymous: the revolution is an improper revolving, a turn into the improper, a definitive moment of errancy. The improper journey is more than an allegory of the revolution; it is the trope by which Wordsworth reads its unreadability and locates its violent dislocation of the world.[3]

❧ I

This lapse or turn was not quite as sudden and definitive as these later texts suggest. The outbreak of war did not silence the political poet entirely; as John Williams argues, the terms of *Salisbury Plain* are inherited from the poems written in protest of the American war, poems in turn rooted in the long tradition of opposition to the Whig government and its wars ("Salisbury Plain" 164–79; *Wordsworth* 69–80). The female vagrant's story repeats certain familiar motifs: the carnage of the American war, the death of husband and children, the loss of home, family, income, and self-respect. It also rehearses longstanding grievances of the poor, especially with regard to the arbitrary cancellation of traditional agreements whereby the poor could make a living; the vagrant's father, for example, is denied his "little range of water" (258), his right of access to fishing grounds. In the final stanzas, of course, Wordsworth assaults the government of Pitt in all of its aspects, attacking its tyranny, imperialism, militarism, superstition, and corruption in the name of reason and enlightenment.

Thus *Salisbury Plain*, along with the "Letter to the Bishop of Llandaff," a prose tract written a few months before (perhaps by February or March of 1793), locates Wordsworth within the political tradition of the English Real Whigs or Commonwealthmen of the late seventeenth century.[4] This political tradition, revived and extended in the eighteenth century by those opposed to the growth of Whig ministerial power (especially under Walpole), financial speculation, and colonial expansion, demanded the end of the system of patronage and corruption whereby the king's ministers could control even a freely elected Parliament. The alternative society they proposed was to be the haven of civic virtue, an agrarian republic in which every (male) freeholder could participate in public debate and could either elect or serve in a legislature free of interference from the king or his ministers. This Real Whig constitutionalism, which never gained much power within England, became the primary political language of the United States in its revolution against England and later inspired the Girondin constitutional proposals in France familiar to Wordsworth during his sojourn there. Wordsworth appropriated this tradition in conceiving of the Lake District as a region set aside for civic virtue and rustic innocence, and adhered to an anti-Whig, country politics throughout his life.[5]

It was this tradition, of course, which joined England and France in Wordsworth's mind and made it possible for him to support the French Revolution while remaining faithful to what he admired in the English tradition. But by mid 1793, when he began to write the first version of the Salisbury Plain poem, he admired neither the Pitt government in England nor the Jacobins in France (J. Williams "*Salisbury Plain*" 168, 172). The constitutionalism that certain groups in the two nations had briefly shared evaporated in the face of a war between governments that both expressed increasing hostility to Wordsworth's political tradition.

Although this political tradition powerfully informs *Salisbury Plain*, showing that Wordsworth does not entirely abandon his political stance, the poem foregrounds not the female vagrant but the experience of crossing into an alien terrain. Wordsworth places the vagrant's tale within the framework of the traveler's journey, as if to reinterpret her homelessness as one aspect of a larger disorientation. Accordingly, he moves from the anti-war genre to a different genre concerned with wandering onto strange ground, turning disorientation itself into his theme. As Samuel Schulman points out, this poem, written in the Spenserian stanza, follows in the neo-Spenserian tradition of such authors as Thomson, Warton, Beattie, Shenstone, and Burns. Wordsworth focuses on the antiquarian strain of this tradition, exemplified by Thomas Warton, who invents a barbaric, ghoulish past he may contemplate with pleasing horror, pleasing in part because the horror is safely in the past. Wordsworth, however, dissolves the antiquarian's dream by shattering the contrast between that absolute past and the present (222–26). The critique of secure analogy implicit in Wordsworth's prefatory materials becomes explicit in this poem, which consciously literalizes the figure and recognizes the antiquarian's imagined past in contemporary reality.

Warton's antiquarian poetry is implicated in a Hobbesian conception of cultural history, insofar as it imagines that culture institutes a great divide between itself and the violent state of nature which preceded it. To reverse Warton is also to reverse Hobbes; if indeed the barbaric past has returned, then the social contract itself has, on one level or another, been dissolved. Since Hobbes's metaphor for the state of nature was war (183–88), Wordsworth can easily imagine the outbreak of war as itself the return to the state of nature and the dissolution of culture in its opposite. This level of concern in the poem becomes clear in the first four stanzas, where, as James K. Chandler demonstrates, Wordsworth rehearses the argument, proposed in Rousseau's Second Discourse, that the poor vagrant is in a worse state than the savage, who never knew a better life (130–31). The mere comparison between the vagrant and the savage implies that the war has stripped its victims, England's poor, of their position within culture and returned them to a precultural condition. Because the poor have it *worse* than savages, however, Rousseau indirectly suggests that the Hobbesian state of nature, of devastating violence and brutality, is not a precultural but a postcultural condition, the result of culture's corruption. In effect, by following Rousseau here, Wordsworth cancels the difference between culture and the state of nature, carrying out on the level of political theory what the rest of the poem performs in relation to poetic antiquarianism. In both cases, the difference between culture and its opposite are dissolved; culture itself now seems to be the state of nature or the barbarism against which it had once defined itself.

Alan Bewell, discussing several later texts (such as "The Discharged Soldier") argues that the poet appropriates Rousseau's Second Discourse in further ways. Wordsworth's solitaries, like Rousseau's, wander about in a world recently devastated by the deluge (72, 78–81). Although Wordsworth does not mention the deluge explicitly in *Salisbury Plain,* he does link the plain directly with the sea: "'Twas dark and waste as ocean's shipless flood / Roaring with storms beneath night's starless gloom" (109–10). To cross into the dark, stormy plain is nearly to be drowned in a landscape barely distinguishable from the flood, as if the traveler walking by the seashore of the Isle of Wight has stepped into the sea, itself transformed from a "glassy" surface into storm. Here again is a crucial indeterminacy; if culture hovers on the brink of nature, nature itself threatens to return to primordial chaos. Moreover, this is a "shipless flood," a deluge without Noah's ark, as it were; neither nature nor culture is provided a guarantee of safe passage through these waters. The traveler on this plain has been hyperbolically cut off from his station, from an ontological ground, discovering that even the ground under his feet is no more stable than the sea.

Or, to use another figure, he has extravagantly stepped off the "selfsame path" into "another region," a process Wordsworth narrates in the fifth stanza onward. Turning back to glimpse the "distant spire" (39) of the village, which soon disappears in "the blank sky" (41), looking around on the plain which is the sheer negation of the inhabited world (note the insistent negatives of stanza six), this traveler soon yearns for the minimal shelter of "a shepherd's lowly thorn / Or hovel from the storm to shield his head" (59–60), but none appear; "the wet cold ground must be his only bed" (63), certainly a "fenceless bed" like that of the first stanza's savage (9). Fenceless bed: a shelter without boundaries, without a mark to set it apart from nature. To cross into the plain is not merely to cross a boundary; it is also to cross from a world defined by boundaries into one which is not. The plain is bereft of shelter, to be sure, but more fundamentally of symbolic markings that set one thing apart from another. This other region is the domain of nondifference, of a blank sky and a "vacant" plain (62), the domain in which the tremendous energies of figuration have never struck ground but wheel about, like whirlwinds, in the gales of the storm which will soon follow (65).[6]

For a moment, however, as the world slides into darkness, the traveler does glimpse another person: "And see the homeward shepherd dim appear / Far off—He stops his feeble voice to strain; / No sound replies but winds" (50–52). Here Wordsworth alludes to the famous opening of Thomas Gray's "Elegy Written in a Country Churchyard," in which "The plowman homeward plods his weary way, / And leaves the world to darkness and to me" (3–4). This allusion places the traveler's journey in the context of Gray's next line: "Now fades the glimmering landscape on the sight" (5), on which Charles J. Rzepka comments:

> The phrasing of line 5 bears emphasis: not the light, but the very "land-scape" is extinguished. It is almost as though . . . the plowman no longer remained "out there," in the dark; rather, the "glimmering" world itself "fades," like a dimming picture on a mental screen. "Glimmer" and "fade" become indices not simply of dusk but of a world being reduced to its image in the mind, becoming gradually insubstantial, and finally nonexistent. Gray's "Elegy" opens with an experience quite close to solipsism, to making the world one's dream. (3)

The proximate cause of the world's loss is the departure of the plowman, who

> represents "the Other," that conscious presence, real or conceived, through which we become self-conscious by considering ourselves as another would. . . . As the plowman departs, the world of others disappears, and with it, the sense of being an object and participant in their world. (4)

Rzepka's analysis clearly applies to the traveler's predicament on the plain; the landscape disappears, over several stanzas, into sheer vacancy. But here Lacan's notion of the Other, to which Rzepka refers, has greater resonance than in Gray; if the Other is the domain of language and the symbolic order, then its effacement involves the loss not only of others but of the system of cultural differences, boundaries, demarcations by which the self is given a name and identity. In this poem the loss of the shepherd is precisely the loss of language; the traveler calls out to the departing figure, but "no sound replies but winds . . . Or desert lark that pours on high a wasted strain" (52, 54). Here language is wasted in the winds, or perhaps the winds themselves are a language of waste, of endless expenditure of meaning without reserve (cf. Bataille 116–29; Derrida *Writing* 251–77).

The dissolution of linguistic boundaries is also, as Rzepka argues, the undoing of "the physical boundaries of the person," the loss of the senses, such as "mere sight, which ordinarily establishes a reciprocally determinative relation between self and world." Gray's line, "And leaves the world to darkness and to me" ("Elegy" 4) "suggests . . . that the poet is akin to darkness—something shapeless, obscure, indefinable, the very negation of embodiment" (3–4). Here Rzepka rehearses cultural dissolution on the level of the self, as if the fall from culture into barbarism or from language into vacancy may also be figured as the self's fall from the body into sheer negation. Perhaps this fall is simply death. In stanza 8, Wordsworth's traveler enters into mortal conflict with the storm:

> He stood the only creature in the wild
> On whom the elements their rage could wreak,
> Save that the bustard of those limits bleak,
> Shy tenant, seeing there a mortal wight
> At that dread hour, outsent a mournful shriek
> And half upon the ground, with strange affright.
> Forced hard against the wind a thick unwieldy flight. (66–72)

The bustard, who seems to be the traveler's own displaced self-consciousness (or Other), recognizes that the "dread hour" has arrived for the "mortal wight." Its grotesque struggle against the elements figures the traveler's own animallike battle to survive. Here we are at the body's limits of resistance to death.

And yet the traveler does not die; somehow he endures in the following stanzas. Were he to die, he would cross the boundary between life and death and arrive at a symbolically secure condition. Culture treats death as if it were readable, appropriating it for its own purposes through the rites of memory and the writing of epitaphs (such as those in Gray's Churchyard). Death may be the quintessential institution of culture, insofar as the symbolic order is founded, as Jacques Lacan has argued, in the name of the dead father (*Écrits* 67, 199, 217). Simply to enter culture, to take on the father's name, is to inscribe the body in the order of the name and thus to undergo a kind of symbolic death interpreted by psychoanalysis as the castration complex. But culture has no language for pain, which, as Elaine

Scarry has demonstrated, exceeds any system of representation and un-
makes the world (20, 36–37 and passim). In pain the body forgets its
boundaries, as all of the senses (not only sight) dissolve in the sensation
of the body's self-dislocation and dismemberment (see 53). But pain also
unsettles cultural boundaries; it is as if pain is precisely the unmaking of
the symbolic order itself since it marks the body's refusal to give up its
bodily experience and become symbolic. If the body would only die, then
culture could read its blankness for its own purposes, but the language of
pain is an unreadable blankness that nevertheless insists on being read as
the sign of an annihilating, incommunicable sensation. Pain is thus one
experience of the living body which one could describe as solipsistic or as
absolutely solitary (cf. Scarry 53); like Rzepka's dark selfhood, the body in
pain inhabits the shapeless darkness outside of language, or rather the
darkness of a shapeless language, a figuration without shapes or words, an
invisible troping or turning akin to the whirlwind's. The body in pain is
indeed like a bustard that "half upon the ground, with strange affright /
Force[s] hard against the wind a thick unwieldy flight."[7]

How might the traveler resist this movement into darkness and pain?
Could he not turn back to the village for shelter and cross the plain some
other time in the light of day? Not this traveler, whose journey into the
plain is also figured as the world's journey into night. Moving through
space and through time have become identical; the traveler can prevent his
further progress onto the plain about as easily as he can keep the night from
falling. Incapable of controlling his own movement, this traveler, like the
horseman of "Strange fits of passion," is carried by an alien temporal force
toward the loss of light and the thought of death. Moreover, because for
Wordsworth the plain is both a hostile space and an other time (*illo tem-
pore*)—the region of whirlwinds and the disastrous night glimpsed in anxious forebodings—to cross this space *is* to journey at the wrong time. Only
someone out of his right mind, no longer in control of his actions, would
embark on such a journey. Like the protester who has lost control over his
own rhetoric so that it now writes him, this traveler is taken away by the
journey he wished to take. For Wordsworth extravagance is not precisely
the action of going beyond the bounds but the passive experience of being
swept away, of losing control. In a strict sense, hyperbole makes one passive; to depart from the self, to lose one's active control over the will, is to
fall under the sway of something else, perhaps an alien or demonic self.
Thus from the very beginning of his involuntary journey, the traveler
stands ec-statically outside of himself (or gradually steps outside) under the
spell of a strange power—a power that has no proper shape but may simply

be the power of self-estrangement and the dissolution of the proper. The dreaded hyperbolic moment, which seemingly is about to take place, has already occurred.

Thus there seems to be no way to ward off the coming of night, the "dread hour" (line 70) or "nightes dread" of the eighteenth-century evening poem. As Geoffrey Hartman has argued, in the latter genre the evening star would rise to fill the "dangerous interval" between sunset and moonrise ("Evening Star" 152); but Hesperus is absent in the "starless gloom" (110) of this plain. Later, discussing a poem of dawn, which like sunset threatens the "continuity of self (in time)," Hartman remarks that the poet needs "a rite, and specifically a rite of passage" (171). Perhaps I should take the liberty of juxtaposing *Salisbury Plain* and *The Prelude* in order to remark that even the rite of the sunset cannon at the Isle of Wight only drew Wordsworth further into his night thoughts of "woes to come, / And sorrow for mankind, and pain of heart" (305–6). Rather than resisting nightfall, this rite (or antirite) seems to captivate the unwary man, carrying him away by his own rhetoric, his forebodings of disaster. The traveler is less likely to perform a rite than to become a sacrificial victim of his own fears, sliding as it were from obsession into hallucination; at nightfall, his proleptic pain of heart will appear before him literally as the body in pain.

As soon as the sun "unheeded" sets (73), the traveler, caught in the dangerous interval when symbolic acts become their opposite, immediately encounters signs of an ancient warlike culture ("Strange marks of mighty arms of former days") and hears "A voice as from a tomb" warn him away from an enchanted castle created by demons (81). The voice goes on:

> "For oft at dead of night, when dreadful fire
> Reveals that powerful circle's reddening stones,
> 'Mid priests and spectres grim and idols dire,
> Far heard the great flame utters human moans,
> Then all is hushed: again the desert groans,
> A dismal light its farthest bounds illumes,
> While warrior spectres of gigantic bones,
> Forth-issuing from a thousand rifted tombs,
> Wheel on their fiery steeds amid the infernal glooms." (91–99)

Here is the vision of cultural self-estrangement toward which the poem has moved. In place of language, there are the strange marks of war, a kind of antilanguage which, instead of creating boundaries, gouges the landscape. The castle that promises shelter is nothing other than Pandemonium, suggesting that the traveler has entered Milton's hell.[8] Here sacrifice, conceived as a rite that expels violence and safeguards the cultural body, becomes barbaric human sacrifice, the dismemberment of the body in pain. Specters break forth from tombs, the memorial shelters that establish the difference between life and death. The voice which, as Hartman suggested, could ward off this darkness, speaks here either as from a tomb (as if it were one of the specters recently returned from the dead and who evidently groan as they wheel across the desert) or in the moans of the great flame, perhaps the final state of the body in pain.[9]

The body in pain, the body returned from death; the voices of these two bodies may be a single voice, that of the body on the threshold between life and death, where the tormented body and the ghost begin to blend. The body in pain is beyond the living body without yet dying; the ghost evades the condition of the dead body without becoming alive. (As if to emphasize this resemblance, Wordsworth gives both the sacrificial victims and the ghosts bodies of fire.) The two bodies nearly meet in the middle of the stanza, where only a brief hush separates the moans from the groans. Perhaps the victims die only to reappear a moment later as ghosts. One might even read the stanza as a sequence from life to death, except that the body never arrives at death; it remains caught on the threshold of the tomb, not quite arriving at the condition of the symbol and of language. Thus these voices will never enter language; their condition is that of the great flame or fiery wheel, the undifferentiated energy of sheer trope.

Wordsworth's readers have usually been embarrassed by these kinds of Gothic passages in his early poetry. Yet in this stanza Wordsworth departs from the typical rendition of human sacrifice as demonic violence. In effect, he argues that Druidic sacrifice is less the practice of cruelty for its own sake than the sign of a failure to turn sacrifice into a symbolic act. Wordsworth implicitly argues that sacrifice is truly symbolic only when something else (an animal, perhaps) is substituted for the human victim; for him, human sacrifice is far too literal a form of violence for it to stand in for any other violence, and thus it cannot genuinely be sacrificial, a making sacred. Here human sacrifice begins to resemble war, which, as Scarry argues, "is one of the few structures" of culture in which the "very first form of substitution" of the animal for the human body "has never occurred" (139). Wordsworth's critique of human sacrifice is thus, as he makes explicit elsewhere, a critique of war, which resembles human sacrifice so closely in this stanza that the poet does not even have to propose an analogy between them.[10]

But how, precisely, is war a form of human sacrifice? Scarry argues that war erupts in a crisis of substantiation, when the claims of different polities conflict so sharply that they lose credibility and become mere fictions (131). To legitimate its version of the world (124), to make it once again authoritative, to carve it into the real, a country substantiates itself by means of physical force on actual bodies, the privileged site of substantiation (62). "[A] military contest," she writes, "differs from other contests in that its outcome carries the power of its own enforcement" (96). By means of this enforcement, the fictional world naturalizes itself as reality—the made-up becomes the made-real (146)—and creates a new and seemingly indisputable consensus. This analysis of war suggests what Scarry never states; after the war is over, the new cultural edifice founds its authority on the basis of the prior violence against real bodies. One major difference between war and sacrifice, then, is that in war we see sacrifice from the perspective of its victims because we are caught in the midst of a violence which has not yet achieved a complete and official form. Once it arrives at that form, the new consensus will read the seemingly random deaths according to a carefully fabricated narrative of cultural value, in effect turning violence into a form of sacrifice, whereby (according to a familiar myth) some lay down their lives that others may be free. Meanwhile, from the perspective of its victims war remains organized violence; instead of legitimating a cultural order, it exposes the latter's fictional status and its foundation in cruelty and murder. The impersonal and eternal authority of the dead father suddenly seems to be very personal and contingent, as if in order to preserve their power the dead must arise from their tombs to terrorize the living.

But according to this analysis, war is not merely a form of human sacrifice; it exposes the violence of sacrifice itself, a violence sanctified by cultural myth. The scene on the plain is supervised, after all, by the Druid priests at their altars, early counterparts of the Anglican clergymen who, according to Wordsworth's account in *The Prelude*, prayed for English victory in war (10.263–274). Here Wordsworth follows John Toland, the early eighteenth-century deist and Commonwealthman, in condemning Anglicanism as a modern form of the same superstitious mystery religion practiced by the Druids.[11] Wordsworth insists that priests of the Eucharist are predisposed to celebrate the carnage of war. At this juncture the protest against war (stated in the Advertisement) becomes a more radical critique of the violent basis of cultural institutions generally, extending the Rousseauist attack on culture initiated in the first four stanzas. Wordsworth again reverses Hobbes; instead of depicting war as the return to the state of nature, he argues that the social contract creates and perpetuates barbaric violence and is itself the institution of war.

In this critique of sacrifice, Wordsworth's text begins to anticipate the work of René Girard, which shares much with that of Scarry. Scarry's *crisis of substantiation*, in which cultural constructs lose their status as reality, resembles Girard's *sacrificial crisis,* in which the foundational gesture of sacred violence has lost its efficacy, depriving culture of any mechanism whereby it can resolve disputes in the name of a determining authority (*Violence* 24, 49). In this crisis, according to Girard, the entire system of cultural differences dissolves, everyone accuses everyone else of precipitating the crisis, and various attempts to save or to subvert the community become indistinguishable (135). Culture emerges from this condition by reinventing what it had just lost, the scapegoat mechanism whereby the members of the community arbitrarily choose a surrogate victim, a substitute object for their generalized and indeterminate hatred, on which they can unanimously place the blame, claim innocence for themselves, and reestablish a cultural order (77–80). Girard argues that the community remains symbolically grounded and secure as long as it keeps itself ignorant of the violence at its foundations (135)—in Scarry's terms, ignorant of the lie at the basis of cultural fictions. Whereas for Scarry the power to believe in fictions depends on the capacity to substantiate them in real bodies, for Girard this power depends more precisely on the capacity to accept the logic of substitution, which displaces real pain and death from oneself to someone or something else and thereby substantiates the fictions without endangering all the members of the community.

Thus the traveler's extravagant step beyond the proper bounds, already a figure for England's descent into war, enacts culture's precipitous loss of the capacity to mystify itself, to deny the illegitimate violence on which it is based. It is not violence as such, but the recognition of the originary position of violence, which sweeps culture from its secure ground. The traveler's hyperbolic journey beyond himself figures culture's absolute estrangement from itself, its transformation into anticulture.

For Wordsworth, then, the scene of sacrifice reveals not only the monstrousness of war but also the illegitimacy of all cultural institutions. The horror of war only makes more visible the violence that inheres in social relations generally. In the poem, as in the Advertisement, he links war's effect on the poor to their treatment in peacetime. Although war kills the vagrant's husband and children, everyday class prejudice and injustice had already stripped her father of his livelihood even before the onset of war. Wordsworth suggests that a culture divided by class is always at war with itself, allowing wealthy landowners to dispense with the poor without a pang. For proof of the endurance of sacrifice, Wordsworth says, look at the poor: "How many by inhuman toil debased, / Abject, obscure, and brute to earth include / Unrespited, forlorn of every spark divine?" (439–41). On this level Wordsworth anticipates Marx's theory of surplus value, which Jean-Joseph Goux has interpreted as a theory of sacrifice whereby one class lives on the surplus labor and pain of another (158, 211, 233).[12] In its broadest political concern, this poem uses war as a metaphor for the general situation in English society, which regularizes sacrifice as a necessary element in the system of class differentiation.

When Wordsworth goes beyond writing an antiwar poem and begins to write a poem that equates culture and war, implicitly he wishes to protect humanity from the ravages of culture itself and to envision a utopian alternative. Written in the hope that a future collective could do without victims of any kind (perhaps not even animals, as we shall see later), that it could dispense with phallic mastery and its attendant castration rituals, this poem resembles the later texts of Girard, who argues in a utopian Christian vein for the renunciation of all forms of violence (*Scapegoat* 100–212). The hyperbolic vision of the illegitimacy of culture modulates into a hyperbolic politics that seeks to surpass all known forms of culture and to create a new one based on Enlightenment ideals.

The problem with this project, of course, is that it counters violence with a violence of its own; in his case, as in that of his exact contemporary Robespierre, a total critique of culture very easily modulates into a total violence against it. For Wordsworth, one cannot transform culture without harrowing hell, without destroying its basis in a barbaric past. Accordingly, in the final stanza he calls for Truth and Reason to "uptear / Th'Oppressor's dungeon," to "let foul Error's monster race / Dragged from their dens start at the light with pain / And die," and to eradicate every trace, except Stonehenge, of the reign of superstition (541–49). The longing to eradicate the source of generalized oppression demands that he return to the Druid circle and do battle with the dead. All he needs for the task of killing Error and her monster race, he claims, is the dazzling light of Enlightenment, of total critique.

No doubt Wordsworth intends the final stanza to overturn the moment of dark hyperbole earlier in the poem. Isn't this light the very one that sank unheeded at the dread hour? Isn't this the Truth that fell prey to Error at Stonehenge? The poet wishes to restage this scene with such a force on his side that he can blind the realm of the dead with light as they inundated the world of the living with their darkness. The symmetry of this reversal, however, should give us pause. To destroy the past with an absolute, killing light seems as excessive and as inhumanly violent as what it attacks. The defense against profane violence is another version of the same. Perhaps those who moan are the victims not of the Druids but of the "Heroes of Truth" (541) or, perhaps, of both of them at once.[13]

The ease with which absolute light metamorphoses into absolute darkness, and vice versa, suggests that extravagant excess has no determinate meaning. Taken beyond their proper bounds, darkness and light, violence and the attempt to defend against violence, become indistinguishable. As Mileur argues, "just as . . . hyperbolic depths are perspectivally indistinguishable from hyperbolic heights, so are wanderings from the true path indistinguishable from true quests." If hyperbole leads to darkness and the dismemberment of culture, it also "leads to quality, sublimity, greatness" (*Romance* 31–32). What may seem to be culture's dissolution in violence may also be, from another perspective, the moment in which it eradicates error. It may be both of these, or neither, or as Timothy Bahti has suggested in his reading of the Arab dream, both *and* neither, both/neither ("Figures" 620). The meaning of hyperbolic excess is indeterminate precisely because hyperbole exceeds the limits of meaning. Thus all of these terms for the properly hyperbolic fail; as Mileur points out, all of our "words for hyperbole (itself a word tending toward the pejorative or suspect) are already judgments on something—a desire, an experience, a mode of writing—to which they refer but which none succeeds in naming" (*Romance* 32). They are all names for the unnameable, for what exceeds language.

If absolute darkness and light are implicated in each other in this way, then the poem's final stanza is already inscribed in the stanza on human sacrifice as its necessary and inevitable counterpart. How could one respond to the knowledge that culture is based upon violence except in this violently utopian way? What other political stance could follow from the vision of a culture that is anticulture? In that case, then, the scene of sacrifice already articulates a total critique of culture; what seems to trigger a political response is already the product of an interpretive act. Far from being the historical truth concerning the war that England will wage against France, the scene of human sacrifice is the literalization of Wordsworth's hyperbolic fear that the war would bring about the dismemberment of culture, his linking of war with Warton's barbaric past or Hobbes's state of nature. That scene is not a historical referent but the product of his fear (and his desire) that a coming historical event could bring about the monstrous (and utopian) end of history. It registers not a hyperbolic event—an unprecedented, apocalyptic violence—but rather an extravagant interpretation of events.

In *Salisbury Plain,* Wordsworth continues with this interpretation, meeting the supposed threat of absolute violence with an equally violent rhetoric. As it turns out, the whirlwind has not entirely cut Wordsworth off from his station, for he still invokes political traditions inherited from figures such as Toland and Rousseau and still feels innocent of the horror he attacks. The traveler never becomes implicated in the violence, neither as Druid nor as victim, never has to witness it, and bears no burden of ghostliness as he leaves the scene. Like Wordsworth at the Isle, he has been warned away by a monitory voice, barely preserved from the violence he foresaw. By virtue of its horror, the astonishing vision has remained in another discursive space, unassimilable even in this poem, and must be spoken by the dead. At certain moments, Wordsworth does pause to recognize that something is indeed unassimilable in this poem; in the final line he writes that his heroes of truth will destroy all superstition "Save that eternal pile which frowns on Sarum's plain" (549). Some residue of the archaic past, it seems, is ineradicable. Yet by so resolutely opposing the superstition that the eternal pile represents, he reestablishes the symbolic opposition between enlightened dissent and oppressive government, in effect founding his own version of enlightened culture on the destruction of error. Thus arises the directly political message of stanzas 48 through 61, in which the practice of human sacrifice is attributed solely to tyrants and priests. Accusing the government of transforming England into a savage state, he uses sacrifice, as did many of his contemporaries on both sides of the Channel, as a privileged term in what Alan Liu has called the *poetics of violence* (*Wordsworth* 138–63).[14]

I I

In his revision, *Adventures on Salisbury Plain* (1795–96) (henceforth *Adventures*), Wordsworth sustains but subtly alters the tone and focus of the poem. He removes most of the overtly political passages, including the first four stanzas and the final political section. But he adds a new level of political concern: an antiwar story about the traveler, now a sailor. As Stephen Gill argues, in the sailor's story Wordsworth protests against the frequent practice of impressing men who had just been discharged from service: the "sailor is pressed after already giving 'two full years of labour hard'" ("Protest" 53; see stanza 9). Since most press-gangs operated in seaports, a sailor would be a likely victim of this practice. Worse yet, he is not even paid for his labor (lines 91–92). Here Wordsworth incorporates complaints, heard early in the war years, that the government sometimes failed to pay its servicemen (Emsley 34). The sailor, enraged by this mistreatment, totally destitute as he nears his home, cannot bring himself actually to return to his family and robs and murders a stranger instead (97). Attributing crime to the injustices of the war, Wordsworth aims in Godwinian fashion "not to excuse the crime but to explain why it was inevitable" (Schulman 235). The fate of the sailor's family, left without any means of support and forced to leave home, also demonstrates the injustice of the government's treatment of the poor: "Like many others [the sailor's] wife had discovered the weakness of the outdoor relief system, which is that local officials, following the letter of the law, can deny relief and move the vagrant on." And finally, again following Godwin, "Wordsworth attacks the appalling barbarity of penal practice," which completely ignores the circumstances of the crime (Gill "Protest" 53–56). Gill also suggests that Wordsworth depicted the sailor's kindness to the old man (stanzas 1–5) to emphasize the sailor's "innate sympathy with the suffering of others" (58). Even more than *Salisbury Plain,* this poem demonstrates that England's militarist government destroys the nation, uprooting its people for unjust wars and punishing them for the consequences of its own actions. The state that should be the bulwark of society is its undoing.

This poem reflects Wordsworth's broadening political concerns and, as Schulman points out, his willingness to follow a change of taste in political poetry (230). But on another level, Wordsworth's decision to make the sailor a criminal indicates his deeper engagement with the problem of cultural dissolution and violence which he explored in *Salisbury Plain.* In contrast to that poem, here he is willing to admit that he cannot escape guilt, implicating his protagonist and himself in the savagery of the plain. Rather than walking away from violent scenes, this protagonist participates in them; he commits murder "In sight of his own house, in such a mood / from his view his children might have run" (95–96), as if he could have murdered his own children. His crime is, in effect, the sailor's version of human sacrifice, his way of profaning the symbolic acts that constitute home, family, and culture. By committing murder on the threshold of his own home, he makes it a fenceless (or defenseless) place, stripping it of the properties that make it a home and returning it to the state of nature. Yet he is not simply a murderer. We are encouraged to sympathize with his plight rather than judge him. Even the political terms of the poem shift toward the indeterminate, from the accusations of the final section of *Salisbury Plain* to the investigation of the psychology of sympathy (Schulman 232–23; Rieder 327), from a strict demarcation of innocence and guilt to the fluidity of mutual identification. Wordsworth even hints that the sailor embodies a peculiarly innocent guilt, or guilty innocence; he kills the stranger in part because of his great love for his family and his rage that he cannot fulfill his obligations to them, because he, "Death's minister" (84), cannot encroach on the inviolable domain of home, or as John Rieder writes in a slightly different context, "[h]e is excluded from society by the same internal power which ties him to his fellow human beings" (335).

These revisions to the poem mark a crucial shift in Wordsworth's practice. Rather than a hyperbolic poetics, with which he attempted violently to attack violence, he writes a poetics of hyperbole—one that recognizes that these opposites are identical, that he is implicated in what he attacks, and that finally there is no escape from cultural dismemberment. In short, he begins to take his own extravagant interpretation of culture seriously; if one can no longer distinguish between culture and anticulture, then one can no longer distinguish between the hero and the Druid, the good man and the murderer, oneself and one's enemy. Although much of the Real Whig political tradition will continue to influence him, his renunciation of a reason whose light will instantly kill the monsters of superstition suggests that he has truly become poet of the whirlwinds, of errancy, of dark romance.

The shift in Wordsworth's poetics does not undo the excessive interpretation of contemporary events with which he began. He is still convinced that the war between England and France undoes culture itself; if anything, he now takes this wild reading for granted. But now he extends the logic of that reading even further, applying it to the discourse that would lament or contain it. He is now, as it were, at a double remove from strictly topical concerns. Having already regarded vagrancy as a product of a generalized social war, he now regards even the means of protest against it to be an aspect of it as well. As a result, the political ramifications of his stance change dramatically. His poetic shift apparently follows from an implicit critique of a totalitarian politics, a Terrorist rationalism, but it also deprives him of the very political discourse that seemed most congenial to his poetics. He is both more and less than political, at once seeing through the claims of insurrectionist ideologies while lapsing into an almost passive acceptance of cultural dismemberment. Thus despite the level of topical political and social concern which will remain a hallmark of his work, Wordsworth begins to write allegories of cultural dislocation. Vagrants are not just vagrants but also representatives of a certain universal homelessness, and divided families figure the shattering of the entire kinship system. Social phenomena are not just themselves, nor do they reveal power's absolute war upon its subjects, because they speak forever of society's traumatic, irreversible dislocation from itself.

Wordsworth already provided a map of the indeterminate paths of extravagant romance in a stanza in *Salisbury Plain* which came soon after the vision of sacrifice. Revised and placed in its new context, that stanza sets the terms of his wide-ranging poetics of disorientation:

Beneath that fabric scarce of earthly form
More dreadful was the whirlwind's rage extreme.
All track quite lost, through rain and blinding storm
Three hours he wilder'd on, no moon to stream

> From gulf of parting clouds one friendly beam,
> Or any friendly sound his footsteps led.
> Once did the lightning's faint disastrous gleam
> Disclose a naked guide-post's double head,
> Sight which, though lost at once, some glimpse of
>   pleasure shed.   (163–71)

In this stanza Wordsworth moves from familiar images of tropological excess ("the whirlwind's rage extreme"), errancy ("all track quite lost"), and the absence of language (darkness, silence) toward the stunning image of an irreducible duplicity, the "naked guide-post's double head." Here the both/neither structure of hyperbole is reduced to a sign that points in two directions, toward heights and depths, true and false quests, simultaneously. In effect, the sign saves the sailor from the empty excess of figuration, the "whirlwind's rage extreme," by figuring tropological excess as doubleness or duplicity. Out of its depths the storm of wordlessness brings forth a doubled word similar to the "antithetical primal words" of Freud (*Papers* 4:184–91). To show the sign, of course, the storm must briefly illuminate it in a flash of lightning, thereby setting it apart from the darkness of namelessness which surrounds it. This privilege of the sign makes it in effect the representation of the storm itself, one that names the unnameable as a doubled name.

If we follow this reading further, we might recognize in this sign something proper to Janus, the god of gates and thresholds. Since this sign is also a signpost, something intended to give directions, it literalizes meaning in spatial terms, reducing the both/neither movement of errant wandering to the stasis of a singularly doubled space. This sign might also prod us into interpreting the sailor himself as Januslike; he and his counterpart in *Salisbury Plain* tend to look backward as they proceed forward: "the distant spire / That fix'd at every turn his backward eye / Was lost, though still he turn'd, in the blank sky" (*Adventures* 48–50); "Till then as if his terror dogged his road / He fled, and often backward cast his face" (*Salisbury Plain* 127–28). The double-headed sign takes over for the sailor's turning head, as it were, and makes the movement of turning or of trope into a frozen doubleness.

And yet the sailor is not on a track, not even this one: "all track quite lost," he encounters this sign, which signifies not that there must be some track here, but that this is both/neither a track and/nor a trackless waste. Although the sign promises to differentiate between two directions, it fails to do so, for it cannot name them, cannot say which is the true or the false path. By reducing tropological excess to duplicity, the sign images the relation between trope as pure excess and as meaning, between trope as unreadable (*naked* sign) and readable (naked *sign*). It thereby reduces direction and indirection, going somewhere and going nowhere, to the same thing. By being posted on a Januslike threshold between two unnamed spaces, it creates a more radical threshold between place and placelessness. If there can be any pleasure in glimpsing such a sign, it would be the distinctly ambivalent pleasure of recognizing that, having truly lost one's path, one has finally found it.

Thus Wordsworth places us on the threshold between language and excess, culture and its negation, giving us in this unique image his own version of a deconstruction of culture which, like Derrida's deconstruction, dissolves the structure of language without finally dissolving it. Moreover, he provides this theory in a truly grammatological form, reducing writing itself to an object that models the operations of a readable/unreadable sign.[15] In a similar scene, once again slightly revised from the first version, Wordsworth expands on these terms as if to capture the duplicity inherent in the term *deconstruction* read as an amalgam of *construction* and *destruction*. A deconstructed enclosure, one might argue, is both a structure and a houseless waste; it is a shelter without a ground or foundation, an enclosure that is not enclosed.[16] It would thus resemble the curious building the sailor encounters as the moon rises:

> At length, though hid in clouds, the moon arose;
> The downs were visible: and now revealed
> A structure stands which two bare slopes enclose.
> It was a spot where, ancient vows fulfill'd,
> Kind pious hands did to the Virgin build
> A lonely Spital, the belated swain
> From the night-terrors of that waste to shield.
> But there no human being could remain;
> And now the Walls are named the dead house of the Plain. (181–89)

The spital is the two-headed sign writ large; here the clouded moon reveals a bare two-sloped enclosure, much as the faint lightning disclosed a naked double-headed sign. But duplicity does not a shelter make. If only "two bare slopes enclose" the spital, it cannot be entirely enclosed; made to "shield" the benighted traveler from the night terrors (or ghostly warriors of *Salisbury Plain*), it may be more like a literal shield, a purely defensive set of walls, than a complete structure. Or perhaps the two slopes position the spital at a kind of crossroads, the spot at which place and placelessness meet. Accordingly, it is truly uncanny, which (as Freud has famously argued) is both *heimlich* and *unheimlich,* homely and unhomely (*Papers* 4:368–

407): it is reserved for the "belated" traveler and built where no one can live, a shelter outside its due time and place. Although "kind pious hands" intended that it be a consecrated site symbolically set apart from the waste, one that could provide hospitality to lonely wanderers and welcome them back briefly into society, as a lonely spital it has itself become a solitary on the waste, more like a homeless shelter than a home.

Outside its due time and place, the spital is a hyperbolic structure, the shape structure takes when it is dislocated from itself. Much as the demonic castle or Druid circle of *Salisbury Plain,* it images cultural dislocation as the failure to symbolize. The shelter is not fully itself because it has failed to differentiate itself definitively from the violence of the plain; it is the site not of hospitality but of hostility (cf. Scarry 45). Accordingly, it is a threshold, a crossroads, the very spot of violence; it is, in short, the threshold spot where the sailor, incapable of entering his home, committed murder. He has stumbled back onto the scene of his crime, or rather its aftermath: a profaned shelter haunted by the ghost of the murdered man. When the sailor enters the spital, he wakes the vagrant who, glimpsing the "shape" of the sailor "with eyes in sleep half drown'd" (218), thinks she has seen a ghost, partly because she has heard the story of the place:

> Had heard of one who, forced from storms to shroud,
> Felt the loose walls of this decayed retreat
> Rock to his horse's neighings shrill and loud,
> While his horse paw'd the floor with furious heat;
> Till on a stone that sparkled to his feet
> Struck, and still struck again, the troubled horse.
> The man half-raised the stone with pain and sweat,
> Half-raised, for well his arm might lose its force
> Disclosing the grim head of a new-murder'd corse. (208–16)

The dead house of the plain is a haunted house, an unclosed tomb in which the unquiet dead can cause an agitation so fierce it shakes the walls. It is thus a version of the demonic, Druid spot in *Salisbury Plain;* the moans in the scene of sacrifice have become the horse's "neighings shrill and loud," and its great flame the sparkles at the horse's feet. Collapsing the living and the dead together, Wordsworth images in the "new-murder'd corse" at once sacrificial victim and unburied dead.

The slide from naked sign to unenclosed shelter to haunted house suggests that a text concerned with the deconstruction of culture inevitably begins to sound like a ghost story or at least to borrow on its narrative conventions. As Karen Swann argues, the vagrant's story elicits precisely the response one expects from narratives like this: recollecting it, the vagrant traumatically repeats the effects of violent death. She instantly applies the tale to the sailor, whom she casts in the role of "corse" . . . while she herself becomes stony, like the discloser of the dead, like the stone covering the dead, and like the corse ("cold stony horror all her senses bound" [220]). What frightens is perhaps not so much murder as one's vulnerability to the shocking return of the dead. ("Transport" 813)

The absence of a boundary between the dead and the living means that at any time the dead may not only return but may cross over into a living body and turn it into a cold stone. The antimemorializing ghost story, like the unclosed tomb, allows the dead to wander not only on the plain but in the spaces of narrative and in the relations between people. The social structure, no longer rooted in the name of the dead father, is now haunted by his ghost, which wanders unhindered through its many paths.

As I suggested above, Wordsworth departs most dramatically from *Salisbury Plain* when he extends this uncanny logic to the characterization of his protagonist, who is now an utterly errant figure. If there is no difference between the living and the dead, then perhaps the sailor is both living and dead, at once a murderer and a ghost. Swann points out that later in the poem while the sailor is in a trance, "the dead, formerly contained in [the vagrant's] superstitious tales, venture onto the natural landscape" of the poem, giving "the impression that in the pause between parts 1 and 2 the life that had animated the sailor is transferred completely to 'ghosts . . . on nightly roam intent'" (407; "Transport" 814–15). Referring to Freud's notion of the primary process, "a movement Cynthia Chase connects to the turning of tropes," Swann argues that the entranced sailor is "suddenly exposed as trope or figure—as one signifier in a structure like an unconscious" (815). As a threshold space between life and death, the sailor is a duplicitous figure, like the double-headed sign, personifying the turnings of trope in a single body.[17]

The context of the sailor's trances, however, suggests a more precise interpretation of his doubleness. In the gibbet scene earlier in the poem, as pivotal in this text as the scene of sacrifice was in *Salisbury Plain,* the spectacle of a dead man "Nor only did for him at once renew / All he had feared from man, but rouzed a train / Of the mind's phantoms, horrible as vain" (120–22). Here the mind's phantoms, its inner ghosts, are linked with the sailor's fear of punishment. The mind's phantom is the sailor's victim, the "new-murder'd corse," threatening retribution for his death. The sailor is double, two people, because he has incorporated his own victim, identified with him so profoundly that he can no longer tell himself apart from the other. The other can thus appear in the guise of the sailor's own future death, a punished man hanging in a gibbet. Similarly, the spectacle of the mutilated body haunts him like a phantom, suggesting that when a phantomlike subjectivity looks in the mirror, it sees a corpse. Here the body in pain is equated with the ghost, such that those who moan and groan are the same, their sounds blending in the "sudden clang" that rings across the desert (112–13). Insofar as the sailor himself is a threshold space, as I have argued, he is caught on the bloody threshold and frozen in the moment of his crime, embodying neither murderer nor victim but the violent relation between them. Himself a scene of sacrifice, he is also the scene of the return of the dead, as if the "warrior spectres of gigantic bones" wander about the plain in the bodies of people like him. His subjectivity, it seems, is the tempestuous site of the gibbet, at once external and internal, the apparitional sight of "A human body that in irons swang, / Uplifted by the tempest sweeping by, / And hovering round it often did a raven fly" (115–17).

The specular element in this scene demonstrates that the social relations on the plain have regressed to the level of Lacan's imaginary order, in which each person becomes the specular double of another. Rzepka points out that the poetry of encounter does "reveal an abnormal fascination with and fear of the eye as an instrument of public self-confirmation and definition" and goes on, quite correctly, to argue that this specular encounter is so unstable that it at once confirms and threatens the self (27). The sailor's gibbet scene is an odd but telling instance of this kind of encounter. Unlike the vagrant, for whom the difference between life and death disappears via narrative, the sailor, glimpsing the "spectacle" of the corpse, immediately blends his identity with that of the dead man and goes into a trance: "He fell and without sense or motion lay" (125). This encounter with the spectacle of the subject follows the course of Lacan's mirror stage, in which the ego takes shape when the infant recognizes itself in the mirror and identifies with the external image as itself. The singular coherence of this image rescues the subject from a "primordial Discord" of "motor unco-ordination" and the fragmented body by giving it the "rigid structure" of a paranoid, defensively unified, ego (Lacan *Écrits* 3–4, 20). On this level, the sailor's trance rescues him from sheer formless subjectivity. In a dismembered symbolic order, in which culture has apparently disappeared into something like the fragmented body, the sailor can represent himself, it seems, only through this specular identification with another.

But, as Lacan argues, this "primary identification" with an external image defines the subject as another, makes him "a rival with himself" (*Écrits* 22), and gives him both narcissism and an "ambivalent aggressivity"

(20), the tendency both to incorporate the other and to attack him.[18] On another level, then, the attempt to escape cultural dismemberment and find an identity via representation ironically captures that dismemberment in the form of an identity permanently hostile to itself. In this poem the sailor murders the other and incorporates him, pushing the logic of ambivalent aggressivity as far as it can go. The gibbeted man is less the sailor's victim than his visible, specular form, the indeterminate self who is at once the sailor's victim and the sailor victimized in the poem's final lines. Wordsworth telescopes the entire imaginary scenario, capturing both specularity and aggression in the gibbet spectacle; to see the spectacle is to identify with the murdered rival and to represent oneself as a corpse. In this imaginary social order, every subject is at once irreducibly unique and the double of every other, as if even unreadable facelessness can be replicated indefinitely throughout society.

The structure of the sailor's haunted subjectivity suggests that for Wordsworth there is no such thing as absolute solitude. To live without the Other, without the social structure that provides a name and identity, is to live in a world constituted by rival others. Rather than being subject to the law of the symbolic father, one incorporates the phantom image of the rivals one has killed. Solitude, it seems, is also a social relation or, more precisely, a site in the fractured, mutilated body of social relations. The famous male solitary of Wordsworth's poetry, it turns out, is not nearly so self-determined or asocial as many have claimed; he is, rather, an embodiment of a particularly riven cultural condition.

Although he may not be entirely solitary, the sailor remains quite male, implicated in some minimal version of gender difference. Wordsworth envisions other forms of dislocation and solitude for women in this text—forms that at once reinforce the ideology of female dependence and provide instances of more hopeful possibilities for dismembered culture. The female vagrant, whom the sailor encounters but who is not his specular rival, seems partially to escape the problematic that dominates elsewhere in the poem. Linked to the wife who lived at home and will be discovered in an inn, herself discovered sleeping in the spital, the vagrant is, despite her vagrancy, identified with the comforts of home. Of course, the war has victimized her as thoroughly as the sailor; she and he wander through the same spaces. But because she has not directly violated the sanctity of home, she retains a level of innocence which the sailor has lost. Since Wordsworth represents the sailor's wife as neither the criminal nor murderer, but rather the ground of culture which is lost when violence breaks out, she can, it seems, wait patiently for her husband's return and embrace him as soon as he manages to cross the threshold. Similarly, the vagrant represents what culture abandons when it goes to war and what it returns to when the war ends.

On some level, then, Wordsworth's solitary women are presocial, akin to the primordial women of Freud's *Totem and Taboo,* whose only function it seems is to await the outcome of the battle between the father and the sons. In this version of culture, women enter society only when they become wives, just as nature becomes social when it turns into exchangeable property.[19] When their husbands leave for war, their link to the symbolic becomes tenuous, the shelters associated with them begin to decay, and they gradually revert to a precultural condition.[20] Of course, just as an abandoned dwelling is not identical to its ground, the abandoned woman is not directly grounded in nature; she too is homeless, but because her name already comes from elsewhere, from her father or husband, she experiences her namelessness in a different way than does the solitary man.

To some extent, the abandoned woman resembles Rousseau's savage rather than his poor and miserable vagrant insofar as the collapse of the symbolic returns her to a condition she can experience as other than total deprivation. Departing somewhat from his overall account of women, Wordsworth explores this condition in a section of the vagrant's story, absent in the original version of the poem, in which she recounts her joining a band of gypsies. Because these gypsies wander as a matter of course, they make wandering their home and purge it of its extravagant character. At home without a house, the gypsies are figures of a Rousseauist natural society that flourishes without a symbolic enclosure and all that it implies (legitimacy, law, sacrifice, phallic power). Although Wordsworth generally sees the loss of secure ground as a disaster, the gypsies' homelessness seems utopian because it frees them from property and government: "How kindly did they paint their vagrant ease! / And their long holiday that feared not grief, / For all belonged to all, and each was chief" (507–9). Soon, however, the vagrant states that the gypsies pretended to be peddlers when they were actually thieves, living outside, instead of without, the law. At this point Wordsworth voices a prevailing attitude of the time, which, as David Simpson has shown, held that the wandering bands were native Englishmen who posed as gypsies to escape hard work, duty toward their superiors, and all forms of edification and improvement (44–47). By describing the gypsies at least partly in utopian terms, Wordsworth suggests that their resistance to labor and to enlightenment may have been the strategy of a natural society attempting to survive in the midst of civilization. Despite this attempt, however, for Wordsworth the gypsies are finally parasites on civilized culture, offering only a spurious alternative. They are errant criminals after all, and accordingly the vagrant leaves them to wander on her own, becoming the more typically Wordsworthian woman of the spital. Although it opens up hopeful possibilities, femininity cannot ultimately escape the lawlessness and homelessness of the plain.

Although the vagrant is not the sailor's specular rival, the similarity between her story and his suggests that they are versions of the same. By now, all of the stories on the plain have begun to sound alike. The collapse of the symbolic order inevitably implies the undoing of narrative as well. We have already seen that the spital is another version of the sailor's home, the vagrant akin to his abandoned wife, and it follows that her dead husband is a version of the sailor victimized by war and even her father a form of the old Soldier in the poem's first stanzas. Later episodes such as the family quarrel at breakfast and the sailor's final encounter with his wife continue this pattern. By taking this text beyond narrative, hyperbole can only name the unnameable repeatedly, as if caught in the logic of imaginary self-replication, disrupting the Odyssean tale of the husband's departure and return again and again.[21]

In that case, how does this poem offer itself for our reading? What would a tissue of naked signs look like? Insofar as Wordsworth conceives of the dismemberment of culture as the return of a prior, archaic condition (Warton's barbaric past, Hobbes's state of nature), he also imagines poetry's dissolution as the return of an archaic, Spenserian poetics (see Schulman 224–25), depicted in the poem as the "Strange marks of mighty arms of former days" (*Salisbury Plain* 76). This is the arrival not merely of language's archaic past but of something alien within language, something that refuses to become subject to the symbolic order, the domain of grounded differences and meaning. As Swann argues, all of those traces of language on the plain, the effaced marks, lines, measures, and turns, refer to "the demands of that most elaborate and repetitive of poetic forms, the Spenserian stanza" ("Transport" 817)—a form that captures the "nonsignificative formal and mechanical effects" of language which resist "the conventions of eighteenth-century realism—naturalistic description, cause and effect plotting, delineation of character, pathos, and so on" (818). Such nonsignificative language is alien even to psychological consciousness. *Adventures*

> dramatizes Spenserian form so that it can in turn make legible that which inhabits subjectivity as something foreign, archaic, and received, or alternatively, so that it can stand for that "other" field which the subject inhabits as figure or trope. . . . To borrow a French formulation, he lets "it"—the unconscious—speak. ("Transport" 819)

The Spenserian stanza allows Wordsworth to conceive of a nonsignificative language of metrics and rhyme, rhythm and repeated sound, the organization and dispensation of words akin to syntax or counting.[22] In this poem metrics have overwhelmed signification, so that we have entered a realm in which meaning disappears into positional markers and repetitive effects. This mechanical, inhuman language seems to take us beyond or before the Lacanian symbolic order; yet, as Swann points out, in such a language (to allude to Lacan) "it speaks," the voice of the Other and of the symbolic as such. But how can the Other speak if it has been shattered? At this juncture we should remind ourselves that Lacan conceives of kinship relations as an instance of the syntactical laws of language and of number; the symbolic is a "combinatory," an instance of the abstract logic of combination and sequence (*Écrits* 141–42). Nevertheless, the passage from kinship to syntax, from Oedipus and the law of the father to abstract combination, requires a shift from a particular symbolic formation to the abstract capacity of cultural figuration. Swann's argument suggests, then, that Wordsworth, having lost his position within the conventions of his culture, encounters the alien and mechanical logic of a figuration prior to convention. Instead of receiving an identity from the particular symbolic formation, entering the kinship system and inheriting the name of the father (according to the familiar Lacanian paradigm), the Wordsworthian subject loses his way in an abstract symbolic field that he "inhabits as figure or trope." Language's state of nature is not vacancy but the combinatory, the sheer sequence, repetition, and counting of syllables into which the poet can dissolve himself.

As we have seen, however, the whirlwinds of abstract figuration have their dangers. We might read the Lacanian combinatory as a logic of generalized and uncontrollable violence, whereby any one term or identity can, via the turns of rhetoric, become any other. Culture is not based in a founding act or figure, since that figure is merely an element in the general capacity of figuration. Accordingly, Wordsworth refigures the oedipal scenario not as the narrative of initiation and foundation but as the articulation of an alien, repetitive logic. As the sailor and vagrant head out on the plain in the morning, they stumble across an oedipal scene, listening to a mother tell how the father beat his son, who had taken his seat at breakfast (see stanzas 68–74). The sailor attempts to scold the father for his violent ways, but as he reaches for the injured child he recognizes his own violence:

> Nor answer made, but stroked the child, outstretch'd
> His face to earth, and as the boy turn'd round

His batter'd head, a groan the Sailor fetch'd.
The head with streaming blood had dy'd the ground,
Flow'd from the spot where he that deadly wound
Had fix'd on him he murder'd. Through his brain
At once the griding iron passage found;
Deluge of tender thoughts then rush'd amain
Nor could his aged eyes from very tears abstain. (640–48)

This wound repeats the wound inflicted on the sailor's victim, making explicit the oedipal dimension of his crime, briefly hinted at before (his anger would have frightened his children [95–96]), and linking it to the scene of Druidic sacrifice or castration. Moreover, because the sight of this wound injures him, "locat[ing] him in the positions of batterer and sufferer" (Swann "Transport" 822), it also makes explicit what we described above as his guilty identification with the victim and, less obviously, his specular identification with himself as victim. Here Wordsworth repeats the poem's basic tale yet again, assembling its characters in a single scene: the narrating woman, the violent man, the victim.

On another level, however, this scene repeats Spenser; as Schulman argues, the "unhappy family *tableau* with accusing mother, snarling father, bloodied child" seems to come straight out of Spenser. "This is the world of the *Faerie Queene*, where travelers chance upon weird sights and arresting sounds" (237). The most compelling repetition comes in the phrase *griding iron*, which alludes via Milton to Spenser. Swann traces out the implications of this phrase, which "functions less like a Spenserian allusion" with a precise exegetical meaning "than a nodal point in fantasy or dream." Following a certain dream logic, she argues that the injured child is like Spenser's Ruddymane, whose bloody hands cannot be washed and who is "guilty by parental crimes," by the stain of original sin ("Transport" 823–25). On the largest level, then, the crime repeats an archaic, nameless crime that predates even Spenser: "'gride' insists that every wound remarks a prior effraction: even the moment when Satan first knew pain is marked by the archaic 'gride.'" This insight leads Swann, citing Lacan, to argue that "the subject is from the first invaded by meanings that predate it and that can only be recognized, gridingly and retroactively, in fantasy." To explore this insight she appeals to Nicolas Abraham's theory of the phantom, whereby the guilty acts of the father reappear in the unconscious of the son, who carries on the repression, guilt, and fate of the father (825–27).

Abraham's theory of the phantom, we might argue, reformulates Lacan's theory of the symbolic: the son inherits not the father's name but his unconscious, his guilty secret. Swann's argument implies that Wordsworth depicts culture not as the symbolic reproduction of the social order but as the imaginary repetition of a disordering rivalry and violence. But if every wound is a repetition, then the originary act is murder, that is, sacrifice understood as profane rather than sacred violence. Because this violence is fated to return with every generation, it is much more than merely profane, merely a random or arbitrary wounding. The necessity of repeating the violence locates it on the threshold between sacred and profane, founding act and murder; failing to mark a great divide between it and the violence that came before, the violent act is caught in the process of origination which it never succeeds in bringing about.[23] Wordsworth's plain is finally neither Hobbes's state of nature prior to the social contract nor the space of the social contract understood as a primordial imposition by the sovereign upon his subjects but the space in which the social contract and the state of nature collapse into each other and become indistinguishable. According to this poet, culture has never been founded; it merely repeats, in countless acts like that of the father at breakfast, the ineffectual gesture of profane beginnings.[24] Or, more precisely, it makes the violence of the state of nature programmatic and gives it a determined, nearly explicit form.

In this passage, the means of repetition is the language of poetic romance. Rather than founding his poetry in Spenser's and thereby inheriting the authority of the English poetic tradition, Wordsworth's allusion understands language as the drama of wounding, whereby words and names are handed down in the gesture of slashing or stabbing. Hyperbolic and transgressive, the language of romance reenacts the moment of violence and the identification with the victim. It is as if Wordsworth verges on Harold Bloom's theory of the anxiety of influence, staging poetry as the encounter of poetic fathers and sons, yet already he has historicized that anxiety as a particular form of cultural dismemberment.

The close of the poem replicates the logic that dominates throughout, tracing once again the shape of an absolute disorientation. Caught within the domain of repetition, Wordsworth restages the basic dramatic situation: the sailor crosses into a shelter (the inn) in which he encounters yet another female vagrant telling her story. This vagrant, of course, is his wife, and her story is in part his story. Recognizing her and pleading for her recognition in return, the sailor replays the recognition scene at the spital, where the vagrant thought she saw a certain ghost, the return of a figure in one of her stories. Moreover, the sailor's longing to be forgiven and welcomed back into his wife's arms belongs to the economy of charity and (ho)spitality, the annulment of guilt and the remarriage of man and woman, which were promised and betrayed at the spital. At the inn, the woman's gesture of forgiveness is interrupted by her death, which once again interposes an ineradicable violence between the sailor and his home. This time, however, his own wife is the victim of that violence, burdening the sailor with an enormous guilt that he cannot withstand. He has murdered not only on the threshold of home, but has killed home itself; accordingly, he turns himself in and welcomes his punishment. Hanging at last in the gibbet, his identification with the dead man seems complete and the romance narrative at an end.

It seems that in this last section Wordsworth finally appeals to the order of law and judgment in order to escape the indeterminacies of the poem. The married couple living in the inn seems to personify the cultural security that eluded the sailor and his wife; no wonder they are so bent on accusing him of the crime: "'He is the man!'" (806). His death might finally free culture of the plague of violence, instituting it in a kind of sacred violence. Such a death would fit nicely into an officializing narrative, which, as Teresa de Lauretis has shown, rehearses oedipal conflict and resolution (103–57).[25] But if we read the final stanza carefully, we can see that even at its end this poem refuses closure:

> They left him hung on high in iron case,
> And dissolute men, unthinking and untaught,
> Planted their festive booths beneath his face;
> And to that spot, which idle thousands sought,
> Women and children were by fathers brought;
> And now some kindred sufferer driven, perchance,
> That way when into storm the sky is wrought,
> Upon his swinging corpse his eye may glance
> And drop, as he once dropp'd, in miserable trance. (820–28)

This text operates on three levels. First, the sailor's death reestablishes a minimal family security, so that a father might take women and children to the scene as if to witness the basis of their kinship. Second, Wordsworth follows Godwin's critique of capital punishment, ordered by the authority that bears "the violated name" of "Justice" (819) and of the "dissolute" crowd that seems indifferent to the sufferings of others (cf. Gill "Protest" 56–57, 62–63). Finally, this critique of indifference leads to the rhetoric of imaginary sympathy, whereby the spectator identifies with the gibbeted corpse and collapses in a trance. As Swann argues, at this point the reader, "kindred sufferer," reads the dead man as kin, recognizing "not that crime will out, but that *l'autre, c'est moi*" ("Transport" 831). In that case, however, the poem ends not on a note of moral solidarity but of captivation; if identification subverts narrative and undoes the judgments of the law, it also structures kinship as specularity rather than familial togetherness. The last word or gesture here is reserved for another person who, like the sailor, is drawn onto the plain "when into storm the sky is wrought," suggesting that the poem is about to begin again in the reader, who will retrace the criminally extravagant steps of the sailor in his or her reading, and that the constitutive violence of the poem will be repeated endlessly beyond its literal end. The relation between this poem and Spenser, demonstrated in the griding iron passage, will also structure the reader's relation to *this* text, so that the series of wounding identifications will extend beyond or across the boundaries of the poem into the mind of the reader, who, in the absence of symbolic differentiation, can no longer distinguish him or herself from the figures in the poem.[26]

This scene exemplifies the complex shape of Wordsworth's poetics. In some ways, the poem is vigilantly radical, following Godwin in exposing the illegitimacy of law and the coercive nature of any system that practices capital punishment. An anarchist ethic demands that we sympathize with the executed criminal. Yet this sympathy quickly transforms into specular identification and occasions trance. Here one who wishes to carry out a total critique of culture becomes captivated by the violence he abhors; to refuse the violence of law is to claim that he, too, deserves death. One who wishes to find a cure for cultural trauma begins to find pleasure in the wound instead. The hyperbolic politics that subjects even law to its searching gaze quickly modulates into a politics of captivation, such that protest dissolves into the aesthetic excess of dark romance. Although this latter turn threatens the authority of political critique, it never effaces it but prefers to leave it intact, to register it as the self-present, proper language from which it deviates. The result is a sedimented text that voices several projects at once—topical, utopian, and romantic—but finally subsumes all in the specular entrancement of the final lines.

Passing beyond the Visible World

Self-wounding in *The Borderers*

✥ In many ways *The Borderers* offers to interpret itself as the dramatization of a hyperbolic condition. It is set on the border between countries, a
border that does not divide the land clearly between different regions of
authority but opens up a space outside the law, as Wordsworth mentioned
in the Fenwick note: "As to the scene & period of action little more was
required for my purpose than the absence of established Law & Government—so that the Agents might be at liberty to act on their own impulses"
(Osborn 814). Yet it is not entirely without law, since Mortimer and his
band still rule the territory with a semblance of legitimacy. Moreover, the
drama is set in the thirteenth century, as if midway between the Druids
and Wordsworth's present, on the border between archaic and modern
England. The borders are an equivocal space, where law is not quite law,
boundaries not quite boundaries. Such a condition is familiar to us, of
course, from the Salisbury Plain poems, and much more in this play is just
as familiar, for example, the many wanderings outdoors in inclement
weather, the encounters with strange figures telling stories, the attempt to
find guides to lead through unknown land, and near-murders in old castles.
The dramatic action of the play in which Rivers seduces Mortimer into
half-committing murder extends the thematics of crime which I explored
above. Beyond the bounds, out of place, *The Borderers* rigorously displays
the condition of a society that has gone beyond itself.

More than restaging the scenario of the Salisbury Plain poems, however, in this play Wordsworth explores one possible response to that scenario. Would it be possible, he asks, to master one's hyperbolic condition
by reinterpreting it as the means of entry into a privileged condition? Could
one escape being subjected to its impersonal logic by willing it, repeating
its violence through one's own conscious action? Could one subordinate

that logic to one's own ends, transforming it into a feature of a style of excess? With these inquiries Wordsworth touches on issues later taken up by philosophers of excess such as Nietzsche, Artaud, and Bataille, anticipating the project of radical amoralism. But this anticipation comes with a critique; in this text of ruthless negativity, he dramatizes how both embracing and refusing asceticism fail to master hyperbole. With this play Wordsworth establishes a tenuous relation to philosophies of excess, resisting a mode of writing which he cannot foreclose as one possible direction for his own poetics.[1]

Wordsworth sets the terms for his analysis of the cultural borderlands through his covert allusions to contemporary plays. Reeve Parker examines these allusions in two essays, arguing in the first that Wordsworth may have been influenced by performances in Paris of Jean-François Ducis's antiaristocratic version of *Othello* ("Reading" 300–304). This version of Shakespeare's play focuses on the struggle between Desdemona and her father Brabantio, whose opposition to her marriage to Othello "dominates the action throughout" and is "given fierce political edge when the Venetian Senate construes her father's apoplectic hostility to Othello as madness endangering the republic" (303). Suggesting that Wordsworth owes much of his plot to Ducis, Parker goes on to argue that Herbert may be another Brabantio enslaving his daughter out of a crazed hostility to Mortimer. In that case, Rivers's charge against Herbert in the first lines of the play may be right; through his tales about how he saved Matilda's life in her infancy, Herbert creates and reinforces "the very bondage of gratitude and pity that leads her, reciprocally, to sacrifice herself in the passionate action of protecting and saving him in old age" (305). This ruthless possessiveness directed toward his daughter is incestuous. Each time Herbert tells the story about how he rescued her from the fires of Antioch, barely reaching the doorway of the building where her mother (and infant brother) died, he chooses Matilda over his wife, in effect killing the mother and embracing Matilda instead (306). Matilda returns this passion, longing not for the dead mother but for the narrative of rescue which takes her place, a narrative that amounts to a "family romance that denies the mother" (309)—a mother who reappears, ghostlike, in the form of the female beggar. This familial tale, however, screens a deeper tale about how the baron abandoned his responsibilities to his people and departed with the crusaders for distant lands. The local usurpation of his lands, about which he complains in the play, results from his own abdication and self-usurpation (308–11). In the later pages of this essay Parker links Herbert to Prospero of *The Tempest*, another figure who has made himself illegitimate as a father and a duke

(317–22). Overall, Parker argues, in these plays narrative arises from "the usurping of self" implicit in the killing of the mother and the abandonment of domestic responsibility (321).

What Parker calls *narrative* is not the oedipal narrative described by de Lauretis, which legitimates paternal and political power, but a tale engendered by an act of violent self-division akin to that of the sailor in *Adventures,* who, in the final stanzas, also becomes responsible for his wife's death. Here again Wordsworth situates the act of familial violence on the threshold or doorway and links it to destruction by war and fire. His mode of narrative is again antinarrative, exposing the illegitimacy of the symbolic order and the violence at its foundations. As Parker emphasizes, the destabilization of the family and the state comes not from elsewhere but from the very powers supposed to anchor it, the father and the baron; as in the Salisbury Plain poems, society subverts *itself.*

This self-usurpation of legitimate authority leads, as in those poems, to repetition. Parker argues that "tales everywhere in the play function to bind their hearers into similar structures of repetition, generating in them both passions that lead them to reenact the actions of the tales and characters that mirror the characters of the tellers" (304). The power of these tales is so strong that they "use the dramatic persons of Matilda or Mortimer to repeat and reenact themselves" (313). Here we can see the familiar logic of "strange repetition"; like the traveler of the first stanzas of *Salisbury Plain,* these characters are under the spell of an alien logic whose movements they cannot resist.

Parker admits that his reading of the play is extravagant (304, 309), as hyperbolic as the charges Rivers levels against Herbert. Indirectly, then, he admits that one must read Herbert hyperbolically to read him as an instance of hyperbole; Rivers participates in society's self-usurpation as much as Herbert. One might even say that this kind of reading is already produced by the tale it reads and participates in the self-replication of the tale. Much as Brabantio is a crazed father because the radical playwright Ducis reads him that way, so also Herbert is a fraud because we see him through Rivers's eyes. Revolution and self-usurpation are two versions of the same unnameable extravagance, whereby the two generations, the father and the suitor, cooperate to unsettle the old familial story.

In that case, Rivers and Mortimer are characters as suspect as Herbert. Wordsworth's suspicion of them can be measured by his distance from Friedrich Schiller's *Die Räuber,* an immensely successful play about the outlaw hero Charles Moor, leader of a band of robbers. The original version of this play had quite an effect; in act 5, for instance, Moor announces his criminal identity to his dying father and murders his beloved Amelia to preserve the loyalty of his men. Such acts horrified and captivated the audience. In another essay Parker demonstrates that in the first account of the play for a British audience (in a lecture published as "Account of the German Theater"), Henry Mackenzie falls prey to the audience response he criticizes elsewhere ("Spectacles" 372–76). Such captivation is given a directly political edge in two French translations of Schiller: Nicolas de Bonneville's *Les Voleurs*, never performed, the version on which Mackenzie depended in his account of the play, and Jean-Henri Ferdinand LaMartelière's *Robert chef de brigands*, a rather loose imitation of Schiller, performed five or six times during Wordsworth's stay in Paris late in 1792 (377–84). Bonneville, a prominent Brissotin and an associate of some British radicals including John Oswald, the British radical whose name Wordsworth used in the 1842 version of *The Borderers* (Erdman 22–23), remained faithful enough to Schiller's play to doom it for the revolutionary stage. But LaMartelière modified the play substantially, making the robbers into brigands and removing the final murder of Amelia. Performed more often than any other play during the revolutionary era, *Robert* seemed to "epitomize the tendencies of revolutionary theater—or even of the revolution itself," so closely did it resemble the "spectre of regicide" (379). Evidently its critics read *Robert* as a decidedly Jacobin play, arguing that it linked radicals and brigands, revolution and outlaw justice (380–82). In hindsight in 1802, moderate historians of the revolution suggested that the judicial tribunals of the brigands prepared the way for "such a revolutionary tribunal as the Jacobin Committee of Public Safety" (382). Parker implies that from Wordsworth's perspective, someone struck by this play would also be captivated by the spectacle of regicide and Terror.[2]

Even this cursory review of Schiller's play enables us to see how Wordsworth could present his critique of Schiller's outlaw hero in terms that resemble his seemingly radical critique of constituted authorities like Prospero and Herbert. The power of Charles Moor, it turns out, is as illegitimate as that of Herbert; he too murders a woman (Amelia) in a bid for power and masks outlaw rule as the reign of (a new and liberating) law. In *The Borderers* Rivers's crime against the captain causes his daughter to go mad, in a lesser version of the murder of Amelia, and his stories captivate and enslave just as much as Herbert's, contributing to the pattern of repetition. These two figures of false authority, the old and young man, resemble each other enough that we might read them as repetitions of each other (à la the griding iron perhaps) in the registers of supposed authority and supposed enlightenment. Wordsworth seems to suggest that in the absence of legitimate authority there is little difference between the false father and the ambitious son, the pious fraud and the violent liberator. Dislocated and errant, like the gypsy band of *Adventures*, the society that attempts to live without law ends up beyond the law, ruled by impostors or brigands.

In the absence of the traditional forms of legitimation, what enables these impostors to rule? Only their power to win assent, to find listeners, to captivate an audience. Violence alone could never win them followers; they must put their violence into a narrative that disguises it as rescue (from Antioch or from tyranny), in effect turning profane into sacred violence and explaining their usurping acts as modes of establishing a cultural order. Thus one concern of the play is the mechanism of captivation whereby the audience accepts the impostor's claim, designates him as its hero, and sets him apart as its representative. Wordsworth embarks on a fundamental examination of tragedy as a genre, taking up problems explored later by Freud and Girard, both of whom read tragedy as a version of more archaic rites that mimetically reenact the story about the death of the primal father (Freud *Totem* 174–81, 192–94) or the designation and expulsion of the scapegoat (Girard *Violence* 68–88).[3]

Wordsworth carries out this project in part by exposing the mechanisms of spectatorship as such. As David Marshall argues, "The play asks us to consider what it means (or what it would mean) to be an eyewitness of *The Borderers*" by staging spectatorship visibly within the play itself. Throughout the play, "characters are represented and described in terms of looks, appearances, eyes, sights, and spectacles" (392–93). "Whether envisioning the eyes of other characters, the vulgar crowd, the eye of Reason, the eye of God, or an audience of devils, the characters in *The Borderers* (like Hamm in Beckett's *Endgame*) seem to share a sense that they are being watched" (394). At certain moments, the characters refer directly to the play's ostensible spectators. Take Rivers's account of the captain's death as an instance:

> 'Twas a spot—
> Methinks I see it now—.   .   .
> It swarmed with shapes of life scarce visible;
> And in that miserable place we left him—
> A giant body mid a world of beings
> Not one of which could give him any aid. (4.2.37–43)

This passage gestures "to the shapes of life and world of beings that come together in the theater" (394–95). Scenes like this "[implicate] the audience in the scene of the crime of *The Borderers* and [make] the play a critique of (what Geoffrey Hartman calls) 'the ethics of complicity'" (395, quoting Hartman *Wordsworth's Poetry* 130). Rivers, Mortimer, and Robert commit the crime in this play not by physical assault, but by "a failure to assist, a failure to give any aid," acting out on the stage the passivity of spectators who are necessarily "complicitous in the act of not saving someone's life" (396). Here, Marshall argues, Wordsworth links theatrical conventions, which place the spectators in an entirely passive role, with murder and carries out his own version of Rousseau's assault in *Lettre à d'Alembert sur les spectacles* on the way theater immobilizes spectators in a dark cavern (397–98).

But Wordsworth's target is not only the passivity of spectators in a theater. Having arrived at the theater to see a spectacle, the audience has, like the ship's crew, demanded a plot and organized a conspiracy to deceive Rivers into killing the captain. In Girard's terms, the mass of people in the audience can only signify its coming together in the modes of scapegoat rituals and must therefore stage its unity as a reenactment of the tales of sacred violence. Passivity is more characteristic of those on stage, who are bound to act out tales generated by an overwhelming if unstated demand of the social totality, in this case the audience, which has always constituted itself symbolically by means of narrative.

Nevertheless, by emphasizing the fact that the play's crime is not physical assault but abandonment, Marshall complicates this Girardian (or Freudian) reading. The actions of the play do not adhere to the conventions of Girardian tragedy, since the moments of violence never become truly symbolic. Rivers and Mortimer do not carry out a heroic deed that inspires the audience's wonderment, for in abandoning the captain and Herbert, refusing to save them, they perform a deed that every spectator performs as well. Instead of metaphorically substituting themselves for the social totality, they merely stand in for any one spectator metonymically, doing what he does.[4] Willful passivity and murderous activity now become indistinguishable. As a result, the spectators cannot project their guilt for the deed onto a hero, either idealizing or blaming him as the case may be, but must remain aware of their role as originators of the deed. The blame for violence continues to circulate amid the social totality, finding no surrogate victim, no substitute in which it can disappear. Like Girard, Wordsworth makes visible the knowledge of violence that culture attempts to bury in the rites of sacrifice—a knowledge voiced, perhaps, in one of the better-known lines of the play: "The world is poisoned at the heart" (2.3.344). It is almost as if Wordsworth has restaged the drama of the primal crime in *Totem and Taboo*, except that after the murder of the dead father the brothers cannot unite and form the cultural order. In this version of the tale, the conventions of tragedy or ritual misfire, captivation creates no heroes, and sacred violence becomes the illegitimate violence of hyperbolic self-usurpation whereby culture exceeds itself without constituting itself in a new way.

The abandonment of the paternal figures bears upon their symbolic status as well. Because they are abandoned, rather than physically assaulted, they do not quite die; the ship leaves the captain on the island, where he is last glimpsed "not dead nor dying, / But standing, walking—stretching forth his arms: / In all things like yourselves" (4.2.45–47), that is, like the members of the audience (Marshall 395). The old men are deprived of the distinctive status of the dead; they, too, are merely like us. They have not been set apart in the realm of the Other but simply placed on the threshold between our world and the blankness beyond it. Rather than becoming Lacan's dead father, in whose name culture can found itself, they are isolated, unburied beings akin to ghosts who are caught on the threshold of the tomb. Physically absent but not yet symbolically other, they continue to haunt the spectators in the form of their guilt for the crime, remaining alive and demanding vengeance until someone can be blamed for it.

Thus the play is not about parricide, a crime that (according to Freud) leads quite readily to the restoration of paternal authority, but about culture's abandonment, in the literal sense, of that very authority. Apart from its consequences for the criminals and victims of the play, abandonment has a specific cultural (or anticultural) significance. If we accept Parker's extravagant reading of the play, Herbert enslaved his daughter by saving her life. Rescuing her from the fires, he blinded himself and forced her to incur an obligation that she will never cease to repay. In this context, the refusal to save Herbert's life may be a perverse but appropriate way to release Matilda from her enslavement. Rivers, the character who first proposes this perverse reading of Herbert, indirectly hopes that by persuading Mortimer of this reading he will free himself from his obligation to Mortimer, who had earlier saved his life. Thus the Herbert-Matilda plot joins with the Rivers-Mortimer plot around the problem of obligation. If saving someone's life is coercive because it forces that person to owe what can never be repaid, *not* saving a life is irresponsible and murderous because any critique of obligation in the name of liberty or the independence of the self risks canceling all social bonds. Perhaps Herbert's rescue of his daughter's life is an allegory of the way parents give life to their children, who apparently become obligated to their parents simply by being born. Society may be, as Edmund Burke argued, a "contract" or series of obligations that bind together "those who are living, those who are dead, and those who are to be born" (194–95). From the perspective of Rivers or Parker, however, the tale of this obligation is pure myth; through it the father takes for himself what his daughter owes to no one or perhaps to the biological giver of life, her mother. Herbert's matricide may be an allegory of the Lacanian symbolic moment whereby the father gives his name to the child and creates a symbolic rather than biological system of obligations. Thus the symbolic order tyrannizes culture, forcing everyone who wishes to become a member of society to define his or her life as something owed to others. But to undo this order in the manner of Thomas Paine, who assaults Burke's notion of a permanent obligation to the dead, is to define culture as the collection of independent people without any necessary obligation to each other (40–45).[5] In Wordsworth's rendition of that post-Burkean world, nothing can prevent the individual who pursues freedom from becoming an isolated, nameless consciousness. Exposing the lie of paternity may simply lead to the equally dangerous lie of independence. Refusing both Herbert and Rivers, Burke and Paine, Wordsworth ultimately finds an intractable violence in the constitution of society.[6]

If no hero or victim convincingly substitutes for the community and all obligations seem coercive, the now indifferentiated mass of people cannot represent itself except in the failure of representation, the undoing of symbolic gestures. The critique of the conventions of heroic tragedy thus revisits the problem of cultural dismemberment, already presented in *Salisbury Plain* in quasi-dramatic terms:

> And oft a night-fire mounting to the clouds
> Reveals the desert and with dismal red
> Clothes the black bodies of encircling crowds.
> It is the sacrificial altar fed
> With living men. (181–85)

The "black bodies" of those "encircling crowds," much like the "idle thousands" who seek a glimpse of the hanged sailor in the final stanza of *Adventures,* are members of the ritual audience gathered together to witness a more archaic version of the violence displayed on the stage of *The Borderers.* One might almost argue that these spectators, like the black bodies, have gathered in Pandemonium, the demon castle depicted earlier in the poem (82–85); they would therefore be those to whom Mortimer refers in the lines, "Yes, look, my friend: / The devils at such sights clap their hands" (5.3.76–77; see Marshall 394). Apparently the poet depicts the theater as Pandemonium not to launch a Rousseauist attack upon it, but to suggest that culture itself is a hellish edifice.

Wordsworth's attention to the role of audience in *The Borderers* extends his interest in the Druidic worshippers and demonstrates that for him the audience is anything but passive. By now, he has considerably com-

plicated his first conception of spectatorial guilt; the initial distinction between the traveler and the scene of sacrifice, reported by the voice of the
dead, collapsed in *Adventures,* where the sailor is implicated in the crime
and thus guiltily entranced by spectacles of horror. A similar entrancement
organizes this play. The griding iron passage of *Adventures* reappears in the
multiple strikings of the climactic scene of *The Robbers* discussed above (see
Parker "Spectacles" 374), where again the sight of a physical wound strikes
the spectator and implicates him in the act he witnesses. And the final
stanza of *Adventures,* in which Wordsworth, preparing an incipient critique
of romantic drama, in effect suggests that anyone who is struck by deeds of
barbarous heroism has, like the sailor, already participated in them, leads
readily to those moments in *The Borderers* when the spectator sits immobi-
lized, captivated by the spectacle of his crime.[7]

Thus the disappearance of the tragedy of substitution, which sets the
hero apart from the audience as its representative, leads to the tragedy of
specular resemblance, by which the members of the audience identify with
the actor as an image of themselves. Wordsworth again shifts from the
symbolic to the imaginary order, from narrative to specular encounter. But
this time Lacan's theory of the imaginary subject, whose identification of
himself as another "determines the awakening of his desire for the object
of the other's desire" (*Écrits* 19) and leads him into an aggressive rivalry
with the other for this object, shades into Girard's theory of mimetic desire,
whereby "the subject desires the object because the rival desires it" (*Violence*
145; original in italics). One reader of *The Borderers,* without appealing to
Girard, traces the patterns of mimetic desire in the relations between Mortimer, Herbert, and Idonea. Using the 1842 edition of the play, R. F. Storch
argues that Mortimer is not very interested in Idonea until Rivers, pointing
to Herbert's incestuous love for his daughter, gives Mortimer a rival for
her love. Throughout the play, she remains "no more than an intermediary
between him and Herbert" (347). To emphasize the identification of the
two characters, "Herbert is actually accused of parricide, though there is
nothing in the play at the naturalistic level to explain this (2.895–902)"
(349). In fact, the two characters look like each other, "and it is this resemblance that puts the scheme of murder into Oswald's [Rivers's] mind" (350).
Like Girard, like Lacan on the imaginary, Wordsworth transforms the
conflict of father and son into the rivalry between doubles, rewriting oedipal initiation as imaginary aggression.

This shift from the symbolic to the imaginary also marks the shift
from what Eve Kosofsky Sedgwick calls *homosocial desire* to what she describes, in her discussion of the Gothic, as *homosexual panic.* Amplifying
and radicalizing Girard's notion of mimetic desire, she writes that "in any

erotic rivalry, the bond that links the two rivals is as intense and potent as the bond that links either of the rivals to the beloved" (21). There is "an inherent and potentially active structural congruence" between such bonds and "the structures for maintaining and transmitting patriarchal power" (25). A form of male rivalry and bonding, a certain homosocial structure, is built into the symbolic order. But this play tips the balance decisively toward the rivalry and attachment between men—such that interest in Idonea is almost transparently a pretext for male competition—and thus takes up the mode of the early Gothic, which, according to Sedgwick, emphasizes intense, unmediated relations between men, at once raising and homophobically disclaiming the possibility of homosexual desire (91–92). *The Borderers* fits easily into Sedgwick's list of classic early Gothic texts, such as *Caleb Williams, Frankenstein,* and *Confessions of a Justified Sinner,* each of whose plots "is about one or more males who not only is persecuted by, but considers himself transparent to and often under the compulsion of, another male" (91). In these terms, the play's critique of the norms of substitutive tragedy, heterosexual narrative, and oedipal identification shatters the terms of normative homosocial relations, bringing into play not only the specular but also the homosexual, or at least violently homosocial, encounter.

The Borderers does not entirely fit into this model, however. Sedgwick explains the emergence of Gothic as an effect of the increasingly homophobic policing of male relations, particularly of aristocratic male sexualities, in the eighteenth century (83–96). The Gothic, it seems, raises the specter of desire that it insistently and hatefully proscribes; it arises from an intensively negated sexuality. It polices dangerous desires on behalf of a homophobic patriarchal order, which models normative male relations through a programmatic exclusion of homosexual desire. But this play exemplifies the possibility that the Gothic arises from precisely the reverse: a sexualized hatred, an eroticized violence. What fuels *The Borderers* is not the policing of dangerous desires but the sadomasochistic desire for something dangerous, perhaps deadly, not panic at the thought of intimacy but the pleasure in creating such panic, in crossing the borders of another self. Rather than serving the purposes of various social codes, it participates in their total critique, dramatizing the illegitimacy of the symbolic order and of paternal masculinity. It suggests that men may come to take pleasure in the Girardian sacrificial crisis, where charges of parricide, hints of matricide, and forms of criminal deception proliferate. It arises from Wordsworth's overall tendency to sexualize trauma, remain fascinated with the scene of violent wounding, and fixate on the radical loss of phallic power.

Wordsworth sketches this deviant eroticism most clearly in his inquiry into how one might respond to an utterly disorienting, unwilled guilt. In the face of the primal crime or the sacrificial crisis, how can one expel the knowledge of violence?[8] As Wordsworth writes in his prefatory essay to *The Borderers,* a young man "goes into the world and is betrayed into a great crime" (Osborn 62). What then? The sailor's answer is to submit himself to legitimate authorities who condemn the crime and punish him. But since these authorities have violated the name of justice (*Adventures* 819) and are not legitimate, his submission merely reproduces the violence it was intended to lay to rest, reenacting the crime with himself as the victim. Because this strategy fails and because legitimacy seems to have no other basis, perhaps it will have to be constructed out of the only thing available, hyperbole itself. The longer Wordsworth worked on the play, the more this strategy interested him and the greater he focused on the character of Rivers, both in the play and the prefatory essay (Osborn 15).

   The most explicit account of this strategy comes in Rivers's confession speech to Mortimer in act 4. There Rivers describes how, after abandoning the captain to die and then learning that he had been deceived, he returned from the voyage to find his reputation and chances for heroism ruined (4.2.63–77). Retreating to a convent, he "dozed away the time" (93–94) until "A fresh tide of crusaders / Drove past the place of my retreat" and provoked him:

                                        three nights
       Did constant meditation dry my blood,
       Three sleepless nights I passed in sounding on
       Through words and things, a dim and perilous way;
       And wheresoe'er I turned me, I beheld
       A slavery, compared to which the dungeon
       And clanking chain are perfect liberty.
       You understand me, with an awful comfort
       I saw that every possible shape of action
       Might lead to good—I saw it and burst forth
       Thirsting for some exploit of power and terror. (99–110)

Echoing the project of the crusaders, self-usurpers who have already wandered too far from home, Rivers takes his own errant journey through or beyond the familiar world of words and things, as if retracing the traveler's path into the waste spaces of Salisbury Plain. With an "awful comfort" he relieves himself of guilt for his crime by reenacting it on a grander level, defining himself not as a mere criminal who broke the law, but as a mind resolutely opposed to the very principle of law. To be released from the

burden of guilt, he need only reverse the meaning of his crime; to be outside the law might also mean to be above the law, capable of determining
by himself what actions "might lead to good." Taking advantage of the indeterminacy of hyperbole, Rivers redefines criminality as heroism, dispensing with the framework of legitimacy altogether and consciously embracing
hyperbole as his proper condition. With this simple act of "seeing" his outlaw status from a new perspective, he extravagantly "burst[s] forth" from
obscurity to terrible power.[9]

This self-usurpation still bears traces of traditional heroic myth. Rivers meditates for three sleepless nights in a parody of Christ's three-day
ordeal of crucifixion and resurrection, drying his blood and negating the
body for the sake of spiritual transformation. On some level he imagines
that his self-sacrifice, like Christ's passion, cancels the old law and opens an
era of genuine liberty. Similar traces of myth appear later in his confession,
especially when he reinterprets the crime in classical terms. When he tells
Mortimer that "one man / Was famished and ten thousand have been
saved" (172–73), he implicitly links his deed with heroic parricide or tyrannicide and the revival of something akin to the Roman republic. But these
appeals to the heroism of liberation immediately dissipate in the face of
Rivers's uncontainable ambition; his transformation will enable him not to
save the world but amaze it with "some exploit of power and terror," and
he refers to tyrannicide in the context of reminding Mortimer "wherein
[he] differ[s] / From common minds" (170–71), justifying his crime not as
the means of freeing the world, but of expressing his own distinctive
greatness.

Elsewhere in the play Rivers extends this pattern. Lacy suggests to a
receptive Mortimer that the band convene the people to pass judgment on
Herbert so that "he shall be sacrificed" in the light of reason (2.3.418–28),
hoping to legitimate the violence against Herbert as an exercise of law or
communal justice. Lacy envisions, of course, something like the trial of
Louis Capet by the revolutionary Convention in December 1792 and Janu-
ary 1793. But Rivers is no Jacobin. Revealing his thoughts in a soliloquy a
few moments after Lacy's proposal, he scorns legal proof in favor of the
judgments of passion, primarily because he wants to intensify the "storms
and anguish of [Mortimer's] spirit" and "dissect" his mind further (see
3.2.1–32). Even revolution is too confining for Rivers. The whole point of
his strategy is to set Mortimer apart from others; instead of persuading him
of Herbert's guilt in the terms of legitimate sacrifice he tempts Mortimer to perform an improper deed that will isolate him and set him beyond
the law.[10]

The refusal of heroic myth or legitimate violence transforms the role of hero itself. In one passage of his confession Rivers disrupts the complex stance of the *pharmakos:*

> I had been nourished by the sickly food
> Of popular applause. I now perceived
> That we are praised by men because they see in us
> The image of themselves; that a great mind
> Outruns its age and is pursued with obliquy
> Because its movements are not understood.
> I felt that to be truly the world's friend,
> We must become the object of its hate. (4.2.150–57)

According to Girard, the classical *pharmakos* is blamed for the community's crimes and driven from the city, but because he enables the community to eradicate its violence and guilt he becomes honored as its savior. He is the substitute victim of the community's ambivalent love and hatred for itself (85–88, 94–99). Rivers nearly takes upon himself this role, claiming that as the world's friend and savior he becomes the object of public scorn. But he differs from the *pharmakos* in at least two ways. First, rather than being blamed for communal violence or made an image of all it must destroy, he is merely misunderstood, someone who is neither a hero/victim nor a part of the community. Second, since no one actually accuses him of wrong-doing, he achieves this ostracized status only in fantasy, inventing an imaginary hostility that he interprets as a sign of privilege. For a public, symbolic violence he substitutes the fantasized violence of self-usurpation, creating a hyperbolic selfhood by turning against the internalized sources of social approval for his actions.

Rivers articulates the disruption of the *pharmakos* role in his "extravagant" reading of Herbert, who like the hero of *Oedipus at Colonus,* enters the play a blind man led by his daughter (Hartman *Wordsworth's Poetry* 131). If, as Hartman suggests, "Herbert's blindness suggests a visionary faculty that cannot be mutilated," making his strength "invulnerably founded beyond nature" (131), it can only be because like Oedipus this criminal has become a holy man, a *pharmakos.* But almost immediately, in the play's first scene, Rivers begins to demystify Herbert's holiness by exposing his crimes, as if turning the blessed old man Oedipus back into the man who committed parricide and incest. Rivers resists the logic whereby the criminal becomes holy, setting this play into motion as one that demystifies classical tragedy and committing himself to a hyperbolic heroism akin to his extravagant reading.

By resisting the tragic hero's ascent to symbolic status, Rivers turns blindness, which marks Herbert's difference from all of the spectators within the play, into the unpredictable, reversible condition of failing to see or to be seen. He spurns the opinions of the spectators and attempts to take himself out of their line of sight:

> When from these forms I turned to contemplate
> The opinions and the uses of the world,
> I seemed a being who had passed alone
> Beyond the visible barriers of the world
> And travelled into things to come. (4.2.141–45)

Rivers contemplates the world from a stage conceived as an invisible space, the domain of the future, whence he can become the privileged spectator of his audience. To be on stage is not to represent an action but to pass beyond the barrier between audience and stage, to enter into a nameless condition that may as well be curtained off from view. A kind of anti-*pharmakos* in an antitragedy, Rivers does not represent the social totality but exceeds it. Even if the curtains were pulled back, there would be nothing to see; because Rivers cannot name his ambition to himself or tie it to any specific purpose, he could not represent it for our view.[11] Like one of Nietzsche's ascetics, he would rather "will *nothingness* than *not* will," and accordingly his ambition is intransitive, aiming into the beyond (Nietzsche 97, 162–63). He wishes to transform his involuntary ghostliness into a consciously willed condition of originality and greatness, to read the precipitous disorientation of revolution as a passage "into things to come" (4.2.145).

But as Wordsworth makes clear, for Rivers to gain such powers he must sacrifice his own body, perform his own death. Choosing the radical self-division into mutilated body and ghostly consciousness which befell the sailor in the moment of his crime (compare the blinded body and ghostly fatherhood that befell Herbert in the moment of violence at Antioch), he must wound, perhaps even castrate, himself.[12] He must not only dispense with his social identity, his resemblance to other men (or to their "image" of themselves [153]), and his position in the domain of the Other generally, but also the visible, corporeal body that belongs to that world. He must blind himself, become like Herbert (conceived not as saint but as ascetic), or alternately turn blindness into privileged insight by imagining that everyone else is blind and cannot see his essential and invisible self. His mind no longer seems to depend upon his body—"I mounted / From action up to action with a mind / That never rested—without meat or drink / I have lived many days" (120–23)—and takes on the substantiality of the body: "my very dreams / Assumed a substance and a character" (124–

25). By surpassing the limitations of the social self and its body, it seems that he discovers a realm of limitless possibilities: "I stood astonished at myself—my brain / Was light and giddy, and it teemed with projects / Which seemed to have no limit" (115–17). These projects have no limit, of course, because they will never materialize as any specific project; in a world where all is bare, white, and formless, every project and no project is possible (a situation that returns later in Wordsworth's career, for example, in the crisis depicted in the first book of the 1805 *Prelude*). The originality for which he sacrifices his identity is ecstatic and dizzying, but also directionless, empty, and wasteful.

But here as always Wordsworth derives this hyperbolic subjectivity from the logic of dismembered culture; this, too, is the subjectivity of another, violated body. Ironically, when Rivers claims to have surpassed humanity and crossed into the future, he identifies with the captain, whom he abandoned in a domain similarly "beyond the visible barriers of the world":

> One day at noon we drifted silently
> By a bare rock, narrow and white and bare.
> There was no food, no drink, no grass, no shade,
> No tree nor jutting eminence, nor form
> Inanimate, large as the body of man,
> Nor any living thing whose span of life
> Might stretch beyond the measure of one moon . . .
>
> . . . .
>
>   'Twas a spot—
> Methinks I see it now—how in the sun
> Its stony surface glittered like a shield:
> It swarmed with shapes of life scarce visible;
> And in that miserable place we left him—
> A giant body mid a world of beings
> Not one of whom could give him any aid,
> Living or dead. (4.2.22–28, 37–44)

Rivers refuses food and drink, as well as the "sickly food / Of popular applause," because on some level he wishes to be famished like the captain, placed permanently beyond the "opinions and the uses of the world" and its "words and things" in the bare, white, lifeless, formless domain of the world to come. He wishes to find a place in the midst of nothingness, an "island / But by permission of the winds and waves" (57–58), a location barely distinct from the storms of the deluge. In reinterpreting his crime, he unconsciously reenacts it as his own victim, as if he were a captain who asked to be abandoned because he scorned his crew and preferred nothingness to their company. Like the sailor of *Adventures* who is entranced by any sight that reminds him of his crime and cannot distinguish between himself and his victim, Rivers retrospectively (and unconsciously) identifies with the captain in that Lebanese convent and relives his ordeal in a trance that lasts three days.

In the very interpretive gesture with which he seizes a privileged subjectivity, Rivers becomes another version of the man he murdered. Despite his intentions, his interpretation of his crime as greatness is itself an act of hyperbolic disorientation. Strangely enough, the attempt to master the crime repeats it on the level of interpretation. The will to mastery, it turns out, is inseparable from the will to repetition. Yet clearly Rivers wishes to repeat with a difference. In claiming greatness for himself, he wishes to distance himself as far as possible from the obscurity of the abandoned captain, and in claiming a more than mortal status he wishes to attain the opposite of the latter's spectacularly exposed condition. For him, to master the crime is to repeat it self-consciously while denying that he is in the same traumatic condition as his victim.

The drive toward masterful repetition leads Rivers literally to restage his crime, this time on his own terms and for his own ends. Accordingly, he needs another captain, another desolate place, another crew who will watch another person like himself abandon the old man. With these new figures playing the old roles, he will in effect direct his crime as a play, coaching especially one new actor (Mortimer) in his lines and creating effects that will satisfy the demands of that other crew, the theatrical audience. Wordsworth's conception of the manipulative Rivers thus marks another self-reflexive dimension of the play: if tragedy somehow enacts crime, then directing or stage-managing a tragedy amounts to planning and carrying out a crime. But Wordsworth stages less the crime itself than Rivers's attempt to restage it. As readers of the closet drama rather than spectators of stage action, we witness the disembodied intelligence, akin to the author's, which operates behind stage without appearing there, the obsessive mind of a theatrical management or criminal conspiracy that would insist, as long as another audience would come, on repeatedly reenacting the crime. In this way Wordsworth not only continues his critique of theatrical convention and production but also begins to sketch the shape of an invisible authorship out of reach of popular applause but still within the line of sight of the solitary reader, his specular counterpart. The action of the play, never actually staged in Wordsworth's lifetime, disappears into the pattern in which the figural author shadows the minds of his characters, as if doubling his own activity through the gestures of his surrogates, and in which the reader doubles it again, shadowing the author in the hidden space of the closet.

In staging Rivers's attempt to restage his crime through the actions of others, Wordsworth must also dramatize the way Rivers mediates his ascetic triumph over the body in his relation to Mortimer. Reinventing himself in an imaginary mode, he deems it sufficient to shape the life of a specular counterpart whom he experiences vicariously as his former consciousness. This desire to image his invisibility, which seems by definition to be impossible, derives from the structure of specular relations already glimpsed in *Adventures;* by giving an external image (often a corpse or ghost) to nameless subjectivity, the face of the criminal's imaginary other makes the latter visible, saving it from its giddy, limitless condition. What results here is the uncanny relation between these two characters which critics have often noted and which so closely resembles the Gothic plots mentioned by Sedgwick: Rivers guides another mind as if it were his own, and Mortimer is haunted by someone who seems to know his every thought. Thus mediated, Rivers's self-wounding narcissism becomes the project of forcing another to become an unwitting criminal and traumatically attain a hyperbolic consciousness. At some point the violence of this manipulation begins to overshadow the crime it is meant to restage; Rivers's narcissistic pleasure in manipulating himself, as in the mode of autobiography (cf. Mileur *Romance* 68–72), gives way to the pleasure of subjecting another mind to his own ends. This pleasure derives not from a dramatically closeted genital sexuality between men, as Sedgwick might argue, but from the pleasure of reproducing one's mind in another, of mastering it, shadowing it in its closet, and effacing its otherness. Nor does it derive from sadism, for it expresses the longings of an almost entirely disembodied subject, the precipitate of the internalized dead captain, who, like a predatory ghost, wishes to image his invisible condition.[13]

In his account of Rivers's project, Wordsworth carries out a critique of self-consciously extravagant authorship. By attempting to master the subjectivity of Mortimer, Rivers is mastered by the inhuman subjectivity of the abandoned captain, and by trying to master his hyperbolic life, he falls prey again to the alien logic of hyperbole. Wordsworth's concern is not to take issue with Godwin's rationalism or to interpret the Reign of Terror but to demonstrate that choosing errancy merely replicates it in an even more unmasterable mode. The play marks his critique of those who would choose for cultural dismemberment, who would, like the decadents or the high modernists, celebrate a certain dislocation, or would, like all those who wish to enforce the knowledge of violence, painfully unsettle the consciousness of others, forgetting that in this very act they repeat the violation of themselves.

How, then, should one respond to one's radical self-estrangement? By the end of the play, Mortimer, like Rivers before him, is faced with this question, for Rivers has succeeded very well in causing him to kill Herbert unintentionally, to experience the crime as a loss of the body (3.2.72–74), and to identify with his victim (in the trance of 5.1.16–22). The resort to law is again impossible, and the punishment of Rivers resolves nothing, because the band's capture of him in the final scene merely forecloses Rivers's response to his condition, not that condition itself. In his final speech, Mortimer proposes a response:

> Raise on this lonely Heath a monument
> That may record my story for warning—
> SEVERAL OF THE BAND (*eagerly*) Captain!
> MORTIMER No prayers, no tears, but hear my doom in silence!
> I will go forth a wanderer on the earth,
> A shadowy thing, and as I wander on
> No human ear shall ever hear my voice,
> No human dwelling ever give me food
> Or sleep or rest, and all the uncertain way
> Shall be as darkness to me, as a waste
> Unnamed by man! and I will wander on
> Living by mere intensity of thought,
> A thing by pain and thought compelled to live,
> Yet loathing life, till heaven in mercy strike me
> With blank forgetfulness—that I may die. (5.3.262–75)

Here Wordsworth assembles all of the terms of errancy familiar to us so far: wandering; the shadowy or invisible, bodiless self; the absence of shelter, food, rest; the dark and uncertain, or dim and perilous, way, where there is no clear path or direction; the waste vacant of names or boundaries; the ascetic solipsism of pain and pure mind; and the threshold condition between life and death. Mortimer even posts a warning monument, a monitory sign like the sunset cannon or voice of the dead, near the threshold of extravagance. As a captain going into exile, he is both the abandoned captain and Rivers, who chooses the captain's fate retrospectively. All of these terms are subsumed under the trope of self-condemnation, whereby Mortimer interprets the hyperbolic condition as exile from the community he values. He attempts to restore legitimacy indirectly by judging himself according to the terms of the law and by erecting a monument in order to prevent the community from crossing over with him. But even this effort is bound to fail. Like Herbert, Mortimer abdicates his responsibility and leaves the community to its own devices. The monument is at best a negative sign, warning culture away from a certain path instead of positively establishing a new cultural order, and at worst a sign of cultural negation, a haunted gravestone marking a ghostly presence which wanders beyond sight or sound in a painful intensity of thought.

Failing to restore culture, the condemnation of errancy simply marks its lawlessness, giving the waste "unnamed by man" the name of "the border" where "established Law & Government" are absent (Osborn 814). Ending with a kind of antimonument, the play refuses closure, setting up in its final lines yet another version of the exile of the captain, Herbert, and Rivers. We cannot leave this play; like Mortimer walking off the stage at the end, the spectator departs the theater not into the real world but into the invisible space of exile already captured in the play's scenes of heroic invisibility. To leave the theater is to repeat those moments in *The Borderers* when the actors depart into the (anti)theatrical space of pure interiority, a specular counterpart of the space of hyperbolic authorship and readership.[14] Although he renounces romantic drama's power to captivate its audience through scenes of criminal heroism, Wordsworth captivates the audience in a more fundamental way, which the specularizing reader of this play cannot easily resist, locating the audience inescapably within the domain of the undoing of tragedy and the dismemberment of culture.

THREE

"Oh misery! oh misery!"

Masochistic Repetition in "Incipient Madness,"
The Ruined Cottage, and "The Thorn"

In the summer of 1797, when William and Dorothy Wordsworth moved to Alfoxden, Coleridge's influence upon Wordsworth's ambitions began to alter the direction of his work. Coleridge planned to write a millenialist theodicy, modeled generally on what Alan Bewell has called the Enlightenment *philosophical poem*, the "vast anthropological epic that would show, through an analysis of human nature and its powers, how mankind, left on its own, had advanced from a state of nature to society" (6). Inspired by Coleridge's work on "The Brook," Wordsworth planned his own epic, *The Recluse*, which would describe man, nature, and society as part of a benevolent design given by a principle immanent in nature or society itself (6–13). In certain hands, such a project would imagine society as a product of human history and therefore something that contemporary political activity might improve or even redeem. By naturalizing a radically different distribution of power and property, for example, it might provide a disciplined rationale for British radicals to challenge the authority of entrenched state interests, or it might lead to the poem that Coleridge urged Wordsworth to write "in blank verse, addressed to those who, in consequence of the complete failure of the French Revolution, have thrown up all hopes of the amelioration of mankind, and are sinking into an almost epicurean selfishness" (*Collected Letters* 1:289).

It is not surprising that Wordsworth took the idea of the philosophical epic to heart and decided to write *The Recluse*. After all, he was familiar with certain strands of eighteenth-century moral philosophy, shared many of Coleridge's concerns, and had already written poems that registered a philosophically informed radicalism. But as we have seen, the most pronounced tendency of his work had been to articulate his sense of the dismemberment of culture. To write an Enlightenment epic, he would have had to imagine how to return his errant poetics to a true home, to the security of grounded political or philosophical discourses—the very ones, according to his own totalizing interpretation of events, which had lost all legitimacy and transformed into their barbaric opposites.[1]

Despite the difficulty of the task, Wordsworth did take hold of this ambition to write some version of a hopeful poem. Toward the end of 1797 and the beginning of 1798, he found himself in an odd position, at once taking culture's dismembered condition for granted and hoping to find a way beyond it. As a result, he had little choice but to pursue the general strategy of *The Borderers*, deciding that in the absence of legitimate discourses the best response to hyperbole lay in hyperbole itself. Yet the texts of this period depart from the mode of that play. Although certain motifs remain—such as fascination, repetition, identification, ascesis—their tone changes, for now hyperbole is figured not as crime but as abandonment.[2] The totalizing interpretation of culture's undoing leads in this case to the sense that the world has disappeared and left one alone in a featureless domain. What befalls the hapless subject is not unwitting guilt but utter isolation in an alien landscape. Here Wordsworth returns to the problematic of radical dislocation sketched in *Salisbury Plain* and complicates it considerably; in "Incipient Madness," *The Ruined Cottage*, and "The Thorn," the subjects of this chapter, he provides a sketch and a critique of a complex of male fantasies surrounding the abandoned woman, and in "The Discharged Soldier," "The Old Cumberland Beggar," and the biography of the pedlar, the concerns of Chapter Four, he reconceives of extravagant wandering. In these closely related texts he explores the possibility that excessive suffering eventually produces an infinite indifference, a more than human calm. Although he addresses such topical concerns as the consequences of war for the poor, begging, and peddling, he nevertheless remains at a great remove from them, treating them as figures in allegories of the reconstruction of culture, aspects of his own distinctive brand of secular theodicy.[3] Rather than hopeful politics or enlightened philosophy, he examines and, to a certain extent, deconstructs a singularly perverse model of ascetic redemption.

I

The initial statement in this series of texts is "Incipient Madness," a short poem that Wordsworth wrote in 1797 but never published in his lifetime. Setting the terms of a problematic that will concern him in *The Ruined Cottage* and "The Thorn," he figures errancy not as the transgression of a boundary or law, but as the subject's radical contingency in the landscape. Subtly altering the terms of the Salisbury Plain poems, he suggests that the wanderer need not stray from the proper path to become hyperbolic, for he is, it seems, out of place from the start, already abandoned and exposed in an inhuman terrain. This subject images its displaced condition not in a gibbeted corpse, which would suggest its complicity in the violent transgression of a boundary or law, but in a "speck of glass" (23); within an uninhabited, ruined hut, similarly abandoned and solitary in these waste spaces, it sees "At a small distance, on the dusky ground, / A broken pane which glitter'd in the moon / And seemed akin to life" (5–7).[4] Its vexed counterpart is no longer the horse of the Female Vagrant's ghost story, who struck a spot where a murdered man lay half-buried, but the restless horse of this poem, the "dull clanking" of whose chains mix with the sounds of wind and rain (26–34). No grave provokes this agitation, which seems as sourceless as the winds. Apparently effacing every trace of violence, the speck of glass and the dull clanking nevertheless captivate the traveler, who, falling prey to an alien consciousness, returns obsessively to the ruin.

What in these images and sounds, which seem to precede all reference to the symbolic order or its undoing, could so captivate this wanderer? Wordsworth intimates that something in them calls upon an old grief, a preoedipal wound. Commenting on the broken pane, he writes, "There is a mood, / A settled temper of the heart, when grief, / Become an instinct, fastening on all things / That promise food, doth like a sucking babe / Create it where it is not" (7–11). The comparison between instinctive grief and the babe's search for the mother's breast is more than a simile; this babe is on the verge of discovering that it is separate from the mother and that the presence on whom it depended might become absent. Through separation anxiety the babe splits from the mother's body and from itself, falling into a grief or "settled temper of the heart," perhaps the primordial mood of consciousness. As Wordsworth goes on to suggest, this mood pertains to the problem of presence and absence: "From this time / I found my sickly heart had tied itself / Even to this speck of glass. It could produce / A feeling as of absence [ ] / [ ] on the moment when my sight / Should feed on it again" (11–16). This passage, itself compounded of present and absent words, figures presence and absence in the traveler's departure and return; his heart is "tied" to the glass, almost as if he reels himself out and back toward it. Here Wordsworth writes his own version of Freud's famous *fort-da* scene in *Beyond the Pleasure Principle*, tossing the traveler, rather than the object, back and forth in order to master the mother's absence (8–11).[5]

In this treatment of presence and absence, Wordsworth borrows from his earlier account of disorientation. The passage in which the traveler steps into the "still and dark" hut and glimpses from amidst the darkness

"A broken pane which glitter'd in the moon" (3–5) alludes to the lines in *Adventures* where the "lightning's faint disastrous gleam / Disclose[d] a naked guide-post's double head, / Sight which, though lost at once, some glimpse of pleasure shed" (169–71) and in *Salisbury Plain*, where the double head is the "Sole object where he stood had day its radiance spread" (108). The glass, which pleasurably images presence and absence, recalls the two-sided sign posted on the threshold between place and no place. The anxious wanderings to and from the glass act out the sign's doubleness in the form of spatial movement; captivated by the gleam, the traveler falls under the spell of the ungrounded reversibility of absence and presence. The both/neither indeterminacy of errancy leads ultimately to the back-and-forth game of *fort-da*.

However ungrounded the reversibility of this game, it at least fastens itself to a determinate object. Like the Freudian child who plays with the little bobbin, the traveler represents repetition in a determinate form in relation to the pane of glass. Wordsworth's account here closely resembles that of Lacan; according to the latter, through repetition the child moves from the domain of unsatisfied physical need into that of representation. Instead of expressing "some need that might demand the return of the mother, and which would be expressed quite simply in a cry," the child "[repeats] the mother's departure as cause of a *Spaltung* [split] in the subject" (*Concepts* 62–63). In this moment, "desire becomes human" and "the child is born into language," because "his action destroys the object that it causes to appear and disappear in the anticipating *provocation* of its absence and presence" (*Écrits* 103).[6] More specifically, what represents (or repeats) the "vacillation of being" (*C* 258) in relation to the mother is the subject's "self-mutilation" (*C* 83) or violent separation from himself "through the function of the *objet a*" (*C* 258)—for example, the child's bobbin—which Lacan describes as "a small part of the subject that detaches itself from him while still remaining his, still retained" (*C* 62). One could fancifully read the *broken* pane of glass as Wordsworth's sign for the object's origin in violent self-alienation; the piece of glass is, as it were, a shard of the self.

It is no accident that the privileged object in this poem is a pane of glass "which glitter'd in the moon / And seemed akin to life" (6–7). As Lacan remarks, "the most characteristic term for apprehending the proper function of the *objet a*" is the gaze (*C* 270), which, in his anecdote on the subject, appears in the field of vision as a "gleam of light" (*C* 96). According to Lacan, in the field of vision the subject is not the geometral point of perspectivist painting, but the person who finds something missing in geometral landscapes: a lack, a hole, an element that eludes vision (*C* 72–73, 108), a lack, in short, which constitutes the subject.[7] This elusive, unapprehensible (83) element is the gaze, the light that looks at the subject "from all sides" (*C* 72) and shows the images in dreams (*C* 75). The subject, out of place in the geometral picture, can locate himself only if he finds an image of the lack, an *objet a*, in a point of opacity or perspectival disturbance (i.e., anamorphosis [*C* 79–90]) where the gaze can reveal itself.[8]

To illustrate his theory, Lacan tells the anecdote mentioned above about a trip he took as a youngster with a poor Breton fisherman, Petit-Jean. Spying a sardine can floating on the waves and glittering in the sun, Petit-Jean said, "*You see that can? Do you see it? Well, it doesn't see you!*" Lacan muses that the can was "looking at me, all the same. It was looking at me at the level of the point of light, the point at which everything that looks at me is situated," in short at the point of the gaze. Furthermore, Petit-Jean is highly amused by his remark, and Lacan less so, because Lacan, "at that moment—as I appeared to those fellows who were earning their livings with great difficulty, in the struggle with what for them was a pitiless nature—looked like nothing on earth. In short, I was rather out of place in the picture."[9] Out of place in a picture that nevertheless was looking at him, Lacan saw, in the glittering sardine can, what it was that gazed at him. What mediates the unapprehensible gaze in the picture is the opaque surface of the can, which provides a point for the "play of light and opacity" and locates the gaze in "the ambiguity of the jewel" (*C* 95–96).

Oddly enough, by designating the subject's lack, the object rescues the subject from the radical disorientation occasioned by that lack. The point "where the subject sees himself caused as a lack by *a*" is also the point "where *a* fills the gap constituted by the inaugural division of the subject" (*C* 270; cf. *C* 144–45). The *a* is at once the product of self-division and the object that covers over that division. In his anecdote, Lacan is out of place, has wandered beyond his proper place, and does not belong in the picture. But in the glittering can he finds an image of what in him exceeds the picture: the alienated and improper subjectivity that appears so ridiculous to Petit-Jean. By making the improper into an image, by representing self-alienation as an external self, the *objet a* gives the hyperbolic subject a proper, if illusory, shape.

A similar process takes place in Wordsworth's text. The traveler is caught on a "dreary moor" under the all-pervasive moonlight (1–2), alone under the sky like the solitary wanderers on Salisbury Plain. As Karen Swann states, here "a slightly paranoid or agoraphobic feeling of being exposed and dissolved on a landscape . . . resolves with the subject's unnerving but perhaps also consoling encounter with an uncanny look" ("Suffering" 91).[10] To be out of place, to be exposed or naked under a pitiless sun or moon, is to be singled out as the object of the world's gaze (or its ridi-

cule) and is to verge on becoming its sacrificial victim. Through the metaphorical self-mutilation of the *objet a* the traveler wards off the possibility
that the gaze will mutilate him, that the daylight will metamorphose into
the violent blaze of sacrifice. The subject who is in danger of being the only
opaque surface, the only disruptive element in the picture, welcomes the
appearance of the gleaming object onto which he can project his own improper subjectivity. Thus the poem's speaker says that the speck of glass,
"Still undisturb'd and glittering in its place," was "more precious to my
soul / Than was the moon in heaven" (22–24), more intimately related to
his subjectivity than the source of light.

As a visible image of the subject, the gleaming *objet a* is a version of
the mirror image in which the subject recognizes an external, alien form of
himself. The traveler's obsession with the glass is thus a version of what
Lacan calls "the trap of imaginary capture" (*E* 211) whereby the subject first
images himself and forges an identity (*E* 18–19). "From the moment
that this gaze appears, the subject tries to adapt himself to it, he becomes
that punctiform object, that point of vanishing being with which the subject confuses his own failure" (*C* 83). The purpose of the traveler's obsessive
return is not merely to play with the glass as if it were a bobbin, but to
identify with it, vanish into it, and become the gaze. He wishes to disappear into the light, whose lunar source seems seems inseparable from the
mechanical logic of repetition, from the impersonal rhythms of its rising
and setting.

On one level, then, the traveler submits to an alien temporal logic
akin to that of the first stanzas of *Salisbury Plain*, where his journey into
the waste is measured by the sun's trajectory toward the horizon. Once
again, to depart from the self is to become the passive plaything of an alien
self; instead of tossing the bobbin back and forth, Wordsworth's travelers
are thrown to and fro by that intimate stranger. Yet, as we have seen,
through the metaphorical self-mutilation of the specular relation the traveler in this text intervenes in the process of his subjection and wards off its
sacrificial culmination. Imaging the alien temporality of celestial objects
through the broken pane, he turns the impossibly distant mechanism into
a repetitive practice in which he can participate. During "many a long
month" his "eye / Did every evening measure the sun's height / And forth
[he] went soon as her yellow beams / Could overtop the elm-trees" (16–20).
As Swann argues, the traveler becomes the "impresario of his own captivation" by "plotting the coordinates of moon, glass, and eye, discovering the
laws governing their alignment, and then metamorphosing into part of the
mechanism" ("Suffering" 88).

No doubt the traveler performs his repetition in a conscious, even strategic mode, as Joseph C. Sitterson suggests in another context (102–5), but because he is playing with the sun (instead of a bobbin) his metaphorical language is tied to movements he cannot control. Having signified self-alienation in the *objet a,* the broken pane, he goes one more step and projects the game of repetition onto nature, alienating even language from himself. The traveler adds another level to the dynamic described by psychoanalysis: it is repetition that he wants to repeat, it is captivation itself that captivates him.[11] The object of his desire is no longer the shard of glass, but rather the exercise of repetition itself. The early simile in the poem may be a simile after all; the traveler may simply be *like* the babe, recalling the pleasures of infantile repetition for adult purposes.

Projecting the language of repetition onto nature in order to make it a source of pleasure, the traveler makes images into his words, natural repetition into his syntax. In effect, he transforms natural processes into a language of alienated subjectivity. Nature ceases to be nature and becomes, like the Spenserian stanza, an impersonal mechanics of repetition. The sun's rising and setting are as rhythmic, regulated, and serialized as any stanza form, and its nonsignificative markings of time's passing give syntax to the day and night. Its endless motion (to speak a pre-Copernican language) captures the errancy of romance in a deviance that circles back upon itself, such that the traveler, perpetually wandering from his true self, treads always the same path fastened to the image of his self-alienation. If the traveler creates his own story in this language of repetition, he cannot help telling it again and again, as if he wants to become merely the personification of a story told from elsewhere, a bobbin spun around in the syntax of the sun. He has been captivated by a figure that mechanizes subjectivity. Already implicit here is the strange logic of Coleridge's *Rime of the Ancient Mariner* and "Christabel," where characters seem to be personifications of an ungrounded figuration, and of Wordsworth's "The Thorn," where an evanescent woman materializes out of a collection of images and a repeated phrase.[12] What results in this case is the subject's total absorption into nature. Creatures of light (the glow worm) and sound (the linnet) come and go, but the speaker, now nearly disembodied, remains alone with "the winds of heaven" and the beams of dawn and sunset (36–49). The blackbird who nests in the thorn, which obscures and displaces the ruin (40), gives way to the uncanny figure who will reappear in the vicinity of another thorn. On the verge of madness, the subject blends not with the gaze but with the inhuman rhythms of the sun.

Wordsworth's treatment of separation anxiety, the *objet a,* and captivation marks a new phase in his engagement with the problem of cultural dissolution. "Incipient Madness" demonstrates that a dismembered culture does not return to the stable ground of nature. When the symbolic order of the dead father has dissolved, culture finds itself not with the mother's body, but with the specular object that represents her absence. All too easily the heart recovers the settled temper of the infant's grief and plays at the old game of repetition. Although certain theorists would postulate that the return to the preoedipal period would allow the subject to indulge in a se-miotic, rather than symbolic, language (Julia Kristeva) or in a literal lan-guage of touch and nonsense sounds (Margaret Homans), in that domain Wordsworth finds only what Lacan calls "the radical vacillation of the sub-ject" (*C* 239).[13] For Wordsworth, if one refuses institutional, patriarchal language one gets not natural language—the goal he seeks in 1798, one we will discuss below and in the next chapter—but the site of a breach in nature which provokes an ungrounded language to come into being.

Although the house of culture falls into ruins, it does not return to the soil; at the bare minimum, culture endures as a ruin, a splinter of glass, and the sound of rattling chains. It is thus reduced to what separates the subject from the mother and what differentiates the traveler from the glow worm or the wind. Strictly speaking, one cannot call this condition *culture* at all, for it is caught in between the break from nature and the entry into culture, in the interval between the mother's body and the father's name. In this condition, subjectivity is baffled on one side by repetition and on the other by extravagant wandering, two versions, perhaps, of the same errancy. As Wordsworth suggested in the early Rousseauist stanzas of *Salisbury Plain,* the errant vagrant is akin to the savage, who "happier days since at the breast he pined / He never knew" (12–13). Like the speaker of "Incipient Madness," who self-consciously returns to the infantile game of repetition, the destitute wanderers on Salisbury Plain recapture the mood of savages who have lost the mother. The undoing of the symbolic, it seems, abandons the subject to a fundamental homelessness, to a figuration without ground.[14]

❧ I I

Expanding on the problematic introduced in "Incipient Madness" and further rewriting the Salisbury Plain poems, in *The Ruined Cottage* Wordsworth returns to the problem of war's consequences for the poor family, especially for the woman abandoned by her husband. Depicting the hardships endured by those workers who could not profit from the labor shortages of 1798 (Emsley 75), he gives his poem an immediate political relevance. But this time the cultural dislocation provoked by war and poverty takes the shape of a repetition compulsion tied to one spot, the ruined cottage. The devastating political injustices of English society, already displaced onto the problematic of culture's violent dismemberment, is displaced further onto the radical vacillation of the subject.

By now the setting of this poem, along with everything it implies about the cultural status of women, is familiar. Once again we encounter an abandoned woman in a ruined cottage that is about to sink back entirely into the landscape. The two places associated with the female vagrant— the idealized home of her youth, complete with a "garden stored with peas and mint and thyme" (*Salisbury Plain* 236) and the lonely spital on the plain—fuse into a single dwelling here, as if the cottage that was once home has become another spital, a homeless shelter. Apparently, when her husband leaves, Margaret becomes a vagrant without even having to leave the cottage. Moreover, in her husband's absence, nothing will prevent the cottage from becoming a total ruin; gradually it decays into the hut of "Incipient Madness" where the gaze reveals itself ("four naked walls / That stared upon each other" [31–32]; cf. Reid 546) and where culture is reduced to a minimal difference from nature. Margaret, too, decays into a counterpart of the speaker of that poem, inventing her own games of repetition and eventually disappearing into the grass.

The pronounced link between the fate of Margaret and her cottage makes explicit the comparatively subtle identification we saw in the Salisbury Plain poems between woman and place. Whereas the vagrant can wander, Margaret cannot; like Martha Ray of "The Thorn," she is permanently rooted to a place, defined not as a home but as a spot in the landscape. When her husband departs for war—when she is, according to a familiar Wordsworthian logic, deprived of her position within the symbolic order—the house that happened to stand on that spot decays, her garden goes wild, she gradually loses the power to work or to speak, and she eventually reverts to a prehuman condition. Like the woman of "The Mad Mother," this abandoned mother goes mad with grief and solitude, as if her reason had departed along with her husband. She neglects her duties, becomes ever more distracted, and finally submits entirely to an obsession with her husband's absence. Readers familiar with "Incipient Madness" are not surprised when the pedlar describes one of the activities of the later stages of Margaret's grief:

> Seest thou that path?
> (The green-sward now has broken its grey line)
> There to and fro she paced through many a day

Of the warm summer, from a belt of flax
That girt her waist spinning the long-drawn thread
With backward steps. (457–62)[15]

Swann links "this portrait of Margaret as a human bobbin" to the *fort-da* game in Freud, describing it as an instance of the mechanics of "reelism" which compelled the repetition compulsion of "Incipient Madness" ("Suffering" 85–89). In the final phases of her deculturation, Margaret becomes a female version of the obsessed speaker in that poem, playing a kind of maternal or wifely version of the infant's game around the spot of her husband's absence.

If Margaret resembles the obsessed traveler of that poem, the pedlar does as well; as Peter Manning points out, his "seasonally recurring visits . . . are the [speaker's] obsessive returns to the hut" (20). As many symptomatic details in the pedlar's biography reveal, he shares the speaker's fantasy of reuniting with the mother, but he expresses this fantasy vicariously through Margaret's obsession with her husband (16–27). In effect, then, the traveler of "Incipient Madness" has displaced his own obsession onto a female figure, now located in or near the hut (20–21).[16] Yet the pedlar's obsession is not entirely vicarious because he too is homeless, is plagued by wandering thoughts, and returns repeatedly to this spot. In this poem, Wordsworth splits the repetition compulsion between two characters. Swann argues that "Wordsworth personifies the coordinates of his technical apparatus and then partly dismantles the machine, giving independent causes to the poet's wanderings, the peddler's rounds, and Margaret's restless pacing and shaping." In this reading, Margaret is "neither flesh nor apparition" but a "personified geometric coordinate, sign mysteriously 'akin to life,'" like the broken pane of "Incipient Madness" ("Suffering" 89), and the pedlar, by extension, the personification of the mechanical return to that sign. Perhaps the characters of this poem give faces and names to positions within the vacillation of the subject.

But these characters are not even stable enough to be personifications of any given coordinate. They move between coordinates, trade places, and take up each other's identities so readily that for most of the poem it is difficult to differentiate between them. On one of the pedlar's visits to the cottage, for example, he arrives when Margaret is absent. He wanders through her garden, noting how it is beginning to go wild. "Ere this an hour / Was wasted. Back I turned my restless steps, / And as I walked before the door it chanced / A stranger passed, and guessing whom I sought / He said that she was used to ramble far" (320–24). Here the pedlar becomes

Margaret, looking restlessly for someone who should be in this house, speaking with passersby about the missing person, and, like her, wasting his time (cf. 352). Margaret, it seems, has become Robert or perhaps the pedlar, rambling far afield.

Wordsworth has more in mind, however, than this elementary exchange of roles. The pedlar continues: "The sun was sinking in the west, and now / I sate with sad impatience. From within / Her solitary infant cried aloud. / The spot though fair seemed very desolate, / The longer I remained more desolate" (325–29). By association the impatient pedlar becomes an abandoned infant crying out for the mother. At this point all roles become confused. For one thing, this scene gives the pedlar an infantile dependence upon Margaret and implies that his wandering is a version of the infant's attempt to recover the mother. But since in this scene the pedlar has already been acting as Margaret, as we just saw, then the infant and the pedlar together represent Margaret's cry for help in the midst of desolation. For another thing, this scene takes place because Margaret, trying to recover the lost object (seeking what she "cannot find" [351]), has abandoned her child. To overcome abandonment, to wander, is in turn to abandon another. But since Margaret has been playing the part of the pedlar, this truth also extends to him: this man who wanders back to the cottage, trying to recover the mother, has abandoned nameless others elsewhere just as he abandons Margaret every time he departs. He may simply be another Robert, who abandons her to find what he has lost, a job and its attendant dignity, perhaps the job of peddler.

In this scene the abandoned cannot finally be distinguished from the one who abandons; according to a bewildering logic, each role duplicates every other, and the game that attempts to master abandonment reproduces it. Wordsworth even suggests that infants do not take up the game of presence and absence inevitably and on their own but in imitation of their errant parents: "Her infant babe / Had from its mother caught the trick of grief / And sighed among its playthings," its little bobbins perhaps (409–11). In a strange counterpart to the griding iron passage, these lines suggest that even separation anxiety is a cultural inheritance sighed down from mother to child across the generations. Each generation, hoping to find the lost object, becomes the lost object for its children. As if to invert Nancy Chodorow, who argues that mothers reproduce their own childhood as they nurse their children, Wordsworth hints that they reproduce the much darker experience of separation and abandonment (Chodorow 191–209). At this point we might imagine that Wordsworth is an especially perverse psychoanalyst. Having already turned Lacan's symbolic order upside down in favor of Nicolas Abraham's theory of the phantom, Wordsworth goes on to overturn Chodorow in favor of a darker theory of motherhood.

One effect of this reading of the poem is that the pedlar's narration, which has been read as a successful mediation between the reader and the overwrought emotions of the tale itself (e.g., Hartman *Wordsworth's Poetry* 135–40; Averill *Suffering* 116–17), becomes implicated in them. Margaret's gradual decay into nature and death is not supposed to threaten the reader because the pedlar's calm acceptance of her fate guarantees cultural survival. To implicate him in the obsession, then, is to remove all grounds for complacency and to plunge women *and* men, nature and culture, into a repetition compulsion without reserve. The "fascinating technics" of repetition, Swann argues, "endures through all efforts to gentle or abandon it"; the narrative frame which is supposed to humanize the sensational tale ends up reproducing that tale on another level ("Suffering" 89, 84).

Wordsworth does not place the pedlar and Margaret within precisely the same logic of repetition. Certain crucial differences between them remain. Of course, Margaret falls silent and dies, whereas the pedlar endures to tell her story, but this works out in poetic time the relation that generally obtains between them: Margaret circles around her lost husband, and the pedlar returns to watch the progress of her obsession. Here, as in "Incipient Madness," it is captivation that captivates the speaker, it is repetition that he wants to repeat. If he was the "impresario of his own captivation" before, he is now, as Swann says, the "impresario of her comings and goings, whose calm acceptance of her loss is purchased by her transformation into a repeating, repeatedly abandoned figure" ("Suffering" 86). The strange arrangement of that earlier poem, whereby the traveler could signify his own obsession through the movements of the sun and moon, is now the oddly intimate division between the pedlar and Margaret whereby the pedlar can map his own repetition through hers. In this way he hopes to experience his pain as her pain and remain immune from its ultimate consequences.

Yet because Margaret embodies the repetition that captivates the pedlar, he still depends upon her as the anchor of the system that he pretends to control. Rather than being a personification of the *objet a* to which the pedlar can return at any time, she too is in search of that object and wanders from the cottage where the pedlar expects to find her. Thus she can, in a sense, abandon him. In the scene discussed above, Margaret's absence threatens his privilege so profoundly that he nearly finds himself in the position of the abandoned child. Her return not long after, however, saves him from total identification with her plight and restores his precarious distance from her. Clearly, by making repetition its own object, the pedlar displaces the problem instead of resolving it, acting out her obsession on another level.

Thus in *The Ruined Cottage* Wordsworth sketches a complicated version of the logic of repetition. The pedlar is obsessed with Margaret's obsession, which he both shares and does not share. To sort out this complexity, we should pause here to rethink the dynamics of the *fort-da* game. In his discussion of that game, Freud first suggests that the child is acting on an instinct for mastery over the mother's absence. His second interpretation, as Leo Bersani argues, "is more a revised repetition of his first interpretation than a genuine alternative to it" (58). He speculates that the child throws the spool over the edge of the crib in order "to revenge himself on his mother for going away from him. In that case, it would have a defiant meaning: 'All right then, go away! I don't need you. I'm sending you away myself'" (*Beyond* 10). Bersani comments:

> This of course sounds very much like a form of mastery, but the desire to dominate the situation rather than passively submit to it is now inseparable from an impulse for revenge. That is, the urge to master is affectively charged; it includes what can only be read, it seems to me, as a pleasure at once sadistic and masochistic. The child enjoys the fantasy of his mother suffering the pain of separation which she originally inflicted on him. And to say this is to be reminded that revenge here must include the avenger's own suffering; by making his mother disappear, the child has just as effectively deprived himself of her presence as he has deprived her of his. But the child's suffering is now inseparable from two sources of pleasure: his representation of his mother's suffering, and what I take to be the narcissistic gratification of exercising so much power. In reality, there is no sequence here; rather, there is a single, satisfying representation of a separation painful to both the mother and the child. In other words, mastery is simultaneous with self-punishment. (58)

Like Lacan, Bersani reads the *fort-da* game as a form of self-mutilation whereby the child separates off a part of himself when he represents his mother's absence. But Bersani emphasizes that this self-punishment is inevitably painful. The little bobbin, the *objet a*, is not merely the absent mother, but a mother *made* absent, a suffering and abandoned mother. The child (gendered masculine in Wordsworth and Freud) enters language not merely by representing her absence but by making her absent through representation. Representation inscribes not the child's loss but its aggression, its delight in inflicting and experiencing pain. Lacan argues that the *objet a* represents the "eternally lacking object" (*C* 180) that desire will never find, giving desire the characteristics of an unappeasable longing. In contrast, Bersani implies that the subject desires the absence of the object, depicting desire as a kind of bitter satisfaction. For him, the moment desire becomes human it also becomes masochistic because it takes pleasure not despite the mother's absence but because it wills that absence; the child, it seems, is the first ascetic.[17]

In *The Ruined Cottage* Wordsworth stages a drama of desire very similar to that in Bersani's Freud. Like the masochistic child, the pedlar is obsessed with the image of the suffering mother, whom he desires precisely because he imagines that he has abandoned her. Perhaps he is a Robert in disguise, returning to observe the effects of his desertion. Bersani's theory enables us to understand the complexity of the pedlar's position in this poem. He attempts to master his own sense of abandonment by representing the abandonment of the mother, thereby at once duplicating his own obsession in the mother's and remaining distinct from it in his sense of narcissistic mastery. In short, he attempts to reverse his condition, to impose abandonment onto the mother who abandoned him. In this way he makes the abandoned child into someone who abandons, and the mother who abandons into someone abandoned, creating the apparent confusion of identities which becomes pronounced in the scene discussed above. Ultimately, however, these identities are not lost in a delirium of endless duplication but are organized around the pedlar's fantasy of masochistic revenge.[18]

In the male fantasmatic of this poem, the greater Margaret's distress and the further she wanders in search of what she will not find, the more the pedlar feels both the delight of revenge and the pain of losing her. As Bersani argues, "revenge here must include the avenger's own suffering; by making his mother disappear, the child has just as effectively deprived himself of her presence as he has deprived her of his." The same abandonment that inflicts Margaret hurts the pedlar as well, and thus the experience of her suffering is also his own. This "mechanics of inverse proportion," Swann argues, is an instance of the "reelism" of the *fort-da* game which *The Ruined Cottage* inherits from "Incipient Madness" (85–86). But now the game of "reelism" is fully gendered; in the poem on Margaret Wordsworth departs from sheer repetition, moving as it were from Lacan to Bersani and interpreting repetition not as an impersonal logic but as a game of revenge on the mother. The *objet a* is no longer the broken pane, a splinter of the subject, but the maternal phantasm; and Margaret is not, as Swann states, an "abstract person, personified geometric coordinate" (89), but rather the suffering woman of the pedlar's masochistic fantasy.[19] This poem takes the game of signification to a new level; we might say, turning Bersani back into Lacan, that by inflicting his pain on another the pedlar *represents* it as the fantasy of a woman's suffering.[20] This gesture enables the pedlar to become the impresario of his own pain across the slight gap between himself and Margaret—the gap that is the split in the self.

This masochistic scenario does not replicate itself indefinitely; by aligning himself with the unnamed speaker of the poem, Wordsworth distances himself from the pedlar and sustains an implicitly critical distance from his fantasy. Nevertheless, the poet is inevitably implicated in the fantasy. At one point the pedlar pauses to admonish his listener and himself that it is improper to take pleasure in a tale about the sufferings of others (221–36), strangely enough borrowing terms such as *wantonness* and *dalliance* from Courtly and Cavalier love poetry as he does so (Barron and Johnston 71–72), but he would not be compelled to make these remarks if he were not in the act of engendering such pleasure even as he speaks. Here as elsewhere Wordsworth denounces sensationalism, refusing to sanction pleasure in suffering, but by giving these words to the pedlar he places his refusal in the context of a sensationalist fantasy, implicating his stance in what he wishes to avoid. Despite his best efforts, then, he ultimately registers the captivating effects of trauma. Wordsworth is not alone in this plight; initially it was war trauma that troubled Freud as well and provoked him into writing *Beyond the Pleasure Principle* (see 6–8), in which he attempted to defend the pleasure principle from a potentially explosive insight by assigning war trauma to a newly invented principle, the death drive. Yet as Bersani argues, at various junctures Freud's argument baffles itself and nearly identifies sex and death, pleasure and shattering (61–64). In a similar way, Wordsworth's attempt to denounce sensationalism ends up revealing all the more how desire becomes fixated on what terrifies or shatters the subject.

Despite his disclaimer, the pedlar is deeply implicated in Margaret's suffering. By dallying with it, he risks falling prey to his own kind of incipient madness. Representing his pain through hers, he alienates his language of repetition from himself and becomes captivated by the captivation that she represents, wishing to move according to her inhuman rhythm, to become a figure in the story that she tells. Susan Wolfson points out several passages in which the pedlar nearly identifies with Margaret (106–7). Instead of bringing her comfort, the pedlar relies on her own sources of consolation: "I had little power / To give her comfort, and was glad to take / Such words of hope from her own mouth as serv'd / To cheer us both" (275–78). Her words, it seems, come from his mouth, perhaps even now as he tells her story. Similarly, at one point her expressions of grief seem to come almost from his own body: "While by the fire / We sate together, sighs came on my ear; / I knew not how, and hardly whence they came"

(385–87). Later, she attempts to draw him into her obsession: "in such sort / That any heart had ached to hear her begged / That wheresoe'er I went I still would ask / For him whom she had lost" (440–43). In all of these cases, the pedlar registers his desire that he become subject to the ghostly mechanics of his own alienated suffering, to speak with a mouth no longer his own.

A passage late in the poem suggests that this fantasy of an alienated, improper speech is implicated in a similarly uncanny practice of reading:

> The windows too were dim, and her few books,
> Which, one upon the other, heretofore
> Had been piled up against the corner-panes
> In seemly order, now with straggling leaves
> Lay scattered here and there, open or shut
> As they had chanced to fall. (404–9)

Although this mode of untamed reading seems to trouble the pedlar, it closely resembles the reading practices of his own childhood (Swann "Suffering" 91–92).[21] Here again the pedlar's official stance belies his pleasure. More importantly, however, by extending the logic of the pedlar's fantasy to the scene of reading, this passage reaches beyond Margaret and the pedlar, beyond the framework established by the poem's anonymous speaker, to include the author and his audience as well, unsettling the officializing written text that Wordsworth offers to his readers. The poem that is supposed to become part of *The Recluse* and thus presumably contribute to a philosophical or moral explanation for the human condition becomes an instance of excessive, sensationalist reading. The scattered books with their "straggling leaves" suggest that the masochistic reader refuses to be satisfied with texts that merely inform or instruct. Like the Lacanian subject, which cannot find itself within the perspectival field and looks for the gleaming object that signifies its lack, such a reader searches for something unnameable that escapes any discipline of knowledge. In certain moods, Wordsworth is already Bersani's Freud, whose normalizing theoretical arguments inevitably collapse and reveal "those forces which obstruct, undermine, play havoc with theoretical accounts themselves" in a logic akin to that of masochistic sexuality (Bersani 3–4).[22] As if to resist the project of intellectual mastery, Wordsworth images a bitter revenge on knowledge itself for failing to satisfy what is demanded of it. The books are scattered on the floor, open or shut, in part because Margaret has abandoned them, thrown them away from her like so many versions of the infantile bobbin.

This protest against intellectual mastery undermines a normatively political account of suffering. In the logic of the pedlar's fantasy, Margaret cannot accept any discourse that would explain the loss of her husband as the result of social injustice because she experiences it as an absolute loss to which she can respond only in the absolute terms of self-estrangement and death. Thus *The Ruined Cottage* suggests that when the dismemberment of culture ruins those discourses that could make it readable, it creates (anti)-discourses of masochistic obsession, texts bent on a darkly pleasurable revenge against textuality itself.

Rather than attempting to reconstruct a normative textuality or to write a politically responsible version of *The Recluse,* Wordsworth in effect embraces the masochistic scenario dramatized in this scene, playing it out, albeit from a critical distance, to construct a kind of secular theodicy out of the very problematic that threatens it the most. In the further reaches of the pedlar's fantasy, masochistic revenge, submitting itself entirely to the death wish, resolves itself in a kind of ghostly closure. Through most of the poem, this wish exerts an enormous pressure on Margaret, who gradually but inevitably descends into death. Repetition becomes a kind of progressive intensification of masochistic pleasure; the pedlar's obsessive return to her cottage allows Wordsworth to divide up her decline into discrete stages and ultimately to frame a static repetition within the temporal progression of her decline. The reader follows step by step as Margaret relinquishes a long series of characteristics that link her with the human world: her husband, her children, her capacity to work or to cultivate her garden, her capacity to speak, and finally her life. In Bersani's terms, this ruthless pressure takes masochistic revenge to extremes, as if the child risks his mother's death as he plays the game of repetition. Yet as Bersani also argues, the child imagines that the mother grieves over her separation from the child and that her sorrow expresses her matchless love for the child she can no longer find. It follows that the more intensely she suffers in the child's fantasy, the more loved the child will feel.

The final goal of the masochistic wish would be the mother's death, which in the child's fantasy would show that she loved the child enough to die for him. Only through her death would she be given over to her love without reserve. But because the mother of fantasy remains the child's entire definition of the world, her disappearance would also be directed at the self, as if the child were to say, "Because you have abandoned me I want the whole world to disappear." This wish is nearly fulfilled on that evening, discussed above, when the pedlar finds Margaret absent, searches for her, and finally sits down on the cottage steps to wait for her return: "The sun was sinking in the west, and now / I sate with sad impatience. From within / Her solitary infant cried aloud. / The spot though fair seemed very desolate, / The longer I remained more desolate" (325–29). In these lines we can easily recognize the terms of the Salisbury Plain poems, with their relentless pressure toward the onset of darkness. Once again the sun sinks toward the horizon, the world gradually becomes more desolate, and the protagonist hears a cry of pain. It is no surprise that at this juncture the pedlar looks around and sees "the corner-stones / Till then unmark'd, on either side the door / With dull red stains discoloured" (330–32), an image that is at once associated with and contrasted to images of founding sacrifice, of blood on foundation stones. Here the death wish threatens to abandon Margaret and the crying infant both to utter darkness and to destroy the world in a blaze of masochistic pleasure.

But this moment of death takes an unexpected form. In the next lines, a strangely changed Margaret silently appears a few steps away, in the manner of ghosts: "The house-clock struck eight; / I turned and saw her distant a few steps. / Her face was pale and thin, her figure too / Was chang'd" (336–39). Later in the scene, Margaret tells the pedlar what has changed her: "I have slept / Weeping, and weeping I have waked; my tears / Have flow'd as if my body were not such / As others are, and I could never die" (354–57). In the logic of masochistic desire, the mother's death marks her disappearance into an implacable, nearly demonic grief that possesses her body with a weeping that never ends. Rather than abandoning the mother and itself entirely, then, the child transforms her into an internalized image of perfect love, whom he can reel in on demand whenever his isolation becomes too threatening. On the other side of the world's dissolution, the child discovers an imaginary mother of undying devotion, a phantasm of perfect love which substitutes for the absolute maternal body.

The absent mother's reappearance as a ghost surprises the child, as Wordsworth hints in a *Prelude* passage toward which he is working in this poem:

> For now a trouble came into my mind
> From unknown causes. I was left alone,
> Seeking the visible world, nor knowing why.
> The props of my affections were removed,
> And yet the building stood, as if sustained
> By its own spirit! (2.291–96)

Hartman remarks, "The troubled astonishment of the child may have expressed a defeated expectation, even perhaps a frustrated death wish. Nature should not have survived! The reality bond of motherly affection, being dissolved, should have meant the collapse of everything!" But because the world survives, the child decides that the newfound, ghostly mother is ineradicable and that she cannot abandon him even if she tries. Her presence becomes absolute: "The fixated or literally animistic mind feels that if nature remains alive when what gave it life (the mother) is dead, then the mother is not dead but invisibly contained in nature" (*Unremarkable* 22).

Wordsworth records a version of this surprise in *The Ruined Cottage.* The pedlar's memory of Margaret's ghostliness provokes him a few lines later into an uncharacteristic digression:

> Sir, I feel
> The story linger in my heart. I fear
> 'Tis long and tedious, but my spirit clings
> To that poor woman: so familiarly
> Do I perceive her manner, and her look
> And presence, and so deeply do I feel
> Her goodness, that not seldom in my walks
> A momentary trance comes over me;
> And to myself I seem to muse on one
> By sorrow laid asleep or borne away,
> A human being destined to awake
> To human life, or something very near
> To human life, when he shall come again
> For whom she suffered. (362–75)

For the pedlar, the total physical loss of Margaret transforms her into a loving psychic presence. Somewhat like the abandoned characters of *The Borderers,* she is neither dead nor alive but asleep, drifting in a state beyond physical existence. The pedlar need not return to the cottage, since even in his wanderings Margaret's presence is near; the *objet a* has been displaced from a spot to a psychic image that he carries with him. Apparently, the captivation with the *objet a* gives way to its incorporation into the subject. Although she is in disembodied form, Margaret remains the anchor of his sense of reality; his spirit clings to her because she is his spirit, the split-off part of the subject in which he recognizes himself. At any time her psychic presence can become so intense that it will yield an imaginary reunion whereby the pedlar, falling into a trance, will blend with her more-than-human life. On some level, the pedlar is comforted because he too is a ghost, someone who has endured the world's loss and returned in an insubstantial form.

The pedlar's incorporation of the mother alters his relation to the scene of Margaret's death. In the final lines of the tale, the pedlar tells his listening friend to cease grieving and find comfort in the visible signs of her presence:[23]

> She sleeps in the calm earth, and peace is here.
> I well remember that those very plumes,
> Those weeds, and the high spear-grass on that wall,
> By mist and silent rain-drops silver'd o'er,
> As once I passed did to my heart convey
> So still an image of tranquillity,
> So calm and still, and looked so beautiful
> Amid the uneasy thoughts which filled my mind,
> That what we feel of sorrow and despair
> From ruin and from change, and all the grief
> The passing shews of being leave behind,
> Appeared an idle dream that could not live
> Where meditation was. I turned away
> And walked along my road in happiness. (512–25)

The pedlar is reconciled to Margaret's death because he turns her presence into the sight of spear-grass, representing her once again through a visible sign. This time the *objet a* is not a punctiform object, a pane of glass, because its brightness is shed through many points of light, the "mist and silent rain-drops" that "[silver] o'er" the grass.[24] This dispersal of its gleam signifies that it is not, finally, visible at all; it is, as Hartman says of the mother, "invisibly contained in nature" (*Unremarkable* 22). Like Margaret, it has transformed from a visible absent object into an invisible present one, and it has precisely the opposite of its former effect upon the traveler. Rather than providing a point to which the radically vacillating subject can return repeatedly in his obsessive reeling, it stabilizes him in the image of a hyperbolic stillness, perhaps of a permanent trance. And in place of the tempestuous agitation and clanking noises of "Incipient Madness" is a silence so great that it effaces the sources of anxiety.[25]

This reversal of the mother's absence into presence comes at some cost. Because the mother remains present even after death and because the desired object is invisibly present, the mind need no longer grieve over ruin, change, and death. But as a result, life and death change places: the dead mother is truly alive, whereas the sorrows of the living belong to "the passing shews of being," the unreality of the phenomenal world. Although this resolution relieves the pedlar of the anxiety of an inevitably errant figuration and convinces him that he is rooted firmly in one place, it also places him beyond the need for figuration or language. As Hartman argues in his discussion of "A slumber did my spirit seal," a poem closely affiliated with the spear-grass vision, Wordsworth's

> stately but static figures barely differentiate themselves from their land-scape. It is hard to *see* them; they move in a blind or hypnotic trance as if they too did not need sight, theirs or ours. . . . At times, therefore, Wordsworth's poetry almost transcends representation, and thus reality testing. It gives up not only the eyes but also touch—tangible words. It seems to exist then without the material density of poetic texture—without imagistic or narrative detail. (*Unremarkable* 27)

In this context we might qualify Hartman's point with reference to the strong imagery of the spear-grass vision. But the visibility of the spear-grass, as we saw above, is a sign of an invisible presence that cannot be represented directly. Thus Hartman's point holds for *The Ruined Cottage*, which Wordsworth conceives from the perspective of these late lines. Earlier in the poem, the pedlar remarks:

> 'Tis a common tale,
> By moving accidents uncharactered,
> A tale of silent suffering, hardly clothed
> In bodily form, and to the grosser sense
> But ill adapted, scarcely palpable
> To him who does not think. (231–36)

Although for the most part the poem is an instance of sensational tales full of moving accidents, as Swann argues ("Suffering" 89), it finally transforms sensationalism into trance, moving beyond the palpable body and its grosser senses into the domain of pure thought. Becoming "uncharact-ered," it risks a move beyond the characters or letters of language and ap-parently offers itself only to a reader capable of finding within these letters, as the pedlar found in the spear-grass, an invisible presence. Through the figure of the pedlar, this text revenges itself so deeply against textuality that it finds an imaginary writing beyond language, a writing that does not an-swer suffering but is immune to it. The *Recluse* project, having reversed the sensational disruptions of an errant figuration into trancelike calm, founds itself not in the discourse of cultural history or political vision, but in an imaginary presence beyond speech.[26]

Although in *The Ruined Cottage* Wordsworth deploys the gamut of terms from *The Borderers*—abandonment, mastery, ascetic self-division, ghostliness, identification through trance—he imagines a different posi-tion by the end of this poem. In *The Ruined Cottage* the subject attempts to master not the abandonment of another (the captain, Herbert) but his abandonment by the mother. Whereas the father's ghostly exile inevitably reminds the subject of his guilt, the mother's disembodied endurance guarantees the subject her undying love. Although the game of masochistic revenge is as harrowing as anything in the Salisbury Plain poems or *The Borderers,* the fact that it arises from a demand instead of an accusation suggests that it can arrive at a fantasy of satisfaction without an appeal to the law and thus without reinstituting the symbolic order. Concerning himself in this poem with the originary split in the subject rather than sacrifice, Wordsworth depicts the fantasy that one can attain a stable psychic and social condition without returning to culture.

In the social context that this poem inherits directly from the Salisbury Plain poems, the strategy Wordsworth examines here becomes disturbing. Rather than imagining an alternative to war, which would require something like the reinstitution of culture, he creates a persona who pushes the consequences of war for the abandoned woman from poverty to death and then turns death into life. The basis for hope here is the reversal of the problem into its own solution by means of a masochism that comes to desire pain and loss and which interprets the mother's death as its ultimate satisfaction. In the interval between the loss of the maternal body and the acceptance of the father's name, the space previously of repetition and errancy, appears an invisible mother who is neither a body nor a name but substitutes for both. Because the mother's body is not lost, perhaps the subject does not need the father, culture, or even language and can dispense with speech and figuration. Ultimately, the vision of spear-grass satisfies everything one would ever want from culture or, even better, presents a utopian vision of a natural culture that could never collapse into errancy.

Wordsworth articulates the political implications of the spear-grass vision more overtly in certain lyrics of March and April 1798, such as "Expostulation and Reply" and "The Tables Turned," which apparently advocate the abandonment of philosophical research and political agitation in favor of a wise passiveness and a spontaneous wisdom that arise from nature. Ironically, by proposing that it might be founded in an imaginary nature, Wordsworth dispenses with the need to complete *The Recluse;* as Averill points out, the attack on laborious study reflects "Wordsworth's rebellion against his own ambition to write the all-encompassing poem" ("'Natural Science'" 244). The trope on the mother's death obviates the effort to encompass cultural history within a narrative of redemption.

III

Even this vision of natural culture, however, depends upon the substitution of the intangible for the tangible maternal body. Because of this substitution, no more stable than any other, the hope for a society without errancy may collapse at any time. In *The Ruined Cottage* Wordsworth hides the figurative basis for the pedlar's vision of a nonfigurative nature. A critique of this poem would not simply point out that it reverses Wordsworth's earlier, political response to socially determined suffering in the Salisbury Plain poems (Chandler 130–39; cf. McGann 82–85) but would expose the strange figure that enables that reversal. In this way it would articulate a critique from within the poem's own terms and demonstrate Wordsworth's uneasiness with its fantastic resolution. But we do not have to carry out such a critique ourselves. As if finally giving voice to the anonymous and nearly speechless narrator of the earlier poem, Wordsworth already provides that critique in "The Thorn," begun shortly after he finished MS. B of *The Ruined Cottage* (M. Reed 27–28, 32; Averill *Suffering* 172).[27]

To make sense of this critique, I will pretend for the moment that "The Thorn" presents a coherent story about Martha Ray, making an assumption that I will later have to challenge. A mere plot summary already suggests that this poem reverses the story about Margaret; this time it is the child, rather than the mother, who dies. In this version of masochistic fantasy, the child gains revenge against the mother through the fantasy of his own death, as if to say, "You abandoned me, so I will abandon you by dying," or better yet, "You abandoned me, I died, and so you have killed me and deprived yourself of me." The child imagines that his death will send the mother into a frenzy of grief and guilt which will entirely possess her. Instead of dying, the mother will disappear into a grief so intense that she will become nothing but the obsessive expression of misery. Already "The Thorn" does not sound that far removed from certain moments in *The Ruined Cottage;* Martha Ray, it seems, is simply a Margaret who remains a ghost of grief possessed by the power of endless weeping—a Margaret who cannot or does not die.

This reversal in the form of the child's revenge transforms the stance of the poem's speaker. Margaret's death keeps the pedlar from sharing her fate and enables him to identify with her suffering from a convenient distance. But in the masochistic fantasy of "The Thorn," the child, who imagines himself dead, hopes to be overwhelmed with the mother's expressions of grief. Where the pedlar incorporates Margaret as a psychic presence, the subject of "The Thorn" will be incorporated into the mother as the source or object of her perpetual lament. In its most intense form, this fantasy would have the poetic speaker overhear the mother's words—as the pedlar hears the ghostly Margaret's sighs—as if he were a part of her body, and accordingly the speaker repeats her words obsessively to himself throughout the poem. Such habits, of course, ostensibly make him far more distasteful to Wordsworth than the pedlar, yet insofar as he embodies the same fantasy he is as much the poet's alter ego as the apparently serene old man.

Thus the poem, saturated with singsong rhythms and repeated phrases, nearly disappears into the rhythms of Martha Ray's lament: "Oh misery! oh misery! / Oh woe is me! oh misery!" Meter, which according to the Preface to *Lyrical Ballads* is supposed to protect the reader from too close an identification with represented suffering, in this poem expresses and intensifies identification. As Adela Pinch argues in an analysis of "Goody Blake and Harry Gill," written around the same time as "The Thorn," perhaps between *The Ruined Cottage* and "The Thorn" (M. Reed 27–28, 32), ballad meter expresses the male speaker's masochistic identification with the suffering woman. When Harry Gill, the strong-voiced landowner, catches Goody Blake, a poor old woman, in the act of stealing firewood from his hedges, Goody curses him with cold, and since that day Harry has never been warm. Losing his strong voice, he falls prey to the involuntary sounds of his shivering body: "his teeth they chatter, / Chatter, chatter, chatter still" (3–4). This chattering, Pinch suggests, "both testifies to the transformation of Harry's body into an old woman's" in a form of masochistic identification "and marks out the rude meter of the poem: the onomatopoetic line—'Chatter, chatter, chatter still'—approaches sheer rhythm as it describes the sheer repetition of unintelligible sound located in the body" (842). The speaker in "The Thorn," like Harry, frequently repeats the suffering woman's refrain ("Oh misery! oh misery!"), which amounts to little more than the endless repetition of a single phrase or one that sounds very similar ("Oh woe is me!"). This phrase is the sound of the endless weeping that takes over Margaret's body; it, too, is "an unintelligible sound located in the body" that chatters in the metrical stanzas of "The Thorn."

In this case, of course, the body speaks in stanzas modeled on the popular German ballads of Gottfried Bürger, which William Taylor had translated and published in the *Monthly Magazine*. Mary Jacobus comments, "It is surely Bürger's 'Tra la la' which lies behind the onomatopoeic verve and grotesqueness of the opening and closing stanzas of 'Goody Blake and Harry Gill'" (*Tradition* 239). Moreover, the language of sensation brought with it the sensational tale of infanticide near a gibbet, pond, and grave in the poem Taylor translated as "The Lass of Fair Wone," which Wordsworth rewrote as "The Thorn" (*Tradition* 242–47). The poet who used an archaic stanza to capture the effects of the nonsignificative elements of language appropriates another neoprimitivist form, the popular ballad, which, in contrast to the Spenserian stanza voices repetition through an imitation of the body's sounds. Thus the stanzaic repetition of the Salisbury Plain poems and the psychological obsession of "Incipient Madness" fuse into the ballad's repetitive chatter. Apparently the ballad speaker no longer needs to be the impresario of his obsession, which organizes itself through an irrepressible disturbance in a physical form that now seems alien to him. Like Harry Gill, the poet seems to be without a voice, in whose place appears a gathering of strange sounds akin to the shriek of the bustard, the moans and groans of the body in pain, the clanging irons of the agitated horse, and "the heavy noise / Of falling rain" carried in the wind ("Incipient Madness" 33–34). Part animal, part bird, part weather, the poet speaks an inarticulate language that is not his own. Reversing the disembodied poetics of *The Ruined Cottage,* "The Thorn" engenders the scandal of the speaking body.

If the speaker of "The Thorn" chatters like Harry Gill, we might guess that he, too, has been cursed by a solitary, witchlike woman. His pleasurable suffering may follow from a previous scene of cursing which never appears in the poem as an event but which remains implicit in the depiction of its major figures. In rural England any woman who had lost her child, sat on the side of mountains outside the village, and haunted a pond as if she were stirring it to produce foul weather, would be accused of witchcraft (Bewell 162–69). According to village superstition, Martha Ray is another Goody Blake, a suffering woman meditating revenge. But because both Harry Gill and "The Thorn"'s speaker take pleasure in being accursed, these witches are products of a masochistic fantasy of being punished by the vengeful mother. In this fantasy, the mother does not submit passively to her abandonment but, like Bersani's child, threatens others with her own suffering. Instead of waiting, like Margaret, for the man's return or displaying her grief to the speaker, the witch curses the male figure with the involuntary, corporeal expressions of that grief. Thus the child imagines not just its own death but also its punishment in the hands of a mother who has learned to be as lovingly spiteful as he has been. The child wants to be the object of his own fantasy of vengeance. Masochistic desire intensifies its pleasures by turning the tables on itself and suffering a punishment that it first directed toward another.

In this context, the witch's curse is merely an adult version of the infant's expression of its vengeful wish; cursing, and perhaps the whole array of superstitious practices visible in "The Thorn," may originate in the fantasies of childhood. We might even interpret the *fort-da* game as a magical practice, akin to poking pins in dolls, whereby the child secretly curses the mother by tossing the bobbin over the edge of the crib. In contrast to *The Ruined Cottage,* in which the child is shocked that the mother might *survive* its death wish, "The Thorn" circles around the shocking possibility that the death wish might *work,* that the child could curse its mother into cursing it in return.

The ease with which the fantasy articulated in *The Ruined Cottage* transforms itself into that of "The Thorn" demonstrates that the former poem fails to establish *The Recluse* on firm ground. Any attempt to found theodicy in an extension of sensationalism surrenders it to the mischievous, reversible logic of errant desire that never arrives at a final or proper form. Almost immediately after conceiving of *The Recluse* as a magnum opus that might restore culture to its proper home, Wordsworth reconceives of it as a study of the extravagant suffering it was meant to heal. The terms in which he tries to recuperate "The Thorn" for philosophical purposes reveal the mobility of his philosophical ambitions. The Note to "The Thorn," published with the 1800 edition of *Lyrical Ballads,* accounts for the poem as an investigation into "the general laws by which superstition acts upon the mind" (Gill 593).[28] At times philosophical poetry may take on the mantle of a secularized prophecy that will save culture from itself, and at other times it poses as a form of protopsychoanalysis that understands the laws of an irrational (and anguished) imagination. Rather than motivating *The Ruined Cottage* and "The Thorn" from the start, these philosophical poses materialize as an aftereffect of poems which originate elsewhere—in a denied obsession with the image of the suffering woman.[29]

By reversing the fantasy of *The Ruined Cottage* and in effect exposing the logic from which it was derived, "The Thorn" opens the possibility that Wordsworth will repudiate the masochistic response to suffering as a potential basis for his poetry. The mocking tone of the poem suggests that he might be tempted to set aside a ludicrously sensationalist poetics and return to the project of writing a secular theodicy that could, for example, at least implicitly map a strategy for reconstructing a shattered culture. Instead, the poem rather brazenly naturalizes masochistic fantasy by deriving it from a nearly primordial condition of consciousness: absolute abandonment. It is time to set aside the assumption, which has enabled the discussion of "The Thorn" so far, that the poem presents something like a coherent tale about Martha Ray. In fact, it merely suggests certain elements of something like that tale when the speaker is forced to give shape to his fantastic surmisings. As Wordsworth suggests in the last paragraph of the

Note, the chief interest of the poem is not that it represents or interprets the mind's passion in any particular way, but that it represents the mind's craving for representation:

> For the Reader cannot be too often reminded that Poetry is passion: it is the history or science of feelings: now every man must know that an attempt is rarely made to communicate impassioned feelings without something of an accompanying consciousness of the inadequateness of our own powers, or the deficiencies of language. During such efforts there will be a craving in the mind, and as long as it is unsatisfied the Speaker will cling to the same words, or words of the same character. There are also various other reasons why repetition and apparent tautology are frequently beauties of the highest kind. Among the chief of these reasons is the interest which the mind attaches to words, not only as symbols of the passion, but as *things*, active and efficient, which are of themselves part of the passion. And further, from a spirit of fondness, exultation, and gratitude, the mind luxuriates in the repetition of words which appear successfully to communicate its feelings. (Gill 594)

This insight into the mind's craving is already extended and complicated in the poem itself. As Jerome Christensen argues, "the 'craving' Wordsworth mentions is evident in the first five stanzas of the poem, where the narrator attempts to describe the spot that so fascinates him." Like the "impassioned feelings" of the Note, the thorn both provokes and escapes representation, so the "narrator's repeated attempts to fix the thorn in a conceptual order . . . communicat[es] not what he sees but his craving to see it as something."[30] In stanza 6, the thorn is impersonated as Martha Ray, who "has an authority that all the other impersonations lack; her appearance condenses all the shifting, anxious passion in the poem because she is herself a figure of passion and propagation." As a result, her cry, "Oh misery," "relieves the anxiety of the narrator's craving for the right words to express the eccentric passion that has impelled him into utterance." Repetition as craving gives way to repetition as exultation; the narrator repeats the cry "to exult in the phrase itself, the thing that has settled an otherwise homeless passion. To be exact, Martha Ray's pain is the narrator's pleasure" (276–77).

Christensen's account of "The Thorn" readily matches the psychoanalytic account of the child's attempt to signify its inexplicable, hyperbolic existence through the *objet a*, specifically through a certain pleasurable repetition oriented toward the image of the suffering mother. His argument enables us to see that in this poem Wordsworth exposes the way in which the masochistic fantasy arises from the subject's prior condition of craving for an adequate representation of itself. Already in "Incipient Madness" he hinted at the origins of the *objet a* in a grief that, "fastening on all things / That promise food, doth like a sucking babe / Create it where it is not" (9–11), but there the craving had so quickly given way to its representation in the gleaming glass that it was nearly effaced by the subsequent exultation in repetition. Wordsworth delays the arrival of the *objet a* in "The Thorn," allowing the mind to search at length for something that would capture in an image or repeated phrase the condition of utter abandonment and homelessness. With this step, he in effect proposes the reading of *The Ruined Cottage* we followed above, revealing that the story of the suffering woman is not a narrative or representation in its own right but rather personifies the mind's craving for representation, its longing to master its radically ungrounded existence. Thus the focus of the poem, as Parrish argues, is not the suffering woman but the thorn, a version of the dark tree that is Wordsworth's favored image of the uncanny natural site (*Art* 106–9). The entire poem follows from its first line, "There is a thorn," which designates subjectivity as a site of sheer disruption and excess. Having figured subjectivity as extravagant wandering and then as obsessive repetition, Wordsworth now depicts it, via the thorn, as a spot where the fabric of being is frayed or cut or meets an unassimilable obstacle (cf. Lacan *C* 55, 63). The originary condition of the subject is to be out of place, inexplicable, alien from itself, and thus without an origin even in absence (since to name absence is already to arrive at the *objet a*).[31] It is, in short, the anxiety of interpretation, the craving for words or signs.

Wordsworth's exposure of the fictional status of the speaker's fantasy extends throughout the poem. Every object by which the speaker attempts to stabilize his fantasy reveals its status as representation. Martha Ray, personifying his own anxious passion, remains a personification rather than a person; in that strange encounter with her he sees nothing but "her face, / Her face it was enough for me" (199–200), as if she merely gives a face to the "mist and rain, and storm and rain" that vex the spot. She is the sign of a body, the human face of an inhuman agitation, the imaginary locus where the storm returns the speaker's gaze.[32] Her repeated phrase consists of sounds so similar and repeated so often that they might simply be the sound of the rain and wind interpreted as speech, the vocal face of the storm. The sighs of Margaret turn back into the wind of "Incipient Madness," but it is a wind heard as a sigh or cry.[33]

A few stanzas later the speaker attempts to represent the spot not as a face but as a crime, Martha's murder of her child. Like the definitive self-mutilation of the *objet a* or the masochistic fantasy of mutual revenge, the fiction of this crime could give the wild energies of the poem a precise form and thus relieve the speaker of his anxiety. Like Lacan, Wordsworth links the fantasy of this crime with the subject's specular self-alienation, replaying it as a kind of mirror scene in which one can look into the pond and see a baby's face looking back (225–31). But this proto-Lacanian moment, rich in implications for our account of the infant's masochistic fantasy, quickly gives way to the insistence that the secret of the spot cannot be made visible.[34] No one, not even the forces of "public justice" (233), can verify the rumor of infanticide, since "the beauteous hill of moss / Before their eyes began to stir" (236–37). The gaze, as always, evades vision, perspective, or judgment, remaining the lack in what the subject can see, but in this case it does not allow itself to appear as a glittering *objet a*. It becomes visible, if at all, as a disturbance in the visual field, something that "slips, passes, is transmitted, from stage to stage, and is always to some degree eluded" in vision (Lacan *C* 73).

Despite his best efforts, the speaker never locates the equivalent of the glittering pane of glass of "Incipient Madness" because the strange ensemble of thorn, pond, and hill of moss refuse to precipitate themselves into a single, punctiform object, just as the speaker never quite makes his point. Because the thorn of "Incipient Madness" "Whose flowery head half hides those ruined piles" (40) has in this poem entirely obscured the hut and its broken pane, we might expect it to have absorbed the *objet a* into itself, but instead it shares its privilege with the pond and hill. The movement from ruin to thorn does not conserve it as an invisible object and distribute its effects through its environs, as in the spear-grass vision at the end of *The Ruined Cottage*, but makes it not yet visible, placing the speaker in the moment before its appearance when the craving for it is most intense.

The speaker proposes these various representations in response to the questions of an interlocutor who prods him into giving ever more explanations for the significance of the thorn. As Christensen demonstrates, the poem is a sequence of questions and answers which generates an imaginary tale out of the unreadable significance of the thorn (cf. Wolfson 56). It is the interlocutor, then, who demands meaning and reference when there may be none. "By the end of the poem," Christensen writes, "the reader feels confident that the interlocutor is missing the point, even though he may not be entirely sure what the point is" (273). But we should not oppose the interlocutor to the speaker, since the latter already longs to stabilize his obsession in an external image and depicts Martha Ray in stanza 6 (56–66) before the interlocutor asks any questions. The interlocutor is simply the voice of his own craving for representation. This craving, moreover, is not an irresponsible flight from the primal condition of the mind but an attempt to survive that condition. Because sheer agitation threatens the subject with disintegration, its highest priority is to discover some way to signify its anxiety to itself, no matter what the form. Building on certain passages in Freud, Bersani argues that sexuality arises in the gap "between the quantities of stimuli to which we are exposed and the development of ego structures capable of resisting or, in Freudian terms, of binding those stimuli." He goes on: "The *mystery* of sexuality is that we seek not only to get rid of this shattering tension but also to repeat, even to increase it. In sexuality, satisfaction is inherent in the painful need to find satisfaction." Nevertheless, by sexualizing organic tension, masochism enables us to defeat biological dysfunction and "to survive our infancy and early childhood" (38–39). Lacan proposes a similar thesis in his account of the mirror stage, whereby the child defends against a certain "organic insufficiency" through the unified body-image in the glass (*E* 4). Whether through masochistic fantasy or the delusory identification with a mirror reflection, the subject fastens itself onto something, finds a reference or invents a story, in order to survive the threat of a purely hyperbolic condition.

At the end of this sequence of texts, Wordsworth's stance in regard to his own aesthetics is more vexed than ever. Although in "The Thorn" he exposes the logic that underlies *The Ruined Cottage*, he does not repudiate the generally depoliticizing mode of that poem or return to the project of writing a secular theodicy. On one level, at least, he questions the very possibility of writing such a poem, suggesting that the subject is out of place in any landscape, that it makes demands that the world will never fulfill. In the Note, he writes as if this may not be cause for despair; the mind's dislocation, its craving for representation, may be the source of great beauty. Our radical homelessness may be the source of greater beauty than can be found in moral consolation. Yet at times he seems to repudiate the stance of "The Thorn" as well. The poem is absurdly and comically excessive in its depiction of the narrator's superstitious foolishness. At the beginning of the Note, Wordsworth mocks him, distancing himself from a potentially embarrassing identification with his persona.

At such a moment Wordsworth could repudiate both the pedlar and the superstitious narrator, renounce a poetics of fantasy, and return to a more normative, politically responsible aesthetic. Yet such a gesture seems inconceivable for one who takes the total undoing of cultural institutions for granted. Thus the poet limits himself to the choice between two fantasies that develop from the premise of abandonment. At times, retreating from sensationalism to an apparently more humane position, he indirectly embraces the pedlar's stance and resists "The Thorn" from the perspective of *The Ruined Cottage*. Alternatively, he demystifies that pious stance, celebrates the pleasures of repetition, and chooses "The Thorn." Together, these poems demonstrate that as long as he insists upon that initial, absolute negation of culture, Wordsworth will be caught within the terms of his own poetics, shifting between apparent opposites—hyperbolic anxiety and inhuman calm—which are, in fact, two sides of the same aesthetic.

FOUR

Ghastly Mildness

Reconfiguring Errancy in "The Discharged Soldier," "The Old Cumberland Beggar," and *The Ruined Cottage*

✤ During the first three months of 1798, Wordsworth set about to rethink the poetics of errancy. As we have seen, in *The Ruined Cottage* of that period he attempted to transform extravagant suffering into its own solution: the death of Margaret would give the pedlar access to an inviolable presence in nature. But since this reading of social dislocation did not envision a way to reunite husband and wife, bring the war or economic hardship to an end, or enable the wanderer to cross the threshold and join the household, it relinquished the attempt to imagine the reconstruction of the symbolic order. At the end of the poem the cottage is still ruined, the pedlar still wanders from door to door, and culture is still fractured. Yet the pedlar is neither a criminal nor a nearly mad obsessive, for his wandering has been transformed into a sign of superior knowledge of life and death. In a series of closely related texts written in early 1798, "The Discharged Soldier," "The Old Cumberland Beggar," and the passages on the pedlar's way of life in *The Ruined Cottage*, Wordsworth extends this logic, exploring the possibility that social dislocation, although depriving the wanderer of much, may give him access to a benevolent force, "the eye of Nature," which does not reconstruct culture but may transform it into a less violent collectivity, a less traumatic encounter between wanderers. Relinquishing the tone of political protest, Wordsworth now openly celebrates the dispossessed condition, regarding the wanderer he encounters not as a specular counterpart of his ghostly subjectivity but as a privileged being, a wanderer who does not err.

To rethink errancy in these texts, Wordsworth must at least indirectly revise his earlier work, including the Salisbury Plain poems and *The Borderers*, and respond to Coleridge's *The Rime of the Ancient Mariner*, already completed, which the mode of that earlier work had inspired.[1] He does so most directly in "The Discharged Soldier," in which he describes the encounter in the public road of an unnamed speaker with an uncanny old wanderer who might as well be one of the undead:

> He was in stature tall,
> A foot above man's common measure tall,
> And lank, and upright. There was in his form
> A meagre stiffness. You might almost think
> That his bones wounded him. His legs were long,
> So long and shapeless that I looked at them
> Forgetful of the body they sustained.
> His arms were long and lean; his hands were bare;
> His visage, wasted though it seemed, was large
> In feature; his cheeks sunken; and his mouth
> Shewed ghastly in the moonlight. From behind
> A mile-stone propped him, and his figure seemed
> Half-sitting and half-standing. (41–53)

This stiff body with hurtful bones and sunken cheeks is already a skeleton; this "ghastly" face, showing white under the moonlight, is ghostly. Yet not all of him is visible as a corpse; this "uncouth shape" (38) is partly "shapeless," giving him the shapeless shape or visible invisibility of a walking spirit. The speaker later remarks that "His shadow / Lay at his feet and moved not" (72–73) to emphasize the soldier's affinity with shadows, with dark, empty shapes. And when they walk together, the speaker "beheld / With ill-suppressed astonishment his tall / And ghostly figure moving at my side" (123–25) as if the soldier is his ghost or shadow (cf. Magnuson 91). At once a skeleton, ghost, and living man, the soldier resembles the sailor of *Adventures* who is caught on the threshold between life and death. His curious posture, which consists of two halves, oddly recalls the Vagrant's ghost story in which the traveler "half-raised the stone with pain and sweat, / Half-raised" it to disclose "the grim head of a new-murder'd corse" (*Adventures* 214 16). That traveler had raised the stone on the urgings of an agitated horse, who reappears in this text as "the chained mastiff in his wooden house / [Who] was vexed, and from among the village trees / Howled never ceasing" (81–83), as any dog might who had spied a ghost. Moreover, the soldier's being propped against a milestone, an image that again associates corpse and stone, suggests that he is an animated dead man leaning against his own gravestone. Perhaps, caught between life and death, he is only half-buried, a "stiff" who has not entirely expired or who does not quite fit into the grave.

The soldier's odd condition extends to his abstracted emotional state.

> His face was turned
> Towards the road, yet not as if he sought
> For any living thing. He appeared
> Forlorn and desolate, a man cut off
> From all his kind, and more than half detached
> From his own nature.
>   He was alone,
> Had no attendant, neither dog, nor staff,
> Nor knapsack—in his very dress appeared
> A desolation, a simplicity
> That appertained to solitude. (55–64)

In this case, hyperbolic consciousness places the soldier beyond desire or apparent need, beyond even his own nature. Like Rivers or the traveler on the plain, he has traveled alone beyond the visible world, but unlike them he apparently does not conceive his departure from the world as a crime or as a form of violent self-division.

Nor is he caught, like the ghostly and solitary ancient mariner, in the domain of textual repetition. He feels no need to tell his tale; when the speaker, finally emerging from his hiding place, prompts him to speak, he tells it as "a simple fact" (99), speaking with "a strange half-absence and a tone / Of weakness and indifference, as of one / Remembering the importance of his theme, / But feeling it no longer" (143–46). We might argue that this indifference toward a merely ordinary tale places the soldier on the verge of being possessed, like the mariner, by a story alien to him, a story that provides its own arbitrary and delibidinal feelings. But it is just as likely that the soldier, long since possessed, has told a marinerlike tale so often that it no longer matters to him. Notice how in place of the soldier's voice is the sound of the body's pain and of the mind's uneasiness: "From his lips meanwhile / There issued murmuring sounds as if of pain / Or of uneasy thought" (69–71). Yet this sound is so mechanical, or rather so natural—like the murmuring of a stream, like noises issuing from lips— that it reduces the mariner's vociferous textuality to a repeated moan, to the language of the speaking body, linking the soldier to the weeping Margaret or chattering Harry Gill: "I wished to see him move, but he remained / Fixed to his place, and still from time to time / Sent forth a murmuring voice of dead complaint, / A groan scarce audible" (77–80). Moans of pain, groans of the dead: the scene of Druidic sacrifice returns here in a sound "scarce audible," a complaint of the dead, suggesting that the soldier has already passed through violence, repetition, and chatter and has arrived at the door of death where even the body ceases to speak for itself.

Wordsworth seems to have returned to Salisbury Plain, where corpses moan, ghosts walk, and discharged soldiers wander without a home. If so, he also revives the cultural analysis of *Salisbury Plain,* complete with its theory of war as a version of Rousseau's savage state. As Bewell argues, "The "Discharged Soldier" follows Rousseau's theory of the origins of culture in the encounters between solitary wanderers in a postdiluvian world (78–93). Like one of Rousseau's giant solitaries (or a figure from a "Romance of giants" [1798 *Pedlar* 71]), the soldier is a foot taller than most people and has long arms and legs and a large face (see lines 41–53 quoted above).[2] Moreover, the traveler encounters him on a road that has apparently just emerged from the deluge, one whose "watry surface to the ridge / Of that sharp rising glittered in the moon / And seemed before my eyes another stream" (7–9). Like the wanderers on the plain, the soldier is a contemporary version of the primitive savage who has endured a natural catastrophe. Bewell's point is strengthened by the connection between the oceanic Salisbury Plain and the seas of *The Ancient Mariner* (cf. Magnuson 75–76), which both reappear as the watery surface of the world. Moreover, this is a discharged *soldier,* a survivor of war, a fact that links natural to social catastrophe and diverts Bewell from Rousseau to Hobbes, who theorizes cultural origins as a state of war (86–87).

The soldier's affinity with the uncanny figures from earlier Wordsworth poems may explain the speaker's odd reaction to him. Although critics frequently point out how strange it is for the speaker to hide behind a hawthorn bush as soon as he spots the soldier, few have attempted to explain his behavior. That reaction is a version of the sailor's entrancement at the sight of the gibbeted man: the corpse is his double, the specular image of the traveler's disembodied, ghostlike subjectivity. In the lines before the encounter, the traveler's mind wanders from the natural imagery surrounding him toward the dreamlike domain of figuration: "What beauteous pictures now / Rose in harmonious imagery—they rose / As from some distant region of my soul / And came along like dreams" (28–31). At first, as Magnuson points out, nature and figure combine together and bring the traveler delight (89). But not for long: "While thus I wandered, step by step led on, / It chanced a sudden turning of the road / Presented to my view an uncouth shape . . ." (36–38). This sudden, "chanced" turn is the moment of unmotivated, extravagant wandering off the natural road into sheer figure, and appropriately it takes place when the traveler allows himself to be led on "step by step" by the seemingly alien force of his own momentum.[3]

In this context, the uncouth shape of the soldier personifies the traveler's figurative powers, bringing into the visual field what Wordsworth, in the guise of the pedlar, saw when he read books as a child:

> But greedily he read and read again
> Whate'er the rustic vicar's shelf supplied:
> The life and death of martyrs who sustained
> Intolerable pangs, and here and there
> A straggling volume, torn and incomplete,
> Which left half-told the preternatural tale,
> Romance of giants, chronicle of fiends,
> Profuse in garniture of wooden cuts
> Strange and uncouth, dire faces, figures dire,
> Sharp-kneed, sharp-elbowed, and lean-ankled too,
> With long and ghostly shanks, forms which once seen
> Could never be forgotten. (1798 *Pedlar*, 65–76)

The strange figures of literature or art have materialized before this traveler, suddenly taking over for reality (cf. Magnuson 89–90), making it the first version of a complex that will reappear in the drowned man episode of *Prelude* 5.450–81. Hiding behind the bush, the traveler reimagines those old woodcuts, marking or carving them in the soldier's form ("I could mark him well" [40]; "I could mark" [53]). The soldier, too, has "long and ghostly shanks" and sharply painful bones (cf. Bewell 85); furthermore, in his pain he resembles the martyrs "who sustained / Intolerable pangs." Later, as he speaks, the "strange half-absence" of his tone leaves his tale "half-told," as if he personifies the "torn and incomplete" volumes on the vicar's shelf. The longer the traveler marks the old man, the more he fears that he has encountered not another person but the personification of his preternatural power of figuration, a figure of figuration. Through most of the poem, then, Wordsworth sketches in slow motion the moment of entrancement whereby the traveler sees another person as the hyperbolic, alienated portion of himself.[4]

The specular, doubled nature of this encounter becomes even clearer if we take a passage from *The Ruined Cottage* into account. When Robert, Margaret's husband, loses his job, he feels strangely alienated from the cottage and its routines and expresses his anxiety by "[Carving] uncouth figures on the heads of sticks" (*Ruined Cottage* 165). It seems the Wordsworthian subject wants to recreate the woodcuts of his youth by carving wood himself. Of course, read differently these uncouth figures represent the strangeness or unreadability of rhetorical figures, which are the appropriate language for Robert's improper and anxious thoughts. Soon after,

Robert becomes a wayward figure himself: "for half a day / He then would leave his home and to the town / Without an errand would he turn his steps / Or wander up and down among the fields" (Butler 83). As Magnuson remarks, "to go on an errand with no object is to be errant" (108). He has become unseasonable, dislocated in time and space: he looks for "any casual task / Of use or ornament" around the cottage and "with a strange, / Amusing but uneasy novelty / He blend[s] where he might the various tasks / Of summer, autumn, winter, and of spring" (167–71). He eventually abandons himself entirely to this errancy, goes off to war, becomes a soldier, and eventually (we might guess) a discharged soldier.[5] Thus Robert's story bears on "The Discharged Soldier" in several ways. The traveler who wanders at night for the sheer pleasure of wandering (1–5), who carves a certain stiff, nearly wooden figure out of the landscape, and who eventually imagines that that figure is his near-shadow (123–25), is another version of Robert, who in turn is another version of the discharged soldier himself.[6] Viewer and viewed, the carver and the carved, are the divided halves of the same subject. We could conflate these two texts and speculate that if the traveler/Robert falls far enough into the trance produced by his figurings, he will soon become the personification of his own figures, a ghostly wanderer on wayward paths. But we need invent no such narrative; the traveler is already this other being, this alien and unrecognizable self.

No wonder the traveler is so anxious to find the old man shelter for the night. To turn the soldier from specular double into a separate person, he needs to establish a social difference between them so that he can "avoid ever being faced with such an encounter again" (Simpson 138). But because the soldier is a figure of the (anti)society of war (or of unemployment), this act requires the traveler in effect to resolve social crises and reestablish culture. Bewell argues that in this text Wordsworth, like Rousseau, writes in the mode of Enlightenment anthropology in order to chart the progression from "the impassioned figurations of primitive perception" to "a domesticated nature grounded on sympathy" (86, 89). But the poet's interest here is not the theory of social origins. As in *Salisbury Plain*, he treats such theories of the savage life as descriptions of the condition of those subjected to the dismemberment of culture: Hobbes's war returns in the 1790s as the war with France. But how might one bring the extravagant traveler back onto the right path or restore an errant culture to its proper home? As Magnuson argues, the speaker's "reaction to the figure marks an effort to master the figure, to relocate it within the natural order" (92). If the passage of the speaker and soldier "In silence through the shades gloomy and dark" toward the cottage (149) alludes to Dante's dark wood (Bewell 88), it also reverses Rivers's journey "through words and things, a dim and perilous way" (*Borderers* 4.2.103). Wordsworth accompanies a ghostly Rivers (a discharged sailor) or, more likely, the abandoned captain on the way back home from his semiburial in the deluge of distant seas.

Insofar as the soldier is a product of Wordsworth's greedy, repeated reading in the vicar's straggling volumes, to turn him into a human being he must read him in another way.[7] Perhaps he belongs not to the romance of giants but to Rousseau's anthropological narrative, which fits giants into the story of the origins of culture. Thus the movement toward the cottage and toward cultural knowledge is also a movement away from extravagant reading toward a domesticated, disciplined form of reading associated with *The Recluse*. Or, perhaps, instead of cultural knowledge this traveler will need knowledge about this particular man. Simply by wrangling the soldier's story out of him, the speaker hopes to defuse the threat of his ghostliness and turn him back into some kind of familiar person. Knowledge and charity shade over into the interrogation of strangers, as if the coherence of community depends on the transparency of each member to every other or on the mutual knowledge of each person's story and name—a core Wordsworth assumption that explains his habit of questioning beggars and other public wanderers (Harrison 24; M. Friedman 182–84) and his bafflement at the anonymity of city life (see *Prelude* 7.117–20). The soldier's half-absence from his own words, however, suggests that he exceeds his own name and story and will not readily be placed within familiar terms.

The tensions between the speaker and soldier culminate, as one might expect, in the scene at the threshold of the cottage. How will the speaker get this ghostly figure, akin to the mariner, through the doorway and back into culture? In relation to wanderers, every dwelling is at least potentially a place of hospitality, as the "kind pious hands" intended the spital of *Salisbury Plain* to be, where the gift of shelter, food, perhaps even friendship will turn relations of violence into those of mutual support. Unfortunately, the spital, the dead house of the plain, marks the collapse of public charity, as does its counterpart in *The Ancient Mariner*, the ship, which at first promises salvation to the mariner and his crew, brings death instead (Magnuson 75–77). For culture to return to its proper condition, the dwelling will have to become hospitable again. Accordingly, in this text the cottage is inhabited not by a desperately poor vagrant but by "an honest man and kind" who, says the speaker, "will not murmur should we break his rest, / And [who] will give you food if food you need, / And lodging for the night" (112–15). This cottage is no homeless shelter but an actual home.

Here Wordsworth explores the possibility that the way from anticulture to culture lies through the rites of hospitality. As Marshall Sahlins and Jean-Pierre Dupuy argue, one strategy to contain the threat of violence is gift exchange, which transforms reciprocity into a mode of mutual recognition (Sahlins 149–83; Dupuy). Following Hobbes, Sahlins conjectures that society emerges from the state of "Warre" and enters the social contract when each person gives up the right to every other and engages in reciprocal, mutual surrender (177–78). We might infer that the moment of hospitality at the end of the poem reworks theories of the social contract and of exchange. The speaker tries to bring the soldier into the network of mutual obligations that constitute the established social realm, telling him that he should "at the door of cottage or of inn / Demand the succour which his state required"—*demand* it, as if it were owed to him—and that, "feeble as he was 'twere fit / He asked relief or alms" (159–62). He could either go on public relief or become a beggar, either way relying on society's obligations to its poor.[8]

By invoking social obligation as a remedy for the soldier's dispossessed condition, the text revisits the thematics of *The Borderers*. Once again the plight of an old wanderer, seemingly abandoned in waste places, challenges the passerby to fulfill the basic duty to rescue even total strangers from death. As if to redeem himself from the crimes of his counterparts Rivers and Mortimer, the speaker invites the ghostly solitary back into the house of culture and goes so far as to instruct him in the ways of mutual concern. But this action promises to alter his status as well. If, as I argued above, it will cancel his specular relation to the old man and establish a difference between them, it will also bring an end to his solitary wanderings, lift the curse of exile pronounced by Mortimer, and in effect bring *The Borderers* to an end.

But the poem turns on the narrative that has apparently motivated it all along. Rather than make any promise to the speaker, the soldier, "with the same ghastly mildness in his look" replies, "'My trust is in the God of heaven, / And in the eye of him that passes me'" (163–65). With that look of ghastly mildness, he chooses to remain a ghost or inhuman wanderer. Astonishingly enough, he refuses to leave his errant ways, to accept charity on its terms, or "to announce his identity and condition in a socially unambiguous way" as the speaker demands (Simpson 138). On one level, the soldier's choice marks Wordsworth's critique of a condescending and intrusive charity (Mileur *Revisionism* 214; cf. Simpson 138). It also points to Wordsworth's critique of the eye of anthropological narrative, "of the customary Enlightenment relationship between the observing philosophe and the observed population of silent marginalized people" (Bewell 90). But because charity and anthropology are the text's two privileged ways of reestablishing culture, the soldier's repudiation of them is much more radical than these readings suggest: he simply does not need culture. The soldier rejects the social identity thrust upon him by the speaker because he is not human in the way that the benevolent man expects. He is beyond charity because he trusts "'in the God of heaven / And in the eye of him that passes me.'"

The soldier's reference to the gaze of strangers breaks the specular relation that held the traveler spellbound and relieves him of his anxiety. The appeal to a generalized, communal eye, perhaps the eye of God, places the soldier under the supervision of a gaze nearly as impersonal as the source of light in "heaven" (as the Lacanian analysis of the gaze would suggest; *C* 91–104). In this way it restores the confident relation to the gaze whose loss abandoned the wanderer to the malevolent forces of *Salisbury Plain* and the murderous spectators of *The Borderers*. As I argued in Chapter One, the departure of the shepherd early in *Salisbury Plain* leaves the solitary without an Other, "that conscious presence, real or conceived, through which we become self-conscious by considering ourselves as another would" (Rzepka 4). Without the Other, he becomes a wanderer beyond the visible world, a disembodied subjectivity liable at any time to encounter himself as ghost. Rzepka suggests that this dilemma did not face earlier generations because in the absence of other people the gaze of the "Divine Presence" (29–30) protected them from utter solitude—and, we might add, from experiencing such solitude as an abandonment to the predatory gaze of others. The soldier's apparently premodern trust in that Presence protects him from ghostly solitude and refers even the eye of strangers to the heavenly eye.

But the soldier's reliance on a benevolent gaze does not mean that he returns home. Although he is housed for the night, he is no more a part of culture than before because he interprets the cottager's hospitality as an instance of a generalized favor that will never cease to welcome him. Freed from errancy *and* repudiating culture, he seems to belong to natural society, the condition of innocence before the fall into social relations or even into language. In place of reading as extravagant figuration or as disciplined obligation is the divine eye, which apparently does not need to read or interpret at all. Under this eye, the soldier belongs neither to romance nor to anthropology but wanders in a space that does not require identity, a space without the improper or the proper.

Where could there be such a space? The soldier utters his final words with the same ghastly mildness as before: he is still a ghost, if not an errant one. Within the poem's terms, the soldier's claim to divine protection is credible because he has endured a suffering so profound that he no longer needs to be rescued from it. Here, as in *The Ruined Cottage*, the solution to errancy is to take it to extremes, to transform it into a death that becomes in turn a kind of disembodied life. The soldier is no longer like Harry Gill, the mariner, or weeping Margaret because he is more like the dead Margaret, "one / By sorrow laid asleep or borne away" (370–71) into the massive tranquillity of nature. He has gone beyond the mass of humanity not into the space of an unnameable excess, but into a different condition entirely, as if his being "cut off / From all his kind" (58–59) sets him apart from ordinary people. If his sublime proximity to death empties him of human feelings, so that he tells his tale "feeling it no longer" (146), it must as a result relieve him of the uneasiness the speaker attributes to him (71). Living without needs and without anxiety, his is the sublime unconcern of the dead.

This depiction of a mild ghostliness, much like that in *The Ruined Cottage,* is the product of an underlying fantasy. This time, however, Wordsworth is concerned not with the condition of being abandoned but with the abandonment of another—the crime of *The Borderers.* Every detail suggests that the captain, abandoned to an utter solitude in the far seas, did not die but became immune to suffering. According to this scenario, Rivers need not reinterpret his crime as a form of moral originality, for he need only imagine that the crime was not a crime at all. Failing to rescue the captain or Herbert is merely to do as the old man himself pleases, for he disdains rescue. He is abandoned but needs no help; he wanders in abject solitude but is not in exile; he is alone in a watery world but fears no deluge. In this version of a familiar fantasy, the new and improved Rivers says, in effect, "So I abandoned him? He didn't need me anyway," thereby absolving himself of his deed and releasing himself from the anxieties of obligation.

The fantasy concerning the soldier is more obscure than that concerning Margaret, in part because Wordsworth avoids any elaborate scenarios and derives the old wanderer's privileged condition more or less directly from his abject suffering. The soldier is a version of the man described in a draft of "The Old Cumberland Beggar" written by July 1797 (M. Reed 27) and published under the title "Old Man Travelling: Animal Tranquillity and Decay, A Sketch" in the 1798 *Lyrical Ballads:*

> He travels on, and in his face, his step,
> His gait, is one expression; every limb,
> His look and bending figure, all bespeak
> A man who does not move with pain, but moves
> With thought—He is insensibly subdued
> To settled quiet: he is one by whom
> All effort seems forgotten, one to whom
> Long patience has such mild composure given,

> That patience now doth seem a thing, of which
> He hath no need. He is by nature led
> To peace so perfect, that the young behold
> With envy, what the old man hardly feels. (3–14)

Wordsworth could hardly spell it out more clearly: the old man has endured life so long that it no longer pains him. Strangely enough, the young are *envious* of this man who is so old and decayed that he is, according to the title, more like an animal than a human being. If Mortimer condemns himself to an exile beyond the senses, to live "by pain and thought" alone so that he may die (*Borderers* 5.3.273), this old man is so numbed that he "does *not* move with pain, but moves / With thought," having so effaced the senses that they can no longer make him suffer. Invoking this poem in the soldier's final speech, Wordsworth suggests that we should not pity but envy him because he has transfigured the human and become either an animal or a being protected by God.[9]

Wordsworth expands upon the logic of these poems in "The Old Cumberland Beggar," in which he clarifies how the old man's excessive suffering can transform the gaze from a hostile to a benevolent presence. Although the beggar seems to see nothing except the scraps of flour he scans "with a fixed and serious look" (10–11), since "one little span of earth / Is all his prospect" (50–51), everyone and everything in the poem sees him, perhaps even the sun under which he sits in solitude (12–15).[10] Nevertheless, because he is so helpless in appearance (25) everyone treats him with great care, placing alms safely in his hat, opening the gate for him, and passing gently by him (26–43). Thus the visibility of helplessness is the old man's best protection: the more obvious his suffering, the less violence he can expect to suffer. The poem ends, appropriately enough, with this blessing: "As in the eye of Nature he has lived, / So in the eye of Nature let him die" (188–89).

In this way, Wordsworth dramatically alters the problematic of his earlier poems, whose errant travelers and abandoned solitaries had "a slightly paranoid or agoraphobic feeling of being exposed and dissolved on a landscape" under the cold light of the gaze (Swann "Suffering" 91), fearing that they were about to become the object of some nameless violence. In defense they oriented themselves toward the *objet a*, thereby entering the game of masochistic violence and obsessive repetition. But the beggar turns the gaze against itself, embracing its violence so openly in the spectacle of his helplessness that it dare not harm him further. By experiencing his own death, as it were, he effaces the source of anxiety and lives in perfect peace.

By embracing his suffering this openly, the beggar seems to endure a sacrificial death: apparently, like the classical *pharmakos,* he submits to the community's violence and thereby unifies it around the spectacle of his suffering (cf. Girard *Violence* 85–88, 94–99). In the topically political section of the poem, added after the first draft was complete (Johnston 5), Wordsworth argues that the villagers do their share to support the old man and to be "kind to such / As needed kindness, for this single cause, / That we have all of us one human heart" (144–46). Perhaps because this beggar has, through suffering, been "cut off / From all his kind" ("Discharged Soldier" 58–59), he can seem to substitute for all his kind and become an emblem of our one human heart.

But even in this text Wordsworth deviates from the structure of sacrifice by preserving the old man from death or even the fear of death. The beggar never crosses the threshold of the tomb in order to become a buried, memorialized representative of the community. He is an example neither of a *pharmakos* nor of institutionalized authority because he remains, in however attenuated a form, a wandering ghost. Instead of uniting the community as its representative in a public ritual, he wanders through the village from house to house, creating a strangely fractured community. Heather Glen argues that in his account of the villagers' response to the beggar (108–24) Wordsworth describes "a society bound together not by fellow-feeling but by a series of separate, identical processes of 'self-congratulation'; one in which men are not questioned by their contact with others, but confirmed in their isolated selfhood," one that is "a collection of finally atomized individuals" (84). Rather than giving these individuals a symbolic unity, the beggar provides them a means to conceive of an atomized society in nonviolent terms. Culture may still be dismembered, but it is not at war. Although an act of private charity resembles the potentially entrancing encounter between wanderers, the displacement of spectatorship onto the eye of nature protects the viewer from a masochistic identification with the beggar and allows him or her to indulge in "a transitory thought / Of self-congratulation" (116–17), a thought not of identity with the beggar but difference. In this way, the beggar preserves the atomized individuals from falling into absolute resemblance with each other, establishing at least a minimal difference between them necessary for social relations.

Thus this poem continues to rewrite *The Borderers,* as if picking up where "The Discharged Soldier" left off. The excessive vulnerability of the beggar to the gaze of passersby makes him subject to a general, even communal abandonment, giving him, like the captain or Herbert, the status of a not entirely dead father, an anti-*pharmakos.* Yet this time the spectators have gathered to witness not his invisible death, but his visible mastery over death. The theater of this village becomes the space of a perpetual self-congratulation or self-absolution, according to a fantasmatic logic that has it both ways: this crime is no crime, this symbolic violence has no victim. Wordsworth challenges the potentially oppositional stance of his earlier poetics, for example in the final stanza of *Adventures,* where a specular entrancement negated the attempt to read the sailor's execution as the restoration of the symbolic order, by imagining that specular relations themselves enable the emergence of a peculiarly entranced model of a restored collective.[11]

They can do so, however, only because the beggar does not depend entirely on passersby. Wordsworth is careful to place him not under the thumb of the villagers but under the "eye of Nature," sustaining the crucial difference voiced in the soldier's final speech. He submits not to the community's charity, then, but to the benevolence of something outside culture. He belongs, like the soldier, neither to the order of specular relations nor to the system of obligations, neither to hyperbolic romance nor the symbolic order. Thus he defies the reader's familiar categories: by appealing to the eye of nature Wordsworth asks us to read him not as a member of any cultural text, whether dismembered or symbolically founded, but as a natural person free of textuality in general. If he no longer experiences anxiety, then he is free of the self's tendency to be out of place in itself or to be oriented toward a lack or absence. Because a benevolent Presence is always watching, he can dispense with the problem of the mother's absence, the *objet a,* and the games of masochistic revenge. He will never be "out of place in the picture" (Lacan *C* 96), never off the right path. Apparently, for him the subject is self-present, lying open and transparent before itself and all the world. Illuminated by a heavenly light, he inhabits a text without figures, a language without writing, a domain of meaning which is identical to itself.

But Wordsworth cannot propose this new way of reading without supplying us with a new reader who has access to the eye of nature. This reader is none other than the pedlar of *The Ruined Cottage,* whose privileged status is described in the brief biography supplied in MS. B, lines 47–105. As a "chosen son" (76), the pedlar has the rare capacity to read nature's language, to find "shades of difference" and a "spirit of strange meaning" hidden in its shapes, forms, and surfaces (95, 85, 83, 96, 100).[12] He does not need the language or system of differences which culture provides through "the dead lore of schools" because he finds it already present in nature (75). Because he can read nature without substituting words for its meaningful forms he gains access to a language free of the instabilities of figuration—to what Wordsworth calls, in other passages drafted for *The Ruined Cottage* during this period, "an inarticulate language" (Butler 261). The way beyond errant interpretation, Wordsworth suggests, is to blend with nature's own senses: if one could only see and hear aright, one would never have to read.

But in that case, one would never need language or even consciousness at all. One could simply submit, like the pedlar, to the "unrelenting agency" of the eye's power that "bind[s] his feelings even as in a chain" (MS. B 102–3). Here, as at the end of *The Ruined Cottage*, the pedlar's privilege comes at a great cost: insofar as his mind is incorporated into the inarticulateness of the winds and stars, he has no human subjectivity to speak of at all.[13] Strangely enough, by being sealed off from normal human anxiety the pedlar becomes another version of the beggar, whose excess of suffering has made him nearly unconscious. If, according to the logic of "Animal Tranquillity," an excess of suffering eventually produces its total absence, there can be no clear distinction between the beggar and one who, like the pedlar, has never suffered.

One section of the pedlar's biography hints at this resemblance:

Though poor in outward shew, he was most rich;
He had a world about him—'twas his own,
He made it—for it only lived to him
And to the God who looked into his mind.
Such sympathies would often bear him far
In outward gesture, and in visible look,
Beyond the common seeming of mankind.
Some called it madness—such it might have been. (86–93)

The pedlar, like the other old men, is the object of the sympathetic viewer's gaze: "poor in outward shew," he has a distinctive "outward gesture" and "visible look" akin to madness, which sets him apart. Like them, he lives under the watchful eye of God in a world that is uniquely his own. The pedlar and beggar blend back into their common source, the discharged soldier, who was at once a sufferer and a wise man.

The resemblance of pedlar and beggar does not end here. We might ask, for instance, why Wordsworth decided that his persona should be a peddler who made his living by wandering on a certain rural itinerary. Wordsworth explains in the Fenwick note to *The Ruined Cottage* that if he had not gone off to college (and become a poet) he would have become a peddler like the old man he describes (Butler 477), but this only raises the question more urgently. Alan Liu accounts for the pedlar in the context of the history of peddling and smuggling in the Lake district (*Wordsworth*

341–47), much as Simpson analyzed the beggar with reference to the history of the debates concerning begging (162–74). But why should *these* two historical forms of localized wandering, peddling and begging, become so important to Wordsworth at the same time? Why should he make their representatives so similar, as if one is the symmetrical opposite or figural counterpart of the other? Both solitaries live at once inside and outside the community. Despite their great poverty, both are rich in access to the wealth of nature. Both wander through rural England to make a living, yet neither seems to cross a threshold or to participate in a truly reciprocal exchange: the beggar receives scraps of flour which he places in a bag in exchange for the good feeling he gives to the "village dames" (8–10), and the pedlar, as we might surmise from his poverty, virtually gives the "wares" from his "long white pack" to the "maids who live / In lonely villages or straggling huts" (MS. B 44–46) in exchange for the knowledge he gains of humankind and nature. Much as the villagers profit from their charity to the beggar, the pedlar profits from his contacts with his customers.[14] If the beggar is the community's exemplary lumpenproletarian, the pedlar is its monarch; but it would not be difficult to imagine both functions united in a single person (the soldier, perhaps) who goes from door to door to watch over all of its members and to be watched by them. This curious resemblance between two seemingly opposed figures verges on the double structure of the Girardian *pharmakos* who suffers death and thus becomes a hero: through his abject submission to nature as poverty and suffering, the beggar gains access to the hidden riches of nature beyond suffering and becomes the pedlar.

Moreover, in his longer biography of the pedlar, written after most of *The Ruined Cottage* was complete, Wordsworth presents the pedlar's wanderings as a domesticated, "habitual" errancy. Around the age of twenty, the youth's "spirit was on fire / With restless thoughts. His eye became disturbed, / And many a time he wished the winds might rage / When they were silent" (1798 *Pedlar* 188–91). Incapable of finding release from this disturbance, he "Found that the wanderings of his thought were then / A misery to him, that he must resign" as the teacher in an adjoining village. "He asked his father's blessing, and assumed / This lowly occupation" (232–36). Clearly, he chooses this occupation as a direct result of his wayward thoughts. Like Robert, he is a haunted, tempestuous, homeless figure, but he manages to contain errancy by making it a way of life. Over the years, "impelled / By curious thought he was content to toil / In this poor calling, which he now pursued / From habit and necessity" (246–49). Like the beggar, who "moves / With thought" ("Old Man Travelling" 6–7) and depends on the way that "the mild necessity of use compels / To acts of love" ("Beggar" 91–92), the pedlar softens errancy down into the ordinary business of getting from door to door. Ultimately, it seems that the beggar and the pedlar are the same person.[15]

Thus the fiction of the eye of nature does not finally undo the specular relation but redefines it as the spectator's identification with someone who has gone beyond suffering. The traveler-soldier relation has given way to the pedlar-beggar relation, which is just as intense and overdetermined. If we conflate all of these closely related texts, we might imagine a scenario that explains this transformation. At a certain moment, perhaps when the soldier rebukes the Wordsworthian traveler, the latter suddenly recognizes that the old man is beyond anxiety and is thus released from his anxious entrancement with him. But this new awareness leads to another kind of fascination with the old man's invulnerability, reviving the specular relation as the identification not with the corpse-ghost but with an old man beyond the thought of death. Insofar as near-death defeats the body's pain and the mind's unease, it also effaces the memory of crime (the sailor) or the unconscious identification whereby one condemns oneself to perpetual wandering (Rivers; Mortimer). The sight of the decayed man heals the spectator's aggressive rivalry with another and creates instead a spectator seemingly incapable of wounding or being wounded. By contemplating the beggar aright, by utterly effacing one's sympathy for him or concern for his condition, one learns to discount all forms of personal anxiety, all attempts to restore culture, and discovers that one need not depend on social relations in the first place. The result is a society of mild ghosts, hyperbolic subjects strangely indifferent to their dispossessed condition.

The pedlar, who embodies this mode of reading, is Wordsworth's answer to the problem of dismembered culture. He can sympathize with fellow mortals without feeling the griding iron of guilt pass through him and can identify with their suffering without imagining that it is his own. According to the logic of this group of poems, he should attain this privileged status because he, like the decayed old man of "Animal Tranquillity," endured a suffering as great as the sailor's and finally became immune to its pain. Because he has suffered more, he can sympathize more with others. But if this experience of his own near-death gives him a unique moral authority, it does so at the cost of placing him at an immense distance from mortal life. Mileur argues that in his later guise as the Wanderer of *The Excursion,* this figure, whose "renunciation of poetic desire" or errant figuration is meant to "humanize and socialize the imagination," becomes someone who "reads—and speaks—as if from a great distance, as if he were receiving a message from the dead. . . . In this curious way, the path of reading aims at well-being only to arrive at death, as if only the dead could possess the answers we seek" (*Romance* 48–50). As we have seen, the pedlar already speaks in this way in the spear-grass vision toward the end of *The Ruined Cottage*, where he appropriates for himself the imagined tranquillity of the dead Margaret.

Because it is his experiential acquaintance with suffering and death which privileges the pedlar of the spear-grass vision, he cannot possess in any familiar sense the symbolic, institutional authority of the dead father. As a result, he cannot be the spokesman for *The Recluse* conceived as the comprehensive statement of systematic knowledge. By trying to defeat the pain of suffering not through a return to the symbolic order but through a change in the perspective on suffering, Wordsworth defines *The Recluse* as the dramatization of a way of seeing rather than the articulation of a stance with philosophical content. At this point *The Recluse* consists of little more than the persona of the pedlar.[16]

Because that persona stems from the transformation of excessive suffering into the immunity from suffering, it remains vulnerable, as did *The Ruined Cottage*, to any new text or interpretation that might transform it back again. Wordsworth is just as capable of writing a critique of the pedlar's biography as he did "The Thorn." But as if to protect from that possibility, late in the biography he tries to exempt the pedlar entirely from suffering. He is exempt both from revolution and from hyperbolic experience: "In his steady course / No piteous revolutions had he felt, / No wild varieties of joy or grief" (1798 *Pedlar* 271–73). It follows that his encounters with suffering do not remind him of his own troubles, since he has none. Unlike the sailor's, his is a nonspecular sympathy: because he "had no painful pressure from within" he "could afford to suffer / With those whom he saw suffer" (281, 283–84). On his rounds he "had observed the progress and decay / Of many minds, of minds and bodies too" (288–89), watching how families "were o'erthrown / By passion or mischance, or such misrule / Among the unthinking masters of the earth / As makes the nations groan" (291–95). But because he, unlike virtually everyone he knows, has never felt the pressure of such misrule, it leaves him so untouched that he merely witnesses it as he passes along. This sort of nonspecular sympathy does not seem to be genuine sympathy at all.

This shift in the pedlar's character is all the more remarkable because Wordsworth once did imagine precisely such a sympathizing figure. Magnuson points out that in early revisions of *Salisbury Plain* Wordsworth describes the sailor as one who could sympathize "because he had committed a crime and experienced the vacillations of joy and fear: 'From each excess of pain his days have known / Well has he learned to make all others ills his own' (*SPP* 116)." When Wordsworth goes on to write *Adventures*, how-

ever, "[t]he sailor has lost most human sympathy; he has not been humanized but has been conquered by fear" (43). Magnuson's argument implies
that Wordsworth's failure to imagine any other fate for the sailor but self-
accusation leads him to create a pedlar entirely free of human troubles. But
if these characters are so closely tied together, they may be versions of each
other. According to the both/neither logic of hyperbole, excessive suffering
and exemption from it are the same. By denying that the pedlar ever
suffered, Wordsworth makes him hyperbolic, out of place in the human
race. Much like Rivers or the "Heroes of Truth" of *Salisbury Plain,* the
pedlar exemplifies a response to "piteous revolutions" so excessive that it
marks him precisely with what it negates.

The hyperbolic claims for the pedlar do not protect him against his
possible reversal back into a personification of errancy but, strangely
enough, bring that reversal about. For one thing, those claims undo the
logic of "Animal Tranquillity," in which excessive suffering becomes indifference to suffering. By taking that logic too far, by reading indifference
to suffering as its absence, Wordsworth demonstrates that he wishes to
write not a secular theodicy—a fully "humanized" (Magnuson 43) response
to "piteous revolutions"—but rather a poetry of an excessive, inhuman response. Similarly, he undoes the logic of the brief passage cited by Magnuson which envisions a criminal who would sympathize, exemplar at once
of the dismemberment and reconstruction of culture. Once again taking
for granted the defeat of any political response to suffering, Wordsworth is
caught between opposite versions of the same: the wanderer must either
sympathize so strongly that he relives his crime or not finally sympathize
at all, never having done any wrong. Claiming too much for the pedlar,
Wordsworth inevitably ties him to his counterpart the sailor, fating them
both to reappear, in slightly different guises, as the Wanderer and the Solitary of *The Excursion.* Much as *The Ruined Cottage* and "The Thorn" are
caught in a spiral of perpetual, mutual critique, these two forms of errancy,
defined respectively by the eye of nature and by the eye of specular rivalry,
will henceforth haunt each other, perpetually reinterpreting revolution as a
total, unendurable event or as an event that never occurred.

FIVE

Characters of Danger and Desire

Deviant Authorship in the 1799 *Prelude,*
Part One

🦋 In Part One of the 1799 *Prelude,* Wordsworth departs from his previous poetry in several ways. No longer attempting to exempt his persona
from traumatic experience, as he did in the biography of the pedlar, he
reads such experience as a sign of his election as a poet. Although this
gesture might seem to revive the logic of *The Borderers,* in which Rivers
transforms the meaning of his crime, in fact it privileges not crime but
punishment, not his violence against another but his subjection to the violent forces in the landscape. In this extraordinarily risky move, Wordsworth
suggests that cultural dismemberment transfigures the world, that the dead
who invade *Salisbury Plain* give him an uncanny, original power when they
wound him. Wordsworth's claims here are both outrageous and perverse;
he at once celebrates cultural disaster and imagines a masochistic vocation.
The world's descent into total violence made him a poet—a magus who
receives his power when invaded by demons.

This shift does not mark Wordsworth's escape from history into the
domain of a lyrical solitude. Far from retreating to a logocentric, phallocentric subjectivity, here he inscribes what he interprets as the total violence of
current events upon a terrorized, nameless subjectivity, interpreting the self
as yet another instance of radical dislocation. This version of autobiography
does not silence or transcend a cultural problematic, as many of Wordsworth's readers have claimed (e.g., Abrams; Liu *Wordsworth* 201–18), because it extends that problematic onto more intimate terrain, demonstrating that the self that is apparently exempt from disaster is produced by it.
It does, however, reverse the apparent import of disaster; as Wordsworth
alludes to his previous accounts of errancy throughout Part One, he consistently uses the idea of poetic election to give a name to his namelessness
and to read the destruction of his conventional social role as the initiation
into something exceptional. As always in his poetry, here the solitary per-

sonifies a shattered culture; this poet speaks not for himself but from elsewhere, for he is occupied by shapes of terror and haunted by the dead. But
now self-alienated solitude is an enchanting mode of being; the archaic
dead reappear in this text as gods of a dark poetry, monitory presences who,
neither moving like living men nor speaking a human tongue, tutor him in
strange ways.

❧ I

Wordsworth does not immediately make such a radical shift in his
stance toward errancy. As he takes up the question of his status as a poet in
the first fragmentary drafts toward what we now call the 1799 *Prelude,* he
draws upon several disparate kinds of authorizing discourses, including the
account of his election as a poet-prophet, the analysis of his mental and
cultural development, and the evocation of his distinctive childhood. In
the process, he brings together vocation, philosophy, and autobiography,
appealing at once to Milton, the Enlightenment, and to his ongoing dialogue with Coleridge. Gradually, in a complex movement that will be my
subject for the first portion of this chapter, he begins to play these discourses off against each other and produce an uncanny disturbance in the
discursive field. Using each context against another, he deviates from them
all, apparently with an eye toward a concept of the author as yet unformu-
lated in its own right. As he proceeds, however, he does more than deviate
from various norms, for he calls upon a discourse proper to deviance.
Wordsworth's authorship, not merely inexplicable in familiar terms, is the
inexplicable itself.

The first lines of MS. JJ are among the most intense evocations of
unnameable disturbance in Wordsworth's canon:

          a mild creative breeze
a vital breeze that passes gently on
Oer things which it has made and soon becomes
A tempest a redundant energy
Creating not but as it may
disturbing things created.—

                  a storm not terrible but strong
with lights and shades and with a rushing power

                     trances of thought
And mountings of the mind compared to which
The wind that drives along th[']autumnal [?leaf]

Is meekness.

> what there is
> Of subtler feeling of remembered joy
> Of soul & spirit in departed sound
> That can not be remembered.   (1–16)[1]

One could read these lines as evidence either of the poetic crisis Wordsworth describes in the first section of the 1805 *Prelude* or of "the powerful
disturbance of mind occasioned by a superabundant flow of inspiration"—
states of mind which are not as far apart as Parrish argues (Prelude 6).
But lacking any supporting evidence or context for these lines aside from
Wordsworth's own retrospective interpretations, one should hesitate to explain them immediately as the expression of a specific biographical experience, whether crisis or inspiration. They read instead as a rewriting of various earlier depictions of errancy and vexation; here again are the breeze,
wind, tempest, and storm of the Salisbury Plain poems and "Incipient
Madness"; the redundant energy of the poems on repetition; the lights and
shades that tend to appear around the *objet a;* the trances of thought of the
sailor or the pedlar; and the curious blend of memory and the lack of memory which appeared in "The Discharged Soldier" (described as "one / Remembering the importance of his theme, / But feeling it no longer" [144–
46]) and in crucial draft passages on the pedlar's life ("the soul /
Remembering how she felt, but what she felt / Remembering not . . ."
[James Butler 371–72; cf. 113]).

But those who explain these lines with reference to a particular occasion may have a point. Those first six lines may refer to the poet's tempestuous mood in attempting to rethink an earlier poem. Could it be that
Wordsworth was already afflicted with the curious disease that would reappear as he attempted to revise *The Pedlar*? Or, to look in the opposite direction, could these lines repeat the self-reflexive moment in the early draft of
"Incipient Madness," where, as Raymond Carney points out, Wordsworth
rehashes the same phrases until he pauses in frustration to remark, "You
will forgive me Sir / I feel I play the truant with my tale" (636–38)? It seems
likely that a similar writing disturbance provokes this fragment, and yet by
itself such a disturbance would not produce it. What generates this text is
Wordsworth's interpretation of disturbed creativity in terms borrowed from
earlier texts. Here a certain restlessness transports neither the reader/spec-
tator (as in *Adventures* and *The Borderers*) nor the surrogate narrator (as in
"The Thorn") but the poet himself, who apparently has lost the power to
displace the unquiet mood onto a persona.

In the next passage of MS. JJ, much as in the biography of the pedlar, Wordsworth attempts to ward off the threat of this exceeding vexation through an appeal to something outside of errancy, the semidivine forces of nature that set him aside to be a "chosen son" (1798 *Pedlar* 326):

> was it for this
> That one, the fairest of all rivers, loved
> To blend his murmurs with my nurse's song
> And from his alder shades and rocky falls
> And from his fords and shallows sent a voice
> To intertwine my dreams, for this didst thou
> O Derwent—travelling over the green plains
> Near my sweet birth-place didst thou beauteous stream
> Give ceaseless music to the night & day
> Which with its steady cadence tempering
> Our human waywardness compose[d] my thought
> To more than infant softness giving me
> Amid the fretful tenements of man
> A knowledge, a dim earnest of the calm
> That Nature breathes among her woodland h[?aunts]
> Was it for this & now I speak of things
> That have been & that are no gentle dreams
> Complacent fashioned fondly to adorn
> The time of unrememberable being. (22–40)

As Magnuson argues, in these lines Wordsworth turns "to a recollection of childhood to calm his tempestuous energy. . . . He invokes childhood to be quieted, to be tempered, to be steadied" (187). Something in the "steady cadence" of the Derwent's music calms "our human waywardness," much as nature soothes the "restless," wandering, "curious" thoughts of the pedlar (1798 *Pedlar* 189, 232, 247). Magnuson also points out that Wordsworth takes over the myth of privileged childhood from Coleridge's "Frost at Midnight," to which he alludes ("my sweet birth-place," the music of the Derwent); the poet even insists, against Coleridge's text, that his childhood is no mere dream but an actual past (187–89). If, as Lucy Newlyn argues, Wordsworth was already responding to Coleridge's poem in the biography of the pedlar, who had a more intimate access to nature than the imagined Hartley of "Frost at Midnight" and who kept that access even into adulthood (38–44), in this poem he extends and personalizes this response, imagining himself as at once a Hartley and a pedlar, someone raised by nature from childhood to be a privileged being.

Yet Wordsworth cannot quite so easily appropriate for himself the claims he makes for the pedlar. Here the idea of vocation takes a curious turn; where the pedlar is a chosen son, set apart from others by "the God who looked into his mind" (*Ruined Cottage* MS. B 76, 89; 1798 *Pedlar* 341), in this poem Wordsworth is a chosen son who has gone awry. John Woolford demonstrates that the repeated lines *was it for this* allude to *Samson Agonistes*. In one passage "Manoa laments the waste of his son's magnificent strength and the reversal of his promised destiny": "For this did th' Angel twice descend? For this / Ordain'd thy nurture holy, as of a Plant?" (361–62). Earlier Samson had asked:

> O wherefore was my birth from Heaven foretold
> Twice by an Angel, who at last in sight
> Of both my Parents all in flames ascended
> From off the Altar, where an Off'ring burned,
> As in a fiery column charioting
> His Godlike presence, and from some great act
> Or benefit reveal'd to *Abraham's* race?
> Why was my breeding order'd and prescrib'd
> As of a person separate to God,
> Design'd for great exploits; if I must die. (23–32)

This repeated question, the memory of specific instances of God's favor to one elected individual, and the sense of failure reappear in the opening of Wordsworth's poem, albeit in naturalized form (Woolford 29–30). Ironically, the appeal to his own privileged childhood does not rescue Wordsworth from the creative disturbance of the initial fragment. Although nature set him apart and soothed his wayward thoughts, he has betrayed his high calling and fallen prey to anxious energies once again.

Already Wordsworth begins to envision a new relation between errancy and poetic vocation. In contrast to the poetry of early 1798, in which he invents a character exempt from waywardness (the pedlar) who will inevitably generate his errant counterpart (the solitary), in this text he imagines a person both privileged and deviant. If he was once given the calm of the pedlar, he has become as anxious as the solitary; if he was once like the Hartley of "Frost at Midnight," he has betrayed the promise of his childhood and become as estranged from nature as the speaker in that poem. But even in failure, Wordsworth is convinced of his privilege; that initial question leads not to a depiction of crisis or to a Samsonlike confession of guilt but to a presentation of the evidences of his calling. Susan Wolfson points out that Wordsworth "expand[s] the syntax of 'was it for this?' from its first rather than its second pronoun, from the past rather than from the present." In this way, he "modulates the syntax of his original question into a confident answering, even exclamation" (148). As many readers have argued, taking their cue from the first book of the 1805 *Prelude,* in writing about his crisis Wordsworth gets his poem started and, in a sense, overcomes the crisis (e.g., Hartman *Wordsworth's Poetry* 208; Chandler 189–90). But he accomplishes much more than this; making deviance from his vocation into a sign of vocation, he envisions a mode of authorship which tolerates errancy and a privilege that can still mark a person who is subject to human waywardness. He need not attempt the impossible and become, like the pedlar, exempt from human suffering or, like the fictional Hartley, inseparable from nature.

On one level, this shift takes shape as a turn from the rhetoric of certainty which dominated Wordsworth's admiring portrait of the pedlar toward the interrogatory, exclamatory rhetoric of MS. JJ. Discussing the episode of the raven's nest, Wolfson writes: "The boy hangs, ambiguously sustained or threatened by the winds of this suddenly alien border world, even as Wordsworth's poetry ambiguously suspends the *what*s of the last three lines between awed exclamation and troubled inquiry" (158): "With what strange utterance did the loud dry wind / Blow through my ears! the sky seemed not a sky / Of earth, and with what motion moved the clouds!" (1805 *Prelude* 1.348–50; cf. MS. JJ 65–67, where the lines are not punctuated). Like this boy and the boy of Winander, who hang ambiguously in the wind or sky (see de Man *Rhetoric* 51–54; "Time" 7–8; Bahti "Theft" 107–8), the rhetoric of the manuscript hangs on the curious question/exclamation that sets it in motion: "the entire JJ draft is nothing but a vast expansion of the question with which it begins, for each of its recollected episodes is controlled by some variant of 'Was it for this?'" (Woolford 36).

On another level, this formula at once poses the problem of vocation and suspends it, invoking the moments of nature's visitations without trying to establish their meaning. Woolford contends that Wordsworth, like Milton's Samson, asks his urgent question to recover the sense of mission implicit in his election, to transform the "parochial episodes" of the past "into a cumulative sign of the progressive future" in which he will write *The Recluse* (35). But by modulating the question into exclamation, Wordsworth "delays answering" (Wolfson 148) and evades the urgent problem of writing a theodicy. Instead of bringing with it the commitment to a redeeming purpose, vocation becomes its own purpose, an intransitive concern that need not be fulfilled in any later action.

An intransitive vocation, of course, is the inevitable result of a *natural* election that, in contrast to the divine election of Samson, conveys no explicit message to the chosen one and imposes on him no particular mission.

Following Woolford, above I argued that the problem of vocation of *Samson Agonistes* reappears in Wordsworth's text in naturalized form. But to naturalize vocation is to transform it entirely; the strange utterances of wind, sky, or mountain may have given Wordsworth a conviction of his special status, but they do not explain what this status might mean for others. The suspension of the vocational question is already implicit in the poet's appeal not to the voice of an angel but to the ceaseless music of the river Derwent. In the absence of a sacred rite, such as the sacrificial offering in whose flames the angel appears to Samson's parents, Wordsworth will remain on the threshold of prophecy, possessing only an empty vocation and a meaningless privilege.

Taken to its logical extreme, the naturalization of vocation deprives Wordsworth of his distinctiveness and makes him a representative or typical instance of the way in which nature fosters the development of the individual mind. Rather than setting him apart for a unique purpose, nature's visitations may simply have shaped his mind for the general purposes of a mature and socialized consciousness. Through its appeal to nature, the poem slides from the Miltonic rhetoric of vocation into the Enlightenment analysis of mental and psychological development. Already toward the end of that first verse paragraph of MS. JJ Wordsworth invokes the Enlightenment myth of the primitive to account for his own childhood, describing himself as a naked savage (50) in lines whose anthropological import becomes more explicit in the 1805 version:

> Oh! many a time have I, a five years' Child,
> A naked Boy   .   .   .
> .   .   .   .   stood alone
> Beneath the sky, as if I had been born
> On Indian Plains, and from my Mother's hut
> Had run abroad in wantonness, to sport,
> A naked Savage, in the thunder shower.   (1.291–92, 300–304)

As Bewell argues, "Wordsworth's belief in the conformities between the child and savage peoples . . . allowed him to transfer to his childhood the modes of inquiry that had traditionally focused on native life" (208). Consequently, Wordsworth read "his individual life as a recapitulation of the intellectual history of the human species" and made the development of the poet's mind "an epitome of the anthropological history of the human imagination." Thus *The Prelude* uses the discourse of *The Recluse*, the "'experimental' language Wordsworth developed in reaction to moral philosophy" (46).[2]

Although Wordsworth briefly refers to the child as a savage early in

MS. JJ, for the most part in that manuscript he is caught within the interrogatory/exclamatory rhetoric of its initial question (Woolford 36–37; cf. Wolfson 148–49). In the first drafts of *The Prelude,* having suspended the rhetoric of vocation, he has little or no context by which to account for the specific qualities of his mind. As Magnuson points out, early in 1799 he wrote two fragments in which he expressed his fear that the episodes of MS. JJ "have no meaning, even a personal meaning to him, that his fragments bear no intelligible whole," and that "he must find the context that would impart meaning elsewhere than in personal experience" (197). Engendered in part as a response to Coleridge's poems, the drafts exceeded that context without arriving at another (198–99). One could follow Bewell's suggestion and argue that a discourse akin to Enlightenment anthropology allowed him to proceed with the poem by organizing the episodes of MS. JJ according to a scheme that classified the stages of his mental growth. In that reading, the exclamatory tone of MS. JJ gives way to the comparatively sober mood of the two-part *Prelude,* in which the poet pretends to trace the effects of nature on the mind in philosophically valid terms. Perhaps the shift in emphasis from the vocational persona to nature's agency eventually enables the poet to focus upon the manner of the mind's formation rather than its purpose or result.

The problem with this reading is that the episodes strain against the interpretive passages that frame them. As Wolfson suggests, Wordsworth attempts to incorporate memories of his childhood into a system that cannot contain them (164–65). This tension between memory and category, lyric and narrative, finally breaks out as the poet introduces the drowned man episode:

> I perceive
> That much is overlooked, and we should ill
> Attain our object if from delicate fears
> Of breaking in upon the unity
> Of this my argument I should omit
> To speak of such effects as cannot here
> Be regularly classed, yet tend no less
> To the same point, the growth of mental power
> And love of Nature's works. (1799 *Prelude* 1.250–58)

Magnuson remarks, "Without the apology, it would be easy to see many similarities between these episodes and those that came before." Yet through this apology, "Wordsworth reveals an urge for the unity of argument and the classification of his experiences and at the same time offers the episode as one that he says does not fit well into the sequence that he is composing" (212–13). Interestingly enough, however, at this point in the poem he has scarcely even mentioned a classificatory scheme; he invokes it precisely when he sets it aside, as if to suggest that the crucial elements in his argument cannot be organized in such a fashion. The apology suggests less that the following episode departs from a sequence than that the entire point of the sequence departs from any classifying scheme; the episodes do cohere, after all, but not in a manner that can be made explicit.

Bewell might explain this move as another instance of Wordsworth's tendency to take moral philosophy "underground" and make it the "silent, informing impulse" of his poetry (12). But why would the poet resist the terms of a discourse that could organize his life in such a coherent fashion? The more aggressive version of the attack on classification in the introduction to the blest babe sequence should give us a clue: "But who shall parcel out / His intellect by geometric rules, / Split like a province into round and square?" (1799 2.242–44). On some level he simply refuses to account for his own subjectivity according to any interpretive scheme. Unlike the eighteenth-century poets of the imagination and poetic development, such as Akenside (*The Pleasures of Imagination*) and Beattie (*The Minstrel*), who treat these subjects as formally defined, external problems for philosophical treatment which do not bear directly upon their status as the authors of these poems, Wordsworth the author claims for himself the imaginative power he is describing. Mental development and imagination are more than philosophical problems for him because they supply the basis for his claims to poetic authority. Although he invests much in a philosophical analysis of the imagination, he subsumes this under the more urgent claim that the imagination belongs to him.

Thus Wordsworth does not finally move from the terms of vocation to those of mental development. Both of these concerns inform *The Prelude*, which everywhere registers signs of the tension between them. If his ambition is to write a definitive study of the (typical) development of the poet's mind, it is also to claim a unique privilege for himself as a poet of nature. This poem thus marks *The Recluse*'s difference from itself, for in it he at once writes that poem and negates it, invoking and contesting the paradigm of mental development at every turn. At various junctures the poem seems to be a poetic study of a conventional subject—education (the five-book *Prelude* of 1804), civic society (Book 7), love of nature leading to love of mankind—but it always deviates in such a way that Wordsworth can assert his privilege—his wayward, accidental education, his exemption from the confusions of Bartholomew Fair, and his love of heroic, solitary shepherds (cf. Bennett 166).[3] This overall tension emerges in nearly every episode, since the poet is unsure whether his memories demonstrate a general pattern or are uniquely his own.[4] Although the poet might like to read himself as a representative man and use "autobiography as the basis for a universal inquiry into the nature and powers of mankind" (Bewell 46), he cannot do so because he experiences the self not as a case history or as allegory of the human but as something truly exceptional, something that fits no existing discourse.[5] Because it has no proper discourse, the authorial self can appear only as an impropriety in other discourses, as what perpetually exceeds philosophy and philosophical accounts of one's life. Thus in the very moment when Wordsworth deviates into what seems to be autobiography, he also deviates from autobiography understood as narrative that traces the contours of a unified life into what Paul de Man has called "autobiography as de-facement" (*Rhetoric* 67–81)—into a life that consists of the "accidents of disfiguration" (Chase 13). At least in this instance, the poetic self marks the limits of philosophy and anthropology because it refuses to be reduced to anything besides itself.[6]

The only way to write such a self is to reduce it to the irreducible. Wordsworth's conviction of his uniqueness depends upon his sense that nature is an unpredictable, accident-prone guardian of youth. Nature deviates from the proper duties of the tutor or parent, coming to the child unsought, by chance, in moments of delight *and* terror. Because nature's visitations are unwilled and do not depend upon the voluntary participation of the boy, Wordsworth can interpret them as a sign of more than human favor, as proof that he is a poet not merely because of talent or ambition. In short, nature's *deviance* from the dominant codes of guardianship and narratives of development convinces Wordsworth that he has distinctive poetic powers. Capitalizing on this deviance, he turns the secular discourse of development into one of vocational privilege, reconstructing a Miltonic poetic identity in a language borrowed from, but resisting, the Enlightenment. He invents a counterdiscourse, based upon memories that could be only his own, of a development that proceeds through a series of disruptions toward an unnameable and finally unknowable quality of mind. By means of the exceptional, the errant, and the inexplicable, Wordsworth reconceives prophetic vocation as hyperbolic authorship.

This transformation of errancy from a problem to a source of power takes place with astonishing rapidity in MS. JJ. In the second verse paragraph, which includes the raven's nest episode mentioned above, Wordsworth links the tempestuous, redundant energy of the initial fragment, an energy that presumably disrupted his prior sense of vocation, with the force that elected him. The "loud dry wind" that speaks to him "with what strange utterance," the sky that "seemd not a sky / Of earth," and the strange motion of the clouds (MS. JJ 65–67) recall the "storm not terrible but strong" of the initial lines, not to mention the "trances of thought / And mountings of the mind compared to which / The wind that drives along th[']autumnal [?leaf] / Is meekness" (7, 9–12). The tempest that distressed the poet seems to be at the center of his power.

What this passage implies becomes explicit elsewhere in the poem. It is not the calming influence of nature's sounds, its gentle visitation, that inspires Wordsworth but its "Severer interventions, ministry / More palpable" (1799 *Prelude* 1.73, 79–80). In a later passage, he expands on his conception of this ministry:

> Ye Powers of earth! ye Genii of the springs!
> And ye that have your voices in the clouds
> And ye that are Familiars of the lakes
> And of the standing pools, I may not think
> A vulgar hope was yours when ye employed
> Such ministry, when ye through many a year
> Thus by the agency of boyish sports
> On caves and trees, upon the woods and hills,
> Impressed upon all forms the characters
> Of danger or desire, and thus did make
> The surface of the universal earth
> With meanings of delight, of hope and fear,
> Work like a sea. (1.186–98; cf MS. JJ, 80–96)

In direct contrast to the poem's opening lines, in which the river Derwent gives the child access to a musical expression free of wayward or fretful thoughts, here the genii and familiars minister to the boy through a very different kind of natural writing: "the characters / Of danger and desire." To be sure, this natural writing sets him apart from "the mean and vulgar works of man" (1799 1.135), much as it kept the pedlar from the "littleness" of "Low desires, / Low thoughts" (1798 *Pedlar* 126, 130–31), but all too easily the pedlar's capacity to "see" rather than read "the writing" of nature (123) becomes the child's incapacity to determine what that writing means. Rather than saving the child from the dangers of figuration, the ceaseless music of this earth-sea inundates him with a language whose characters will never quite become the letters of a readable text. The nature that promised to relieve the child from anxious thoughts becomes the privileged expression of errancy, flowing uneasily among delight, hope, and fear.

Yet it is precisely the dangerous unreadability of the world that sets this poet apart as a "favoured being" (1799 *Prelude* 1.70). Here the initial question "Was it for this?" nearly becomes the assertion "It was *through* this": the workings of the earth-sea and the redundant energies of the storm made him a poet. This much is clear in nearly all of the episodes of MS. JJ or of Part One of the 1799 *Prelude*, which I will discuss in the second part of this chapter; the child encounters the spirits of nature when he steals birds or a boat, is mildly shocked by the silence of the owls, watches a drowned man suddenly surface, loses his way and stumbles onto a mould-ered gibbet, and waits in a rainstorm near a crossroads not long before his father dies. In such episodes Wordsworth makes the characters of danger and desire the source of his poetic power, thereby reversing the terms of his earlier poems. Perhaps the text of the world is unreadable because it is writ-ten by the unknown, nameless powers of earth who disdain to use the vul-gar languages of men.

By invoking such powers, Wordsworth seems to be locating a Mil-tonic source of inspiration in a secular domain without relinquishing its sacred power. Through some sleight of hand, he seems to have it both ways, finding a way for the prophetic voice to resonate in the words of the auto-biographer without ceasing to speak of more than human things. Yet Wordsworth refuses such an idealizing reading. Receiving the prophetic mantle would make him one more instance of a familiar type, the prophet. He defines himself instead as a failed prophet or rather someone whose relation to prophecy could only be described in terms of deferral or failure. His conception of the authorial self is not comforting; it is the site not of vatic fullness nor of despairing emptiness (another version of the same), but rather of what Frances Ferguson, in another context, has called the "noncoincidence of the subject with itself" (117).[7] It is neither present nor absent but both/neither present and/nor absent, positioned where it is not and absent where it is, never capable of being isolated in its proper place. Wordsworth neither escapes the terms of the many discourses that inform his text nor remains entirely circumscribed within them; in a baffling and complex way, he marks a new moment in the history of authorship not with a new discourse (a new psychology, a new concept of vocation) but with a new way of deploying existing discourses, shifting between them from a phantom site, from the place of an authorship which does not prop-erly exist. IIis is an authorship, or antiauthorship, of errancy.

I I

If Wordsworth transgresses a variety of discourses in *The Prelude* and makes them unreadable, he also provides an allegory of transgression and brings into view the lineaments of an unreadable textuality. The Enlighten-ment coherence that errancy disrupts on one level returns on another as the difficult but coherent logic of errancy itself. Although the well-known episodes gathered in MS. JJ and in Part One of the 1799 version of the poem do not adhere to the received narrative of personal development, they refer so consistently to each other, build so directly upon each other's images and themes, and move so rigorously toward a more and more explicit formulation of their shared concerns that together they provide a counternarrative of the (de)formation of hyperbolic subjectivity out of the primal impropriety of the self. Appropriating from his earlier work not only specific episodes and images, as many of his readers have pointed out, but also the entire complex of concerns imbedded in them, including extravagance, the profanation of ritual, the specular encounter, hyperbolic subjectivity, matricide, and masochistic repetition, Wordsworth reconfigures them in the mode of disfigured autobiography. Preferring impropriety to the proper, namelessness to the name, the Wordsworthian child refuses to identify with the oedipal father and inherit his power, choosing instead to provoke the father's anger and take pleasure in the punishment that follows. In several homoerotic, masochistic episodes, this counternarrative dramatizes the child's growing captivation by a nonsignificative language and a disfigured culture, by the pleasurably terrifying power of the undead.[8]

Already in the bird theft episode, the first section that follows the poem's opening lines (and the reference to the savage child), Wordsworth describes his boyhood self as a transgressive wanderer. It was his "joy / To wander half the night" where the woodcocks ran in order to entrap them or to steal them from the traps of others (30–31). "In thought and wish, / That time, my shoulder all with springes hung, / I was a fell destroyer" (33–35), a dangerous figure from the world of romance.[9] With an eager, erotic anxiousness, he tries to provoke the spirits of the place with a forbidden act:

> When scudding on from snare to snare I plied
> My anxious visitation, hurrying on,
> Still hurrying hurrying onward, how my heart
> Panted; among the scattered yew-trees, and the crags
> That looked upon me, how my bosom beat
> With expectation. (37–42)

Jonathan Wordsworth argues that the "onomatopoeic anxiety of the rhythms" of the repeated words demonstrates that the child is terrified by a dark and accusing nature; "despite his predatory wishes, the child himself is the hunted animal" (*Borders* 43). But we should not hasten to decide whether the child is joyful wanderer or anxious fugitive, hunter or hunted; for this child, these apparent opposites are identical. Like the errant figures of "The Thorn," this onomatopoeic, anxious figure is acting out not merely a "fantasy of violence" (*Borders* 42), but a masochistic fantasy in which desire and aggressivity blend together in mutual, pleasurable violation. As in that poem, masochistic fantasy attempts to represent a subjectivity conceived as sheer excess or disruption, what Timothy Bahti calls an "impropriety amid nature" ("Theft" 95), as Wordsworth emphasizes in the lines added in the 1805 version of the passage: "moon and stars / Were shining o'er my head; I was alone, / And seemed to be a trouble to the peace / That was among them" (1.321–24).[10] Merely being in this landscape is already to intrude upon it and to be threatened by it. The child is hyperbolic, out of place, a person without origins or name. Caught between the landscape and language, nature and culture, he becomes pure figure, a repeated and anxious bodily gesture (hurrying, hurrying) akin to the chattering or burring of earlier texts. The child formalizes his impropriety, his antagonistic relation to nature, through the fantasy of mutual predation. To stretch a point, we might even read the child's game as a version of *fort-da*, whereby the child, trying to recover what has been denied him, does not toss the mother away in an act of revenge but steals her—for, as James Heffernan points out, "in the later versions of *The Prelude* birds typically appear as mothers" (259; cf. Bahti 94–95)—and hopes someone will come and steal him back.

In this version of the game, the mother has become a counter in a contest between the child and a third as yet unnamed figure that gazes at him from the yew trees and crags. The child is less worried about being with the mother than possessing her (cf. Heffernan 259), less interested in a reunion with her body than the contest with other trappers:

> Sometimes strong desire,
> Resistless, overpowered me, and the bird
> Which was the captive of another's toils
> Became my prey; and when the deed was done
> I heard among the solitary hills
> Low breathings coming after me, and sounds
> Of undistinguishable motion, steps
> Almost as silent as the turf they trod. (42–49)

The child cannot directly take possession of the mother, for possession is necessarily a symbolic, cultural relation to nature or the mother. Truly to possess her, he must enter the symbolic order or at least challenge its law, appropriating for himself, in oedipal fashion, the power which rightfully belongs to the Other or the gaze. Yet the child does not finally desire to possess her; his strong desire is rather to play a masochistic game with the uncanny presences of the hills, to become their rival and provoke them into a potentially violent response.[11] The point of the episode is not to deter-mine proper ownership through law or force but to disturb the fixed, haunting presences and set them in motion, to put them in play. The child transfers the masochistic dynamic of the *fort-da* game onto a proto-oedipal rivalry, refusing a grounded or established system of signs, a determinate symbolic, in favor of a mobile and ungrounded game of signification.

Appropriately enough, the "sounds / Of undistinguishable motion" which participate in his fantasy represent an indeterminate version of the symbolic and its language, a signification that is emptied of all meaning except for its capacity to signify itself. As Bahti demonstrates in his rigor-ously de Manian analysis of the last two clauses, if the meaning of the *motions* is undistinguishable, if the sounds are almost silent or almost non-signifying, then "the consequence of this first theft is the appearance of signs without apparent meanings." Discussing a line found in one of the MS. JJ drafts of the scene—"When shape was [?not ?no] figure to be seen" (leaf B^r)—which he reads as an allusion to Milton's personification of Death in *Paradise Lost* (2.667–70), Bahti argues that the "shape is literally a shape of a figure, but the figure of the shape, the personification, cannot be understood." In short, it is "a sign of a sign and of its process of significa-tion" (102–5). What chases the child is neither a person nor a personifica-tion but the mobility of pure figuration, the undistinguishable motion of an ungrounded language or, as Mary Jacobus suggests, of trope (*Romanti-cism* 108). Similarly, what breathes on those hills is not the punishing father of the law of property and kinship but a windy, ghostly figure akin to Mil-ton's Death; as Jacobus remarks, the "uncanny animation" and "indetermi-nate physicality" of this scene make it "an intimation of the ghostly" (108–9), a "ghostly life beyond the image" which never arrives at the fixity of "the dead letter" (105) or, we might add, of the dead father. Much as in *Adven-tures,* here Wordsworth dissolves a particular symbolic structure into the abstract tropological and syntactical capacities of the symbolic combinatory (*Écrits* 141–42), into the nonsignificative aspects of signification.

Wordsworth extends the dynamics of this scene in the raven's nest episode that follows in the 1799 *Prelude.* He dramatizes the child's position within figuration as his uncanny capacity to hang from the wind—to be "Suspended by the blast which blew amain" (61)—or, in other words, to take his placeless place within sheer motion (cf. "and with what motion moved the clouds!" [66]) and within a meaningless language ("With what strange utterance did the loud dry wind / Blow through my ears! [64–65]; cf. Kneale 79–80). Here again the text passes beyond the image, arriving not at the symbol but rather at something that is other or more than the image: "the sky seemed not a sky / Of earth" (65–66). As Bahti argues, this phrase suggests that the sky "does not appear as itself" but is "improper to itself, or quite simply improper—figural, in the realm of appearance rather than of being or identity" (109–10). The sky loses its literal status and becomes somehow significant without signifying or representing any meaning; in the terms of the celebratory passage that follows the bird theft episodes in MS. JJ, it is an instance of the literal language of "the visible imagery of all the worlds" painted by the "eternal spirit" (124–27), a purely natural or imagistic language deployed in the tropes or "motions of the sense" (136).

Wordsworth rewrites the bird theft episodes in the boy of Winander sequence that follows them in MS. JJ (and which was not included in the 1799 *Prelude*). Like the yew trees and the crags of the woodcock sequence, the supervisory presences of the "rocks / And islands of Winander" know this child well (MS. JJ 171–72). Once again the boy is alone beneath the stars—"When the stars began / To move along the edges of the hills / Rising or setting would he stand alone" (174–76)—but this time he does not seem to be a trouble to their peace, nor do the admonitory presences seem to trouble him in return. This time the child plays a game not of mutual predation but of mimicry and response, which signifies his conviction that nature's voice is an echo of his own. Nature's silence is not a threat, for the boy can readily transform it into responsive sound; when he would blow "mimic hootings" to the silent owls, they "would shout / Across the watry vale & shout again / Responsive to my call with tremulous sobs / And long halloos & screams & echoes loud / Redoubld & redoubld" (179–84). Here signification enters the imaginary, enabling the child to reduplicate his voice indefinitely in nature's echoing sounds.[12] The affirmative quality of this game apparently cancels the threat of the mother's absence, for the child and the owls exchange their calls across a "watry vale" similar to the "three long leagues / Of shining water" from which the child drank "New pleasure like a bee among the flowers" in the previous verse paragraph (MS. JJ, 162–65; cf. 1799 1.409–12). In this interpretation of the imaginary, the oral mother is at once beyond reach (the child is no longer engaged in "mute dialogues" with her "by intercourse of touch" [2.312–13]) and yet close enough for the child's eyes to drink her in.

But silence disrupts this imaginary game:

> And when it chanced
> That pauses of deep silence mockd my skill
> Then, often, in that silence while I hung
> Listening a sudden shock of mild surprize
> Would carry far into my heart the voice

Of mountain torrents: or the visible scene
Would enter unawares into my mind
With all its solemn imagery its rocks
Its woods & that uncertain heaven rece[i]ved
Into the bosom of the steady lake (MS. JJ 185–94)

In this reprise of the raven's nest episode, the child again hangs in a space
associated with torrents and an uncertain heaven. We might therefore read
these lines as presenting a more explicit version of the passage from sound
to voice, from scene to solemn imagery, from phenomenal world to signification. Andrzej Warminski offers such a reading at one point, suggesting
that "the direct entry of *voice* into the Boy's *heart*—by-passing the ears—
and the *visible scene* into his *mind*—by-passing the eyes" represents the
"passage *from* a mimetic, representational language faithful to sense experience *to* a figural language that takes advantage of, violates, the senses," a
passage from perception to reading (995–96) or from speaking to writing.
But since the boy's game with the owls was already a signifying practice, it
seems possible that their silence provokes the child to move from one practice of language to another, from an imaginary or imagistic practice that
attempts to signify voice as sound to a symbolic practice that separates
voice from sound. If one accepts this reading, one might argue that the
provisionally phenomenal language of mimicry gives way, via a sudden
shock or rupture, to a symbolic language based upon a silencing of nature.
Wordsworth suggests as much in his revision of the episode for the 1805
Prelude, where, after a brief pause, he added an account of the poet's mute
contemplation of the boy's gravestone (5.414–49). To enter the symbolic
is to experience a kind of death and to become subject to the epitaphic,
memorializing language of the dead father. As Warminski argues, "death
is precisely the poem's name for that which makes, marks, a difference between sound and speech, silence and muteness, speaking and writing"
("Missed Crossing" 995). Perhaps the graveside scene makes more explicit
the deadly qualities of the silence that shocks and surprises the boy—a
shock that, as in nearly all of the privileged scenes in *The Prelude,* intervenes in his life by chance ("And when it chanced" [MS. JJ 185]), as if coming unsought to him from elsewhere, perhaps from the admonitory genii
of the place.

Yet this reading goes too far; in the MS. JJ version of the sequence,
the owls' silence confronts the child not with a fully developed symbol (or
word) but with the more general capacities of symbolic signification.[13]
Warminski suggests that because the boy has already made the owls' hooting into a form of speech, he "has no choice but to take [their] pause of

silence as a '*measured* break or rest' (one dictionary definition of 'pause')—
articulate silence or muteness, not the *absence* of sound but the *deprivation*
of speech" ("Crossing" 997). Rather than initiating the boy into the symbolic by giving him a name or cultural status, the pause surprises him with
an instance of sequencing, spacing, or articulation as such, presenting him
with the resources of syntax rather than any particular identity.[14] As a result, it does not displace the imaginary but articulates it anew, making the
elements of what seems to be the perfect imaginary scene—complete with
a reflection in the mirrorlike surface of the lake, which in turn is associated
with the maternal bosom—into the counters of the elementary figural language of the mind and heart. In this way nature's own form of signification—its capacity, for example, to make itself artful and picturesque in the
reflecting surface of the lake or to hint at language in the sound of mountain torrents—can become an articulate, syntactical language without submitting entirely to the substitutive relations of culture.[15]

The further Wordsworth gets into this counternarrative, the more
explicitly he evokes the violent dimensions of this nonsymbolic language.
Immediately following the boy of Winander sequence in MS. JJ, and following soon after the bird theft episodes in the 1799 *Prelude,* is the episode
of the stolen boat (MS. JJ 195–241, 1799 1.81–129). Here again the child steals
something from its "usual home" in an "act of stealth / And troubled pleasure" (1799 1.84, 90–91) as if eager to provoke a response from the presences
in the caves, mountains, and trees that look on him. The poet emphasizes
what the child shares with figures from romance; Jonathan Wordsworth
argues that behind the "stilted, iambic rhythms and . . . incongruous image" of the lines "Just like a man who walks with stately step / Though
bent on speed" (89–90) one "hears another simile, equally dominant in its
different rhythm," from the *Ancient Mariner:*

> Like one, that on a lonely road
> > Doth walk in fear and dread,
> And having once turn'd round, walks on
> > And turns no more his head:
> Because he knows, a frightful fiend
> > Doth close behind him tread.[16]

Moreover, "the link with Coleridge is confirmed within a few lines when
the 'track / Of sparkling light' [95–96] recalls (and rhymes with) the 'tracks
of shining white' made by the water-snakes" (*Borders* 46). These allusions
to Coleridge link the fantasy of mutual predation with the anticulture of
the Salisbury Plain poems and the *Ancient Mariner,* in which every man is
potentially the murderer or victim of another. The line "I . . . struck the

oars, and struck again" (87) alludes, more hauntingly, to the ghost story told
in those early poems, in which the horse "Struck, and still struck again" the
spot in the floor where a murdered man was buried (*Adventures* 213). Taken
together, these allusions demonstrate that Wordsworth is fully aware he is
revising his early poems in these apparently autobiographical episodes. In
fact, he goes so far as to subsume the anxieties of the Sailor and the agitated
horse of *Adventures* and "Incipient Madness" in the child's troubled pleasure. Even his emphasis on the rhythmic "cadence" (88) in which the child
strikes the oars can be taken as a reference both to the child's mastery of
syntax, spacing, and metrics (as if he learned the lesson of the Winander
episode, which resonates here in "the voice / Of mountain-echoes" [91–
92]) and to the uncanny, violent nature of a nonsignifying textuality (akin
to the Spenserian stanza as described by Swann ["Transport" 817–19]). To
be given the gift of syntax, it seems, is to be plunged into the realm of
hyperbolic romance.

The overtones of oedipal insurrection implicit in the child's pleasurable theft of the boat become explicit later in the episode as a sexual challenge to the father. Rowing the boat—now described as an "elfin pinnace"
or penis—figures a kind of masturbation or of penetration of the watery,
maternal body: "as I rose upon the stroke, my Boat / Went heaving through
the water, like a swan" (103–6; cf. Bahti 114–15). But this is not simply auto-
erotic pleasure; at this point in the original draft of the passage, Wordsworth broke off and wrote the passage cited above—"It was an act of
stealth / And troubled pleasure" (Parrish Prelude 89)—as if to emphasize
that the act has less to do with genital sexuality than with an anxious, masochistic fantasy, familiar from the earlier theft scenes, of provoking the father's response. What he desires most is to threaten the father and to
be threatened in return. Much like the revengeful child in Bersani's reading
of the *fort-da* game, he wants to participate in a scenario in which the assault on the father and the father's punishing response cannot be distinguished.

Accordingly, when the "huge Cliff / As if with voluntary power
instinct, / Upreared its head" above the horizon, the child does not stop,
but extends his fantasy: "I struck, and struck again, / And, growing still in
stature, the huge cliff / Rose up between me and the stars" (108–12). Who
is growing in stature in that participial clause? At first, it seems to refer to
the child, who continues to grow (or rise) on the stroke as he did earlier in
the passage, and then it seems to be the cliff, the avenging father's massive
phallus rising into the heavens (cf. Heffernan 260; Bahti 116). When the
cliff "With measured motion, like a living thing / Strode after me" (113–14),

to whose measure or cadence did it stride? Its motion is the counterpart of the child's, its vengeful strides a necessary part of the implicitly murderous stroking ("struck, and struck again"), its fiendish pursuit merely the completion of the child's dreadful knowledge, hidden in the allusion to the *Ancient Mariner,* that "a frightful fiend / Doth close behind him tread." Astonishingly, in this passage it is the threat of castration which makes masturbatory fantasy so pleasurable; if no cliff had arisen to threaten the child, he would have invented one anyway, much as he imagined the undistinguishable motion of silent steps in the woodcock episode—a motion given a distinguishable measure in this version of the fantasy (cf. Bahti 117).[17]

But in the threat of castration lies an even more forbidden possibility of a wounding anal penetration that he would experience in fantasy as at once a punishment and a delight. As before, the child wishes to be stalked from behind, perhaps from close behind. But in this case he also imagines that when the cliff appears it "upreared its head." Is the cliff's head like a rear? Or is its phallic head being forced "up" a rear, from behind, of a trembling, masturbating child? In that case, the child's murderous stroking is matched by the father's wounding assaults, each rising on the stroke. Here Wordsworth conflates murder and sex, oedipal violence and anal intercourse, as if being stabbed, castrated, and penetrated are versions of the same event that demonstrates beyond doubt the father's vengeful love.

This masochistic fantasy culminates in the lines that describe the child's return to shore: "With trembling hands I turned, / And through the silent water stole my way / Back to the cavern of the willow-tree" where he left the boat (114–16). Returning the boat, of course, is like giving up the elfin pinnace or penis, rendering back to the father that which is the father's, and becoming at least symbolically castrated. But the child turns "with trembling hands": like that of Harry Gill, his body's uncontrollable shaking expresses its masochistic pleasure in the prospect of its dismemberment. Once again the nonsignificative measured motion of syntax or meter is located in the "sheer repetition of unintelligible sound" or gesture "located in the body" (Pinch 842)—a sound or gesture that operates through most of the episode as the child's repeated strokes ("struck . . . and struck again" [87]) which are again repeated ("struck, and struck again" [110]). The trembling hands, it seems, are not so different from the masturbatory hands earlier in the episode, a link that demonstrates that the child's troubled pleasure was masochistic all along. Moreover, Wordsworth's use of *stole* here as an intransitive verb (stole my way) suspends the transitive logic of stealing the phallus or being stolen by it, suggesting that the theft arrests an oedipal narrative of purposive confrontation in a nonpurposive, undecidable pleasure.

The episode culminates in the most extensive description yet of the ghostly presences in the landscape:

> after I had seen
> That spectacle, for many days my brain
> Worked with a dim and undetermined sense
> Of unknown modes of being: in my thoughts
> There was a darkness, call it solitude
> Or blank desertion; no familiar shapes
> Of hourly objects, images of trees,
> Of sea or sky, no colours of green fields:
> But huge and mighty forms, that do not live
> Like living men, moved slowly through my mind
> By day, and were the trouble of my dreams. (1799 1.119–29)

At first, this passage seems to verge on the entry into the symbolic. Unlike the boy of Winander episode, this one ends *without* the solemn imagery of sea and sky, without the signs borrowed from the imaginary. The silencing of nature reaches a new intensity, blanking out the visible world entirely. The movement, as Bahti puts it, from the "literally figural" ("undistinguishable motion") to the "purely figural" ("with what motion moved the clouds") and now to the "figurally figural" ("like a living thing" [1799 1.113] which he reads as "a simile of a personification" [117]) arrives finally at a signifying motion allied with death: "forms that do not live / Like living men." These forms, Bahti argues, can only be "'Forms that do not live' 'moving,'" and thus "their only motion . . . can be rhetorical: the movement of tropes" (121–22). The passage associates the castrating father with language or rhetoric, a mode of being based upon the negation of nature and of the body.

Once again Wordsworth conveys a sense not of the institutional authority of the Lacanian dead father but rather a "dim and undetermined sense" of troubling, haunting, ghostly presences. These dead forms have not been buried and memorialized but are rather the giant forms of spectacle, figures that move in the dim spaces beyond the barriers of the visible. Natives of darkness, solitude, and blank desertion, they are akin to the dead who rise in another deserted waste to another solitary traveler on the stroke of darkness, figures who also threaten to assault the unwary male who, compelled by "strong desire / Resistless" (42–43), has transgressed the boundaries of the law. Moreover, in the context of the episode as a whole, they do not punish the child and discipline his desire as much as fulfill his masochistic fantasy and haunt his pleasurably tormenting dreams. Wordsworth writes as if a certain more than natural power enters him in the assault of the undead presences. Hinting that only someone violently homoerotic can become a great poet, he suggests that in the culmination of his fantasy he gains the dark power of a nonsignificative language, of Spenserian or balladic romance.

Wordsworth now celebrates the very features of the earlier poems which seemed most troubling as the source of his poetic power. Following the stolen boat episode with a passage in which he praises the "Beings of the hills" and those "that walk the woods and open heaths," he reinterprets the ghostly dead as the nature spirits who singled him out for a high purpose (see 130–41). Revising the Salisbury Plain poems in a way that should help one interpret the scene of Druidic sacrifice later in *The Prelude* (12.312–53), he imagines the child's transgression as an act prompted by nature's powers (81) and the visitation of the huge and mighty forms as a sign of his election. He wants no institutional authority but rather an emotional power derived from a fantasized violence. He receives the power of the dead not through an officializing rite but in the face of a ghost, whence it passes directly across the (absent) boundary between the dead and the living, the otherworldly and the human, into the phenomenal world, where it shocks and disturbs him. He would rather be haunted by such a ghost than inspired by God.[18]

Skipping over descriptions of various boyish sports—skating, cards, fishing—we must move on to the final sequence in Part One, which includes the drowned man episode and the spots of time and which articulates the stance of this text most thoroughly. Once again the child chances across a scene by a lakeside, as if led by nature ("I chanced to cross / One of those open fields which, shaped like ears, / Make green peninsulas on Esthwaite's lake" [263–65]). In the 1805 version of the passage Wordsworth strengthens the links between this child and the errant wanderer of the theft scenes. Describing himself as "roving up and down alone, / Seeking I knew not what" (5.455–56), he recalls the solitary child plagued by an anxious desire (compare also Margaret's confession to the pedlar: "About the fields I wander, knowing this / Only, that what I seek I cannot find" [MS. D 350–51]). Moreover, this child, somewhat like the boy of Winander, gazes across the lake in the twilight, but instead of seeing his reflection or hearing an echo of his voice, he sees "through the gloom . . . on the opposite shore / Beneath a tree and close by the lake side / A heap of garments, as if left by one / Who there was bathing" (266–70). Bewell argues that in this scene the child "has an intimation of the Underworld. The water grows dark and spectral 'shadows' begin to play 'on its breast.' Then fishes, the traditional conveyers of the dead, come from below to disturb the surface of a now 'breathless stillness'" (see lines 271–74). Perhaps, as Bewell suggests, "[t]he premonitory aspects and phantasmal qualities of the scene do not so much derive from what Wordsworth is actually seeing as from what he knows has happened" (214). But even in that case, this episode picks up with the elements of previous episodes—with a pause ("half an hour I watched" [270]—a phrase echoed in the revised version of the boy of Winander episode [5.421]) over the question of possession ("and no one owned [the garments]" [271]) in the presence of shadows and ghostly silences. The echoes of the stolen boat episode are particularly strong; like the thieving child, the boatmen who probe in the waters the next day insist on provoking, with the action of their oarlike instruments, a response from the as-yet invisible ghost: "The succeeding day / There came a company, and in their boat / Sounded with iron hooks and with long poles" (274–76). If the drowned man's sudden appearance the next day realizes the child's prior intimation (Bewell 214) "as if his death were a fact known all along" (Manning 94), it also realizes the intimations gathered in all the previous episodes. Here, at last, the ghostly figures of the theft scenes show a face: "At length the dead man 'mid that beauteous scene / Of trees, and hills, and water, bolt upright / Rose with his ghastly face" (277–79).

Certain associations of this figure are immediately clear. Ronald Paulson remarks that its sudden appearance "carries with it the memory of the 'huge peak, black and huge' that 'Upreared its head' in the boat-stealing episode" (259), and Manning comments that "[t]his figure, rising phallically 'bolt upright' (278), invites psychoanalytic readings, oedipal and preoedipal" (95). But one disturbing feature of the scene is not so clear. These interpreters attribute the fact that this phallic figure is dead to Wordsworth's experience of the Reign of Terror during the French Revolution (citing a phrase added in the 1805 version's description of the drowned man: "a spectre shape / Of terror" [5.472–73; Paulson 259]) and to the child's confrontation with his own mortality (Manning 95). But the logic of the entire poem to this point makes it inevitable that the oedipal father appears in the form of a dead man.[19] And it is just as inevitable that this ghastly or uncouth figure, like the discharged soldier, trails along behind him a series of texts, whether the pronounced allusion to *Othello* and the nature of seductive storytelling in the 1799 version (the "numerous accidents in flood or field" [280]; cf. "Wherein I spake of most disastrous chances, / Of moving accidents by flood and field" [I.3.136–37]) or the explanation in the 1805 version that as a child Wordsworth was not terrified by the scene because his "inner eye had seen / Such sights before, among the shining streams / Of Fairy Land, the Forests of Romance" (5.475–77).[20] The dead man bears texts because he personifies textuality; here at last appears, in the phenomenal world, one of the "huge and mighty forms, that do not live / Like living men," one of those ghosts of trope and rhetoric, for he is, according to the 1799 version, an instance of the "forms / That yet exist with independent life / And, like their archetypes, know no decay" (285–87). As Cynthia Chase suggests, "the insistent literalism of *decay* refers back to the decay of the risen corpse" (25); it is as if Wordsworth denies that this is a literal corpse that will decay and reads it instead as a personification of the more than mortal status of the mind's archetypes or symbols. Here the drowned man's death signifies not simply death but the transition to another kind of life, the nonphenomenal life of words or stories.

Yet if the phallic father can only appear in this text in the form of a dead man, he must also be an unburied dead man, a specter. He personifies not textuality in general but that of Othello's stories or of Spenserian romance (the allusion is unmistakable: "the shining streams / of Fairy Land, the Forests of Romance"). To designate this kind of textuality, Wordsworth need not have gone so far afield; in these allusions he covertly refers to his own texts, *The Borderers* and the Salisbury Plain poems respectively. Even without these allusions, one reference, at least, would be clear enough; this ghastly corpse recalls the discharged soldier, and beyond him the corpse-ghost of the gibbet scene in *Adventures*. He is not the dead father but the anxious rival of the child, indeed the specular double of the errant wanderer. This mutilated body, in short, personifies the nonsignificative textuality of hyperbolic romance, the world not of perpetual life but of endless, anxious, and mobile violence: of "numerous accidents in flood or field," errant chances and mischances, unplanned and fearful visitations.[21] True enough, this episode is in part about the Terror and about the confrontation with one's own death (not to mention the outbreak of war with France, parricide and regicide, and the spectral nature of nonsymbolic subjectivity), but it interprets them all according to its vision of dismembered culture.

Even this reading, however, does not exhaust the episode. The allusion to *Othello*, in which a man seduces a woman by means of his stories and then kills her, brings into this text a plot suspiciously similar to the one in *The Tempest* which, according to Reeve Parker, influences *The Borderers* ("Reading" 317–22).[22] Wordsworth is continuing the process, already begun in "The Discharged Soldier," of entangling the thematics of *Adventures* and *The Borderers*. But in the context of the 1799 *Prelude* to this point, the implications of this allusion remain unclear. One of Wordsworth's tasks in the spots of time which follow is to elucidate this dense constellation of concerns.

In the first spot of time, "some mischance / Disjoined" the child from his guide (304–5), dislocating him from the man who could lead him down the proper path. "Through fear / Dismounting," the boy led his horse off that path onto untracked ground, "stumbling" "down the rough and stony moor" (305–7) until he

> Came to a bottom where in former times
> A man, the murderer of his wife, was hung
> In irons; mouldered was the gibbet mast,
> The bones were gone, the iron and the wood,
> Only a long green ridge of turf remained
> Whose shape was like a grave. I left the spot,
> And, reascending the bare slope, I saw
> A naked pool that lay beneath the hills,
> The beacon on the summit, and more near
> A girl who bore a pitcher on her head
> And seemed with difficult steps to force her way
> Against the blowing wind. (308–19)

Having strayed extravagantly, the child descends and ascends, moving hyperbolically between depths and heights. In the 1805 and 1850 versions, Wordsworth emphasizes the boy's disorientation: "I fled, / Faltering and faint, and ignorant of the road" (1850 12.246–47), suggesting that he dizzily wandered on, beyond a familiar experience of the senses and beyond any sense of direction "Through words and things, a dim and perilous way" (*Borderers* 4.2.103). In this domain something divests the landscape of its normal attributes, making the slope bare and the pool naked and removing nearly every trace of the old skeleton and gibbet—perhaps the wind that, in the second writing of the scene, threatens to strip the girl ("The woman and her garments vexed and tossed / By the strong wind" [326–27]; cf. Weiskel 178–79; Reid). It seems that the Wordsworthian traveler, now in the guise of a child, is back on a certain waste where, on the verge of the dread hour, a bustard "Forced hard against the wind a thick unwieldy flight" (*Salisbury Plain* 70, 72).[23] But the dread hour of transgression beyond the boundaries has already arrived; the child stumbles onto the site of murder and punishment once marked by a gibbet mast, a site that recalls the gibbet scenes of *Adventures* and, through them, the entire problematic of war, sacrifice, crime, and punishment of the Salisbury Plain poems (cf. Williams *Wordsworth* 115–16; Liu *Wordsworth* 201–10).

In this immediate context, however, the gibbet scene is associated with the gibbeted corpse-ghosts of *Adventures*, a version of which just surfaced in the drowned man episode. This passage expands upon the concerns of that episode; its description of the criminal as a murderer of his wife refers once again to *Othello,* suggesting that in this sequence of Part One the drowned man and the gibbeted man are the same. Later Wordsworth indirectly reinforces this link; as Kneale points out, when the lines on numerous accidents were removed for the 1805 *Prelude,* "so too was the detail that this particular man had murdered his wife" (132). Conflating Othello the storyteller with Othello the murderer, Wordsworth reads him as another version of Herbert and of Prospero: a man whose enslaving narrative power is directly related to the murder of his wife. Wordsworth's reading of Shakespeare here is perceptive; one could argue that *Othello* explores better than *The Tempest* the problem of matricidal poetics, for in this text it is the same woman, Desdemona, who is both seduced and murdered. Apparently, to be seduced by narrative *is* to be killed by it. Or, conversely, to tell romantic tales in a certain echoing and repeated cadence, to voice an anxious pleasure with a certain measured motion, is to kill a woman.

Building on the autobiographical texture of these episodes and on Richard Onorato's genetic psychoanalytic reading of *The Prelude,* James Heffernan interprets Wordsworth's reference to matricide as an expression of a private, psychological obsession: his resentment concerning his mother's death and his unconscious tendency to blame it on his father. Like Othello, Mr. Wordsworth killed his wife, and the child takes pleasure in the possibility that the father is punished for his deed (259–63). This search for a genetic explanation ignores not only the context of *The Borderers* (and with it *Othello* and *The Tempest*) but also the series of poems in which Wordsworth focuses upon a man's abandonment or murder of a woman: *Adventures,* "The Somersetshire Tragedy," *The Ruined Cottage,* and "The Thorn." Perhaps even the pedlar, who founds his complacent poetics on the death of Margaret, is another version of the matricidal poet, in which case he is vulnerable to Wordsworth's own critique of the apparently saintly old man in *The Borderers.* The issue here is not Wordsworth's private resentment but his engagement with the problem of the way in which male-centered narratives violate the maternal body or, in larger terms, the way in which culture, even a dismembered culture, violates nature. This is one major concern of all the episodes we have discussed from Part One: by turning the maternal body (the mother bird or the lake) into a counter in the game of rivalry with the castrating and castrated father, the child helps to negate its physical, bodily nature and transform it into a collection of images and signs.

It would be just as misleading, however, to turn Wordsworth's concern into a typical instance of the paradigm, described by post-Lacanian theorists such as Margaret Homans, according to which the boy is severed from the maternal body when he joins the symbolic order (*Bearing* 1–11).

Rather than taking this passage into the symbolic for granted, Wordsworth remains aware that it necessarily violates the maternal body, that the "symbolic order is founded, not merely on the regrettable loss of the mother, but rather on her active and overt murder" (*Bearing* 11). In a reprise of the strategy of *Salisbury Plain*, here Wordsworth performs a critique of the symbolic from the perspective, as it were, of its victims, the mother and the child, exposing the violent imposture or self-usurpation (Parker "Reading" 321), which grounds the father's symbolic and linguistic authority. What may seem to be Wordsworth's private resentment about his mother's death is more likely to be a far-reaching resentment about the way the symbolic order attempts to found itself in the eradication of the maternal body.

In the 1805 version of this passage, Wordsworth carries out this critique in a different fashion. He depicts the violence of romance narrative not with reference to the gibbeted man's crime but through the appearance of a violent language directly on the spot itself:

> The Gibbet-mast was mouldered down, the bones
> And iron case were gone, but on the turf,
> Hard by, soon after that fell deed was wrought,
> Some unknown hand had carved the Murderer's name.
> The monumental writing was engraven
> In times long past, and still from year to year
> By superstition of the neighborhood
> The grass is cleared away; and to this hour
> The letters are all fresh and visible.
> Faltering, and ignorant where I was, at length
> I chanced to espy those characters inscribed
> On the green sod: forthwith I left the spot. (11.291–302)

In a cursory reading of this passage, one might conclude that here at last the child encounters the symbolic order. The monumental letters manifest "forms / That yet exist with independent life / And, like their archetypes, know no decay" (1799 1.285–87); they are the permanent expression of the law in written form. Insofar as these letters at once pronounce judgment and constitute a proper name, they might be read as a version of the Lacanian name of the father, which grounds the law of the father, the symbolic order. Such a reading of these letters implicitly proposes a complex scenario that one might simplify as follows: once the child's masochistic fantasy of rivalry with the father both effaces the maternal body and culminates in the father's death, a new force, an unknown hand or impersonal law, intervenes to put an end to the child's destructive game and to punish him for his wish, as if the living father must be killed, at least in fantasy, before the dead father or the law of culture can assert itself in an authoritative fashion. Where Lacan's displacement of the Freudian father from any actual man to the abstract name of the father was a theoretical gesture, a correction of the master's work, according to this scenario Wordsworth locates this displacement in the child's fantasy of the father's death, when the father ceases to be a jealous, anxious, personally interested figure and becomes the impersonal, dead personification of the law.

True, such a reading is suggested in the 1799 version of the passage, in which the culmination of the fantasy is already old news. The child arrives on the scene long after the gibbet itself has mouldered into a shape like a grave. Perhaps now the unburied ghosts are finally buried in a grave of their own—a site marked in the 1805 version by a kind of epitaph. This marked ground may be another version of the boy of Winander's grave, these monumental or admonitory letters (cf. Kneale 137) another version of the memorial stone positioned as a warning near the end of *The Borderers*. Moreover, no specular encounter, it seems, can take place here, not even with the ghastly face of the criminal; the father is now apparently Other, possessing a gaze that does not look back from what Heffernan calls "the patriarchal eye" of the Penrith Beacon, which looms over the second scene of this spot of time (264). Perhaps the spectral, specular faces of the earlier passages—the upraised head of the cliff and the ghastly face of the drowned man—give way to the monolithic, phallic beacon, which, marking a boundary between different realms (and thus putting the disturbances of *The Borderers* to rest), apparently stabilizes culture under the vast sweep of its eye.[24]

But this reading unravels very quickly under closer analysis. These letters do, in fact, know decay; they endure only because "from year to year / By superstition of the neighborhood / The grass is cleared away." The idea that certain cultural archetypes are permanent is a fiction, for their survival depends upon an endless process of return and renewal. Here, much as in the final stanza of *Adventures*, the judgment that seems to bring a Gothic violence to an end actually renews it in the form of an excessive and repeated condemnation. What might that "superstition" be? Why keep recarving those letters? Is it possible that this is not really a grave, even though "its shape [is] like a grave," because it merely consists of the mouldered remains of the dead man and his gibbet?[25] Without a coffin, without a proper burial, this dead man threatens to become a ghost, and only the engraved characters keep him in his proper place. The unknown hand carves the murderer's name not to memorialize him (to give him an epitaph) but, out of vengeful desire or superstitious fear, to keep him from returning to haunt the living. As a result, the anonymous engraver must continually return to this spot, haunt it, and become the living counterpart to the ghost that he fears. But who is this engraver? As Kneale points out, even talking about him as an unknown hand "has the effect of disembodying that author," of making him a "ghost-writer writing a ghost-word" (139). Perhaps the ghost that writes is that of the dead man himself; as Kneale points out, the perpetual reinscription of the name "from year to year" recalls Othello's rehearsal of his tale ("Her father lov'd me, oft invited me, / Still question'd me the story of my life, / From year to year"), a link that suggests that the wife killer still tells his story through these letters (143–44). Of course, the unknown hand could just as easily belong to the superstitious villagers who, like Othello, keep alive an old tale of one particular accident in flood or field.

If the villagers return from year to year, they not only keep Othello's way of telling stories alive but also renew the matricidal violence of his crime, inscribing language or narrative on the body of nature. Rather than substituting the name for the body, they carve the name onto the body, making language intervene directly into the phenomenal world instead of taking its place. The powers of earth, which, like a printing press, "On caves and trees, upon the woods and hills, / Impressed upon all forms the characters / Of danger and desire" (1799 1.193–95; cf. Kneale 86–87) have been at work here, engraving and inscribing these characters directly in the turf, as if, for once, to make them fresh and visible. Ironically, in this way the name loses its symbolic status and becomes merely phenomenal, something seen and not read. Far from constituting the name of the father, the basis for language and for reading, this proper name collapses into merely visible letters and becomes unreadable (cf. Kneale 181). Accordingly, these carved letters become uncanny, even uncouth figures, monumental shapes akin to the "huge and mighty forms that do not live / Like living men." No wonder the child, glimpsing them, flees as if he has seen a ghost. Strangely enough, once the indistinct forms of the earlier episodes in Part One finally materialize as a name—once the more than phenomenal presences become symbolic—that name immediately dissolves back into a disturbance in the phenomenal field.

Here, as in the episodes of the stolen boat or the drowned man, the symbolic is reduced to a certain violent intervention into the world of the senses, an intervention that reappears in the form of the beacon, another monumental, dead, and phallic form. Isobel Armstrong, using the added passage of the 1805 version, which refers to "the naked pool and dreary crags" and "the melancholy Beacon" (11.321–22), suggests that these fearful presences are displaced versions of the gibbet (35) or, we might add, of the cliffhead (cf. "dreary crags"). As a physical counterpart of the communal discipline exercised in the carving of the letters, the beacon embodies not the gaze of the Other but the specular gaze of the anxious father. Rather than drawing a boundary or imposing a law, the beacon brings into this text the outlaw energies and matricidal poetics of *The Borderers,* over some of whose scenes it presided (*Borderers* 3.4; Osborn 202n)—a lineage that Liu has sketched in detail (*Wordsworth* 201–10).

When the child turns away from this scene of matricide and ascends the bare slope, he sees a gathering of images, one of which is an image of the oral mother—a "girl who bore a pitcher on her head" (Onorato 205–19; Manning 13–15). Something about these images is so compelling that Wordsworth pauses to look at them again:

> It was in truth
> An ordinary sight but I should need
> Colours and words that are unknown to man
> To paint the visionary dreariness
> Which, while I looked all round for my lost guide,
> Did, at that time, invest the naked pool,
> The beacon on the lonely eminence,
> The woman and her garments vexed and tossed
> By the strong wind. (1799 1.319–27)

Magnuson argues that in this passage Wordsworth "interrupts stark narration to admit the poverty of language to convey the feelings of the child." This interruption "signals a shift from naturalism in time and image to the literary and figurative. It destroys the illusion of realism and the accuracy of narrative" (214). As Kneale writes, here "Wordsworth, as the little boy on the hill, stands on that verge where words abandon him" (181). But just as the child's being abandoned prompts him to search for his lost guide, the poet's abandonment by language produces a craving for words, one that expresses itself, as in "The Thorn," through repetition. Already this passage repeats nearly the same words and images of the previous lines (313–19), and in the 1805 version they are repeated again (11.316–26).[26] Thus the suspension of narrative does not bring the poem to a halt but deflects it into the repetitious rhetoric of vexation. It is as if Wordsworth finds himself back in "The Thorn"; here again the craving poet circles around a pond, a woman vexed by the wind, and—to include an image from earlier in this spot of time—a gravelike mound (see J. Wordsworth *Borders* 59). Even the beacon becomes one more image in that game, one more object of the abandoned child's desire. These images are even more inexplicable than in "The Thorn," for in this text there is no interlocutor to ask what they mean or who this woman is (J. Wordsworth 59; cf. Christensen 272–73, 279). As he admits later, Wordsworth the poet and interpreter is truly lost in these images ("I am lost": 1805 11.330).

When the child turns from the ungrave (1799) or the name that is not a name (1805) toward the pool, beacon, and woman, Wordsworth the poet turns from the nonsignificative language of hyperbolic romance to the language of imagistic repetition, from the violent father to the abandoning mother, as if recapitulating the turn from the Salisbury Plain poems and *The Borderers* toward *The Ruined Cottage* and "The Thorn."[27] It would be tempting to read this as a turn from matricide to the maternal body or, with Thomas Weiskel, as a "displacement or regression from the order of symbol to that of image" (179). Such a reading would emphasize the contrast between these orders and propose that the imagistic language of the maternal body somehow saves the child from the violence of the gibbet scene and transforms it into a sublime "visionary dreariness" (cf. Weiskel 179–80, 185). But violence and death remain in the order of the image, in the Penrith Beacon and in the allusions to "The Thorn." There is no escape from parricide, matricide, or for that matter infanticide in this text. The brief ascent up the bare slope does not deliver the child from murderous, hyperbolic romance but draws him into another telling of the same tale, a telling that by effacing the name also sidesteps the problem of crime and its punishment but as a result creates a craving in the mind for some representation of the significance of the visionary dreariness. The displacement from symbol to image is from one form of repetition, the periodic reinscription of the criminal's name, onto another, the poet's anxious review of inadequate images, and brings together in a single problematic what had been in his previous texts the separate problems of the dismemberment of culture and the absence of nature.

Wordsworth blends these problems together through the use of similar images in the two sections of this spot of time: the gibbet and the beacon, the ridge of turf and the hill of moss. If one collapses these two scenes together and throws the drowned man in for good measure, one gets something like the landscape of "The Thorn":

> some will say
> She hanged her baby on the tree,
> Some say she drowned it in the pond,
> Which is a little step beyond,
> But all and each agree,
> The little babe was buried there,
> Beneath that hill of moss so fair. ("The Thorn" 214–20)

The landscape is the same, but the criminals and victims have changed. One could speculate at length about the basic elements of what seems to be Wordsworth's primal scene: to hang from a tree/gibbet (or to be stunned by the eye of cliff/crags/beacon), to drown in a pond/lake, to be buried in a hill of moss/a ridge of turf. Evidently Wordsworth can manipulate these elements in several ways, shifting the persons of the fantasy around (who kills whom? who is buried in that mound?) and encoding the tale in different signifying practices (repeated images, monumental letters). But precisely because these images are so easily manipulated and so conventional (how else might one be killed in a pond?) they hold little clue to the complex of fantasies that they help signify. The real problem is not the blending together of the images but of the fantasies, oriented as they are in two different directions: toward the father/culture, and toward the mother/ nature.

In the second spot of time these fantasies come together. Again the "Feverish, and tired and restless" child wanders the fields, looking for the horses that will take him and his two brothers home for Christmas (332). To look for them better, he perches on "the highest summit" of "a crag, / An eminence which from the meeting point / Of two highways ascending overlooked / At least a long half-mile of those two roads" (341, 335–38). By ascending this height, the youth becomes hyperbolic; he has in effect climbed the Penrith Beacon to appropriate its gaze; he too is perched on a summit (cf. 316) or eminence (cf. 325) associated with crags (1805 II.321–22) and overlooks, if not the boundaries between two nations, the meeting point of two roads. Heffernan remarks, "In thus taking up the station symbolically assumed by his father in the boat stealing episode, he unconsciously threatens to usurp the father's authority" (265). Like the boy of the breakfast scene in *Adventures*, he takes the father's seat and thus implicitly challenges him to oedipal battle (*Adventures* 604–66). Moreover, he positions himself at the crossroads, the classic site of the oedipal confrontation since *Oedipus Rex* (Bewell 180)—a site at which the son contests the father's right of way. The violent clash evoked and suppressed in the image of the "naked guide-post's double head" (*Adventures* 170), which might as well be posted at this crossroads, under this "naked wall" (1799 1.343; cf. the "naked crag" of the raven's nest episode [62]; Reid 542–43), has become nearly explicit. Taking the father's seat, intruding upon his path; in either case, the son challenges the father's claim to physical precedence. Hyperbolic ascent and transgressive journeying, tropes of the same error, have arrived at the nodal point of violent encounter.

Yet on the heights of usurpation, the youth seems to be a figure in "The Thorn," perhaps another version of Martha Ray:

> 'twas a day
> Stormy, and rough, and wild, and on the grass
> I sate, half-sheltered by the naked wall;
> Upon my right hand was a single sheep,
> A whistling hawthorn on my left. (1799 1.341–45)

As Bewell argues, these evocations of "The Thorn" suggest that the boy perches over a crossroads because he is a kind of witch. According to folk traditions, "[o]ne went to the crossroads to meet devils or demons; they were places where magic was practiced; and it was believed that witches met there for sabbats." According to the *Malleus Maleficarum,* witches could raise "hailstorms and tempests" by sacrificing "a black cock at two cross-roads" at midnight or could by similar means gain the power to fly to a witches' sabbat (179–83). Although the youth is in no obvious sense a witch, his presumption that simply through wishing devoutly enough, through having a sufficient "anxiety of hope" (357), he might make something happen is, as we saw in our discussion of "Goody Blake" and "The Thorn," the infantile, fantastic basis for the array of adult superstitions and magic practices associated with witchcraft.

Wordsworth's perverse rewriting of the normative oedipal tale becomes clearer in the rest of the passage. Before the holidays were over, his father died:

> And I and my two Brothers, orphans then,
> Followed his body to the grave. The event
> With all the sorrow which it brought appeared
> A chastisement, and when I called to mind
> That day so lately passed when from the crag
> I looked in such anxiety of hope,
> With trite reflections of morality
> Yet with the deepest passion I bowed low
> To God, who thus corrected my desires. (352–60)

That event could be a "chastisement" only if the boy had desired his father's death; here Wordsworth almost explicitly admits to the youth's unconscious oedipal wish (cf. Weiskel 182–83). Furthermore, he articulates as an actual sequence the logic implicit in the first spot of time; only when the son's wish for the father comes true (this time not in fantasy) does the impersonal law of the dead father or of God intervene to discipline his desire. But, as Weiskel asks, "In what sense does Wordsworth stand corrected? Far from repenting—or repressing—the spectacles and sounds which are linked to his desires, Wordsworth repairs often to them" (183–84). Weiskel chooses to emphasize how Wordsworth "is aware of the triteness and the ritual conventionality of the gesture" of bowing low, as if he is not disciplined at all (184). But more perversely, I find in this gesture of bowing *low* in *deepest passion* a homoerotic pleasure in abasement, a masochistic delight in God's discipline.[28] What is trite is not the discipline itself but the idea that discipline is somehow moral rather than pleasurable. Here, as in the first spot of time, Wordsworth subsumes even the judgments of the law to the passionate economy of discipline, transforming the punishment of desire into the desire for punishment. And in an extension of the homoerotics of the stolen boat episode, he regards God not as the final arbiter of justice but as the most frightful and most wonderfully invasive of all punishing figures. More clearly than ever, Wordsworth suggests that he was elected as a poet, set apart not merely by the gods but by God himself, in a moment of masochistic wounding.

As if to emphasize that this mode of repentance for his desires is a form of taking pleasure in them, Wordsworth again interrupts the narrative to return to the scene of desire and indulge in a little repetition:

> And afterwards the wind, and sleety rain,
> And all the business of the elements,
> The single sheep, and the one blasted tree,
> And the bleak music of that old stone wall,
> The noise of wood and water, and the mist
> Which on the line of each of those two roads
> Advanced in such indisputable shapes,
> All these were spectacles and sounds to which
> I often would repair, and thence would drink
> As at a fountain, and I do not doubt
> That in this later time when storm and rain
> Beat on my roof at midnight, or by day
> When I am in the woods, unknown to me
> The workings of my spirit thence are brought. (361–74)

As David Ellis points out, in this second rehearsal of the spot of time Wordsworth emphasizes visionary sounds—the "bleak music" of the wall, the "noise of wood and water," the sound of "storm and rain" that "Beat on [his] roof at midnight" (30–33). These tempestuous sounds and sights, reminiscent of "The Thorn," hint that in this passage Wordsworth nearly becomes a witch; as Bewell points out, he has whipped up a good storm and claims that the beating *midnight* rains can transport him, by the witchlike powers of imagination, back to that crag (182–83).

This passage evokes the pleasures of agitation with such a rare intensity that we should suspect it harbors another masochistic fantasy like that of the *fort-da* game. Kneale, following one of Hartman's suggestions, traces one etymology of the word *repair* to *repatriare*, "to return to one's fatherland" (177). Wordsworth repairs to this scene in order to recover his fatherland, his father. And yet this is, by his own account, the scene in which he wished for his father's death. By repairing to the scene he repeats the act that apparently killed his father: "Thither I repaired / Up to the highest summit" (340–41). How can one recover the father by wishing for his death, by taking his place? Only if that wish is, as in the *fort-da* fantasy, a retrospective wish to master one's abandonment by willing it. Wordsworth's father, like his mother, had abandoned him by dying—"And I and my two Brothers, orphans then, / Followed his body to the grave" (353–54)—and like the vengeful child he responds, "All right then, go away! I don't need you. I'm sending you away myself'" (Freud *Beyond* 10). The seemingly Freudian passage in which Wordsworth admits to desiring his father's death covers over the deeper logic of the episode; it is not a confession but a symptom of the fantasy at work here.[29]

This odd kind of *fort-da* game with the *father* is, however, a simple extension of the games of mutual predation which appeared in the stealing episodes earlier in Part One, or rather is the appropriation of those early games to meet the challenge of a new and entirely unforeseen crisis. In his fantasy, the youth hopes to provoke the absent father into making an appearance by taking what should be his—in this case, his life. If, as I argued above, the logic of masochistic fantasy culminates in the gibbet scene of the first spot of time, in this second spot Wordsworth captures the satisfactions that he finds in such a scene, using one childhood episode to interpret and expand upon another. These two spots may on some level be the same; Bewell suggests that Wordsworth associates the witchlike, demonic qualities of these crossroads with the Gibbet Moss, a crossroads gibbet that was believed to be haunted and certain details of which contributed to the first spot (180–81).[30] The tempest that surrounds this gibbet in *Adventures* (112–17) and the horse's tempestuous agitation on the spot of murder in that poem (208–13)—stormy disturbances suppressed in the first spot—now noisily invade the text and circulate around the site of violence at the crossroads. In fantasy, at least, the son *did* meet the father at the crossroads and kill him, but now it is clear that he did so in order that the father's ghost, which apparently haunts the spot, would hunt him down. He seems to get his wish; like the "questionable shape" of the ghost in *Hamlet* (1.4.43–44), a certain spectral, misty figure advances down those roads in "indisputable shapes" (367; De Selincourt 615; Weiskel 182–83; Kneale 182–83). An indisputable shape of mist; here is a version of the undistinguishable motion of the bird theft episode (cf. Jacobus *Romanticism* 104) or more likely of the shape without figure of a canceled line ("When shape was [?not ?no] figure to be seen") which, as we saw above, Bahti links with Milton's Death. A ghostly Death is still coming after the boy, as he has so often before, and accordingly the youth feels with extraordinary intensity an anxious, troubled pleasure in the prospect of the father's vengeance. Even now this pleasure at times transports him back to the scene, puts him into a trance, as if the spectacle of that gibbet still gives him, as it did the sailor, a pleasurable "shuddering pain" and rouses in his mind a more satisfying "train / Of the mind's phantoms, horrible as vain" (*Adventures* 119, 121–22).

Yet because Wordsworth is now abandoned by both parents, the absent father fuses with the absent mother. Repairing to this scene, Wordsworth "thence would drink / As at a fountain" (369–70), as at a lake or pitcher that gives him the satisfactions of the oral mother. Returning to the fatherland or the motherland; it is all one fantasy now. The gibbet storm is a witch storm too and revives the ghost of the mother as much as the father. Like the pedlar, this youth often returns to the scene to glimpse the abandoned mother or, like the gossip of "The Thorn," to hear the cry "Oh misery," which still whistles in this wind. Homoerotic and heteroerotic masochism blend here in similar fantasies that the parents, overwhelmed by the child's abandonment of or assault on them, meditate a perpetual, loving vengeance upon him. Although no one seems to weep, shudder, or chatter in this scene, a less articulate and less physical agitation survives in the workings of Wordsworth's spirit, suggesting that the spirit, etymologically linked to the wind, masochistically identifies with its pain and becomes "a tempest, a redundant energy" (cf. MS. JJ 1–12).

Wordsworth's use of the word *workings* should give us pause. Are these workings, brought to Wordsworth without his knowledge by storm and rain, responsible for making "The surface of the universal earth / With meanings of delight, of hope and fear, / Work like a sea" (196–98)? If so, they have also "Impressed upon all forms the characters / Of danger or desire" (194–95). What works in Wordsworth's spirit is also what impresses characters on all forms and perhaps what carves the characters in the turf. The subtle links between these passages suggest that it is Wordsworth who returns (if only in fantasy) to the gibbet scene to reengrave the father's name in the earth, thereby at once repairing the letters (renewing the condemnation) and repairing *to* the letters, finding in them at least a trace of the absent father. Or, more precisely, it is only by making the father's name into an instrument of fearful vengeance, into a site of mutual haunting, that he can recover it at all.[31]

Thus Wordsworth becomes as vengeful and haunting a figure as the unburied father, appropriating the power not of his name but of his ghostly subjectivity. If, as Kneale suggests, the wife killer still tells his story from year to year in the letters of his name, and if it is Wordsworth who, by superstition, returns to reengrave those letters, then the dead man and living engraver are the same; here again is a scene of specular, entrancing identification, whereby the poet becomes the counterpart of the Othello-like dead man. This identification resonates through the entire Othello sequence and emerges most explicitly in that first allusion, immediately following the drowned man episode, in which Wordsworth speaks as Othello: "I might advert / To numerous accidents in flood or field" (279–80). Wordsworth, too, tells the story of his life in words or characters of violence, seducing us with his misadventures and his encounters with unknown and exotic forms. Although in this sequence Wordsworth exposes the matricidal violence at the basis of the symbolic order, he also demonstrates that there is no innocent or natural alternative in the maternal body, in which the scene of violence reappears, and that the subject, threatened at every turn by dangerous forces, has little choice but to transform this violence into a source of pleasure and even of affective and affecting power. Making the characters of danger into those of desire, Wordsworth becomes a self-usurping poet, one whose literary powers are based upon a seductive violence: of others toward him, of him toward himself, and of himself toward his readers.

Telling his own story with these words, inscribing his life in these letters, Wordsworth writes a *mise en scène,* mirroring the autobiographical writing that is *The Prelude* (Kneale 144; Jacobus *Romanticism* 18). More radically, however, he demonstrates that autobiographical writing is an effect of cultural dismemberment, a local instance of hyperbolic romance. Making that text out of the dissolution of the father's name into characters, the first spot of time demonstrates that the self becomes autobiographical when its symbolic identity collapses. Like Rzepka's ghostly self, the autobiographical subject appears when the Other disappears, when all other names for the self have failed, when, in effect, it can create a (non)identity for itself only by making itself up out of the various mischances of its life. Because the self that writes itself (or, as other passages in Part One suggest, searches for evidences of how it has been written) is still alive, this tale always remains incomplete and this identity unstable; writing itself from year to year, it can never represent itself adequately in any text or symbol and thus becomes, for itself and others, a set of unreadable characters. Moreover, in the attempt to make life into a text, it renews the violence of textuality, demanding a textual coherence of lived experience. Where the symbolic kills the mother once and for all, substituting itself for nature, the autobiographer obsessively renews the death of the body, repeatedly turning into a text what persists on remaining alive. By trying to write itself as a text, the self inscribes not its name but what exceeds names and produces a double, a specular counterpart of its ghostly selfhood (cf. Johnson). To write oneself, it seems, is to haunt oneself as another in the manner of an unknown hand that returns to the place of the unburied dead.[32]

Thus by the end of the major sequence of Part One, it is clear that Wordsworth the poet does not claim for himself a vocation founded by the symbolic order, an oedipal, phallic power rooted in divine correction, but rather aspires to embody the tempestuous energies that circulate around the site of cultural dismemberment. He embraces the poetics of errancy, unreadability, repetition, and even crime, abandoning himself to the unredeemed rhetoric of romantic error. If he truly wished to possess a prophetic vocation, to become a figure of institutional authority, or to hand down a finished, readable, philosophical poem, he could have retrospectively accepted divine correction, submitted to at least a symbolic castration, and received the name of the father; in that way the culminating passages of Part One would have confirmed the pretensions with which it began. Like Samson's parents, he could have presented God an offering on the altar. But in a demonic parody of holy sacrifice, in the last spot of time he participates in his own version of the witches' ritual at the crossroads, as if offering up himself and his parents to a sadistic God, to the devil. Rewriting and affirming the Druidic sacrifice of *Salisbury Plain,* he identifies himself as poet not with Samson—not even a failed Samson—but with the dark storytellers whose powers are based on profane violence: the Druids, Prospero, Othello, the chattering Harry Gill, and Martha Ray. Refusing all discipline, all social and moral purpose, the poetics of Part One makes trauma into a source of pleasure; it does not protest parricide, matricide, infanticide, or castration but desires them, chattering poetically at the thought. It celebrates no homecoming, no heterosexual reunion with the beloved, but the longing for unspeakable, shattering, sacrilegious violation. It is the occult, queer face of Romanticism, a poetics that, anticipating the avantgarde of our century, wishes to transfigure normative subjectivity. It is inherited not from God's messengers or nature's benevolent spirits but from the undead, the specters who uprear their ghastly faces and shatter nature's calm. It speaks not the creative word that brings the world into being but a dark fiat, a word that threatens to destroy the world (Hartman *Unremark-*

able 107). It is not a divine power but the divinatory power of the self-usurping magus (cf. Bloom *Anxiety* 61), the incantatory power of the witch. In a deep refusal of theodicy, it celebrates the fact that the world is lost, that we know not who we are, that alien presences inhabit the world. It no longer hopes to heal but only to take a wounded comfort in the dismemberment of culture.

SIX

Unfinished Covenant

The Disruption of Tradition in "Michael"

❧ When Wordsworth takes up the problem of the endurance of the rural community as he writes "Michael," he seems to shift his focus away from the scenarios of violence or captivation familiar in his earlier work. His concerns seem more mundane: kinship, property, obligation, and the persistence of memory in rural communities. Yet here, as before, culture is a systemic war, a machine of disorientation which one cannot finally escape; this poem's economy is one of accident, disruption, loss. As if to rewrite *Salisbury Plain,* Wordsworth even revives the question of human sacrifice, interpreting it more explicitly as the effect of desymbolization, the unraveling of those gestures of symbolic violence which found institutions.

To carry out this project, on one level he gestures toward a theory of culture, reading the operations of kinship exchange, economic obligation, and familial affection as aspects of a unified system of symbolic exchange— a general economy. This move is of interest in its own right, for it anticipates several later theorists, including Mauss and Lacan, and proleptically challenges them by finding in their disparate models a common underlying logic. But in a more characteristic, negative gesture he offers a total critique of this general economy. In "Michael" an unexpected obligation disrupts the traditional household, vitiates the sacrificial rite and disfigures the entire structure of inheritance. What disturbs that structure is the structure itself; not only does obligation intrude upon the system of obligations, but the desperate attempt to ward off its threat creates the dispossession it attempts to forestall. In this account, culture is inherently hyperbolic, bound to destroy itself precisely when it wishes to ensure its survival. Despite the claims of the poem's opening lines, in the end the poem refuses Wordsworth the role of the traditional storyteller and makes him instead the poet of extravagant dispossession.

"Michael" derives one of its first cultural concerns from the "Poems on the Naming of Places" composed in 1800, for it is similarly preoccupied with the problem of making places in the landscape signify. Like a name, the "straggling heap of unhewn stones" with which it begins marks a spot, makes it significant, and provokes the passerby to wonder what story is associated with it. On some level, in these poems Wordsworth attempts to construct a theory of natural signification, whereby the landscape captures and preserves the associations of communal memory almost without human intervention. Yet because neither a name nor a mute sign is complete without its accompanying story, because each marks significance without spelling it out, each depends entirely on the capacity of living people to explain what it means.[1] As a result, its meaning may be no more permanent than the memory of a circle of acquaintances; it is always about to revert back to a mere sign without a story, an unreadable mark. If the community disappears, then the sign will collapse back into the landscape as the mute debris of a forgotten culture.[2]

In his own way, Wordsworth demonstrates that signs cannot be grounded in nature; if anything, nature is hostile to signs and continually threatens to ruin them (cf. Manning 46). The heap of stones, the image with which "Michael" begins, hints more at the disappearance than the stability of signs. In a fragmentary draft Wordsworth describes it as "a shapeless crowd of unhewn stones / That lie together, some in heaps, and some / In lines, that seem to keep themselves alive / In the last dotage of a dying form" (*Poetical Works* [henceforth *PW*] 2.482). Such a ruin threatens the coherence of poetry; as Reeve Parker points out, *lines* and *form* suggest an identity between the sheepfold and verse, as if the collapse of signs would necessarily involve the dismemberment of verse ("Finishing" 60).

If nature or memory is an insufficient base for the endurance of signs, they must be founded instead in the survival of culture. Accordingly, in "Michael" Wordsworth submits the poetry of place to the discipline of an oral tradition. As one might expect, in this poem about place Wordsworth begins with the sheepfold itself and then moves on to the story that pertains to it (18). Moreover, in that first verse paragraph he begins to elaborate in a familiar manner on the nature of rural tales; this one, he claims, was the first that spoke to him of shepherds, whom he had formerly loved "not verily / For their own sakes, but for the fields and hills / Where was their occupation and abode" (24–26). To use the terms of the 1805 *Prelude*, this tale led him from the love of nature to the love of man:

And hence this Tale, while I was yet a boy
Careless of books, yet having felt the power

> Of Nature, by the gentle agency
> Of natural objects led me on to feel
> For passions that were not my own, and think
> At random and imperfectly indeed
> On man; the heart of man and human life. (27–33)

Because the tale incorporates human passions in natural objects in the manner described in the Preface to *Lyrical Ballads*, it enables the boy's love for nature to modulate into a sympathy with the passions of others, and thus to join the "general sympathy" which is, for Wordsworth, the best definition of rural culture (Preface 603).

So far the terms of this introduction are familiar: society emerges from nature through the "gentle agency / Of natural objects" themselves. But in the next lines Wordsworth introduces something new:

> Therefore, although it be a history
> Homely and rude, I will relate the same
> For the delight of a few natural hearts,
> And with yet fonder feeling, for the sake
> Of youthful Poets, who among these Hills
> Will be my second self when I am gone. (34–39)

Here again is the idea of a stock of tales shared among a small group of friends. But now it seems that their shared memories will not die out; by telling this story, the speaker will give it to youthful poets who will carry it on after his death. These lines extend and revise the "Poems on the Naming of Places"; to signify a memory in a more or less permanent fashion, one must not only substitute a name or sign for it but must also find a second self, another mind that can remember when one is gone. Here signification, or the substitution of sign for memory, gives way to the substitution of one person's memory for another, or more precisely of tradition for memory. Evidently, signification cannot become signification until some mechanism subsumes individual minds and memories within an impersonal cultural order that will survive them all. In short, signification requires the symbolic order.

The entire poem spells out the operations of such an order; much like the speaker of the introduction, Michael hopes that his son Luke will be his second self and carry on when he is gone (cf. Simpson 147). Thus the poem, which is supposed to initiate young listeners, is directly about the problem of initiation; the poem's function and its story are the same. The introduction collapses into the poem, or vice versa, in such a way that the tale becomes an allegory of its own transmission. Somewhat like the speaker of "The Thorn," Wordsworth generates a poem entirely out of his own anxieties. Although, as he later states, the poem "was founded on the son of an old couple having become dissolute and run away from his parents; and on an old shepherd having been seven years in building up a sheepfold in a solitary valley," the blending of these two tales around the central covenantal scene is his own invention (*PW* 2.478).[3] Coming across the unfinished sheepfold, he makes it not only into a sign of an oral narrative but also into the site at which narrative is handed down in a scene of initiation from father to son. If these stones represent at first the unreadability of culture, he hopes to make them represent the very opposite.

To do so, however, Wordsworth must actively suppress not only the stones' persistent unreadability but also their subjective counterpart, the errancy of his playful, associative mind. As Parker argues, while Wordsworth was completing the final version of "Michael," he expunged a number of passages that display this errancy. In contrast to Michael's strenuous purpose "To further without stop or one stray thought / The business of the present hour," the "freaks / And pastimes of the boy would intersperse / Short fits of idleness" which inevitably would meet Michael's "Habitual opposition" (*PW* 2.483). Parker remarks, "Measured against the extraordinary totality of Michael's purposefulness, Luke is, as it were from conception, always already dissolute" ("Finishing" 58). Of course, this passage may simply dramatize Wordsworth's familiar contention that rural life disciplines the errant mind (cf. Simpson 59–60). But as Parker also points out, in other draft passages Wordsworth has Michael "let loose / His tongue and give it the mind's freedom" or has the curling locks of his hair "teaze and fret him" about the face (*Letters* 268; *PW* 2.484). Accordingly, Wordsworth removes such passages and takes care to point out that he writes not with a loose tongue or errant spirit, "Not with a waste of words, but for the sake / Of pleasure which I know that I shall give / To many living now" (131–33; Parker "Finishing" 61–63).

This strenuous attempt to expunge errancy from the poem has a curious effect; as Susan Eilenberg puts it, "the telling of the story baffles itself repeatedly. The narrator resists narration and substitutes, when he can, description or moralizing for the tale he has promised. Again and again he signals that he is about to proceed in his story, only to turn aside from his task" ("Property" 17). The resistance to errancy is in part a resistance to the disruption necessary in any story and thus to narrative itself (cf. Brooks 108; Bennett 150–51). As a result, when the necessary crisis takes place, it has an extraordinarily disruptive effect. Michael's discovery that he must make good on the debt of a kinsman "breaks in upon the quiet poem . . . as an importunate absurdity, something that should have nothing to do with him, an accident," partly because it is "a consequence of something that has happened to someone of whom we have never before this heard a word." Similarly, when Michael admits to Luke that he had been in debt until he was forty (384–85), "it is news to the reader, who has been led to assume that the land had always been the secure property of Michael's family." Here, as before, what the poet repressed "comes out now with the effect of a sudden and uncanny interruption."

Oddly enough, this second interruption reveals that Michael's dilemma is "less strange or unfamiliar than it looks, for Michael has faced it before" ("Property" 17–19).[4] The errant or accidental is part of a larger pattern of economic hardship or debt; the narrator attempts to repress not only looseness or freakishness of mind but also the unpredictability of a rural economy founded in hard work. Errancy does not interrupt Michael's purposive labor, for it is an inherent part of the system of property which he serves. The effect of Michael's admission, then, is "like that of reading a palimpsest: a suppressed writing begins to disturb what is written over it" (Eilenberg "Possession" 211). Beneath the prologue's conception of a securely founded symbolic order begins to emerge an uncanny conception of dismembered textuality, loose speech, and an economy of accident; in short, a culture of errancy.

Such a culture may be nothing other than the one that is supposed to defend against errancy. Insofar as Michael's life is disrupted by obligations to his kinsman, the system constructed for the preservation of the local tradition proves to be the source of its undoing. Obligation works both ways: the people on whom one depends might depend on one in return, and what seems good may become the source of evil ("Michael" 246, 247). If the symbolic order defends against errancy, it also channels its disruptive energies in certain predicable ways; it gives structure not only to culture but to what subverts it. Despite Wordsworth's best intentions, a Gothic poetics of errancy returns in this text; the poem he wrote to replace "Christabel" in the 1800 *Lyrical Ballads,* to oust Coleridge's improper and extravagant text from his own apparently domesticated collection, becomes another version of it (cf. Eilenberg "Possession" 212–14). Here again errancy does not remain safely outside the door but is found inside the threshold, within the household or kinship system itself.

Eilenberg demonstrates that the tales in these poems are strikingly similar: "The families in both poems are destroyed by pleas for help from the children of brothers." Sir Leoline is more concerned with his old friend and his supposed daughter, Geraldine, than with his own daughter, Christabel, and Michael gives up his own son to pay for the error of his brother's son. "In both poems, the evil associated with the old friend's or kinsman's child corrupts the son or daughter . . . The rival child displaces the true child from his [or her] secure place in the family, and the true child, abandoned, takes on the characteristics of the rival" ("Possession" 213–14). This myth of the rival child is a counterpart to the familiar folk motif of rival parents (the good mother and bad stepmother) which, according to a familiar Freudian interpretation, expresses the child's ambivalence about his or her parents (Bettelheim 66–70, 111–16), providing in effect a folk tale for parents who are ambivalent about children. Coleridge offers this interpretation in the Conclusion to Part II of "Christabel" (1816), a section that substitutes for a narrative conclusion to the poem, when he describes a moment in which the father, overwhelmed with delight in his child, "Must needs express his love's excess / With words of unmeant bitterness" (664–65). Whereas Coleridge explains the father's words with reference to psychological contingency (Mileur *Vision* 63–66), Wordsworth places the rival child in the context of an errancy embedded in the processes of culture itself. A father interested in preserving his family tradition cannot help being ambivalent about a child, who at once promises to sustain that tradition and threatens to disrupt it entirely. Children might model themselves on their parents (Luke on Michael, Christabel on her mother) but they might refuse to submit to the parental law and, like the nephew or Geraldine, become the embodiment of uncontainable dissolution or figuration. In effect, the tradition can defend against its disappearance only by producing a new generation, which in turn raises the possibility of its disruption.

Thus what bursts through into "Michael" is no more than the possibly errant results of any tradition's attempt to replicate itself. A tradition is less an endless succession of perfectly reproducing second selves than the site of potential conflict between the generations. Much as the suppressed writing that emerges in this text resembles the nonsignificative writing of the Salisbury Plain poems, it brings with it the oedipal violence of those poems as well; once again, as in the breakfast scene, a bad child dares to challenge a father who responds by injuring or at least abandoning his son. But here Wordsworth elaborates on this basic scene; by displacing the child's rebellion onto Michael's nephew, he makes clear that such a rebellion disrupts not merely the immediate family but also the whole network of kinship relations. It does not matter much where the rebellion comes from, for in any case the extended family is threatened and must defend itself. "Michael" suggests that to generalize relations between individuals into a codified system of relations is to generalize the resistance to that system as well. The displacement from the familial (and psychological) to the cultural extends the private oedipal drama into legal and financial relations.

Yet the narrator, or at least the narrator of the prologue, hopes that the system can respond to this resistance in a successful way. Rather than injuring his son, Michael can make a covenant with him to forestall any further disruption. In fact, the oedipal break indirectly serves Michael's purposes. Without it, he would never initiate Luke into the tradition of his forefathers; an initial disruption is necessary before paternal discipline can intervene. The son's entry into the symbolic order is not automatic; it first requires his threat to the system. In effect, then, the symbolic order is structured as a response to a necessary crisis and takes its meaning only in relation to that crisis. If it produces disruption by trying to reproduce itself in another generation, it also incorporates that disruption within the ritual of its containment.

In its most archaic form, the requirement both to have children and to discipline them for their inevitable rebellion took the fearsome shape of child sacrifice, a practice that demonstrated quite openly that the preservation of the tradition was much more important than the survival of any given child. Even in modified versions of child sacrifice, this priority remains clear; given the impossible choice between God's covenant and the life of the only child who embodies a potential succession, Abraham chooses God and nearly kills his own son. This is virtually the same choice that faces Michael, and he decides in a similar fashion (Eilenberg "Property" 21).[5] Of course, Abraham is released at the last moment from this choice by the providential appearance of a ram, a sacrifical substitute for Isaac, and in this way he can at once fulfill the covenant and keep the possibility of covenantal succession alive. The tradition's ultimate answer for oedipal disruption, then, is the symbolic violence of animal sacrifice.

Michael attempts to perform a similar symbolic act at the sheepfold as he says farewell to Luke. He could, of course, rely on the strength of the "domestic affections" which Wordsworth describes as the primary cohesive force of rural society in his discussion of the poem in the letter to Charles James Fox (1801; *Letters* 261). But evidently, those affections are not strong enough on their own to bind Luke to Michael's purposes. In the covenantal scene, as in the introduction to the poem, the society of sympathy must be grounded in something more archaic: "the unconscious 'links of love' must be reinforced by transforming them into a conscious 'emblem' if they are to suffice against the pressure of temptation and evil men" (Manning 41). Apparently the welter of complex, ambivalent, inarticulate feelings that obtain between father and son must be formalized and resolved through a ritual act, and unconscious hatred must be given an object before love can be made secure.

Curiously enough, however, Michael introduces the covenant less in the language of discipline than of gift exchange:

> —Even to the utmost I have been to thee
> A kind and a good Father: and herein
> I but repay a gift which I myself
> Received at others hands, for, though now old
> Beyond the common life of man, I still
> Remember them who loved me in my youth. (371–76)

Here Wordsworth extends the logic of the poem's introduction by suggesting that even affection is part of the succession; one receives and gives love in much the same way as an old story or a family name. As Eilenberg remarks, "in order to mean anything, to be worth anything, a story must be told, listened to, and—the teller hopes—told again" ("Possession" 209). Kept to oneself, love is no more valuable than a good story. The oral tale is thus the perfect example of the general logic of gift exchange as described by Marcel Mauss: when one accepts a gift one incurs the obligation to give again, such that possession is identical to debt (Mauss 10–12, 37–41; 30–31, 51). For Michael, too, what one has is what one owes to another. The land is not mere property in the sense of something that can be bought or sold in a monetary economy but rather the physical form of the obligations that obtain between members of the familial succession. There at the heap of stones Michael wishes to initiate Luke into this succession; if Luke will admit his obligations to his forefathers, then in turn he will be made their legitimate heir and receive what is owed to him. In this version, initiation is primarily an act of symbolic exchange.

The symbolic death of the son which looms over this scene, however, takes the logic of gift exchange one more step, for it suggests that the son's life belongs not to him but to the succession. Rescued from death by God's gift of the ram, Isaac owes his life to Abraham and his God and, one assumes, will not dare to violate the covenant. This ruthless enforcement of traditional authority locates obligation on the most intimate level of the self, as if the son can receive the name of the father only if he submits to a symbolic violence even greater than castration and repudiates his native, nameless subjectivity. Here Mauss and Lacan begin to sound very similar; the boy receives the father's name and thus his cultural identity as a gift, which in turn he will transmit to another. One might say that Luke receives the gift not directly from Michael but from Michael's forefathers, the third party in their affective relations, and thus from the Lacanian dead father.

But one could just as easily say, à la Mauss, that Luke will give the gift to unborn heirs; like the *kula* exchange of the Trobrianders, Michael's gift "is given only on condition that it will be used on behalf of, or transmitted to, a third person, the remote partner" (Mauss 22). Whether the name of the father that interposes into the boy's dualistic, imaginary relations (cf. *Écrits* 23) or the unborn son, this third party inevitably transforms the gift from a directly personal exchange between Michael and Luke into the rather impersonal operation of a symbolic economy that surpasses them both. The most powerful force in this scene is not Michael, who is simply another person defined by the system of obligations, but that economy itself. Land and name are the possession of neither father nor son but are items in the overall system of exchange between the generations, a system identical to kinship relations. The son's entry into kinship, then, is also into a system of symbolic exchange; name, identity, and property all belong to a single overall symbolic order in which, as Lacan writes, "I is an other" (*Écrits* 23). To paraphrase Wordsworth, the self is already a kind of second self, something that one inherits from elsewhere and which will remain after one is gone. Property, propriety, and the proper name, so often linked in general usage up through the eighteenth century and in Wordsworth's texts, are here revealed not as the unique possession of the private self but as the inscription upon it of what is proper to it by an order at once religious, economic, legal, patriarchal, psychoanalytic, and affective.[6]

Ultimately, when Michael interprets his affection for Luke as an instance of gift exchange, he casts his obligation to his kinsman in a new light. It is as if Michael is liable to pay surety for the debts of his kinsman simply because he is kin. But by the same token, the kinship system will contain the forces that disrupt it. If Michael is obligated for his kinsman's debt, then Luke in turn is obligated to Michael, and the kinsman in the city is obligated to help them both. As Michael says to Isabel, "We have, thou knowest / Another Kinsman, he will be our friend / In this distress" (257–59). Interestingly enough, Michael simply assumes that his urban relative will help them out, making his decision without having contacted that relative (Lea 63). Obligation, having already become a threat, turns back into a source of support. In this way the symbolic economy can contain nearly anything that challenges it.

The system can respond in this fashion only if it is a truly symbolic order, if Michael can sacrifice something besides his son. To all appearances, however, there is no ram at this sheepfold. Yet Wordsworth smuggles a sacrificial logic into the poem in a secular guise. In a note appended to the poem, Wordsworth explains that the sheepfold "enable[s] the shepherds conveniently to single out one or more of [the sheep] for any particular purpose" (Gill 701). Parker comments: "Transgressing the utilitarian function of the note is a drama of culling, a shadowy agenda of separation and, perhaps, sacrifice" (61). A covenantal drama staged near this enclosure suggests, however indirectly, that a sheep (perhaps a ram) is about to be singled out as a substitute for Luke. The hidden logic of this scene is spelled out in an odd episode Wordsworth originally wrote for "Michael" and first published as the "Matron's Tale" in the 1805 *Prelude* (8.222–311; De Selincourt 578). According to the tale, a father and son looked together for a lost sheep until at length the son left the father to retrace their steps alone. As a rainstorm began, he "spied" (8.270) the sheep on an island in a stream—a sheep, Wordsworth pauses to point out, who "Had left his Fellows, and made his way alone" to this remote spot (8.276)—but when he leapt onto the island the sheep sprang forward into the stream and was borne away. Surrounded by the "tempestuous torrent" and caught like "A prisoner on the Island, not without / More than one thought of death and his last hour" (287–89), the boy cried out for his father who, having already returned home, set out again in search of the child, "espied" the boy in the middle of the stream (303), and rescued him. Clearly, the father's actions duplicate the son's; he too retraced his steps, spied someone singled out in danger, and in his case rescued the child. The strong parallels between their actions suggest that one substitutes for the other; the sheep is lost that the son may be saved. The tale surreptitiously casts into narrative form the sacrificial logic of the covenantal scene, further teasing out its affiliations with the story of Abraham and Isaac.

But Wordsworth is not content with a loose analogy between the scenes of rescue and sacrifice. To emphasize their strong resemblance, he stages them on virtually the same spot. Poetically speaking, the stream of the "Matron's Tale," "whose course / Was through that unfenced tract of mountain-ground / Which to his Father's little Farm belonged, / The home and ancient Birth-right of their Flock" (8.260–63), is "the tumultuous brook of Green-head Gill" which flows near the sheepfold, the symbolic center of that birthright ("Michael" 2). Moreover, to find this spot one struggles along the brook ("Michael" 1–4; 8.264–65, 301–2) until one finds "a place / Remote and deep, piled round with rocks where foot / Of man or beast was seldom used to tread" (8.271–73), an "utter solitude" marked by "a straggling heap of unhewn stones" ("Michael" 13, 17). Here a sheep and boy, having left their fellows, single themselves out on the dangerous island or are singled out in the fold for a particular purpose: to slay a sheep that the boy may live. Following an Old Testament logic even in the remote corners of his text, Wordsworth hints that animal sacrifice and the redemption of the son are the same.

Nevertheless, these evocations of substitutive sacrifice are so indirect that they are barely discernible. Moreover, as if ashamed of the "Matron's Tale," Wordsworth at first decides not to publish it in "Michael" and later removes it from *The Prelude*, expunging it from his published works altogether. In the context of Wordsworth's other writings in 1800, one can see why, for in "Hart-Leap Well" he voices his opposition even to secular versions of animal sacrifice. Here as elsewhere he interprets sacrifice from the perspective of its victim; the shrine built on the site at which a deer expired at the end of a long hunt fills him with sorrow, and toward the poem's close he looks forward to "the coming of the milder day" when "These monuments shall all be overgrown" (171–72). But a man who kills and memorializes a deer is not so different from one who would kill a sheep and build a covenantal sheepfold on the spot; the sheepfold, too, is at least potentially a shrine founded in blood. It seems that the poet honestly prefers a heap of stones to any monument or shrine and would like to dispense with sacrifice altogether.

Oddly enough, then, Wordsworth's attempt to imagine a way in which the sympathetic relations of rural society could be preserved over the generations leads him directly toward sacrifice, which is, however, precisely the kind of officializing gesture he most resists. The poem works at cross-purposes both to embrace and to refuse symbolization. For the covenantal scene, Wordsworth invents a version of the ram and then disposes of it, at once imagining an Abrahamic covenant and robbing it of its only means of expression. Although he has exposed the violent nature of sacrifice, he senses that he cannot do without sacrifice of some kind if he wishes to sustain the tradition. Thus he is faced with an impossible choice: whether to commit human sacrifice or to abandon the tradition entirely.[7] Ironically, the critique of sacrifice leads back to Abraham's impossible and absurd choice between the tradition and his son, to the situation of culture before the appearance of the ram. Trying to achieve symbolization without symbols, Wordsworth cannot help but go to extremes, to present a radically violent figure or renounce figuration altogether, and thus to make "Michael" a massive overstatement or understatement, an exemplary instance of hyperbole.

The rhetoric of hyperbole pervades this text. Much as Michael and Luke cannot quite symbolize their affections, Wordsworth tells us with some urgency that the poem is important but cannot articulate exactly why it is so. In the opening lines of "Michael," he adds gratuitous exclamation points as if to emphasize the significance of something we might otherwise miss (lines 6, 17). A similar rhetoric infects the "Matron's Tale"; at the crucial point in his description of how the father spied his son in the middle of the stream, Wordsworth writes: "The sight was such as no one could have seen / Without distress and fear" (8.307–8). Concerning "Michael," Sydney Lea remarks, "In the rhetorical vehemence where none seems appropriate (why the exclamation point?) is our first clue that the writer anticipates indifference, asks us to bear with him until he can justify the importance of an observation which may strike us as trivial." This urgent tone gives way later in the opening section to the rhetoric of litotes; the poem is "unenriched with strange events" and is "not unfit . . . for the fireside / Or for the summer shade." This "vacillation in tone—from portentous to self-effacing" informs the entire poem and suggests that Wordsworth fears that "he may *himself* be the victim of error, delusion," that "he passes on a doubtful legacy" (55, 57, 60). Eschewing symbolic violence, Wordsworth unleashes rhetorical violence in a poem that continually says too much or too little, suggesting that the tradition will now be held together by vociferous speech and strenuous effort. As Mileur might argue, without religious foundation his belief becomes hyperbolic, more like an assertion against doubt than a participation in a confessional practice with chances for survival (cf. *Romance* 21–22, *Revisionism* 39).

Wordsworth allegorizes this strenuous assertiveness in the character of Michael. His affections are almost too strong; his fields, which are more to him "Than his own Blood," give him "A pleasurable feeling of blind love, / The pleasure which there is in life itself" (76, 78–79), and he bears toward Luke such an "Exceeding" love that he treats him as "The dearest object that he knew on earth" (161, 160). Michael's affections exemplify those of the idealized statesmen he describes in his letter to Fox; among the "proprietors of small estates which have descended to them from their ancestors, the power which these affections will acquire amongst such men is inconceivable" (*Letters* 262). Moreover, he, Isabel, and Luke work so hard that they become "a proverb in the vale / For endless industry" (96–97). Even their lamp is excessive: it was "An aged utensil, which had performed / Service beyond all others of its kind" (117–18). Of course, Wordsworth intends to suggest that inconceivably strong affections and endless industriousness provide an excellent basis for the endurance of this family; an excess of virtue should make the likelihood of its survival exceedingly high.

But in this poem, such hyperbolic virtues alone cannot sustain the family. As Michael admits, superhuman effort cannot ward off disaster: "Our lot is a hard lot; the Sun itself / Has scarcely been more diligent than I, / And I have lived to be a fool at last / To my own family" (243–46). Moreover, once disaster hits, Michael's ingrained extremism proves to be the undoing of the family. He performs the most brazenly hyperbolic act of the poem, deciding to send Luke away virtually at that very moment: "let us send him forth / To-morrow, or the next day, or to-night: / —If he could go, the Boy should go to-night" (290–92). He acts as if the only way to respond to an unwilled calamity is to become even more endless in one's industry, to get to work much sooner than is viable. In this way he calls his son to a task before he is ready, much as he had earlier in the poem, where Luke, only five years old, served as the watchman of the flock, "And to his office prematurely called," was "Something between a hindrance and a help, / And for this cause not always, I believe, / Receiving from his Father hire of praise" (197, 199–201). As Manning points out, once again Michael imposes a responsibility upon Luke "before the bearer could sustain it" (47). Michael's excessive love for the family tradition compels him to commit an untimely, improper act, to ask Luke to save the tradition before he even belongs to it.

Michael's precipitous decision to send Luke away so soon profoundly disrupts the putative initiation ritual that follows. Given the poem's opening lines on the virtues of an oral tradition and the lines early in the scene on the inheritance of affection over the generations, we expect Michael to initiate Luke into the tradition before sending him away. But as it turns out, this is impossible. One cannot say, with J. L. Austin, that this ceremony is carried out at the wrong time and without the full understanding of both participants and is thus infelicitous (cf. 25–38). Rather, this scene suggests that the process that might lead even to an infelicitous ritual has been rudely interrupted. The fact that Michael says farewell to Luke at the site of a sheepfold they were to build together demonstrates that both their common work and the necessary preparations for Luke's initiation are incomplete. Because Michael cannot now make a covenant with Luke, he can only promise to do so later on: "When thou return'st, thou in this place wilt see / A work which is not here, a covenant" (423–24). Evidently, Michael is so bent on getting Luke to work that he is willing to postpone the covenant, and thus the urgent demand to save the family tradition disrupts the process of handing it down.

Here a hyperbolic investment in the tradition directly threatens its continuity and suspends its familiar mode of reproduction. As the lines on the five-year-old Luke suggest, Michael's untimely intervention into Luke's life *creates* the disturbance he fears; if the boy were old enough, he would not annoy the father with his ineptitude. The father's urgency to raise his son too fast in order to get him to work makes the boy improper, out of place at the "gate or gap" (196). Similarly, the prematurely enacted ritual produces a legacy of the premature (or the immature), branding Luke as someone who will necessarily be out of place in the kinsman's house; he will become, as it were, another rival child. The excessiveness with which Michael tries to preserve the family from the rival child only recreates him. Where the father in "Christabel," inspired by the excess of love, speaks improper words to his child, Michael utters an improper child, as if Luke were an outrageous figure of speech, the extravagant effect of hyperbolic love.[8] Here the tradition subverts itself; like the sailor of *Adventures* and Robert of *The Ruined Cottage*, who are so overcome by love and rage at trying to sustain families without money that they commit acts that ultimately unsettle those families, Michael is so desperate to preserve his family from debt that he uproots his son and drives him away from home. The tradition does not contain the disruptiveness of the rival child through symbolic obligation after all, for in this case disruption forces the system to be precipitous and, in setting aside its rituals, to become its own worst rival.

Yet unlike his counterparts in those earlier texts, Michael seems to be aware of the consequences of his precipitous act. He realizes that sending Luke away at this point interrupts more than their shared work, for he designates the unfinished sheepfold as the emblem of the deferred covenant. By having Luke lay the cornerstone of the sheepfold, he makes this untimely ritual into a pact of deferral, subsuming the postponement of the covenant in an agreement to postpone. Setting aside the symbolic act, which involves a third party, he exchanges promises with Luke, hoping in this way to master premature departure with proleptic return and to make separation a figure of reunion. As a result, however, covenant disappears into the slippery logic of the promise, the pact with the dead into one with the living. Perhaps, then, the sheepfold scene becomes a ritual after all, for even a promise is a kind of ritual gesture (cf. Austin 9–11 and passim). But because this pact does not bring Luke into the tradition, in effect it formalizes the impossibility of doing so and makes the disruption of the tradition official.

Michael's willingness to send Luke away even if it means postponing the covenant demonstrates that he puts more faith in hard work than in symbolic action. The sheepfold scene suggests that the family's extraordinary industry masks a profound suspicion of the tradition and its system of obligations. This suspicion becomes explicit in Michael's farewell speech to Luke in which he voices his dissatisfaction with the way the traditional arrangements have worked out. Looking back over his life, he admits that his faithfulness to the land and to his kin has availed him nothing: "I wished that thou should'st live the life they lived. / But 'tis a long time to look back, my Son, / And see so little gain from sixty years" (381–83). Despite his great efforts, he is back where he started and is about to bequeath to his son the same debt-"burthened" lands he received as a young man

(384). This fact should encourage Michael, for if he believes in the virtues of his son, he should be confident that despite all accidents of fate Luke will clear the land of debt just as he did. But Michael does not want Luke to relive his life, for he must feel that his effort ("I toiled and toiled" [387]) is simply not worth it. It is as if he has never existed, so little has changed from his birth. Simply reproducing the tradition and passing on what one has received is not enough; he wants to have made a mark of his own, to show some gain from all his toil, and to bequeath something unique to his son. Although he does not see the land as mere capital, something he could sell for his own private gain, but rather the embodiment of what he owes to another, his eagerness to clear the land of financial debt and make it free (388) shows that he chafes against this obligation and hopes to make the traditional lands better than they already are, less burdensome to those who would inherit them. There is something in his efforts that resists obligation and counterposes the unique self to the inherited proper self. Rather than disappearing from the poem, the loose or errant Michael of the fragmentary drafts reappears as the excessively industrious shepherd, a second self or rival Michael who is restless with the tradition and desires more than it has given him.

Oddly enough, then, at the very scene in which Michael is supposed to bring his son into the tradition, he suggests that Luke does *not* owe his life to his forefathers. Expressing concern for his son's fate, he imagines Luke's departure as a mode of liberation, admitting that it may be better for him never to return; the land "looks as if it never could endure / Another Master. Heaven forgive me, Luke, / If I judge ill for thee, but it seems good / That thou should'st go" (389–92). As if recalling the scene of Abrahamic sacrifice, Michael asks the God of covenants to forgive him for *not* sacrificing Luke to the tradition. He resists becoming another Abraham, even though he knows full well that by foregoing sacrifice he relies on links that will be too weak to bring Luke back home: "Luke, thou hast been bound to me / *Only* by links of love, when thou art gone / What will be left to us!" (411–13; emphasis added). With these words, he makes the ritual of untimeliness into one of affectionate disownment, an anticovenant that releases the son from all symbolic obligation.

Yet just at this point Michael breaks off and returns to the business at hand: "—But, I forget / My purposes. Lay now the corner-stone" (413–14). Faced with Abraham's absurd choice, he was about to give up the tradition, and now he returns to the purpose of giving up his son. But what is the difference between these actions? Has Michael truly forgotten his purposes, or has he fulfilled them by forgetting them? To send Luke away is both/neither to preserve and/nor to destroy the tradition. The covenantal moment that follows is as much a rite of farewell as of promise ("Now, fare thee well" [422]). Michael does not know what will become of Luke and does not expect to see him again: "a covenant / 'Twill be between us—but whatever fate / Befall thee, I shall love thee to the last, / And bear thy memory with me to the grave" (424–27). The scene hovers on the edge of anticipation and renunciation, the beginning of a work and its end, and becomes as indeterminate and unreadable as the heap of stones. Here ambiguous rite and uncanny spot come together; already in Michael's words the absent sheepfold is reduced from sacred site—a place where tradition is handed down—to an "emblem of the life thy Fathers led" (420), a mute reminder of a vanished tradition. Much as the rite is at once farewell and promise, the sheepfold is at once sign and sacred site or, more precisely, the sign *of* the covenantal altar, a place that marks the incompletion and deferral of the tradition. Rather than reverting entirely to the condition of the unreadable marks in the landscape, the unfinished sheepfold marks the failure of the tradition that would keep their significance alive.

With Luke's departure, the poem finally unleashes the extravagant energies it has so far held at bay. A few lines later, Luke falls into corrupt city ways and is so overcome with ignominy and shame that he is "driven at last / To seek a hiding-place beyond the seas" (454–56). Here Biblical parable and Real Whig rhetoric converge: Luke is a prodigal son (Manning 42) who has gone astray in the dissolute city (453). But unlike the prodigal son, Luke never returns. The rival child finally disrupts the system of obligations in such a way that it cannot respond.

The prodigal Luke is an instance of pure extravagance, a hyperbolic figure created by an anxious Michael. But Wordsworth affiliates this extravagance with the city and with the cultural formation it represents, considerably extending the reach of the poem's concerns. Chandler states, "In the context of a poem where illiteracy plays so beneficial a role, we should probably have expected such an end as soon as we learned of Luke's letters home": "and the Boy / Wrote loving letters, full of wond'rous news" (441–42). "As the son grows in literacy and in knowledge of the world, the unwritten reminder of the life of his fathers is readily forgotten" (Chandler 166). One might say that writing makes signs into texts whose significance does not depend upon the survival of living memory. As Bourdieu argues, literacy makes the rituals of oral transmission unnecessary, for its capacity "to preserve and accumulate in objectified form the cultural resources it has inherited from the past" frees it from the constraints of "individual memory" and oral poetics (186–87). Simply by joining literate society, Luke poses a threat to Michael and his world; literacy enables cultural institutions to

survive independently of particular agents, and accordingly it can dispense
with more direct means of cultural transmission.

Similarly, as the center of a burgeoning economy, the dissolute city
introduces into traditional property relations an objective medium of exchange which, much like the text, sustains wealth in its own right apart
from actual properties. Writing and money are homologous; writing enables the accumulation of cultural capital and money of economic capital
(cf. Bourdieu 183–84, 187). Here, as in cultural history generally, "[a] mode
of writing is representative of a mode of signifying exchange" (Goux 72,
italicized in the original); because wealth, like cultural memory, survives on
its own, it no longer requires the system of gift exchange and can dispense
with the difficulties of moral obligation or symbolic exchange in favor of
monetary exchange (Mauss 52; Bourdieu 171–72). Moreover, literate, capitalist society gathers in the city because it creates the social counterpart of
the objective institution; much to Wordsworth's despair, city society, having codified relations between total strangers, no longer depends upon the
mutual acquaintance, affection, or sympathy of its members, such that
"Even next-door neighbors, as we say, [are] yet still / Strangers, and
[know] not each other's names" (*Prelude* 7.119–20), much less their stories
and family traditions. Wordsworth implies that with the advent of such
objective institutions, the tradition ceases to be grounded in the obligation
to a third party, whether the dead father or the unborn child, and no longer
sustains itself primarily in the archaic form of the symbolic order. What
sustains culture is less the commitment to preserving and transmitting it
than certain mediating institutions, which are, according to Bourdieu, the
educational institutions of literacy, the juridical apparatus, and the state
(183).[9]

Of course, the rural economy of "Michael" is already implicated in
these objective institutions. Michael reads and writes, is familiar with property law, and has been in and out of debt before. To pay off a debt of a
wealthy relative, who probably lives in the city, he must send Luke to the
city as well, for there is little money in the country; the city is an inescap-
able part even of the rural economy. Moreover, Michael assumes that even
inherited land should remain economically viable, lamenting that he has
not gained much from his efforts. In this respect, Wordsworth remains
faithful both to the realities of the contemporary rural economy, which was
gradually becoming integrated into the national economy of agrarian capitalism, and to the realities of traditional economies generally, in which gift
exchange is implicated in economic interest and calculation, however disguised and negated they may be (Mauss 1–2; Bourdieu 171–83). Rather than

naively celebrating an imaginary past, he admits that no society is innocent of economic relations.

But Wordsworth also suggests that traditional culture attempts to preserve itself from the potentially corrosive effects of purely economic relations. Like the societies described by Bourdieu, Michael wishes to subsume economic within symbolic or at least affective exchange, to personalize the impersonal logic of culture as much as possible. One might say, following Bourdieu, that his land is fully symbolic capital, something valuable at once in economic *and* symbolic terms, or more precisely *affective capital*, the reservoir of inconceivably strong affections. For Michael, as for the societies interpreted by Bourdieu, "a piece of land will sometimes take on a symbolic value disproportionate to its economic value, as a function of the socially accepted definition of the symbolic patrimony" (182). Such societies resist not the bare idea of a monetary economy but the destructive effects of conceiving of culture in its terms; if one imagines that social relations are finally relations of production or labor, one can dismiss affective relations as secondary or inessential.

However deeply he sympathizes with this resistance to the economic, Wordsworth exposes its weaknesses in his tale of Michael's extravagant defensiveness. By regarding as an interruption what is already present in the symbolic economy, by attempting to discipline the self-interest that at times motivates even himself, Michael inevitably creates the mythic dissolute city, the site at which traditional relationships are bound to dissolve. Through a strange logic, the destructive force of capital arises from the excessive attempt to preserve society from it. Insofar as Michael's defense of the family's land produces the errant Luke, the attempt to preserve symbolic economy at all costs creates the specter of an antisymbolic economy, a capitalism equivalent to the dismemberment of culture.

Michael's fate in the poem's final pages exemplifies this reading of capital. Because it reproduces property impersonally, capital actually *deprives* one of a cultural function, takes away one's proper self, sets one adrift. According to "Repentance: A Pastoral Ballad" (written 1804), the family members who sell their patrimonial fields lose their birthright, feel like strangers near their land, and without a tradition to hand down, can give their son no role but that of a "wanderer" (*PW* 2.46–47, lines 24, 13, 26; cf. M. Friedman 194–95). In "Michael" the opposite occurs: the father gives up his son rather than selling "A portion of his patrimonial fields" (234), as if selling his son to keep his land (Eilenberg "Property" 23–24; cf. Levinson 68). On one level, this monetary sacrifice of Luke apparently pays off; after hearing of his son's fate, Michael attains the status of the nearly deified shepherd of *The Prelude* 8.312–428 and is never bothered again about the payment of the debt. The land is clear, and in a late, idealizing passage (457–81), he is a heroic solitary once again (Bushnell 251–52). But ultimately Michael's gesture works no better than that of the family in "Repentance": when Luke departs, becomes dissolute, and fails to return, the family's entire tradition collapses. The fact that Michael's solitude comes at the expense of his cherished tradition belies his apparently heroic status. Much as war displaces the sailor and the discharged soldier, economic disruption uproots Michael and makes him a wanderer on his own land, just as alienated from it as he would be if he had sold it. Here the economic relations that, according to Locke, free the self from traditional obligations, make it independent, and enable it to possess itself as its inalienable property in fact deprive the self of all that is proper to it, making it alien to itself and others.[10]

Much as the absence of the dead father or the proper name displaces the young men of "Repentance" and "Michael," so also the absence of an heir and of unborn future generations displaces Michael and, by extension, all of his forefathers. The rival child's refusal to fulfill his obligation to his ancestors unsettles the entire system of gift exchange, and as a result the dead father also becomes homeless and self-estranged. The old shepherd becomes an uncanny figure, sitting there by the heap of stones:

> 'tis believed by all
> That many and many a day he thither went,
> And never lifted up a single stone.
> There, by the Sheep-fold, sometimes was he seen
> Sitting alone, with that his faithful Dog,
> Then old, beside him, lying at his feet.
> The length of full seven years from time to time
> He at the building of this Sheep-fold wrought,
> And left the work unfinished when he died. (473–81)

Without lifting a stone, Michael "wrought" at the sheepfold simply by returning to it obsessively and sitting beside it, as if completing the logic of its incompletion and fleshing out its unreadability. His presence on this spot is obtrusive; one gets the feeling that he too somehow keeps himself "alive / In the last dotage of a dying form," that his death is as incomplete as the labor of building the sheepfold (*PW* 2.482). The poem's final lines do not dispel this strange mood; the fact that the land eventually passes "into a Stranger's hand" (484) should remind us of Michael's comment earlier in the poem that "if these fields of ours / Should pass into a Stranger's hand, I think / That I could not lie quiet in my grave" (240–42). If, with Eilenberg, we read the sheepfold as in part a tombstone ("Property" 22)—an unfinished tombstone, we might add—the effect is complete; Michael haunts this spot as would a dead man not yet given the status and authority of the dead, a father not yet provided a proper burial.

Only at this point do the full repercussions of the incomplete covenant become clear. The hyperbolic urgency that disrupted the ritual of initiation results in the disruption of the burial rites as well. One sheepfold scene leads to another; an incomplete altar is also, inevitably, an incomplete tombstone. Here we should pause to sketch out the logic of the tradition which Wordsworth at once evokes and disfigures in this scene. In that logic, apparently, the ritual of initiation is only one half of a larger sequence of symbolic acts. The initiation or making of the covenant, at which the father hands the tradition of the dead fathers down to his son, implies a second ritual, in which the son buries his father, makes him one of the dead, and fully inherits the land. This sequence is an instance of gift and countergift, an exchange of symbolic acts: the father brings the son across the threshold into adulthood, and the son in turn memorializes the father's crossing the threshold into death. As it turns out, the symbolic order is finally a temporal structure, an interminable sequence of deferral in which each symbolic act requires its fulfillment at a later time in another such act (cf. Bourdieu 3–9; Dupuy 86–94). Thus in one respect every covenant is one of return, for it implies that the initiated son will come back to this spot and make the altar a tombstone.

But "Michael" undoes the entire sequence. Just as it is too early for Michael to finish the altar and initiate Luke, so also it will always be too late for Luke to return, finish the tombstone, and bury his father. As Cathy Caruth argues in her reading of "Vaudracour and Julia," an untimely act at one point in the narrative—Vaudracour's premature promise of love to Julia—leads to another later on—their child's inexplicable death (80–81).[11] Rather than inscribing the tradition within an officializing narrative, "Michael" disrupts it in a series of interruptions and arrested actions.[12] In the final lines, where we might expect an epilogue akin to the poem's prologue, the poem instead shatters narrative into a landscape of obscure, liminal images:[13]

> The Cottage which was named The Evening Star
> Is gone, the ploughshare has been through the ground
> On which it stood; great changes have been wrought
> In all the neighborhood, yet the Oak is left
> That grew beside their Door; and the remains
> Of the unfinished Sheep-fold may be seen
> Beside the boisterous brook of Green-head Gill. (485–91)

This oak, of course, is the "Clipping Tree" where Michael sheared the sheep and disciplined his son (169–86), activities remarkably similar to those planned for the unfinished sheepfold. At least one named place remains, but as Lea remarks, "there is none to comprehend its significance; it can no longer take dominion, and is now a ritual sign stripped of its referent" (66). Thus these signs or symbols turn back into the images of the tree and ruined shelter, images that resonate back through the spots of time, "The Thorn," *The Ruined Cottage, The Borderers,* and the Salisbury Plain poems; all of the associations of infanticide, abandonment, exile, ghostliness, profanation, and errancy hover over this strangely muted scene. Like the ghostly father at the unreadable grave, Margaret at the ruined cottage, Mortimer in exile beyond the monument of warning (cf. "Michael" 416–22), and the homeless wanderer at the spital, Michael haunts this landscape of ruins.[14]

With the death of Michael and Isabel, a family heritage comes to an end. So does the promise of a renewed oral tradition, which would make Wordsworth a modern-day counterpart of the rustic Bard. Many critics argue, in the spirit of the poem's opening lines, that the literate poetic tradition takes over in its stead; Wordsworth replaces Luke and hands the family heritage down to his readers.[15] But the fact that the supposed oral tradition is sustained here in *written* form allies Wordsworth, even within the terms of this poem, with the forces that would destroy it. Perhaps one can overcome this difficulty by claiming that "Michael" belongs to a kind of writing nearly as ancient and venerable as any oral tradition. Judith Page demonstrates that in this text Wordsworth "recalls the style of the King James Bible" in "echoes and stylistic allusions" and borrows "an Old English stylistic tradition" by using compound forms, alliterative phrasing, and the archaic prefix *be.* In this way he tries to recover a "potentially timeless language of natural passion," a language appropriate for his depiction of "a life based on domestic industry and independent labor" (628–33). This strategy suggests that it is the written language of the Old Testament which defines the tradition of rustic life and links Abraham with Michael; here, as in Harringtonian political theory, the rustic republic merges with the Mosaic polity (Leask 34–42). The problem with this argument, of course, is that it makes the written tradition as ancient, and as threatened, as the oral; the disappearance of the evening star implies the end of the Miltonic virtue with which it was associated in the political sonnets (Leask 43–45) and even of the eighteenth-century Hesperian poetry that meditated the tradition's decline (Lea 66–68; Mileur *Revisionism* 198, 207–8).

Perhaps, then, it would be better to face this difficulty by claiming that Wordsworth is a traditionalist, someone who wants to overcome writing's disruptive effects and to refigure literate, post-Enlightenment culture on the model of the oral tradition (Chandler 158–62, 181). But as Chandler admits, this very project is contradictory: "the sense of having to 'go back' to recover the past is itself proof that the desired past is not fully recoverable" (182). Insofar as one hopes not to join the tradition but to value it merely for being a tradition, one appropriates it not for its own sake but to defend against modernity. In this way, one replaces its living continuity with an abstract idea of it, making it an improper figure of itself, a sign of the symbol.

Thus Wordsworth cannot be Michael's heir, cannot substitute for Luke and carry on the family ways. Interestingly enough, however, Wordsworth himself never claims to be such an heir. Perhaps critics have so often argued that he is, in fact, Michael's heir because they rely too strongly upon the claims of the poem's opening lines and identify them too readily with the overall import of the poem. The poem, however, contests those claims, subtly but consistently undermining the conception of rustic poetics introduced in the prologue. It demonstrates that every attempt to master the economy of accident and the rhetoric of hyperbole indirectly extends them. Moreover, by reviving in the poem's final lines the images of the tree and ruined shelter, Wordsworth brings "Michael" into the orbit of his earlier texts, complete with their corrosive poetics of errancy, and in effect responds to the prologue in a nearly silent epilogue, quietly distancing himself from the dream of a communal tradition. What is moving about this poem is not the fulfillment of the prologue's dream but rather the hyperbolically understated way in which Wordsworth evokes the impossibility of such a transmission of culture.

Yet Wordsworth can neither entirely renounce the hopes of the prologue nor entirely escape Michael's fate. By making his critique of archaic culture in such an understated way, Wordsworth shares in Michael's hyperbolic rhetoric, his untimely destiny. If the tract of land is also a poetic tract or text (Eilenberg "Property" 14), if to write the poem is to work at the sheepfold (D. Wordsworth *Journals* 44–54; Parker "Finishing" 58–59), then Wordsworth is another Michael, haunting the scene where texts unravel and hopes disappear. In this sense, "Michael" marks Wordsworth's implication in what he attempted to write, the dissolution of the oral or Biblical tradition, the collapse of the altar and tombstone into an unreadable heap of stones. There is no innocent way to map hyperbolic culture, and so Wordsworth inevitably becomes a hyperbolic poet, writing in the straggling heap another instance of the unreadable books of the Pedlar's childhood and Margaret's decline—the "straggling volume, torn and incomplete, / That left half-told the preternatural tale," the "straggling leaves / [That] Lay scattered here and there, open or shut / As they had chanced to fall" (1798 *Pedlar* 69–70; *Ruined Cottage* 407–9).

Thus despite Wordsworth's ambitions for the poem, "Michael" is finally a preternatural tale. Rather than initiating young minds into the social affections, as the prologue claims, it exposes the failure of precisely such an initiating tale (the one Michael tells Luke). Or, more perversely, it initiates the reader into the tale of how initiation must fail; in a mode exemplified by the griding iron passage of *Adventures*, it hands down the tradition through a wound. In this hurtful tale, it portrays an antisociety composed of unequal and unreturned affections; the sheepfold, Dorothy Wordsworth writes, is built "nearly in the form of a heart unequally divided" (44). This poem, like "The Brothers," displays the "disintegration" of the rural community and "the failure of the actual human relationships" on which it is based. "One after another," the poems of the 1800 *Lyrical Ballads* "end blankly on images of loss and diminution: finally, on a heap of stones" (Glen 324–25, 342). In its understated way, it teaches readers how to contemplate and endure something "which else / Would break the heart" (458–59), to sympathize with the victims of cultural dislocation, and, like the reader-spectator of *Adventures* and *The Borderers*, to identify with the dead. Although it mutely protests the economic dislocation of the poor, in its final pages it too becomes entranced with an isolated figure of dismembered culture.

Destruction by Deluge

Nature against Itself in *The Prelude*

ꝺꝭ In his writings up to 1804, Wordsworth inscribed his totalizing interpretation of cultural dismemberment in a broad range of mutually implicated registers, including symbolic practice, language, politics, economics, and autobiography. Yet until that point he had not fully articulated the sense, hinted at throughout his early texts, that cultural dislocation unsettles what seems most stable and enduring, nature itself. In *Salisbury Plain,* for example, just as culture disappears into its opposite, human sacrifice, so also the landscape dissolves, under the fierce onslaughts of the tempest, into a sea as "dark and waste as ocean's shipless flood" (109). Similarly, the anxious rebels of *The Borderers* abandon their victims (and themselves) on lifeless islands in distant seas or upon barren wastes overswept by storms. When one approaches the scene of the crime, the landscape itself threatens to disappear under the waters of a second deluge. This concern with the deluge, present in these texts but never explored in them outright, becomes overt in the 1805 *Prelude,* particularly in the Arab dream of Book 5.1–165. In this dream sequence, Wordsworth rewrites cultural dislocation almost entirely as natural cataclysm, thereby bringing into this poem a problem that will continue to concern him throughout *Prelude.* As Theresa Kelley points out, deluge imagery resurfaces in a number of climactic episodes, all of which build on the Arab dream in some manner: the crossing of the Alps, the blind beggar ("My mind did at this spectacle turn round / As with the might of waters" [7.616–17]), and the death of Robespierre ("the great Sea meanwhile / Was at safe distance, far retired" [10. 528–29]).[1] It is tempting to claim that from Book 5 onward *The Prelude* consists largely of a series of movements that culminate in the eruption of or the response to the threat of the flood.

The appearance of the deluge in the landscape is of such concern in this poem, particularly in its more famous passages (such as the Simplon

Pass and the ascent of Snowdon), that for some readers the poem's cultural concerns are nearly subsumed into the difficult relation between nature and an apocalyptic imagination (cf. Hartman *Wordsworth's Poetry* 33–69). Yet the opposite is true; rather than enabling Wordsworth to escape his sense of the dismemberment of culture, the language of the deluge or apocalypse inscribes it in the domain of nature.[2] Moreover, the poet consistently refers to cultural concerns in these episodes, using terms and images borrowed from his earlier writings, thereby suggesting that the deluge is homologous with cultural disaster. Yet this preoccupation with the deluge is so unmistakably hyperbolic that it inevitably exposes the underpinnings of his poetic practice. Far from muting his cultural poetics, these episodes write it even larger and thus confront him with its logic all the more. At times, Wordsworth somewhat unwillingly recognizes that what haunts both nature and culture is his own hyperbolic poetics, that the deluge and cultural disaster are projections of his own alien mind.

It may not be obvious that in these episodes Wordsworth extends his cultural concerns into his reading of the landscape; after all, in them he seems to focus primarily on the latter. Readers have shown how in this register, as in every other, he inherits the thought of the Enlightenment; his reading of mountains and seas derives from the eighteenth-century "history of the earth," which also influences his descriptions of the French Revolution in Books 9 and 10 (Bewell 237–79). Similarly, that geological rendering of the revolution derives from an analogy, quite familiar in the 1790s, between natural and historical cataclysm (cf. Paulson 43–47, 49–56). To a certain extent, then, the climactic episodes of *The Prelude* are further installments in the philosophical, anthropological, and now geological project of *The Recluse*. But here again Wordsworth disrupts the philosophical enclosure; the geological interpretation of the deluge is no more a discourse of knowledge for him than that provided by anthropology (in such texts as Rousseau's *Essay on the Origin of Languages* which informs *Salisbury Plain* and "The Discharged Soldier"), because the overall theory—shared by Rousseau and such authors as Buffon, Maupertuis, Holbach, Boulanger, and Erasmus Darwin—that societies must repeatedly assemble themselves after natural cataclysm suggests that culture, far from being grounded permanently in nature, is exposed to its arbitrary whims (Bernhardt-Kabisch 465–66).

By itself, the fear that the world might be destroyed by fire or flood would not produce the distinctively Wordsworthian anxiety recorded in the prologue of the Arab dream in Book 5 because the cosmologies of the world's great religions all anticipate such an event. "What distinguishes Wordsworth's cataclysm from those of traditional myth," writes

Bernhardt-Kabisch, "is that it is not eschatological in nature but itself part of history," the history of earth provided by the theorists of "the heroic age of geology" (464–65). According to this history, natural catastrophe is a routine geological event; the various objects scattered on the earth's surface testify that fires and floods regularly sweep across the world and that cataclysmic events are as inherent in nature as periods of calm. This version of earth's history scrambles the categories of creation and destruction, or (to use Hartman's terms) nature and apocalypse, because it makes the destruction of nature into a regular part of natural processes. This history can be comforting; apocalypse could not truly destroy the world, for nature would absorb destruction as it has many times before: "Yet would the living Presence still subsist / Victorious; and composure would ensue" (5.33–34). But it can also lead to great anxiety, because it makes nature and apocalypse, the ground and the abyss, indistinguishable. To read the history of the earth is to read the signs of nature's perennial destruction and renewal. This secularized interpretation of nature identifies it with its apparent opposite, in effect arguing that it is divided against itself, capable at any time of becoming something radically different from what it is. Geology suggests that nature is not "natural," not at all something that one can take for granted or regard as inevitable or self-identical.

The knowledge of nature's capacity for self-destruction leads to anxiety not because it threatens a literal and immediate destruction but because it destroys the fiction that culture is grounded in something that is ineradicable. The fear of natural apocalypse is primarily a fear for culture, as Wordsworth writes in his prologue: after another deluge, the "living Presence" might "still subsist," but "all the meditations of mankind, / Yea, all the adamantine holds of truth" would not (5.37–38). Perhaps culture is finite, "unique and unrepeatable because grounded merely in language and in originating circumstance" (Bernhardt-Kabisch 469). The characteristics of this anxiety demonstrate that nature was conceived previously as an aspect of culture, as something authored by the same force that founded culture. Never a merely biological or geological domain, a literal ground of meaning which one could take for granted, nature was always a symbolic construct, an extension of a given culture's conception of itself. In the Judeo-Christian tradition, the world begins with an originary symbolic act, the creating word that brings forth a fully intended and interpretable text, a second book of nature. Moreover, the rainbow covenant that God made with humanity after the deluge guarantees that he will hold in check any hostile or unruly force that threatens to destroy creation. Certain passages in the Old Testament and in *Paradise Lost* link these two events, describing the separation of water and land on the second day of creation as the mark-

ing of a boundary that the waters cannot pass.[3] In effect, creation is an act
of founding violence whereby God imposes what one could call a natural
contract upon the elements, which henceforth must remain at peace with
each other and subject themselves to his law. Through the myth of creation
and covenant, culture attempts to make nature obedient to its own demands.

Although Wordsworth's readers have seldom discussed it, this theology of the rainbow covenant is an issue in his work, particularly in the
"analogy passage" that followed the Snowdon episode in the five-book *Prelude* of 1804 and which was removed for the thirteen-book version of 1805.
At one point in that passage, Wordsworth describes how "A large unmuti-
lated rainbow stood / Immoveable in heaven" above a ferocious storm (J.
Wordsworth, Abrams, and Gill 497). As Jacobus argues, this is a covenantal
rainbow that "defends the Coniston landscape against dissolution into
chaos" (*Romanticism* 279) and Wordsworth against the fate of voyagers
such as Columbus, Gilbert, Park, and Dampier, all of whom face the inundating powers of the sea later in the passage (J. Wordsworth, Abrams, and
Gill 498–99). The threat of the deluge, it seems, is inevitably linked with
its corollary, the rainbow of the covenant. This entire problematic, once
crucial for Book 5 (1804), eventually becomes crucial to the overall scenario
of the 1805 version. When Wordsworth removes the "analogy passage,"
writes an even more dramatic scene of inundation in the Arab dream, and
shifts the Snowdon episode to the final book, he expands the original Book
5 to encompass most of the 1805 poem, sandwiching the latter between the
fear of cataclysm and the promise of its containment.[4] In this way, he sets
up a counterpart to the crisis and resolution scenario of Books 9 through
12, giving cultural disruption truly geological dimensions.

The question of the covenant is nowhere explicit in the Arab dream,
but it strongly informs the attenuated theology of the prologue, where
Wordsworth describes God as the poet's "prime Teacher," the "speaking
face of earth and heaven," and as the "sovereign Intellect / Who through
that bodily Image hath diffused / A soul divine which we participate" (5.12–
16). Nature seems to be as subject to the divine will and intention as in the
familiar myths of the Judeo-Christian tradition, and humanity seems to
share in the "soul" of the divine. Yet it turns out that this nameless "living
Presence," far from warding off another deluge, would merely survive it in
the way that nature itself does (cf. 33–34). Rather than enforcing his own
providential law over nature, this God now personifies the law of nature's
own immanent functioning, becoming little more than a metaphysical extension of what he was sworn to discipline. And rather than being nature's
author, this God disappears into an unreadable landscape, a collection of

contingent signs that speak only of the endless process of destruction and renewal. The disappearance of the covenantal God prompts the lament of the prologue's final lines:

> Oh! why hath not the mind
> Some element to stamp her image on
> In nature somewhat nearer to her own?
> Why, gifted with such powers to send abroad
> Her spirit, must it lodge in shrines so frail? (5.7–48)

In pointed contrast to the condition of the "sovereign Intellect," here the human mind has no permanent "image" in the world, no natural dwelling place for its spirit. The capacity of the "living Presence" to incarnate itself does not guarantee the same for the human mind. Moreover, the effacement of the symbolic violence that subjects nature to culture cancels the difference between a cultural artifact (like a shrine) and a merely literal sign or physical object, such that every shrine becomes frail, an abandoned spital or a ruined cottage.

The possibility that nature might destroy itself does not usually lead to undue fears concerning the fate of culture; geological time is so vast, encompassing such huge tracts of human history in its slightest interval, that the possibility that natural disaster could threaten the survival of certain precious artifacts seems remote. The poetry of disaster, however, is precipitated less by mere geological fact than by the fear, felt with a nearly hallucinatory intensity, that the abrogation of the rainbow covenant threatens to unleash the forces of disaster. The dreamer's hyperbolic anxiety is a precise counterpart to that which produced *Salisbury Plain*—so precise in fact that we cannot help but suspect that it inscribes the latter in another register. Within this hyperbolic logic, God's indifference to the deluge makes it almost inevitable that nature, no longer subject to his rule, will dissolve into a war between the elements, a revolt against the natural contract that would never be reestablished by the sacred violence of divine law. Whatever force undoes sacrifice also undoes the rainbow covenant (itself made official through sacrifice [Genesis 8:20–9:17]), making the world vulnerable to nature's version of the return of the dead.

This time, however, hyperbolic anxiety seems so misplaced and takes such an extraordinary form that we become more attentive to it than to its cause. By writing those fears in the form of a dream, by emphasizing its fictive, even hallucinatory qualities, Wordsworth makes his fascination with extravagant anxiety explicit and in the process foregrounds the poetics of errancy as clearly as anywhere in his *oeuvre*. The dream itself begins when the already excessive anxiety concerning the deluge (an anxiety, says the Friend, which results from "going far to seek disquietude" [52]) becomes even more hyperbolic, bringing the reader's fear to such an unusual height (61) that it takes over his consciousness. This force transports the hapless wanderer from reading a text to seeing its figures, from perusing *Don Quixote* to following Cervantes's knight (58–60, 123–24), much as it draws him into hallucinating the vision of human sacrifice or encountering, in the form of the discharged soldier, an "uncouth figure" from his childhood reading.[5] The dreamer also finds himself in a familiar space, an "Arabian Waste, / A Desart" akin to the empty, dark terrain of the Plain, a resemblance emphasized in the 1850 version: "I saw before me stretched a boundless plain / Of sandy wilderness, all black and void" (5.71–72). The prologue hints that this void may result from a "fire" that is "sent from far to wither all / Her [earth's] pleasant habitations, and dry up / Old Ocean in his bed left singed and bare" (5.30–32); here again a "dreadful fire" or "great flame" swallows up the world (*Salisbury Plain* 91, 94). In this void, of course, there are no boundaries, no directions; more vacant even than the Plain, it is a nature entirely stripped of divine intention, one "where the 'speaking face of earth and heaven' has gone blank and become unreadable" (Bernhardt-Kabisch 471). The utter effacement of every mode of signification fills the dreamer with great "Distress of mind" (5.74), because it strips his "immortal being" of its "garments" (5.22–23) and deprives his overall capacity of figuration of any specific sign or image in which it might anchor itself.

Unlike the traveler on the plain, however, this dreamer does not have to search the landscape for signs of human habitation or of the proper direction, for suddenly there appears at his side an Arab who, he assumes, will take over the functions of hospitality and guidance and "lead him through the Desart" (83). The Arab is not much of a guide; he increases the dreamer's anxiety by sharing with him the prophecy of destruction and then speeds away, abandoning the dreamer to his own devices (131–33). Far from being a unitary presence who travels the desert "with unerring skill" (1850 *Prelude* 5.82), the bedouin is himself a two-sided sign, a duplicitous figure akin to the double-headed guidepost. Bernhardt-Kabisch remarks that the rider himself "is in fact a kind of Janus figure, constantly looking forward and backward" (471–72), like the fearful traveler on the plain, the ancient mariner, and the child in the stolen boat episode. Moreover, as a person bearing a stone and shell he resembles "innumerable figures" from "classical, Renaissance, and Eastern" iconography who bear "symbolic objects" in their two hands (469–70), a figure whose emblematic significance is ruthlessly binaristic. In the dream, as in the prologue, Wordsworth invites us to classify nearly everything in culture according to the opposition between stone and shell, "The consecrated works of Bard and Sage, / Sensuous or intellectual" (5.41–42).

But the dream quickly moves beyond binarism toward the more sophisticated conception of the two-sided sign, whose logic, familiar to us from the Salisbury Plain poems, is made more devastatingly explicit here. As Wordsworth writes of the bedouin later in the dream, "I fancied that he was the very Knight / Whose Tale Cervantes tells, yet not the Knight, / But was an Arab of the Desert too; / Of these was neither, and was both at once (5.123–26). The fusion of either/or and both/and, Bahti argues, produces the rhetorical structure of both/neither.[6] In this structure, "a sign can function or mean in at least two different ways—most basically, as literal and figural—without itself being or meaning any one thing" ("Figures" 620, 606). It would be, like the naked signpost, at once naked and a sign, at once a literal object and a figure. Or it would be like the objects the Arab holds in his hand: "I plainly saw / The one to be a Stone, the other a Shell, / Nor doubted once but that they both were Books" (5.111–13). Bahti comments that here the dreamer understands these objects "as both one and the other, material and immaterial" ("Figures" 619). The Arab rider is himself both/neither literal and/nor figurative, or—to take up the larger terms of the dream—is caught, like the post-Enlightenment world generally, on the threshold between literal object and figure, between an unreadable void and a readable text, between the deluge and safe haven. Rather than being the dreamer's guide, then, the rider personifies his anxiety of figuration, his desperate attempt to establish a difference between signification and the void.

But because the Arab cannot depend upon the rainbow covenant and thus cannot establish this difference by means of a definitive, symbolic violence, he cannot finally distinguish between thing and word, object and sign. He will never be able to cross the threshold into signification. Clarifying the structure of both/neither, Bahti compares it with the Moebius strip on which one side "is always already the other side as well" ("Figures" 606–7).[7] Thus signification is a version of unreadability; when the dreamer holds up the precious shell to his ear, he hears an "unknown Tongue / Which yet I understood, articulate sounds / A loud prophetic blast of harmony" (5.94–96), as if the shell gives the void a voice, makes literal sounds articulate and, like the monumental letters of the first spot of time, makes the unreadable readable. Such is the status of a pure and abstract figuration, which, unlike a specific language, can never be comprehended. A few lines later Wordsworth states that the shell "was a God, yea many Gods, / Had voices more than all the winds, and was / A joy, a consolation, and a hope" (5.107–9). Michael Ragussis comments that this multivoiced tongue, capable of soothing "Through every clime, the heart of human kind" (1850 *Prelude* 5.109), "speaks a primal language which is understood by all people. Its 'harmony' is a universally understood order like music" (29). This universal language resembles Lacan's symbolic combinatory, the abstract capacities of signification as such, the reservoir of figures and of syntactic markings which make reading possible but which cannot themselves be read. In its first appearance, it seems, the pure possibility of language is as unreadable as what it would replace, the significance of its many voices as multiple and indeterminate as the desert's grains of sand.[8]

More dangerously, Wordsworth hints that the shell is indistinguishable from the deluge about which it warns the world. Listening to the "unknown Tongue," the dreamer hears "An Ode, in passion uttered, which foretold / Destruction to the Children of the Earth / By deluge now at hand" (5.97–99). Not long after, the Arab and dreamer look back to see the "waters of the deep / Gathering" upon them (5.130–31). This "passage from *hearing* the prophetic Ode to *seeing* the deluge pre-figured by it," writes Warminski, "is a passage . . . from the (pre-)figurative sense to the literal sense. The flood *seen* is a literalization of the flood *heard*" ("Missed Crossing" 1004). The very object that the Arab would preserve from destruction brings destruction in its wake. The Arab's quest is impossible. He will never be able to bury the shell, for he cannot protect the shell from itself. Both/neither figure of the flood and/nor the literal flood, warning and fulfillment, the shell reduces preservation and destruction to a single duplicitous sign. It becomes the perfect emblem of the prologue's conception of nature, one that is identical with its own periodic destruction—one whose other side (cataclysm) is "always already" itself, and vice versa. Through the shell, nature makes its unreadability readable and reveals that it, too, is a two-sided sign.

In a gesture that for the first time lays bare the hallucinatory logic of *Salisbury Plain*, Wordsworth suggests that much as the shell creates the disaster it warns against, so also the Arab's fear of the deluge brings it to pass. Strangely enough, what threatens the world is the anxiety concerning its destruction, the anxiety Wordsworth voiced in the prologue. In the logic of hyperbole, an anxiety taken to such a "height" cannot help but call forth the waters of the "deep" (5.61, 130). This hopeless confusion as to whether imagination is in danger or is the source of danger,[9] this mutual implication of foreboding and disaster, confounds anticipation and fulfillment, thereby destroying the narrative logic of the dream and placing it on a strange temporal threshold. At dream's end, as the dreamer first withdraws to the position of a spectator and then awakens, the Arab remains suspended in the moment before his death and/nor before his rescue of the stone and shell, as if perpetually fleeing the fleet waters (5.132–39). But what is the difference, precisely, between the shell and the flood? If the deluge is "now at hand," as the shell says (99), on which hand is it: there in the shell, or behind him in the waters? Moreover, what is the difference between the desert and the waters, the two elements of the Arab's landscape (cf. 135–36)—between the world at the dream's beginning, the "*dry* chaos" where the ocean has been burned away (Hartman *Wordsworth's Poetry* 230), and at the dream's end, where the waters overtake the earth (cf. Bahti "Figures" 616; Kelley "Spirit" 576)? Has the cataclysm just taken place, or is it just about to do so? The Arab dream occurs in that impossible interval between two versions of the same event, the (anti-)moment when the deluge is (to simplify my syntax) both in the past and the future, the space both before him in the desert sands and behind him in the waters.

The dream's logic of duplicity applies with the greatest force to the figure of the Arab rider, with which (as we have seen) Wordsworth introduces the both/neither rhetorical structure. The rider's two identities suggest two general interpretations of his status on the threshold of signification. In his guise as an Arab, he represents what eighteenth century anthropology regarded as culture in its earliest, most elementary phase. This conception of the Arab, Bewell argues, allows Wordsworth to render him as yet another postdiluvian wanderer and to make the dream itself into another instance of the primitive encounter (258–59). In this reading, the Arab is poised on the threshold between cataclysm and culture, as if he is about to construct language and social relations. In his guise as Don Quixote, the rider is a figure from romance, akin to the Spenserian personages of the Salisbury Plain poems, the magical figures of neoprimitivist ballad poetry, and the adventuring child of the 1799 *Prelude*. Like Cervantes's famed hero, this mad figure (5.151–52) wishes to transfigure a barren, literal reality by means of fictions and thus wanders in the domain between life and art. Overall, then, the mad bedouin appears out of the concerns of Enlightenment moral philosophy and high literary romance, the invention of language and the seductions of artifice, taking shape as someone who is both a postdiluvian wanderer and a questing knight. Such shapes have appeared before in Wordsworth's texts; both Rousseau and Spenser are at stake in *Salisbury Plain,* much as delugic anthropology and marvelous fictions produce the uncanny figure of the discharged soldier.

Yet this text clarifies the mutual implication of these two versions of the Wordsworthian traveler. The rider is both an anxious, harried postdiluvian wanderer, a primitive solitary abandoned in the desert against his will, and a knight who voluntarily sets forth on a mad quest to read fictions as if they were real. This coupling suggests that for Wordsworth Enlightenment speculation is bound up with the fascinations of pure fiction and that a tale about cultural origins spun by a *philosophe* easily metamorphoses into a "preternatural tale, / Romance of giants, chronicle of fiends" (1798 *Pedlar* 70–71). More importantly, Wordsworth's intertwining of primitive anxiety and romantic pleasure recalls the duplicitous logic of masochistic fantasy, according to which the psychologically primitive, Januslike child of the stolen boat episode, for example, purposely summons forth the vengeful presence from which he flees. Perhaps in his madness the Arab/Quixote *challenges* nature to inundate him, much as the child openly defies the brooding presences in the landscape. The entire sequence may be a fantasy; one cannot be sure that the "glittering light" (129) behind the Arab is in fact the deluge, as he claims, for like the child who thinks a cliff is coming after him, he may be interpreting appearances according to the dictates of desire. If, as I suggested above, the Arab's fear of the deluge brings it forth from the deep, is his anxiety somehow a form of perverse *desire* for a cataclysm he cannot prevent? Is the prophecy only a warning or is it an attempt to signify, to lend a voice to, the inevitable disaster?

In response to the prologue which, in a mournful tone, describes a crisis of faith in nature, the dream itself imbricates anxiety and pleasure, transfiguring potential disaster into the site of fascination. It does so, quite simply, by dramatizing the inherently hyperbolic quality of this apocalyptic dread, this insistence that if culture does not survive forever it is worthless. The fear of the deluge gives the world a hallucinatory intensity, poising it on that threshold where one cannot safely distinguish between the world's virulent existence and its utter disappearance. At once real and unreal, the world takes upon itself the fatal charm of a pure fiction, a fabulous illusion, a stunning apparition, or a dream.[10] Strangely enough, by challenging the world to end—to destroy all works of art—one lends it the texture of artifice. The secular anxiety of the prologue becomes a means of transport into the domain of pure surface, where inexplicable figures appear from nowhere, words are uttered by no one, and an indeterminate light glitters on the horizon.[11] Works of art may not be merely physical objects after all, things that survive or are destroyed like the rest, but rather things that appear when one puts the idea of reality into question. What would the works of "Shakespeare, or Milton, Labourers divine" (5.165) be worth if they were carved in adamant and could never disappear? Their poetic fictions are seductive, provide an opportunity for the reader to embark upon a romantic quest, only because they are contained in frail shrines, in such volumes as that "Poor earthly casket of immortal Verse" (5.164).[12]

Although the Book of *The Prelude* dedicated to books begins with the fear that poetry could be wiped out by a deluge, it soon proposes that this very fear is poetic—a version of Quixotic romance. One could hardly propose a more exemplary instance of sensationalist reading; what transports the reader into the dream, it seems, is the attraction of an inhuman anxiety or desire, the fascination with the possibility of transfiguring even nature through artifice. Moreover, through its insistent reference to Wordsworth's prior texts, the dream implies that the poetics of errancy is a product of sensationalist reading—that *Salisbury Plain* and the texts that follow in its wake literalize the fiction of disaster and make real what is as yet only a foreboding of culture's end. But it also demonstrates that such a literalization is utterly fascinating, that Wordsworth's fears for culture, however extreme, culminate in scenarios of surpassing charm. What begins as a poetry of protest ultimately voices a capacity to find beauty in disaster, to be captivated beyond reason by the prospect of the world's loss.

The fact that Wordsworth apologizes for this outrageous dream at length in the following lines (5.166–98) only emphasizes his uneasy awareness that it reveals too much about his capacity to be captivated partly against his will. These lines point to his tendency to deny or negate his investment in errancy, a tendency that will become even more pronounced later in *The Prelude*. Yet this defensive tone soon gives way to the argument of Book 5 as a whole, in which Wordsworth aggressively celebrates hyperbolic romance and attacks the forces that would regulate it according to the strictures of an enlightening, moralizing education. The dream provides an excellent starting place for this argument because in it Wordsworth abandons a geological or philosophical mode of reading for an openly fantastic one. If one can celebrate the Arab dream, one no longer bears allegiance to philosophical discipline and in fact is willing to violate it, to take it to extremes, to confound the known and the unknown, until one has enabled nature to escape all discourses and to become a fabulously unreadable text. What Wordsworth performs in the dream he articulates explicitly in the rest of Book 5, finally opposing a poetics of errancy against the philosophical norms he disputes in a less obvious way in his previous texts.

James K. Chandler argues that this polemic is launched against the educational theories, largely based upon Rousseau's *Emile,* which became popular in France during the Thermidorian period (93–119). But as Joel Morkan demonstrates, the theories attacked in Book 5 prevailed in England as well as France; derived ultimately from the work of Locke, they shaped "the general educational temper of his time." Many authors besides Rousseau, including Kant, Wollstonecraft, Richard Edgeworth, and Mrs. Barbauld, advocated the strict control over a child's learning and especially over its flights of imagination (250–51). What Wordsworth mocks is the educational system based upon the developmental psychology of the Enlightenment, a psychology that he at once borrowed and resisted in the 1799 *Prelude*. Here he defies this tradition, arguing that a child's development should follow no prearranged plan but rather a deviant path full of fearful accidents and mischances. Similarly, a child should read not to acquire knowledge or discipline its mind for adult purposes but to defraud the day of its glory, to indulge in fantasies of omnipotence over a paltry reality, and to take pleasure in dreams and lawless tales (5.512, 530–48). In Book 5 Luke gets a chance to speak and *The Prelude* takes its revenge upon *The Recluse*.

But the implications of the Arab dream reach beyond those passages, resurfacing in the episode of the drowned man, an episode from the 1799 *Prelude* placed in the new context of Book 5 (5.450–81). Cynthia Chase points out that certain figures from the Arab dream are literalized in these lines. Where the speaker of the prologue experienced "Tremblings of the heart" in thinking that "the immortal being / No more shall need such garments" (5.22–23), the autobiographical child "saw distinctly on the opposite Shore" a quite literal "heap of garments" which their owner would no longer need (5.460–61). Similarly, the "literal action of drowning also repeats a poetic figure: a report of a drowned man instead of the vision of 'the drowning world' that opens the book" (14–16). One can easily extend this reading and argue that the entire episode literalizes the Arab dream: the child waits by the lake, much as the reader sits by the sea; he anticipates the discovery of the man's drowning, much as the reader has anxious forebodings of the coming deluge; and he eventually passes from seeing nature to seeing a figure from a text, much as the reader passes into dream, except in this case he sees the figure literally in the face of the drowned man *without* passing into dream (cf. Chase 23). Wordsworth claims that his "inner eye had seen / Such sights before" in his reading of romance; he might as well say he saw it in the Arab dream, the romance to which this episode, placed in its new context, everywhere refers.

In this episode Wordsworth revises the Arab dream, bringing that text of sheer appearance and literary artifice into the domain of the phenomenal world and autobiographical reminiscence familiar in the rest of *The Prelude*. But in doing so, Chase argues, he erodes "the distinction between literal and figurative," for "[w]hat surfaces in the poem with the drowned man's 'ghastly face' is effaced figure—lines one can trace neither as literal nor figurative language, wording that, like the desert traveler in the poet's dream, 'Of these was neither, and was both at once'" (14). This erosion, consistent with the rhetorical structure of the dream, has a different effect here, for by demonstrating that this episode literalizes the figural logic of the dream, Wordsworth suggests that all such episodes in his work already obey a logic from elsewhere, that they realize a dreamlike structure in biographical or historical form. In effect, he admits that his texts are less statements on various topical concerns than embodiments of a hyperbolic textuality. The episode thus refers less to the Arab dream itself than to what it represents: the textual elsewhere given various designations in Wordsworth's texts, whether the Spenserian stanza, the ballad, or Othello's seductive tales. What we read in this passage we have indeed read before.

This episode also literalizes a number of other concerns of Book 5 related to the dream. For one, Chase points out that "the drowned man was, in fact, a local schoolmaster. Wordsworth's polemical argument—do away with the schoolmasters!—gets transformed in the course of Book 5 into an incident that literally does away with one" (31) or rather which transfigures one into a ghastly face from the world of romance. Much as Wordsworth disrupts the text of nature or of philosophy, making it seductively unreadable, so also he mutilates the face of the pedagogue, making it as sensationally unrecognizable as the face of a ghost ("ghastly face"), an apparition, a figure in a dream. No longer a scholarly counterpart of the Lacanian dead father, an embodiment of a grounded and enduring knowledge, the pedagogue now becomes a kind of magus, the master of an illegitimate knowledge and of lawless illusion.[13] Similarly, on another level of concern introduced by the prologue to the dream, where the deluge apparently threatens the survival of the "works of Bard and Sage, / Sensuous or intellectual" (5.41–42), this mutilated face has "decoration and ideal grace: / A dignity, a smoothness, like the works / Of Grecian Art, and purest Poesy" (5.479–81). Chase argues that the "Grecian Art" of this simile "refers particularly to marble statues, to antique nudes," to "the sculpture of classical antiquity" which "is treasured precisely in the condition of defacement or fragmentation in which many such works were found" (24). Much as the voice of the shell made an unknown tongue understandable to the dreamer's ear, so also this reference to Grecian art makes the unrecognizable recognizable to the poet's eye, lending the ruin of this sensuous work of art, drowned as if in the deluge, an even greater grace.

On yet another level of implication, the ghastly face that arises "'mid that beauteous scene / Of trees, and hills and water" (5.472, 470–71) reveals the defacement not only of a schoolmaster or sculpture but also of "the speaking face of earth and heaven" who is the "prime Teacher" of the poet's mind (5.12–13). To parody de Man, this scene is an instance of a theology as defacement, whereby God himself, now disfigured, is recognized not as a speaking but a speechless and unreadable face. To a certain extent, the fears of the prologue are confirmed: a God who fails to keep the covenant and to enforce culture's symbolic difference from nature is a dead God, a corpse. But like the drowned man's face, this mutilated speaking face of nature attains to an ideal grace, as if by disfiguring nature's sculpted form the deluge makes it into an uncouth shape and gives it the charm of romance. Displacing its substantial version, nature becomes its own simulation, remaining animated after its cataclysmic death. Thus the overall defense in Book 5 of lawless reading and mad errands (cf. 5.160–61) becomes that of the prospect of the deluge itself, a prospect that inscribes within the order of the real a perverse extravagance that rescues it from a total subjection to the discourses of knowledge.[14] Here Wordsworth takes his resistance to the forces that would tame and regulate culture to its furthest extreme, suggesting that nature is finally untamed and unknowable.

The concerns of Book 5 spill over into the passage in Book 6 on the crossing of the Alps, in which Wordsworth assembles a wide array of terms, including the deluge, around perhaps the most memorable instance of errancy in his work. The story of how he and his companion lose their way deploys several familiar motifs: the untimely act (of leaving their "noon's repast" slightly too late to join their fellow travelers), the traveler's separation from his guide (compare the first spot of time and the Arab dream), the disappearance of the path or of signs that mark the proper direction (note their perplexity when the "beaten road" breaks off at "a rivulet's edge" [502–3]), the extravagant step off the right path, and the chance event or encounter ("By fortunate chance . . . A Peasant met us" [511, 513]). Yet after bringing these motifs together in such a clear manner, Wordsworth displaces them in the final line, which captures his shock and disappointment on discovering that he had crossed the Alps (524). This particular misadventure, it seems, points to the more stunning error of crossing the Alps without knowing it; an error, of course, that would be more difficult to represent, to locate in time and space, or to comprehend in any way. Where, or when, had he reached the heights? The memory of one extravagant act, of climbing when he should descend, refers to an event he will never remember, the moment when he began to descend when he thought he was still ascending.

But in that case, both errors of mistaking heights for depths and depths for heights refer not to any literal act but rather to the shock of discovering that the heights and depths, the true and false paths, may be indistinguishable. Here Wordsworth expands upon the heights/depths motif familiar from the 1799 *Prelude*, making their reversibility into a crucially unreadable or indecipherable sign; he and his companion have great difficulty believing and translating the peasant's words (520, 523). To accept these words is to move from error to errancy, from a wrong path to the unknowability of the right path; it is, in short, to render the world unreadable, to lose one's faith in the order of things. Much as Oedipus fulfills the oracle's prophecy in the course of escaping it, this traveler misses his goal in the course of achieving it and is nearly as incredulous when hearing the peasant's tidings as Oedipus when listening to Tiresias.[15] For the traveler this news turns the world on its head, because in identifying heights and depths it reveals that the world is other than it seems, that the Alps are not the Alps.

It is this unreadable, impossible world that appears in the Gorge of Gondo passage, where nature becomes its own scene of destruction while remaining itself. Borrowing the terms of Book 5, Wordsworth depicts the landscape as at once permanence and change, security and chaos, creation and deluge:

> The immeasurable height
> Of woods decaying, never to be decayed,
> The stationary blasts of water-falls,
> And every where along the hollow rent
> Winds thwarting winds, bewildered and forlorn,
> The torrents shooting from the clear blue sky,
> The rocks that muttered close upon our ears,
> Black drizzling crags that spake by the way-side
> As if a voice were in them, the sick sight
> And giddy prospect of the raving stream,
> The unfettered clouds and region of the heavens,
> Tumult and peace, the darkness and the light
> Were all like workings of one mind, the features
> Of the same face, blossoms upon one tree,
> Characters of the great Apocalypse,
> The types and symbols of Eternity,
> Of first and last, and midst, and without end. (6.556–72)

Without question, a furiously destructive force is unleashed here, something that tears a hollow rent in the earth's surface, that blasts and shoots as in battle, that mutters and raves like a madman, that mixes the elements in a bizarre fashion (the torrents shoot not from clouds but from the "clear blue sky") and severs them from each other, unfettering not only the clouds but also the entire "region of the heavens" from the earth (so that the sky will truly be "not a sky / Of earth" [1799 *Prelude* 1.65–66]). Yet this force is itself a part of nature's endless functioning, as Wordsworth writes in lines whose logic is perhaps too easily grasped; much as the woods' decay enables them never truly to decay, so also the waters' endless blasting shapes the "stationary blasts of water-falls." Destruction and creation, chaos and order, are the same. Those "winds thwarting winds" hint at what works here, a certain breeze that blows "Oer things which it has made and soon becomes / A tempest a redundant energy / Creating not but as it may / disturbing things created" (MS. JJ 3–6). What appears in the gorge is the decreating power of creation itself, or rather a power that creates *by disturbing* things created, one that, in the terms of contemporary geology, formed these mountains by means of a deluge (Kelley *Aesthetics* 106). The conflation of creation and destruction that Wordsworth articulates in the dramatic episodes of Book 5 now appears in a landscape so spectacularly mobile that once again "The surface of the universal earth . . . Work[s] like a sea" (1799 *Prelude* 1.196, 198).

In the final lines of this passage, according to Isobel Armstrong, Wordsworth defines this curious relation between creation and deluge either as one of opposition (tumult and peace, darkness and light) or of apposition (workings of one mind, features of the same face). But in this way it only sharpens the difficulty; does the scene reveal a clash between opposed forces or aspects of a single overall process? "The great sentence reads two ways": Apocalypse "might be subsumed appositionally into the types and symbols of Eternity"; or it might be opposed to Eternity, "for one is an ending, a destruction, the other is endlessness, permanence, timelessness." The last line either brings Apocalypse ("first and last") and Eternity ("and without end") together in an "affirmation of resolution," or it "breaks" them apart (38). It arrives, in short, at the rhetorical structure of both/neither. Although the scene may be like a vast text, the "Characters of the great Apocalypse, / The types and symbols of Eternity," it also collapses the difference between opposed terms, disfigures this text, and thus speaks, like the shell, in "an unknown Tongue, / Which yet I understood" (5.94–95; cf. Armstrong 36).

In his original draft of the crossing of the Alps, Wordsworth pauses to discuss this kind of disfigured text. After the account of meeting the peasant and before the Gorge of Gondo passage, he interposes the Cave of Yordas passage, later moved to Book 8 (711–41), in which he describes how a traveler, carrying a torch, passes into a cave and sees there,

> or thinks
> He sees, erelong, the roof above his head,
> Which instantly unsettles and recedes
> Substance and shadow, light and darkness, all
> Commingled, making up a Canopy
> Of Shapes and Forms and Tendencies to Shape,
> That shift and vanish, change and interchange

Like Spectres, ferment quiet and sublime,
Which, after a short space, works less and less,
Till every effort, every motion gone,
The scene before him lies in perfect view,
Exposed and lifeless, as a written book. (8.716–27)

Here again the scene moves and works, mingling together light and darkness, potential opposites "that shift and vanish" into each other, that "change and interchange" their shapes. Moreover, the scene does not long remain lifeless; as soon as the traveler looks again, it quickens into a new array of forms, "Like a magician's airy pageant, parts / Unites, embodying everywhere some pressure / Or image, recognised or new, some type / Or picture of the world," forming "A Spectacle to which there is no end" (8.734–37, 741). In this passage, whose terms are interwoven into that on the Gorge of Gondo, Wordsworth favorably contrasts the spectacle of uncertain forms with the perfectly comprehended text of a written book, where oppositions have been secured in a lifeless writing as if mastered by the symbolic authority of the dead. What captivates him in the Alps is not nature as God's second book, a divine writing founded in his covenant, but rather the characters of a Protean and incomprehensible spectacle that will never end. Like the Cave of Yordas and the Arab dream, the Gorge of Gondo is also a tissue of specters, images that interchange between substance and shadow and actions that take place without subjects or objects (who mutters in the rocks? to whom?).[16] Here Wordsworth returns to the argument of Book 5, celebrating whatever unsettles readability, puts the system of differences into play (cf. Derrida *Writing* 289, 292), and gives reality the magic of sheer appearance.

By pausing to write about his Alpine experience in such a way, Wordsworth demonstrates that he finds it necessary to explain it in terms other than its own. What overwhelmed him, he suggests, was no literal disorientation but a certain kind of textual experience. But for some reason it is no longer adequate to describe it in the terms of Book 5, where he similarly interprets biographical experience as the literalization of romantic reading. Something more uncanny has happened here. Accordingly, he puts aside the Cave of Yordas passage and writes another, unprecedented in his canon, in which unreadable textuality takes the shape neither of the face of a drowned man nor of an airy pageant but of his own imagination or soul (6.525–48). This attribution of errancy to his own soul might seem to return him to his proper self, something presumably stable and knowable; but as the following lines demonstrate, his imagination is yet another version of the ghostly traveler (or drowned man). What he encounters in the Alps is hyperbolic textuality, something that exceeds all definite shapes and names. The classic features of errancy and errancy's ghosts return here; the imagination interrupts both the eye and progress of the poem, unsettling what the poet sees and steering him off the proper path. An "unfathered" force, it is at once an inexplicable, sourceless disruption in the symbolic order founded in the name of the dead father; an unfather, an uncouth figure, much like the discharged soldier, who is not yet dead or buried, and thus not yet symbolically the dead father; and a child who, as in the second spot of time, has lost its father (cf. Kneale 161–62). Moreover, in an image perfectly appropriate in this context, the "unfathered vapor" personifies the deluge, inundating the traveler so that he is "lost as in a cloud, / Halted, without a struggle to break through" (529–30).[17] But this delugic force is not truly akin to those unfathers until Wordsworth recovers from total loss and, in a moment of specular identification, recognizes in that errant power the face of his own soul: "And now recovering, to my Soul I say / 'I recognise thy glory'" (531–32).

By naming this mist the *imagination,* Wordsworth recognizes that the unreadable textuality that he insists on finding in the landscapes of history and of the Alps is his own alienated poetics. At the same time he suggests that it is not his own, for it steers him off his proper path, blocks him, inundates him, and comes to him unsought. In effect, he encounters his poetics as a force that befalls him—as if it imposes itself upon him in a way he never intended. In this counterpart to the triumphant myth of the 1799 *Prelude,* the unwilled intrusion of spectral forces is less a sign of his election than a thwarting of his conscious will. When he recognizes in that mist the glory of his soul, however, he retrospectively chooses to have written what at first came to him unchosen. Far from confirming the self-presence of the poetic mind or claiming that its powers originate in a transcendental realm, this passage defines the *imagination* as a poetic mind divided from itself, one that hopes to be haunted by figuration as by an alien force, that intends to be thwarted by what it does not intend. It thus inscribes in imagination the structure of specular self-rivalry characteristic of the Lacanian imaginary. But imagination is more than another instance of such rivalry; since this passage bears upon his entire poetics, including those former passages that describe specular encounter, it ultimately derives the logic of his writing from the texts he has written. Rather than mastering errancy by writing it, his poetics is written by errancy, befalling the poet as if he were a figure in one of his texts.

Rather than writing as if this recognition overmasters him, however, Wordsworth claims that it enables him to recover from his initial disorientation. Strictly speaking, to recognize a disfiguring force does not necessarily enable one to recover from it, since that recognition may simply make the latter all the more visible. But the poet thinks otherwise. Following the logic of hyperbole, whereby depth is indistinguishable from height, he transforms disorientation into the exhilaration of entering an uncharted space. This reversal has dramatic consequences for the rest of this passage. Alan Liu has argued that this passage rewrites Napoleon's crossing of the Alps in order to subsume contemporary history in imagination. But it does much more than that; it transforms Wordsworth's own account of cultural disaster into its opposite.[18] The "dreadful fire" whose "dismal light . . . illumes" the desert's "farthest bounds" (*Salisbury Plain* 91, 96) becomes "the light of sense / [that] Goes out in flashes that have shewn to us / The invisible world" (534–36), and the violence whereby dead warriors rose up to slaughter the living (97–99) becomes a testament to the "banners militant" of the imagination (543).[19] The agents of crime and oedipal insurrection return in the unfathered vapor and the imagination, which has such "strength / Of usurpation," such insurrectionary power. The extravagant departure from the proper path does not make one homeless but rather locates "Our destiny, our nature, and our home" beyond all boundaries in a hyperbolic, unattainable space, in the yearning for what will always remain elsewhere: "with infinitude, and only there; / With hope it is, hope that can never die, / Effort, and expectation, and desire, / And something evermore about to be" (538–42). Even the delugic power that "rose from the mind's abyss" (1850 *Prelude* 6.594) reappears in a positive guise, "like the mighty flood of Nile / Poured from his fount of Abyssinian clouds / To fertilise the whole Egyptian plain" (1850 *Prelude* 6.614–16).[20] In short, all the elements associated with the dismemberment of culture—the departure from the proper path, the onset of darkness, the appearance of specters, the clash of arms, the unfathering of symbolic authority, and the destruction of the world by deluge—metamorphose into elements of the transfiguration of culture.

Thus this passage, like the Arab dream, affirms the charms of disaster. By embracing imagination, Wordsworth finds in the utter disfiguration of the world the lineaments of the infinite. What seems to be a central affirmation in this poet's canon in fact makes the imagination inseparable from terror. Here he takes the general strategy of the 1799 *Prelude* to new heights, transforming not just the mischances of childhood but also the possibility of another deluge into a sign of his calling. Ultimately, the passage suggests what he never states nor would consciously accept: that he finds human sacrifice sublime and regards terror as a sign of hope. Those who argue that in this episode Wordsworth generously finds gain in potential loss verge upon the insight that for this poet absolute loss *is* gain: the unspeakable event is both/neither loss and/nor gain, at once the world's destruction and its transfiguration.

This passage would have a far different import if it followed the Kantian account of the sublime. At first, it seems that it does so, because it moves from loss or breakdown to recovery, from bafflement to a celebration of infinity. The mind seems to recover from a disorder of the senses and of language by claiming for itself the resources of a totalizing, supersensible reason (cf. Kant 86 106). This account, Weiskel argues, recapitulates and thereby reestablishes the Oedipus complex, for in the moment of recovery the mind overidentifies with the force that threatened it and creates a strong superego (92–97). Weiskel's reading demonstrates that the Kantian scenario closely parallels the Freudian myth of cultural origins; in both cases, phenomenal disorientation or physical conflict is resolved through the appeal to symbolic authority. In an act of sacred violence, one lays all merely profane aggression to rest and establishes the nonphenomenal basis for culture in a transcendental reason or in the dead father. In the Simplon Pass episode, such a development would bring an end to the threat of the deluge and return nature to the condition of a readable text.

But this episode deviates from the Kantian scenario. Instead of struggling to break through the blockage and identify with a transcendental power, Wordsworth celebrates the "strength / Of usurpation," the moment of bafflement and disorientation. Weiskel writes: "this strength preserves and indeed depends upon the resistance of sense to its overcoming. Man [sic] achieves or realizes an aesthetic greatness at the moment when his infinite destiny is revealed to him as still outstanding, unrealized, unachieved" (43). The moment of unfathering does not finally lead to the appearance of a symbolic father, nor does the loss of one's path enable one to arrive at one's true, supersensible home. Thus, as I argued above, the *imagination* is an idealizing name for an errancy that, escaping the logic both of the sublime and of the rainbow covenant, more closely resembles the fertilizing deluge of the Nile; it is a proper deviance, an enlightening darkness, a destructiveness that recreates the world. Moreover, despite Hartman's argument concerning the complex relation between imagination and nature (*Wordsworth's Poetry* 33–69), imagination is little more than a face or name—inadequate at that, given the "sad incompetence of human speech" (1850 *Prelude* 6.593), indeed of all symbolic representation—for a radically indeterminate nature that, having lost its ground in the natural or self-identical, has become errant, spectral, unfathered.[21]

But Wordsworth cannot capture the significance of the Alpine crossing entirely in the imagination passage. Whatever hyperbole gives it can take away. As we have seen, the Gorge of Gondo speaks just as fiercely of a darkening enlightenment, a creativity that destroys. In pausing to interpret the hyperprivileged lines on imagination, readers of Wordsworth sometimes forget to go on to the following pages of Book 6, in which the world's dislocation reverberates in further episodes of spectacular disorientation. The lines immediately after the Gorge of Gondo sequence, for example, are nearly transparent in the terms of Wordsworth's early poems:

> That night our lodging was an Alpine House,
> An Inn, or Hospital, as they are named,
> Standing in that same valley by itself,
> And close upon the confluence of two Streams;
> A dreary Mansion, large beyond all need,
> With high and spacious rooms, deafened and stunned
> By noise of waters, making innocent Sleep
> Lie melancholy among weary bones. (573–80)

Like the lonely spital, this shelter does not truly shelter the travelers. "Large beyond all need," it too is hyperbolic, more closely resembling the sublime scenes outside its walls than a human habitation. Lodged by this confluence of raging streams, this natural crossroads or site of violence, one might as well try to sleep through the deluge. What Wordsworth earlier celebrates as the imagination he dreads here; there is something too stunning about the overflowing Nile (548). This is the darker face of a sublimity without resolution, an overmastering of a mind that cannot take refuge in fictions of transcendence. For a moment, Wordsworth displaces the earlier face of hyperbole by verging upon a more haunting personification: "innocent Sleep," occupying a body of nothing but weary bones, is a spirit in a skeleton, a bony ghost that, like the discharged soldier, has barely survived the deluge. He too is "more than half detached / From his own nature," and from him issue "murmuring" or rather deafening "sounds as if of pain / Or of uneasy thought" in the noise of waters ("Soldier" 59–60, 70–71).[22] Unreadable nature is also an uninhabitable shelter and, in turn, an unendurable imagination.[23]

The troubling implications of this brief passage are writ large in the account of the second night's misadventures (617–57), which follows the idyllic recollection of the intervening day's journey along Lake Locarno (581–616). Slightly distanced in this way from the passages on one day's extravagance, this account echoes the latter in a nightly and nightmarish mode, giving sublimity the lineaments of Gothic or darkly supernatural poetry. Once again the travelers leave their quarters in an untimely fashion, misled by Italian clocks into rising long before sunrise, and as a result they again stray from the path, getting "lost, bewildered among woods immense" (631). Stopping on a rock by the lake to wait for day, they are harassed by "the stings / Of insects, which with noise like that of noon / Filled all the woods" (642–44). As on the previous night, a noise out of its due place—or rather time—keeps them awake. The earlier day and night have collapsed together into a singular disorientation without reprieve.

But the passage does not stop there; soon it draws the entire Alpine sequence back into the uncanny landscape of the texts of 1797 through 1799. The untimely noise of noon insects parodies the comparatively benign insect murmurs in the opening of *The Ruined Cottage* (24–25); "The cry of unknown birds" (644) mocks the owls that call to the boy of Winander; these mountains, like those that haunt an adventurer on another lake, glow with a deathly "darkness visible" (645; cf. Part One 108–129; *Paradise Lost* 1.63); the "sometimes rustling motions nigh at hand / Which did not leave us free from personal fear" (650–51) resemble the strange motions that pursue the boy in the theft episodes; and "lastly the withdrawing Moon, that set / Before us while she still was high in heaven" (652–53) disappears as suddenly as the moon of "Strange fits" or the sun of *Salisbury Plain*. Interspersed in these echoes are various images from Coleridge's mystery poems: the moon's "dull red image" that earlier "Lay bedded" on the lake's surface, "changing oftentimes its form / Like an uneasy snake" (636–38), emerges from the complex moon-serpent imagery of the *Ancient Mariner* and "Christabel" (cf. Armstrong 39); and the "clock / That told with unintelligible voice / The widely-parted hours" (647–49) keeps time with the latter poem's castle clock, which, like the cock's crow that accompanies it, prematurely and repeatedly announces the dawn (1–13). Overall, the benighted wanderer loses himself in a series of uncanny images, which in this case he cannot articulate together into any pattern, not even into a scenario of pleasurable repetition.

In this episode Wordsworth carries out a dazzling critique of the Simplon Pass sequence, proposing that in the Alpine crossing, as in a number of earlier texts, the mind is captivated by a figuration alien to it, or rather by a figuration that results from its own hyperbolic self-alienation. An experience of the sublime which never arrives at resolution but remains caught in the moment of breakdown, of unreadability and bafflement, cannot be distinguished from the experience of submitting to a terrifying, implacable force—to whatever brings darkness over Salisbury Plain or to the images that fascinate the unwary traveler of "Incipient Madness." However much he wishes to idealize cultural dismemberment, Wordsworth must also admit that it threatens to inundate the mind with what it can least assimilate or understand.

And yet this deidealization can always metamorphose back into idealization; there is no end to the matter. Accordingly, Wordsworth must bring his account of the Alpine journey to a rather arbitrary end: "But here I must break off, and quit at once, / Though loth, the record of these wanderings, / A theme which may seduce me else beyond / All reasonable bounds" (658–61). To bring a tale of wandering to an end, it seems, is to resist the tale's own tendency to wander beyond the bounds. Perhaps it even requires the claim, made in the following lines, that the entire poem resists errancy,

> that not
> In hollow exultation, dealing forth
> Hyperboles of praise comparative,
> Not rich one moment to be poor for ever,
> Not prostrate, overborn, as if the mind
> Itself were nothing, a mean pensioner
> On outward forms, did we in presence stand
> Of that magnificent region. On the front
> Of this whole Song is written that my heart
> Must in such temple needs have offered up
> A different worship. (662–72)

In this moment of resistance to his own poetic impulses (he is "loth" to quit), Wordsworth inadvertently makes explicit the terms of his poetics of errancy, linking together wandering, seduction, extravagance, hyperbole, expenditure, self-alienation, and captivation by natural figuration, as if, in a massive instance of Freudian negation, he admits everything he wishes to deny and anticipates an interpretation of his work which he would repudiate ("Negation," *Papers* 5.181–85). No theorist has given as exhaustive an account of extravagance as Wordsworth provides in these lines—an account that, despite his protestations, he has been forming in the travel sequence of Book 6. What has he been telling, if not the story about going "beyond / All reasonable bounds"? Here at the book's end, he appeals to the stratagem to which he resorted earlier, attempting to put a pious "front" or face on the poem and to make it a readable, "written" text. Yet this stratagem may simply be a defensive gesture performed by someone who, like "innocent Sleep," is deafened by his own imagination, again represented as the confluence of streams: "whate'er / I saw, or heard, or felt, was but a stream / That flowed into a kindred stream, a gale / That helped me forwards" (672–75). Whatever leads him "To grandeur and to tenderness" (676) does so, he finally admits, "along a path / Which in the main was more circuitous" (679–80); errancy gets the last word.

Although Wordsworth allows Book 6 to close in this way, he cannot allow *The Prelude* as a whole to do so. No matter how seductive hyperbolic romance may be, he seems bent on pacifying its tumultuous energies. When the end of the poem approaches, he attempts to bring his errant journey to its proper destination by reconfiguring the delugic sequences of Books 5 and 6 in the episode of the ascent of Snowdon (13.1–119). In this case, errancy redounds to his advantage; in a precise reversal of the Simplon episode, where he misses his destination by having unknowingly reached it, he reaches an unintended destination (the vision of the moon above the mist) by missing what he went to see, "the sun / Rise from the top of Snowdon" (4–5). In a reversal of the second night's misadventure along Lake Locarno, the moon's untimely appearance in place of the dawn could scarcely be more timely. Moreover, by departing from the guide, "our tried Pilot" (15), by setting out on his own and becoming "the foremost of the Band" (35), he does not lose his way but finds his proper path again.

The cumulative effect of these reversals is to relieve the traveler of the burden of errancy and implicitly to undo those events that threaten to dismember culture. Somehow, he "break[s] through" the "cloud" of bafflement as he steps out of the mist and regains the "light of sense" in the sort of "flash" that once put it out (13.39–40; 6.535). The usurping, un-fathered vapor that thwarted him now appears before him as a literal, exter-nal spectacle—a "huge sea of mist," a silent, "still Ocean," that no longer usurps upon him but upon the "real Sea" "as far as sight could reach" (43, 46, 49, 51). Standing at the "shore" of that sea, "Which, meek and silent, rested at my feet" (42, 44), he survives the deluge, whose waters are too subdued to threaten him any further. The Arab's quest is over, for the boundary between land and sea, self and imagination, is restored. No longer within the landscape, no longer subject to a nameless, hostile gaze, Wordsworth can now gaze around upon the creation like a latter-day Noah to see what else has escaped inundation ("A hundred hills their dusky backs upheaved / All over this still Ocean" [45–46]).[24] Protected from the over-whelming effects of natural imagery, he can see and hear with delight the literalizations of imagination that threatened him during those Alpine nights: the moon, neither serpentine nor in danger of suddenly disap-pearing, "looked down upon this shew / In single glory" (52–53), and the aural confluence of far more than two streams ("torrents, streams / Innu-merable"), rising through "a fracture in the vapour, / A deep and gloomy breathing-place," no longer deafens him with its "roar of waters" (56–59).

It is as if he can watch and listen to the deluge from a safe distance and contemplate from above the "hollow rent" in nature through which he once journeyed (6.559): "in that breach / Through which the homeless voice of waters rose, / That dark deep thoroughfare, had Nature lodged / The Soul, the Imagination of the whole" (62–65). Once again the soul-imagination (cf. 6.525, 531) broods in darkness, and its home or lodging is in homelessness, but now the Wordsworthian traveler is neither homeless nor in darkness because he has escaped that breach and no longer fears that he will be broken himself.

In the Snowdon passage, then, Wordsworth conserves and yet subtly contains the poetics of errancy. Here again the deluge inundates the mountains, as if it is about to produce another Gorge of Gondo and to disfigure the text of nature in an act that is both/neither creation and/nor destruction. But from its delugic expenditure of itself, nature keeps something in reserve. However deep the breach or wide the rent, however vast the sea that drowns the world, creation survives intact. It is not, after all, entirely identical with its destruction. As a result, it provides enough of a space from which one can witness and interpret hyperbolic disruption in peace. Standing on the shore of imagination, the Wordsworthian traveler becomes its privileged spectator, using the authority of his stance to read the lineaments of the mistscape as an allegory of a "mighty Mind" (69) and thereby subsume errancy within a discourse of knowledge. No longer overmastered by imagination, he masters it in this reading, attributing it not to the usurping abyss of his own mind but to that of another mind which is "the express / Resemblance," the "genuine Counterpart / And Brother" of "higher minds" (86–90), in this way drawing a boundary between himself and what thwarts him while still claiming that the latter somehow resembles a power within himself.

By reading the mistscape as another mind, Wordsworth verges upon making it into a metaphor or symbol. Perhaps he flirts with the Kantian sublime, transforming a baffling landscape into an emblem of supersensible reason with which he identifies himself. Or, perhaps, by locating himself upon a secure shore, he finally turns the threshold into a boundary against the waters and takes refuge in the rainbow covenant, to which, as we have seen, he refers in the "analogy passage" that follows in the first draft of this episode. But the scene is an "image" of the mind, not its symbol; it is its "express / Resemblance," not its substitute. Still an unfather, it is the mind's "Brother," its "Counterpart" or equal, rather than a power to which it must submit. Moreover, the traveler has neither entirely crossed the boundary onto dry land nor completely distinguished himself from what he sees: "and we stood, the mist / Touching our very feet" (53–54). No God intervenes to subject land and sea to his will; rather, one suspects that both traveler and mighty Mind are "exalted by an underpresence, / The sense of God, or whatso'er is dim / Or vast in its own being" (71–73). Rather than the anchor of a transcendental reason or the ground of the symbolic order, God is still what exalts or moves the mind, something it senses in itself or in the phenomenal world.

As a visible counterpart of the mind which is not truly different from it, the scene at Snowdon is the mirror image of the mind, its specular resemblance. This scene shows how higher minds can make the world a mirror of themselves: "They from their native selves can send abroad / Like transformations, for themselves create / A like existence" (93–95). In the Snowdon episode, Wordsworth rewrites the encounter episodes on a grand scale, subsuming various specters, undistinguishable mists, and unfathered vapors into its vast sea. But the anxious indeterminacies of those encounters never unsettle this episode; the scene is an image not of Wordsworth's own mind but of the faculty of higher minds generally. Avoiding the autobiographical first person singular, he modulates into the third person, assembling around this mighty Mind a kind of loose brotherhood of similar minds. As in the poems of spring 1798, he undoes the dangerous consequences of the imaginary without reestablishing the symbolic order. The result once again is a strangely fractured community of solitaries, each of which, like the old beggar or pedlar, possesses a privileged relation to God or nature—"Such minds are truly from the Deity" (106)—and an amazing exemption from normal human fears: "Hence sovereignty within and peace at will"; "Hence chearfulness in every act of life" (114, 117). The Snowdon episode so thoroughly tames the errancies of *The Prelude* that it enables the poem to modulate into another version of the pedlar's biography. Like the eye of nature, a certain hypostasized "Power" (84) in nature subsumes images, potentially duplicitous and captivating *objets a*, into its own nonfigural language: it "So moulds them, and endues, abstracts, combines," or "Doth make one object so impress itself / Upon all others, and pervade them so, / That even the grossest minds must see and hear / And cannot chuse but feel" (79, 81–84). Here, as before, Wordsworth's idealizations are so excessive that they point directly to what they would negate, showing that despite his best efforts the Snowdon episode makes sense only in relation to the extravagance it attempts to tame.

In bringing the poem to a close, Wordsworth finds it necessary to contain the problem of errancy which he variously celebrates and resists throughout. Ironically, he transforms *The Prelude* into another version of the very *Recluse* texts it exploded when it first emerged as the two-part poem of 1798–99. Attributing imagination not to himself but to that external agency, he reverses the tendency to find in error the source of his powers and thus limits many of the claims of this poem, especially his sense that certain severer interventions (such as cultural disaster) made him a poet. This gesture demonstrates that he still longs to write a secular theodicy, that on some level he wishes not to write in the mode of hyperbole but to find a secure home. In short, it makes legible the strand of *The Prelude* which is hostile to errancy, which consistently apologizes for extravagant formulations, and which attempts to tame the imagination. Despite his tentative celebrations of hyperbolic romance, Wordsworth gives anti-romance the last word.

EIGHT

A Mockery of History

Unreadable Revolution

۶ۻ If the event that initially precipitated Wordsworth's fears of the dis-memberment of culture was the outbreak of war in 1793, as I argued in Chapter One, then it is no surprise that the poet of *The Prelude* regards the entire cluster of events surrounding the French Revolution as somehow impossible to capture within the framework of any conventional discourse. Alan Liu demonstrates that in the course of Books 9 and 10 Wordsworth narrates his memory of those events in a wide variety of genres, including the tour, romance, drama, Miltonic epic, and the epitaph (*Wordsworth* 362–87). Through the "overall accumulation of genres," the "excess of shapes," he foregrounds what remains for him the irreducible "shapelessness" of the revolution (365). Even in 1804, after a decade has passed, he still holds that the revolution escapes the familiar conventions by which a society attempts to describe or narrate its own past. It is unreadable and thus, on some level, unwritable.

Liu argues that this insistence upon the revolution's inscrutability serves the purposes of an Orphic self that wishes to efface its participation in history (365–66). But Wordsworth is not alone in grappling with the revolution in this way. In fact, the generic sequence of the books on France closely resembles the succession of genres that dominated political discourse in France during the years of political turmoil. According to Lynn Hunt, initially the revolution interpreted itself as an instance of comedy, in which a new social order wins out over an old one to which it is at last reconciled. The Festival of Federation on July 14, 1790 best exemplifies this comic rhetoric, for it staged the king's acceptance of the revolution and the people's reconciliation with him. In the second phase, from around 1792 on, a more radical revolution appropriated the rhetoric of quest-romance to describe its heroic struggle against the villainous forces of the counterrevolution. By choosing for her example a militant speech in the Convention,

Hunt suggests that this rhetoric flourished in public oratory, perhaps in the martial crusading of the Brissotin Girondins who, as Simon Schama remarks, constituted "a battery of orators the like of which had never before been heard together in one room and certainly not in France" (Schama 583). In the next phase, through 1793 and 1794, the obsession with counterrevolutionary plots grew into a full-fledged rhetoric of tragedy. By that time, radicals made a habit of accusing people of every description of forming plots against the regime, and Robespierre, taking this rhetoric as far as it would go, offered himself as a sacrificial victim of the immense forces arrayed against the French nation (Hunt 34–40).[1]

Wordsworth not only follows this sequence in his account of the revolution but also makes the specifically generic characteristics of each phase of the revolution explicit. In Book 6.332–425, he writes of how, landing "at Calais on the very eve / Of that great federal Day" of July 14, 1790, he wended his way through a joyously reborn and festive France, where "benevolence and blessedness / Spread like a fragrance everywhere, like Spring / That leaves no corner of the land untouched" (356–57, 368–70). All of France seemed to be celebrating a kind of May Day festival, dancing and dancing again those "Dances of liberty" (381) in which he and his companion, as honored Englishmen, were welcome participants (406–13), in this way celebrating the marriage of king and people, "the great Spousals newly solemnized / At their chief City, in the sight of Heaven" (396–97). Official fete blends into the rural, nearly pagan Bacchic festival and into the comic plot of reconciliation and marriage.[2] When Wordsworth next returns to developments in France in Book 9, he describes the revolutionary warriors of mid 1792, those brave youths who part from their loves and go to war "with a martyr's confidence" (280), as figures from romance. The personification of the French soldier, Michel Beaupuy, is a latter-day version of Chaucer's meek, sweet Knight (Roe 57–58), someone who wandered through events "As through a Book, an old Romance or Tale / Of Fairy, or some dream of actions wrought / Behind the summer clouds" (307–9), someone who transforms chivalry toward women into a love for "the mean and the obscure" (314) and the discourses of civic republicanism into the enchanting, Platonic voice of "philosophic war" (423).[3] Finally, in Book 10 Wordsworth turns his notes to tragic, bringing the September Massacres into the orbit of *Macbeth*, capturing the rhetoric of accusation in the Louvet episode (10.83–103), and descending into the violence of war and the Terror.

By displaying the literary dimensions of revolutionary discourse so openly, Wordsworth directly anticipates Hunt's analysis. Rather than being caught up in a shapeless eagerness, as Liu implies, he in fact demonstrates that the revolution could never arrive at a definitive narrative interpretation of itself and continued to transform itself over the years. The shapelessness of these books of *The Prelude* is evidence not of the poet's evasion of history but rather of history's resistance to generic categories. No doubt Hayden White is correct in arguing that historians inevitably shape historical narrative along the lines of traditional genres (such as romance, comedy, tragedy, or satire).[4] But if narratives of differing genres can be convincing and societies in the midst of change can rapidly modify the narratives to which they appeal, then history has no intrinsic generic shape of its own. As Louis O. Mink argues, the narrative form and significance of history are not there for us to discover but are rather something that we construct. What Wordsworth captures in the books on France is the chaotic experience of living through a historical moment that, by taking on the shape of too many genres, finally escapes them all.

Wordsworth's account of the resistance of lived history to historical narrative takes his readers back to familiar territory. Insofar as narrative gives events a shape and creates out of them a system of differences and a world of significance, it is an agent of the symbolic order. To get from a purely phenomenal world to the world of narrative, one must cross the threshold of representation. Conversely, a historical experience that never arrives at generic coherence will be caught on the threshold of the symbolic in the space of excess which effaces the difference between comedy and tragedy, heroic romance and nightmarish wandering.

At first Wordsworth writes the revolution's excess as his own hyperbolic condition of being out of place in France. Although the festive French welcomed him and his companion almost as joyously as Abraham welcomed the angels (6.403–4), the youth of 1790 kept his distance, glad that the church spires and the gently flowing Rhone spoke to him "with a sense of peace" amidst the "boisterous Crew" with whom he traveled (6.419–20). On his next arrival in France, he was more disoriented: he "had abruptly passed / Into a theatre, of which the stage / Was busy with an action far advanced" (9.93–95). He explains this in part as an effect of his own ignorance; he "had read, and eagerly / Sometimes, the master Pamphlets of the day" (9.96–97), but because he had not seen

> a regular Chronicle
> (If any such indeed existed then)
> Whence the main Organs of the public Power
> Had sprung, their transmigrations when and how
> Accomplished, giving thus unto events
> A form and body, all things were to me

Loose and disjointed, and the affections left
Without a vital interest. (9.101–8)

For a moment he assumed that things were incomprehensible only to him,
for anyone who had been on the scene as events were occurring would understand them well enough. What he needed was a substitute for experience, a chronicle that would represent recent events and give the nation a
form and body comprehensible to outsiders. But he knew of none, and
perhaps there was none. In the absence of such a tale of origins which
would gather the public "Organs" into a body politic, things remained
"loose and disjointed," as if that body were alienated from itself. Possessing
only "half-insight" into events (98), left "without a vital interest," this wanderer resembles the physically bizarre discharged soldier, who speaks with
"a strange half-absence and a tone / Of weakness and indifference, as of
one / Remembering the importance of his theme, / But feeling it no
longer" ("Soldier" 143–46).

But this scenario of displacement masks the more radical displacement of French society generally. After all, earlier in the passage Wordsworth writes that in his ignorance he

                   scarcely felt
The shock of these concussions, unconcerned,
Tranquil almost, and careless as a flower
Glassed in a Green-house, or a Parlour shrub,
When every bush and tree, the country through,
Is shaking to the roots. (86–91)

The revolution was an earthquake, a geological cataclysm (Bewell 250–51),
a site where nature destroyed itself, where the body politic was itself disjointed, where the drama lost its way in nonsense. Oddly enough, this
stranger fit right in, for no one comprehended the situation any better than
he. In the hidden logic of this passage, a regular chronicle of events was
impossible because events were too irregular to be captured in a narrative;
things were caught on the threshold between the literal and the figurative,
the lived and the written. To arrive at a regular narrative one would first
have to reestablish the social order on secure ground and gather the joints
and organs together into a body politic. The absence of a chronicle, then,
marked the absence of a power that could substitute itself for the nation in
the same way that a narrative would for the nation's history. Of course, a
wide array of factions rushed into this void and competed to gain power
through the pamphlets that Wordsworth mentions. But because none of
them had yet succeeded, the best one could hope for were *master* pam-

phlets, which, having won out over their minor competitors, articulated various semiofficial positions.

In this passage Wordsworth describes a society without a body, a shared experience that cannot articulate itself, a story without shape or meaning. Strangely enough, France begins to resemble the subject that, stripped of the name of the father, represents itself at best through the autobiographical account of its unique development. Of course, such a representation would be provisional and incomplete; any history of the revolution published in 1792 would, like autobiography, impose an artificial closure upon an experience (a history, a life) that had not yet come to an end. But even this provisional account is lacking. Much as Wordsworth writes the self in the 1799 *Prelude* as something that takes shape not through autobiographical development but rather through deviant, anxious pleasures, here he conceives of lived history as the utter disfigurement of any script that would predict how the "action far advanced" might end (95). For him lived history, like autobiography, is the pure disruption of narrative.

The various hints concerning history scattered in this passage emerge much more forcefully in the following section upon the royalist officer (9.127–83), who is a particularly spectacular instance of displacement:

> his port,
> Which once had been erect and open, now
> Was stooping and contracted, and a face,
> By nature lovely in itself, expressed,
> As much as any that was ever seen,
> A ravage out of season, made by thoughts
> Unhealthy and vexatious. At the hour,
> The most important of each day, in which
> The public News was read, the fever came,
> A punctual visitant, to shake this Man,
> Disarmed his voice, and fanned his yellow cheek
> Into a thousand colours; while he read,
> Or mused, his sword was haunted by his touch
> Continually, like an uneasy place
> In his own body. (9.150–64)

The officer is a compendium of the vexed characters of *The Ruined Cottage* and related texts: like Robert and the young pedlar, he is unseasonable, out of place, restless; like the young pedlar and Margaret, he is utterly captivated by what he reads; and like Margaret in the later stages of her decay, he is disfigured and wasted by anxiety. With a greater longing than the disaffected young Wordsworth, he awaits the daily news, which does not clarify the shape of current events but rather agitates him further and increases his suspense. Moreover, like the speaker of "The Thorn" and the child of the 1799 *Prelude,* he apparently derives great pleasure from the prospect of his own destruction. Playing with his sword as if it were a place in his own body, the officer takes a kind of masturbatory pleasure in his anxiety (cf. Mileur *Romance* 67–69). One might think that he touches his weapon to reassure himself that it is still there, that he has not been symbolically castrated. But it is more likely that in a reprise of a familiar masochistic scenario he plays with his sword/penis because, like the child of the stolen boat episode, he takes a very "troubled pleasure" (1799 *Prelude* 1.91) in the thought that it might *not* be there. The pleasure would not be as intense or as physically wasting were he not so overwhelmed with fear, nor would the fear obsess him so much were it not so pleasurable.

Although the royalist officer reminds one of other Wordsworthian figures, he is finally a more outrageous character than any of them. Whereas the speaker of "The Thorn" or the perverse child of Part One attempts to master a largely personal wound through masochistic fantasies, this officer takes his pleasure from the crisis of an entire nation. He sexualizes cultural dismemberment itself. In fact, by means of his fevered fantasy, he registers the rending of the body politic on his own body, its defacement upon his face. Moving directly from his description of the officer to that of the contemporary political crisis, Wordsworth suggests that this man embodies the febrile condition of France:

> 'Twas in truth an hour
> Of universal ferment; mildest men
> Were agitated; and commotions, strife
> Of passion and opinion filled the walls
> Of peaceful houses with unquiet sounds.
> The soil of common life was at that time
> Too hot to tread upon. (164–70)

Everyone is agitated, uneasy, feverish; everyone is out of place, even in formerly quiet homes; even the earth is overheated, preparing to burst forth, through the words of radicals like Carra and Gorsas, in "earthquakes, shocks repeated day by day, / And felt through every nook of town and field" (179, 182–83). Whether royalist or radical, whether in town or in field, everyone is shocked by the spectacle of France's dissolution. But the officer's anxiety also mirrors the nation's undeniable fascination with that spectacle, its pleasure in suffering what it dreads, its desire to hasten and intensify the conflict rather than resolve it (cf. 189–91). In effect, Wordsworth hints at something he will state more explicitly later: that the French body politic unconsciously longed for its dismemberment and at some point was more inspired by masochistic revenge than by the calculations of political reason.

The spectacle of the royalist officer's distemper and the general strife that it embodies prompts Wordsworth to make an explicit statement about written history. If France is indeed a disease, an earthquake, a haunted and masochistic wreck, then it is also the very emblem of what deviates from narrative and confounds representation. Abandoning his wish to possess a regular chronicle, the young Wordsworth concludes that no written history could possibly do justice to his experience of France. But this point immediately gives way to the much more radical claim that no historical narrative does justice to history as it is lived:

> The soil of life was at that time
> Too hot to tread upon; oft said I then,
> And not then only, "what a mockery this
> Of history, the past and that to come!
> Now do I feel how I have been deceived,
> Reading of Nations and their works, in faith,
> Faith given to vanity and emptiness;
> Oh! laughter for the Page that would reflect
> To future times the face of what now is!" (169–77)

If words cannot capture his experience, the poet reasons, then they must always fail. No page can reflect, as in a mirror, the face of what now is because, as the context of the previous passage on the absent chronicle suggests, no narrative can capture the experience of living through a historical crisis in which that retrospective narrative itself is absent. Such an experience is suspended between the familiar generic categories of narrative history, much as the royalist officer awaits the news with feverish uncertainty; everything is indeterminate, capable at any time of undergoing radical "transmigrations" (9.104) or metamorphoses. The "public News," which in the Preface to *Lyrical Ballads* Wordsworth calls "the rapid communication of intelligence" (Gill 599), is the Romantic antigenre *par excellence*, for it puts history's unmasterable volatility into textual form and thereby becomes the focal point for the anxiety of history—the anxiety, which all of us in historical cultures necessarily share, of living in the midst of an unfinished and generically indeterminate tale.

This suspension on the threshold of narrative representation bears directly upon the question of the historical reference of these texts. Recent historicist criticism of Wordsworth has attempted to saturate his texts in the referential field of contemporary events, reading *The Borderers* in light of the rise of illegitimacy rates in England or the Intimations Ode in the context of the Peace of Amiens (Liu *Wordsworth* 225–310; Levinson 80–100). But these passages in *The Prelude* suggest that there are no literally historical events or purely referential facts; such things become significant only when they have been interpreted, narrated, or otherwise represented. Ironically enough, then, the closer one comes to historical actuality, which often moves more quickly than the discourses that would interpret it or, in moments of crisis, exceeds all previous modes of understanding, the less knowable history becomes; it is no longer clear which events are significant, what direction they are taking, or in their context what socially inflected actions might mean. Wordsworth apparently believes that a society in the midst of crisis may be so transported in the delirium of its metamorphosis that it loses track of its referential ground. Like the anxious man who dreams of the world's end by the deluge, it may no longer know the difference between reality and illusion, itself and its own destruction, its past and future.

By repudiating historical narrative in favor of an experience it can never capture, Wordsworth apparently verges upon creating a new and irreducible reference point. He seems to suggest that the experience of the world's undoing is so fabulously real, so shocking and unforgettable, that no page could possibly substitute for it. In that case, one might be tempted to argue that the experience described in this passage is the referential basis for his poetry. But it can serve as no such basis, for as an instance of the textual representation of history which the young man repudiates, it too is printed upon a laughable "'Page that would reflect / To future times the face of what now is'" (176–77), becoming a similar exercise in vanity and emptiness (175). As a result, even history as an unmediated domain of lived experience disappears into the abyss, beyond the historian's reach. Merely by writing in this way, however, Wordsworth ends up representing the impossibility of representation. By representing his failure to represent history, he represents history. It seems that history is present where it is absent and absent where present, according to a logic long since familiar in these texts. Much like the uncanny poet of the Goslar *Prelude,* this laughable historian writes from a phantom space between genres, reflecting in the scenes of the historical past, as in those of his youth, only disfigured faces.

Rather than providing a new basis for or an alternative to articulation in an essentialized present, historical experience disarticulates the written text, rendering it into a set of Protean "characters / Of danger and desire." The logic of these passages on the utter disruption of narrative in Book 9 leads readily to the passage early in Book 10 concerning the September Massacres, in which history appears unreadable:

I crossed (a blank and empty area then)
The Square of the Carousel, few weeks back
Heaped up with dead and dying, upon these
And other sights looking as doth a man
Upon a volume whose contents he knows
Are memorable, but from him locked up,
Being written in a tongue he cannot read,
So that he questions the mute leaves with pain
And half upbraids their silence. (10.46–54)

The absent chronicle has become a locked book, the laughable page a gathering of mute leaves. The echoes begin to multiply; like the dreamer of Book 5, this traveler struggles to understand a message in an unknown tongue, or, like the tourist in the Cave of Yordas, to make sense of a scene that refuses to become as legible as a written book (8.727). Moreover, this site of violence, of the absent yet strangely present bodies of the "dead and dying," is in "a blank and empty area" akin to another waste where the traveler hallucinates a vision of the ghostly return of the dead and the pain of the dying.[5]

These echoes suggest that for Wordsworth the disarticulation of the historical text and the violence of the revolution inscribe within their respective registers a general condition of cultural dismemberment. Before long, the scene of unreadability expands into a full-fledged rehearsal of a familiar Wordsworthian drama. Having retreated from the square, the traveler attempts to calm his anxieties by reading, but here as early in Book 5, solitary reading only intensifies anxiety; fears for the world soon become a hallucination of the world's end:

With unextinguished taper I kept watch,
Reading at intervals. The fear gone by
Pressed on me almost like a fear to come.
I thought of those September Massacres,
Divided from me by a little month,
And felt and touched them, a substantial dread;
The rest was conjured up from tragic fictions,
And mournful Calendars of true history,
Remembrances and dim admonishments.
"The horse is taught his manage, and the wind

Of heaven wheels round and treads in his own steps,
Year follows year, the tide returns again,
Day follows day, all things have second birth;
The earthquake is not satisfied at once."
And in such way I wrought upon myself,
Until I seemed to hear a voice that cried,
To the whole City, "Sleep no more." (10.61–77)

Here the traveler manages to translate the unknown tongue into a prophecy of destruction by geological cataclysm (5.94, 87). Truly reading "at intervals," he places himself between "The fear gone by" and "a fear to come" that it strongly resembles, dreading an event that is both/neither before and/nor after—an event, it appears, which does not destroy nature but, like the returning days and years, follows the rhythm of nature's nonsignificative repetition, the carousel of its redundant energy (MS. JJ 4).[6] In short, he converts unreadability into sensationalist reading, "conjuring" up (around midnight) an apocalyptic fantasy out of an odd assortment of elements. This youth takes over for the royalist officer with whom, evidently, he identified earlier; while reading, he too "wrought upon" himself and "felt and touched" a "substantial dread," managing to make that homeless place one not "wholly without pleasure" (75, 66, 60).

Interpreters of this passage have emphasized its invocation of Shakespeare in the curious lines on the returning earthquake and in the culminating allusion to *Macbeth* ("Methought, I heard a voice cry, 'Sleep no more! / Macbeth does murther sleep'" [2.2.34–35]) and, as I mentioned above, to argue that here Wordsworth enters the domain of tragedy (Liu *Wordsworth* 377; Jacobus *Romanticism* 40–42). But the context of these allusions suggests that he absorbs Shakespeare, as elsewhere he absorbs Cervantes or Enlightenment philosophy, into a masochistic scenario largely of his own making. The drama of regicide which preoccupies him in his "high and lonely" room (10.57) above the square evokes the fantasy of parricide and punishment which the witchlike child conjured up on "the highest summit" (1799 *Prelude* 1.341) over another crossroads, not to mention the unfathered strength that came athwart him on the Alpine heights. Here again he attempts to retreat from the unreadable "Characters of the great Apocalypse" (6.570) into "a large Mansion or Hotel" (10.58) which, because of its proximity to the crossroads of violence (cf. the "confluence of two Streams," 6.576), fails to shelter him: "at the best it seemed a place of fear, / Unfit for the repose of night, / Defenceless as a wood where tigers roam" (10.80–82; cf. Armstrong 36; Liu *Wordsworth* 33–34).

The implications of these echoes are unsettling. Jacobus suggests that through this appeal to poetry Wordsworth distances himself from a threat-eningly real violence and manages to repress and sublimate his fear (*Romanticism* 41–42). But he goes further; as I mentioned above, he hints that through his conjuring, he makes the memory and prospect of violence into a source of pleasure (10.60). He does so by means of a masochistic logic familiar to us from his earlier texts. In the spots of time, Wordsworth admits that he wished for his father's death, and in the Alpine sequence he recognizes the unfathered, usurping power of the imagination as his own. In both cases he attempts to master a chance event—his father's death, a missed crossing—by claiming that he somehow intended it, by willing precisely what threatens him the most. He makes a similar claim here, al-though less directly. When he hallucinates the night cry, he identifies him-self as another Macbeth who, in a frenzy of guilt, imagines that all the world now knows of his deed. He thus takes responsibility for the Septem-ber Massacres and for the regicide to come, fantasizing that he too has murdered sleep, unleashed the tigers, and created the homelessness he now suffers. He distances himself from the threat of an inexplicable violence not by repressing it but by embracing it as his own, as its perpetrator and poten-tial victim.[7] He "reads" the unreadable volume by imagining that he inten-tionally vandalized it and finds a part to play in the "disjointed" and incom-plete drama of the revolution (9.107, 93–95) by casting himself in the role of regicide, the one who assaults the most visible embodiment of the sym-bolic order.

By finding in this text of violence the shape of Shakespearean tragedy, as he did in the spots of time, Wordsworth refashions his masochistic fan-tasy, depicting himself at once as the murderer of sleep and an insomniac, a regicide and one who fears for the king. The unreadable text slides quickly into the aggressive relations of the Lacanian imaginary, in which the poet is his own mortal enemy. The preternatural denunciation he calls down upon his own head he soon directs against another: Robespierre, the true regicide (cf. Jacobus 43). He can hardly wait to begin his case against the famous Jacobin; in the very next lines he recounts how Louvet alone dared accuse Robespierre of seeking absolute power (10.83–103). This con-frontation of two men, each set apart from his peers, exemplifies the specu-lar character of what Hunt calls the *rhetoric of conspiracy*. According to Wordsworth, Louvet "walked singly through the avenue / And took his station in the Tribune" (98–99), as if to look Robespierre in the face; but in this gesture he took the risk of conflating himself with his enemy, phrasing his denunciation in such a way as to suggest that he himself were Robes-pierre: "'I, Robespierre, accuse thee!'" (100). Is Robespierre the subject or the object of this sentence? Is he master or victim of the discourse of accu-

sation generally?[8] Perhaps Louvet is merely aping Robespierre's own manner of accusation by denouncing him in turn. Here, as in Girard's sacrificial
crisis, the accuser cannot distinguish himself from the accused (*Violence*
47). That sentence merely puts into grammatical form the overall undecid-
ability of social relations during the reign of the rhetoric of conspiracy.

This specular quality dominates in the following extended section, in
which Wordsworth recounts how fervently he wished that "one paramount
mind" would arise to contend with those in power in France—by implication, Robespierre—and to clear "a passage for just government" there
(10.179, 185). The emphasis on the power of "single persons" (138) owes
much to Milton's individualist politics, but it also allows Wordsworth to
imagine a heroic counterpart to Robespierre, one who resembles him so
closely that he is virtually his double. The masochistic fantasy that allows
him to take the blame for the massacres and regicide gives way to a fantasy
straight out of the Lacanian imaginary, in which he becomes Anti-
Robespierre, the liberator of France.[9] Despite his status as "An insignificant
Stranger" devoid of eloquence (130–32), he would "willingly have taken up /
A service at this time for cause so great, / However dangerous" (134–36),
offering himself for the good of the country in the manner of his archen-
emy. Moreover, he would have justified his bid for power with arguments
that, however Girondin in spirit, are barely distinguishable from those of
the Jacobins—by appealing to the "Spirit thoroughly faithful to itself, /
Unquenchable, unsleeping, undismayed, / [which] Was as an instinct
among men" (147–49) and by demonstrating from classical precedent "that
tyrannic Power is weak" and can fall at a single blow (see 158–75).[10] In short,
he aspired to a version of the absolute power denounced by Louvet in order
to carry out a project that, in this formulation, is identical with Robespierre's: to quell "Outrage and bloody power" and to create a new state in
the teeth of opposition from within and without (see 176–88). This fantasy
exemplifies how easily opposition to such power, already based upon the
denunciation of power, merely reproduces it; the Robespierre he opposes is
his own alienated, rival self.

Although Wordsworth introduces this section with a suggestion of
indeterminacy in the Louvet episode, for the most part he stabilizes the
imaginary according to a moral dualism, a contrast between good and evil
rulers. Recoiling from the massacres and from the possibility that he resembles Robespierre, he denies the merest hint of complicity in revolutionary violence: "from such thought / And the least fear about the end of
things, / I was as far as Angels are from guilt" (125–27). The situation in
France becomes readable, perhaps far too readable, in the light of the the-

ory of the paramount mind to which the poet adheres even in 1804 ("Creed which ten shameful years have not annulled" [178]). Apparently, the subtle strategies he deploys in earlier episodes allow him to keep alive his sense of innocence; he merely witnessed another nation's drama, was moved by its anxieties, and was stirred to a literary fantasy by its disasters. But when he begins to recount his response to the outbreak of war between England and France, when he is faced with the memory of how both nations betrayed his hopes and robbed him of a sure basis for enlightened political discourse, unreadable excess finally shatters his moral complacency and implicates him in a hyperbolic condition from which he cannot escape.

At this point unreadability ceases to be the object of the poet's thematic meditations and becomes the mode of the poem itself, which Wordsworth now abandons without disguise to the poetics of errancy. The tropes that generate many previous texts—such as errancy and spectacular violence (*Salisbury Plain*), masochistic fantasy ("The Thorn"), and the both/neither structure of duplicity (the Arab dream)—appear directly in their own right, stripped of the web of implications and complications which usually surrounds them. The entire enterprise of reading or writing texts collapses into a few irreducibly hyperbolic terms. His moral revolution, Wordsworth writes in a passage I discussed in Chapter One, was a "stride at once / Into another region" (10.240–41); it created a most unnatural strife of self-division in his heart (250–51); and it severed him from his ground in the English nation "And tossed [him] about in whirlwinds" (257–58). Moreover, at one point it prompted a vengeful fantasy that Wordsworth renders more clearly than ever:

> I rejoiced
> Yea, afterwards, truth painful to record!
> Exulted in the triumph of my soul
> When Englishmen by thousands were o'erthrown,
> Left without glory on the Field, or driven,
> Brave hearts, to shameful flight. It was a grief,
> Grief call it not, 'twas anything but that,
> A conflict of sensations without name,
> Of which he only who may love the sight
> Of a Village Steeple as I do can judge,
> When in the Congregation, bending all
> To their great Father, prayers were offered up
> Or praises for our Country's Victories,
> And 'mid the simple worshippers, perchance,

I only, like an uninvited Guest
Whom no one owned sate silent, shall I add,
Fed on the day of vengeance yet to come! (258–74)

The youth exults in what also grieves him (and pains him even as he writes); where others pray, he in effect curses his country, as if he is another Goody Blake; and in a demonic parody of the Eucharist, he feeds with pleasure on the slaughter of his own countrymen. He fervently hopes to avenge himself on those who wounded him: "Oh! much have they to account for, who would tear / By violence at once decisive rent / From the best Youth in England their dear pride, / Their joy, in England" (275–78). Castrated and dismembered by England's rulers, he wishes to castrate in turn; deprived of his joy in England, he hopes to destroy England's pride in itself. To confirm his love, he tries to destroy what betrayed him.

The conflicted pleasures of this fantasy, Wordsworth suggests, follow the duplicitous logic of hyperbolic excess:

this, too, at a time
In which worst losses easily might wear
The best of names, when patriotic love
Did of itself in modesty give away
Like the Precursor when the Deity
Is come, whose Harbinger he is, a time
In which apostacy from ancient faith
Seemed but conversion to a higher creed. (278–85)

In straying from his proper path, Wordsworth may have taken the true one; in losing his joy in England, he may have gained a better; in plotting vengeance in the midst of his own congregation, he may have joined a higher faith. Wearing the names of both castration and transport, apostasy and conversion, violent excess is, like masochistic fantasy, "a conflict of sensations without name" (265), a whirlwind of duplicity.

Such fabulous disorientation, however, can become a source of pleasure, as the passages on the royalist officer and the September Massacres demonstrate. What Wordsworth only hinted at before he writes openly here. In an especially scandalous passage, he suggests that the Reign of Terror arose from the attempt to intensify the strange pleasures of disorientation. The Terrorists, he writes,

found their joy
They made it, ever thirsty, as a Child,
If light desires of innocent little Ones
May with such heinous appetites be matched,

Having a toy, a wind-mill, though the air
Do of itself blow fresh, and makes the vane
Spin in his eyesight, he is not content,
But with the play-thing at arm's length he sets
His front against the blast, and runs amain,
To make it whirl the faster. (336–45)

Although Wordsworth attempts to separate heinous from innocent appetites, in this simile he in fact brings them closer together, as if to say that the Terrorists themselves were not so monstrous after all or that the "innocent little Ones" are much less innocent than they seem. As in the Note to "The Thorn," he naturalizes a sensationalism he wants to condemn, explaining the spectacle of inhuman excess as an effect of the constitutive perversity of desire. According to the Note, when our attempts to "communicate impassioned feelings" in language fail, we experience a "craving in the mind, and as long as it is unsatisfied the Speaker will cling to the same words, or words of the same character," and luxuriate in their repetition (Gill 594). In a similar manner, when the Terrorists cannot represent power adequately in a name, a narrative, or institutional authority, all of which are lost in the whirlwind of undecidable figuration, they cling to the whirlwind itself, luxuriating in its violent repetition ("Head after head, and never heads enough / For those who bade them fall" [335–36]). As in earlier texts, this violence tears apart the family, severing "the Old Man from the chimney-nook, / The Maiden from the bosom of her Love, / The Mother from the Cradle of her Babe, / The Warrior from the Field" (330–33); but this time the implication is stronger than ever that "Domestic carnage" (329) springs from the deviance of that infantile grief which, "Become an instinct, fastening on all things / That promise food, doth like a sucking babe / Create it where it is not" ("Incipient Madness" 9–11). The rival child of "Michael" returns here in a particularly "dangerous and wild" form (286), breaking up not merely the family of an old shepherd but an entire polity.

Although Wordsworth earlier identified with a figure who took a very troubled pleasure in France's dissolution, it seems he cannot do so here. If he wants to preserve his claim to innocence, he cannot read the Terror as an instance of imaginative excess. Yet as I have just argued, by comparing the Terrorists and the child, he implicates innocent desire itself in monstrous violence. On some level, desire cannot remain innocent; despite one's best attempts to uphold the moral law, the mind may cling to terror nevertheless. More importantly, however, under the pressure of such a trauma the "heinous appetites" of the mind may not remain faithful to pleasure, even to a troubled pleasure, but may fall under the sway of what

Freud calls the *death drive*.[11] Thus the poem gravitates toward those traumatic, "ghastly visions . . . of despair / And tyranny, and implements of death, / And long orations which in dreams I pleaded / Before unjust Tribunals" (374–77)—visions that, Wordsworth claims, disturbed his sleep for years after the Terror. The unreadable text of history now becomes unspeakable—an oration that the dreamer delivers "with a voice / Labouring" and a "brain confounded" (377–78).[12] It seems that an unintelligible extravagance has reached its limits, alienating the mind entirely from itself, or perhaps this is no longer extravagance at all but rather evidence of the mind's capacity to absorb the hostile forces that wound it most.

But here, as perhaps in Freud, the notion of traumatic anxiety wards off the more unsettling prospect that visions of destruction satisfy the pleasure principle itself.[13] This dark prospect arises in the course of an idealizing argument. Trying to put a positive spin to his ordeal, over the next two verse paragraphs Wordsworth constructs the broad claim that from the "heaviest sorrow earth can bring, / Griefs bitterest of ourselves or of our Kind," there can grow "a faith, / An elevation, and a sanctity" unknown before (423–27). At first one might think that he is revisiting the theme of the *Recluse* poems of early 1798 and arguing that through an excess of grief one can overcome grief; whoever allows heaviest sorrow to take its course will emerge purified and gain the peace of mind of the pedlar or the old beggar. However, lines earlier in this passage tell a different story:

> But as the ancient Prophets were enflamed
> Nor wanted consolations of their own
> And majesty of mind, when they denounced
> On Towns and Cities, wallowing in the abyss
> Of their offences, punishment to come;
> Or saw like other men with bodily eyes
> Before them in some desolated place
> The consummation of the wrath of Heaven;
> So did some portion of that spirit fall
> On me, to uphold me through those evil times,
> And in their rage and dog-day heat I found
> Something to glory in, as just and fit,
> And in the order of sublimest laws. (401–13)

Wordsworth claims that what upheld him through the evil times of the Terror was an ancient, almost divine anger. But this sounds less like rage directed against the Terror than the imagined rage of the monstrous Terrorists themselves. Who could have denounced the offenses of evildoers more thunderously than they? Who could have gloried more in a dog-day heat that claimed to be founded in the principles of universal justice and sublimest laws? Renaming the Terrorists *the ancient Prophets* allows Wordsworth to embrace a hyperbolic violence that he would otherwise repudiate. Indirectly he admits that there were personal consolations in the violence of the Terror, just as there were "When Englishmen by thousands were o'erthrown" (10.261). Having already fantasized that he carried out the September Massacres, the execution of Louis Capet, and—by the force of his curses—the defeat of the British armies, now he also imagines that some portion of the spirit of the Terrorists fell upon him.

Wordsworth survives those evil times not by resisting violence but by taking pleasure in it. Exploiting the both/neither indeterminacy of excess, he surmises that the cataclysmic destruction of the world must reveal the laws of a higher world; the dismemberment of culture must be sublime. With this stunning reversal of his reading of the Terror and, by extension, of all of the violence that traumatized him, he in effect declares that when the revolution rent his former self, it transformed him into a prophet, a chosen son. Only such an extraordinarily traumatic instance of error could give him such an extraordinary privilege. Inspired by this reversal, he rewrites the vision of horror in *Salisbury Plain,* suggesting that what he saw "with bodily eyes / Before [him] in some desolated place" was not human sacrifice but "The consummation of the wrath of Heaven." He also takes the logic of the Arab dream one more step; rather than merely listening as a voice prophecies the deluge that it immediately brings to pass, he becomes a prophet of cataclysm himself and immediately witnesses the day of judgment with his own eyes.[14]

However outrageous this passage, it does not violate the overall tenor of *The Prelude,* but rather mobilizes one of its familiar strategies in the context of historical crisis. Like the child of Part One of the 1799 *Prelude,* the young man of these passages is most stirred by what we could call the revolution's severer interventions, the "spectre shape[s] / Of terror" that erupt in the numerous accidents of Books 9 and 10 (1799 1.79; 5.472–73; 1799 1.280). Here again the poet is less likely to describe his former self as an upstanding citizen than a witch, a magus, a connoisseur of chaos. This resurgence of a severe poetics is so powerful that Wordsworth rewrites his anxiety dreams as a visionary episode, finding in those ghastly visions some intimations of grandeur:

> amid the awe
> Of unintelligible chastisement
> I felt a kind of sympathy with power,
> Motions raised up within me, nevertheless,

> Which had relationship to highest things.
> Wild blasts of music thus did find their way
> Into the midst of terrible events,
> So that worst tempests might be listened to. (414–21)

Like the death of his father, the Terror visits upon the young man a certain "chastisement" that he masters by listening, in a high place, to the "bleak music" of the tempest; like the punishing cliffhead of the stolen boat episode, which looms on high over the fearful child, it rouses him so much that certain powerful forms "moved slowly through [his] mind" and "were the trouble of [his] dreams" (1799 1.128–29). These ghastly visions are new versions of familiar dreams; even the sense "Of treachery and desertion in the place / The holiest that I knew of, my own soul" (10.379–80) revives the "solitude / Or blank desertion" (1799 1.123–24) that haunted him as a child and which he still associates with "highest things." Reinterpreted in this way, these visions are less anxiety dreams than fantasies of dismemberment which make the submerged longings of Part One dangerously explicit. "Unintelligible" violence becomes as thrilling as the sounds of undistinguishable motion which chased the thieving boy (1799 1.47–48) because it promises once again to subject Wordsworth to a pleasurably violent chastisement under the aegis of sublimest laws. In that case, perhaps the poet is as "enflamed" as the ancient prophets (10.401) because he himself is going up in flames, receiving upon his body "The consummation of the wrath of Heaven."

In this dense, neglected passage, Wordsworth combines the pleasures of destruction and victimization in a single full-fledged masochistic fantasy. The violence of the Terror allows him to unleash his rage against the world, but it also allows him to imagine the deadly pleasure of becoming the object of that rage. Far from being simply a Terrorist *manque,* a wild-eyed enthusiast of mass slaughter, he finds in violence a nameless conflict of sensations, a prophetic rage that is as likely to wound as to empower him, to render him speechless as to give him voice. Here again the fantasy of revenge yields a distinctly ambivalent pleasure; as Bersani would argue, the more one punishes what one loves, the more one punishes oneself (58). The perverse logic that Wordsworth followed in texts concerning the abandonment of children now organizes his interpretation of events surrounding the revolution. In his hands, these events become parts of a family drama: by going to war, England rends its children (10.276), who respond in the Terror by making the whirlwind whirl faster and rending the family even more (see 10.329–45).

Despite his resistance to the drift of his own text, Wordsworth nearly allows Book 10 to culminate in a celebration of the pleasures of extravagant violence. For a moment it seems that this book, like Part One of the 1799 *Prelude,* will stage its fierce energies in a scene of divination which strangely moves the poet even as its logic escapes his comprehension. Yet the sort of idealizations that surround the spots of time take on a defensive tone here. The memory of rage does not directly fill him with thoughts of highest things as much as it enables him to find something good in evil, some new strength in his affliction (428, 425). Moreover, insofar as this passage implicates him once again in revolutionary violence, he feels compelled, as after the passage on the September Massacres, to reestablish his innocence by blaming that violence upon the absolutely villainous Robespierre. Accordingly, this movement of the poem culminates instead in the extended section upon the news of Robespierre's death, which closes out Book 10 in the poem's final version (1850).[15] By repudiating violence in this way, Wordsworth also turns against a fully articulated masochistic fantasy and, on the broadest level, against the poetics of errancy.[16] It is as if the poet, having strayed further than ever from his proper path, must return to that path with a vengeance.

The result is a passage that flirts much more than usual with the classic strategies of power. Reversing the terms of his earlier works, the poet attempts to undo the dismemberment of culture and to envision in some limited way the return of the symbolic order. According to the "separate chronicle" of that especially happy day (see 466–71), Wordsworth had visited the grave of a beloved schoolteacher in the churchyard of Cartmell. Proceeding onward to the Leven Sands, he heard the news of Robespierre's death and burst forth into a hymn of joy:

> Great was my glee of spirit, great my joy
> In vengeance, and eternal justice, thus
> Made manifest. "Come now ye golden times,"
> Said I, forth-breathing on those open Sands
> A Hymn of triumph, "as the morning comes
> Out of the bosom of the night, come Ye:
> Thus far our trust is verified; behold!
> They who with clumsy desperation brought
> Rivers of Blood, and preached that nothing else
> Could cleanse the Augean Stable, by the might
> Of their own helper have been swept away;
> Their madness is declared and visible,

> Elsewhere will safety now be sought, and Earth
> March firmly towards righteousness and peace."
> Then schemes I framed more calmly, when and how
> The madding Factions might be tranquillised,
> And, though through hardships manifold and long
> The mighty renovation would proceed. (539–56)

The poet who not long before gloried in the rage and dog-day heat of the Terror blames it entirely on someone else. *They* caused the violence; it was *their* guillotine. Since they were dead, peace could come to all; those who remained, of course, were innocent. Here Wordsworth follows the Girardian logic whereby culture, threatened by a unanimous violence, chooses a surrogate victim who bears the blame for violence and sacrifices him in the name of eternal justice or divine law, thereby ousting violence by a more definitive and symbolic violence and bringing the sacrificial crisis to an end.[17] For him, the obvious victim of such a restoring sacrifice is Robespierre, the personification of the Terror, the Girardian monstrous double who brings madness to the land.

Of course, as David Erdman suggests, only someone who had "spent some time under the fascination and inspiration of [Robespierre's] ruthless leadership" (30) or, we might add, who wished to rival Robespierre in the task of liberating France, could rejoice at his death in such a manner. On some level, that event may have fulfilled Wordsworth's longing for personal vengeance against Robespierre and allowed him to claim undisputed victory over his imaginary rival (cf. J. Wordsworth *Borders* 256–57; Hopkins 124). Perhaps it even allowed him to indulge in the fantasy that he would take charge of the revolution and become the good liberator who could frame new schemes for the renovation of France. Yet the poet speaks of much more than a personal triumph in this passage. At least potentially, this event promises to bring an end to imaginary rivalry; although somewhat less directly than in archaic ritual systems, the death of one man promises to unify the madding factions into a single polity and to bring peace to a warring world.

In the context of Wordsworth's overall poetics, the healing of a dismembered culture has implications that reach far beyond the domain of politics per se. Somehow it has restored nature to itself as well:

> Upon a small
> And rocky Island near, a fragment stood
> (Itself like a sea rock) of what had been
> A Romish Chapel, where in ancient times
> Masses were said at the hour which suited those

Who crossed the Sands with ebb of morning tide.
Not far from this still Ruin all the Plain
Was spotted with a variegated crowd
Of Coaches, Wains, and Travellers, horse and foot,
Wading, beneath the conduct of their Guide
In loose procession through the shallow Stream
Of inland water; the great Sea meanwhile
Was at safe distance, far retired. (515–29)

On one level, this is a "naturalized Exodus vision," for Wordsworth implies
that the "great Sea" has retired so that the crowd may cross the stream.
Moreover, the poet's spontaneous hymn "completes the Exodus imagery;
the enemies of the Revolution have been swept away and drowned"
(Springer 244–45). But the passage invokes an even more archaic triumph
over the waters. As Bewell argues, "Wordsworth makes the scene at Leven
Sands an emblem of a history of ritual that extends back, through the ceremonies of the Catholic Church and the story of Exodus, to the earliest of
sacred festivals—those of the survivors of the Deluge" (256). It is as if the
death of Robespierre brings to an end not only a "deluge" of violence in
"Rivers of Blood" (10.439, 547) but also the deluge itself; apparently, the
restoration of sacred violence enables eternal justice to impose its law upon
the elements and to confine them within certain boundaries. In effect,
then, those masses commemorated the establishment of a rainbow covenant, interpreting the perpetual retreat of the tides as evidence of the sea's
continuing submission to that covenant.

As if to emphasize this dramatic restoration of culture, Wordsworth
refigures several major tropes of the Salisbury Plain poems. Where the
travelers on the plain seem lost in its vast, unmarked spaces, the "variegated
crowd / Of Coaches, Wains, and Travellers" that follow their guide across
the stream seem to exemplify a nonerrant wandering, a form of transporta-
tion (or transport) which will not go awry. The sun that plunged the world
into darkness rises again in the youth's hymn—"'as the morning comes /
Out of the bosom of the night, come Ye'" (543–44)—and, as we have seen,
the delugic tempest that overwhelmed the plain now retreats with the ebb
of morning tide. Looming over this scene is another version of the spital,
a "fragment" of a chapel which is "Itself like a sea rock"; half-rock and half-
ruin, this structure is poised on the threshold between nature and culture,
but in contrast to the spital it apparently marks nature's crossing into the
"gentleness and peace" of culture (517).[18] Widening his allusive net, Wordsworth takes care to reverse the Isle of Wight scene, sketched only a few
pages before, which he closely associates with *Salisbury Plain*; the forebod-

ing sound of the "sunset cannon" that he heard "walking by the still sea-shore" (10.301, 299) finds its counterpart here in the prospective sound of morning masses that travelers once heard on the Leven Sands—a sound that, in effect, announces the imminent end of that war.

But the full implications of the Robespierre sequence become even clearer in the Cartmell churchyard scene, which I skipped over above. This brief vignette, which bears no obvious relation to the celebratory passage which follows, in fact completes its logic:

> While we were Schoolboys he had died among us,
> And was born hither, as I knew, to rest
> With his own Family. A plain Stone, inscribed
> With name, date, office, pointed out the spot,
> To which a slip of verses was subjoined,
> (By his desire, as afterwards I learned)
> A fragment from the Elegy of Gray.
> A week, or little less, before his death
> He had said to me, "my head will soon lie low;"
> And when I saw the turf that covered him,
> After the lapse of full eight years, those words,
> With sound of voice, and countenance of the Man,
> Came back upon me, so that some few tears
> Fell from me in my own despite. And now,
> Thus travelling smoothly o'er the level Sands,
> I thought with pleasure of the Verses graven
> Upon his Tombstone, saying to myself
> He loved the Poets, and if now alive,
> Would have loved me, as one not destitute
> Of promise, nor belying the kind hope
> Which he had formed, when I at his command
> Began to spin, at first, my toilsome Songs. (493–514)

There are shades of a Gothic scenario here; something like the dead man's ghost appears near his grave, beckoning to the youth with voice and countenance. His remembered words are strangely unsettling. In a passage so concerned with the Terror, the announcement that one's "head will soon lie low" takes on more than the obvious meaning. Perhaps the old man fears that his will be one in an endless sequence of severed heads, another "grim head" like that of the murdered man of *Adventures* (216), in which case his apparition may rise up to cry out for vengeance. But that voice, speaking as it does of a death that has not yet occurred, might suggest instead that the old man leans against the tombstone in the manner of the discharged soldier, murmuring in pain. More likely, he is at once unburied and a ghost, a drowned schoolmaster with a ghastly face who is thus a "spectre shape / Of terror" (5.472–73). As always, Wordsworth does not finally distinguish between the ghost and the body in pain, both of which haunt the ground of an unreadable violence.

But this passage overturns the Gothic scenario it so subtly evokes. The dead man does not loiter on the threshold of death but perishes in little less than a week. He does not cry out for vengeance but rests quietly in his grave. Despite his haunting words, he is the victim not of the Terror but of a much less violent death. With the execution of Robespierre and the apparent end of the Terror, the young Wordsworth no longer trembles at the prospect of his immanent beheading (as he apparently does in those anxiety dreams) but instead remembers an old man's intimations of mortality. In that case, everything works as if the death of one man enables another to die in peace, as if the ghost accepts his burial because he has finally gained vengeance upon the living. Here Wordsworth depends upon, or rather completes, the logic of sacrifice he spells out more explicitly later in the Robespierre sequence: the dead also satisfy their thirst for vengeance upon a surrogate victim, whose ritual death solemnizes a covenant of peace with the living. At long last, the wars come to an end. The solitary wanderer who may have destroyed his family now manages to rejoin it again in death; the unrecognizable ghost acquires a name; and the drowned schoolmaster, the shape of terror from the realm of unreadable romance, is laid to rest within the tomb of an official textuality. In short, the familiar specter of the early poems enters into the domain of language and kinship, of the symbolic order.

Thus the logic of the Robespierre sequence, and indeed the entire family drama of Book 10, culminates in the Abrahamic plot that Wordsworth attempted to construct in "Michael." The sheepfold is complete, a sacrificial victim is at hand, and the initiation ritual can finally take place. By means of this symbolic act, reciprocal violence transforms into the reciprocal structures of gift exchange (cf. Dupuy); the dead man, having gained vengeance through sacrifice, can now bestow the poetic tradition he received from his own predecessors (such as Gray) upon the fledgling writer, who obeys his command, fulfills his expectations, and renders back the gift of his teacher's love in his affectionate tears. In this scenario, Robespierre becomes the rival child, the wild masochist who takes pleasure in increasing the violence of the Terror, whereas Wordsworth becomes the good child, the proper heir of the tradition. It is as if Michael kills the errant nephew and thereby officially bestows the gift of his love and property upon Luke, who responds by burying and memorializing his beloved father. Sacrifice is completed in memorialization, the altar in the tomb-stone, and the news of Robespierre's death in the visit to the Cartmell churchyard.

The section on the death of Robespierre, taken as a whole, effectively transforms Book 10 into a narrative to which it is the fitting conclusion. Liu argues that the flow of genres over the course of the revolution books stops with what he calls the *epitaphic lyric* of the Cartmell churchyard epi-sode, a generic mode that "contains in seed the whole span of his character-istic lyricism" (*Wordsworth* 365, 382–83). But rather than closing these books with any one genre, Wordsworth attempts to expunge hyperbolic indeter-minacy from the poem and reestablish generic coherence as such. In con-trast to the final stanza of *Adventures,* where the poet refuses to scapegoat the criminal and where, as a result, the text fails to end, the final movement of Book 10 rests easy with a sacrificial logic and thus brings the tale of Terror to an end.

But this passage is not entirely officializing. Unlike Girardian sacri-fice, the execution of Robespierre purges violence from culture without im-mediately creating a new and peaceful regime, and unlike Freudian sacri-fice, it reconciles one with the dead father without returning him to power. Even with Robespierre gone, much work remains to be done; the last we see Wordsworth on the Leven Sands, he is scheming how to pacify the "madding Factions" and to carry forward the "mighty renovation" (554, 556). Culture may be free of the threat of its dismemberment, but it is still poised on the threshold of its future, still crossing the waters on its way toward the promised land. It may no longer be unreadable, but it is not yet written either; it is a prospective history, one that has yet to articulate itself in a truly enduring and official form. In effect, Wordsworth uses the resources of sacrifice to impose limits upon revolutionary extravagance without repu-diating it altogether, much as he appeals to sacrificial narrative not to con-clude the revolution books overall but to bring the thematics of violence to an end. The consequence is a nonerrant errancy, a deviant pleasure without trauma or pain, and a nonviolent looseness or flexibility in culture.

On the strength of this foreclosure of violence, Wordsworth departs from the chronological organization that he has followed so far in the revo-lution books and begins an entirely new rendition of his experiences during those years. It is remarkable that an interpretive tradition that insists that *The Prelude* is in part a record of what he recognizes in the course of com-position (e.g., in the writing of the Simplon Pass episode) should have commented so little upon the curious structure of Book 10 (1805), for Wordsworth's account of his joyous return to revolutionary fervor after Robespierre's death (567–635) leads him into an associated account of his initial enthusiasm for political inquiry (657–756). The famous lines on the revolution's blissful dawn may speak less of any historical moment than of the unfolding of the poem's figural logic, as if the most enchanting dimension of the revolution, its immense promise, can come back to Wordsworth only after he has buried Robespierre. Appropriately enough, he associates this promise with the pleasure, rather than the terror, of an undefined social situation, specifically with the "pleasant exercise" (689) of giving revolutionary enthusiasm the permanence and sanctity of a constitution (666–88). In the wake of the section upon Robespierre, the paternal law itself authorizes an open-ended system, so that everyone can participate in the work of constructing a new social order without taking undue risks (689–727). Now that errancy cannot go astray, the shapelessness of history becomes entirely prospective, the wildest flights of fancy wholly enchanting. Even inheritance sounds oddly like the uninhibited refiguration of the tradition (728–35).[19]

Already the poem's terms begin to shift; now Wordsworth interprets his revolutionary experience not as the impossibility of reading but of writing history. As soon as Robespierre is dead, he imagines himself as a prime agent of revolutionary thought, someone akin to the "paramount mind" missing earlier (10.179), whose task was to investigate the "management / Of Nations" (685–86) and give the world an exemplary model of a new society. But ironically, as he tells this story he is forced to confront revolutionary violence without blaming it upon Robespierre. The problem is not the violence of another, nor some evil force in himself, but rather the violence inherent in the hyperbolic project of reinventing culture; the inquiry into the foundations of the social order led him, he writes, to attack the "living body of society / Even to the heart" (875–76). Here, as in *The Borderers*, perhaps the "dramatic Story" that he mentions in passing (879), he suggests that one can become aware of the illegitimacy of the social order and the violence upon which it is founded not only by identifying with its victims (the more typical scenario) but also by attempting to give culture a new foundation, to reconceive of the order of law, and by discovering that in the process one creates victims, including oneself. To recreate the world, it seems, is to destroy it. Denouncing the projects of his youth, Wordsworth suggests that he who wishes to ground society in unimpeachable evidence and absolute principles will end up believing nothing. Voicing what amounts to a critique of the final stanzas of *Salisbury Plain*, he writes that total revolution and total enlightenment lead only to total loss. In a long passage, filled with the terms of errancy, he recounts how in the pitch of a philosophical crisis, "confounded" and "misguided," confronted with the inscrutability of the mind, "now believing, / Now disbelieving, endlessly perplexed / With impulse, motive, right and wrong," he "lost / All feeling of conviction, and in fine, / Sick, wearied out with contrarieties, / Yielded up moral questions in despair" (887–88, 892–94, 897–900).

In this passage Wordsworth denounces the extravagance of youth ostensibly to contrast it with his temperate manner as a mature poet. He breaks off his account of the crisis in midsentence, denies that he lost his way, and thanks his friend and sister for helping him escape the labyrinth and return to his true and unchanged self (see 904–26). Strangely enough, after attacking himself for deviating so far from his proper path, he claims that he had not in fact left it.[20] Here and in the next three books he constructs *The Prelude*'s overarching myth of fall and recovery, of imagination impaired and restored. Yet this myth, founded upon the distinction between false and true paths, error and truth, betrays the poetics of errancy which so often informs the poem. It is bizarre enough that something impaired, for example, in the September Massacres episode, is restored in the spots of time, where he acts out virtually the same masochistic fantasy. But it is even more peculiar that, in the central trope of this myth, he deplores taking the wrong path, for nearly all of this poem's most celebrated episodes begin when he loses his way or encounters something apparently horrifying by accident. The poem's most consistent figural structure powerfully contests its central myth.

Moreover, this passage intimates that when Wordsworth took his project to extremes and metamorphosed it into its opposite, when his totalizing interpretations propelled him into the dizzying world of the contrarieties, he could neither find his way back to any settled discourse nor escape the both/neither structure and accordingly submitted to errancy as the dominant trope of his writing. By absolutizing political, philosophical, and moral discourses he transformed them into forms of radical self-contestation. He could not return to a safely grounded discourse, for that would derive from a sacrificial logic akin to that of the Robespierre sequence, a logic already undermined by the second half of Book 10. Perhaps, then, he could claim to discover a culture without violence of any sort, one at ease without representing itself in any ritual or philosophical enclosure. This, I think, is his intention: here as in *The Borderers* he attacks the attempt of the French ideologues to master, and perhaps transform, the social mind, implying that it can sustain itself well enough whether one understands it or not (cf. Chandler 216–34). But this point, familiar from the pre-Ideological tradition of Scottish moral philosophy, easily modulates into the darker suggestion that if the social mind finally escapes every discourse, then it prompts the craving for interpretation writ large in "The Thorn" and gives rise to the language of extravagant repetition. In this poet's own terms, to eschew representation is to live with the desperate craving for it; to live in a culture without sacrifice is to live in sacrificial crisis. Ultimately, his account of his crisis shows that he cannot conceive of any but a hyperbolic culture, one identical with its opposite. Wordsworth recovers from philosophical crisis, if at all, by transforming its fabulous disorientation into the characteristic tropes of his poetic discourse, by making its unreadability readable.

This far more characteristic response to trauma emerges later in *The Prelude*. The moment he has cryptically rewritten again and again, the nodal site of hallucinatory anxiety he has attempted to displace in countless ways, he finally addresses in this text—albeit at the end of Book 12, far from its chronological and thematic contexts. As if to repudiate the tale of his crisis outright, he rewrites the scene of sacrifice from *Salisbury Plain* in an idealizing, even celebratory mode, thereby privileging the moment in his writing which best exemplifies how a total critique of culture metamorphoses into total violence against it. In the wake of the 1799 *Prelude* and the passages on the deluge, one is hardly surprised to see that Wordsworth reads this vision of the dismemberment of culture as the exemplary sign of his election as a poet, in effect summing up such previous texts and making their import starkly clear. As I argued above, he began this process in Book 10, interpreting the Terror as "the consummation of the wrath of heaven," a vision of destruction which he, like the ancient prophets, could see with his own eyes (10.401, 406). Here he distinguishes himself even from those prophets, claiming that as an "influx" from the "depth of untaught things," such a vision establishes his originality as a poet-prophet and shows that he "is enabled to perceive / Something unseen before" (12.308, 310, 304–5).

Yet despite his claims in the introduction to the vision, this passage does not confirm an unproblematic conception of the "Orphic" poet's visionary power (cf. Liu *Wordsworth* 365). Here as ever Wordsworth is after something other than logocentric self-confirmation:

> I called upon the darkness; and it took,
> A midnight darkness seemed to come and take
> All objects from my sight; and lo! again
> The desart visible by dismal flames!
> It is the sacrificial Altar, fed
> With living men; how deep the groans; the voice
> Of those in the gigantic wicker thrills
> Throughout the region far and near, pervades
> The monumental hillocks; and the pomp
> Is for both worlds, the living and the dead. (12.327–36)

Although this mind claims an archaic, Godlike power to create by speaking a word, in fact it creates primarily by destroying, as if it has a Satanic power to undo God's creating word. Here, as in the Arab dream and the Gorge of Gondo, the world is suspended between creation (a power that is "Enduring and creative" [311]) and destruction, as if cultural disaster, like the deluge, creates culture by dismembering it, or more precisely reveals that its construction and destruction are part of the same enduring process. Similarly, although the poetic voice claims to master the world of sense, it fulfills itself here, if at all, through a radical alienation from itself. This event simultaneously reveals the poet's power and bestows it upon him; on the one hand, like the dreamer of Book 5, he literalizes his imagination and sees a vision by fiat, demonstrating that he possesses a quasi-divine "power like one of Nature's" (312), and on the other, that vision comes to the poet from the past (320) and unites the worlds of the dead and the living, thereby giving him a chance "to perceive / Something unseen before" (304–5). This passage, like those in Books 5 and 6, is written in the middle voice, posing itself on the threshold between fiat and influx; the word took effect, the vision took all objects, *it took*. The poet, surprised by the fact that his words take effect, indirectly recognizes that his words are alien to him and come from elsewhere. And indeed the voice that calls the vision forth is met by another within the vision itself: "the voice / Of those in the gigantic wicker thrills / Throughout the region far and near."

If the passage clearly demonstrates that the vision sweeps over Wordsworth as much as he calls it forth, if it gives voice to the dying as much as to his mastery, why should he claim that he chose it? What could he gain by saying that he called forth a traumatic event? A whole series of earlier texts has instructed us how to answer such questions: the conflation of fiat and influx, creation and destruction, culminates once again in a masochistic fantasy, whereby the poetic voice thrills in its dismemberment. The poet's strategy, it turns out, is not to appropriate or sublimate the power of spectacular violence but rather to claim, in a self-wounding gesture, that he willed an event that devastated him. Where he once emphasized that the hapless traveler of *Salisbury Plain* went forth into annihilating darkness against his will, now he pretends that he intentionally called forth that darkness. As in the Imagination passage of Book 6, he recognizes the hyperbolic, alienated force that compelled him forward into darkness as himself—as a voice that is at once alien to him and yet himself, at once something that he speaks and that speaks him. This passage is thus the second spot of time writ large, for here he reconceives the Terroristic destruction of the world as if he intended it from the start, as if he were a dark witch or magus who both revealed and received his ancient, untaught, Druidic

power through the spectacle of a midnight darkness, a revolutionary violence. There, on the "monumental hillocks" akin to the ungrave of the first
spot of time, he reads again a "monumental writing" etched by both worlds,
the living and the dead.

This passage does not readily suggest this reading. After all, Wordsworth apparently obscures its import by placing it out of context and takes
no pains to link it with any particular historical event. Yet he is quite aware
of the context he invokes, and the passage's first readers in 1850 would have
had little difficulty in finding here a strong allusion to *Guilt and Sorrow*,
published in 1842, whose Advertisement, as we saw in Chapter One, linked
human sacrifice to war's effects upon the poor. It seems possible, then, that
its historical dimension is meant to be relatively clear. In that case, he
places the vision at the end of Book 12 so that it might at once extend the
majestically demonic conclusion to the spots of time sequence at the end
of Book 11 onto the terrain of history and provide a powerful counterweight
to the idealizing Snowdon episode that immediately follows in Book 13. In
short, this passage may be as crucial a statement as the highly privileged
moments that precede and follow it, contesting them both.

Although in *The Prelude* Wordsworth repeatedly attempts to contain
his hyperbolic interpretation of the revolution or its aftermath, much as he
attempts to refigure errancy in the biography of the pedlar or the Snowdon
episode, here in Book 12 he embraces it without apology. Read in the light
of its many contexts, this passage suggests that he became a poet when he
submitted to an astonishing fantasy; devastated by the possibility of war,
betrayed by the course of the revolution and the martial response of his
own nation, he wished that both of them would expire in flames and that
a midnight darkness would take the whole world from his sight. Like the
child of the *fort-da game*, he imagined he could take a wounded comfort
from destroying what he loved through a feat of magic, in this case a primal
word. Even if, as Bersani would argue, the fulfillment of this fantasy would
eradicate everything he cherished and thus destroy him as well, he would
rather that the world end than accept its betrayal. If history cannot bring
about Utopia, Wordsworth would prefer anti-Utopia, in whose bitter exu-
berance he could still find the satisfactions of an absolute hope. Submitting
to the logic of this nihilistic eroticism, overcome by the alien wish not only
to destroy but to be destroyed, the poet discovers that in the moment of its
disappearance the world reappears as pure spectacle—as a light emanating
from darkness, a word spoken from elsewhere. By destroying the world,
he glimpses its alien beauty in the moment of an exquisite trauma and a
charming disaster.

What speaks in this passage and in the moments of dark romance throughout Wordsworth's canon is that aspect of culture no moral, philosophical, or political discourse can eradicate. According to the final lines of *Salisbury Plain,* once enlightenment has done its work, "not a trace / [will] Be left on earth of Superstition's reign, / Save that eternal pile which frowns on Sarum's plain" (*Salisbury Plain* 547–49). There is something primordial and constitutive about culture which inevitably defeats hope, that resists revolution even from within revolution itself: the longing not to establish justice but to expend life, to exceed the proper bounds, to become more than human. In such dark moments, Wordsworth anticipates and, through the reach of his concerns, offers a proleptic critique of those antihumanist philosophers, including Nietzsche, Bataille, Derrida, and Foucault, whose longing to go beyond "man" still haunts our critical moment, obsessed as it as been with finding those aspects of every text that render it unreadable, those sites where culture exceeds itself, those figures in which hope loses its way.

Notes

Introduction

1. Sources for the epigraphs: Baudrillard *Fatal* 75; Laclau 254; Bersani 60. Here and throughout the book *The Prelude* refers to the 1805 edition of *The Prelude,* unless otherwise noted.

2. Unless otherwise indicated, all quotations from Wordsworth's poetry and prose are taken from Stephen Gill's edition, *William Wordsworth,* published in The Oxford Authors series. For the sake of brevity, I will cite this edition throughout the book using only Gill's name (e.g., Gill 599).

3. I have omitted a chapter on the Preface only for considerations of length and with the greatest reluctance. A reading of that text affords unique opportunities to discuss the politics (or antipolitics) of the literature of sensibility as well as many other public discourses of the late eighteenth century and to challenge a number of recent readings of Wordsworth's politics.

4. For a relevant recent discussion of many of these same issues, including war neurosis, masochism, and nontraditional masculinity, see Kaja Silverman's *Male Subjectivity,* which focuses primarily on film and fiction. Like Silverman, I am interested in the way that war tends to undermine belief in the dominant fiction; unlike her, however, I do not regard that fiction primarily to be the equation of penis and phallus (42–51), for such a conception, I think, reduces the problem of symbolic violence at the basis of any number of institutions to a very narrow focus upon normative masculine sexuality, no doubt one of the most exemplary of such institutions but not in fact the anchor of them all. On war neurosis see 52–121; on masochism, 185–213.

5. Without directly proposing such a theory of culture, Bakhtin sketches out its rudimentary elements in his theory of novelistic heteroglossia (*Dialogic* 3–40 and 259–422). For a useful discussion of the cultural implications of Bakhtin's theories, with particular emphasis on the situation of discourses and audiences in the late eighteenth and early nineteenth centuries, see Klancher 11–14. For a good example of a Gramscian critique of the theories of classical Marxism, Louis Althusser, and Foucault, especially as they apply to Thatcherite Britain, see Hall.

6. I use *flaming* here advisedly, both to invoke the possibility of a certain queer

Wordsworth and to play up the scenes of masochistic pleasure in conflagration, especially in *Salisbury Plain* and *The Prelude,* Books 10 and 12.

7. Despite the obvious differences between his work and theirs, Wordsworth also resembles post-Lacanian feminists, such as Julia Kristeva, Luce Irigaray, and Hélène Cixous, insofar as they attempt to refuse the symbolic so thoroughly that they replicate it. To oversimplify: taking Lacan's map of gender for granted, associating the symbolic order with patriarchy and masculinity, they put women in a nonsymbolic, pre- or anti-cultural space, thereby replicating the sexism (of a poet like Wordsworth) that they wish to challenge. (See Moi *Politics* 102–49 [on Cixous and Irigaray] and Judith Butler 79–93 [on Kristeva].) On some level, then, Wordsworth defines the peculiar impasse of any project defined by the wish absolutely to refuse the symbolic order as a patriarchal construct.

Chapter One: All Track Quite Lost

1. For an excellent discussion of the history of the word *revolution* and its transformation in the hands of Burke in 1790, see Paulson 49–52. On turn, lapse, and revolution, see Bennett 164.

2. On the dating of these poems see Gill *Salisbury Plain Poems* (henceforth *SPP*) 4–12.

3. For a useful discussion of wandering, interruption, scandal, and narrative form in Wordsworth, see Bennett, whose article appeared after I had drafted this book. Bennett discusses the metaphor of walking with greater emphasis on the poet's actual walking practices, narrative form, and the *feet* of poetic lines and reads several texts I do not touch upon in this study. His article provocatively complicates the argument below. He does not, however, treat *wandering* or *scandal* as terms closely related to the undoing of culture, as I do, for he tends to focus upon the disruption of narrative rather than of culture.

4. On the dating of the "Letter," see Owen and Smyser 1.20–22.

5. For discussions of the Real Whig tradition, see Robbins and Pocock. On Wordsworth and the English republican tradition, see Fink "Republican"; Chard 76–91, 138–45, 171–77 (a discussion of the republican tradition and the Salisbury Plain poems); and Williams ("*Salisbury Plain*" and *Wordsworth*). On Wordsworth and the agrarian idealism of the republican tradition, see MacLean 87–103; Leask 34–74; and Simpson 56–78, all of whom emphasize Wordsworth's Preface to *Lyrical Ballads.* For an overview of the closely related tradition of dissent at Cambridge and its influence upon Wordsworth and Coleridge, see Roe 15–37, 84–117.

6. As Williams *Wordsworth* 73–74 argues, in these early stanzas Wordsworth engages the tradition of eighteenth-century pastoral poetry. But his insistent negation of the picturesque terms of Thomson or Beattie suggests that the gradual slide from culture into nature is also one from picturesque into Gothic. In a reading of Wordsworth's major poem in the picturesque mode, Alan Liu argues that *"An Evening Walk* wishes to tell incipient stories of desire and violence excessive of picturesque arrest—stories that threaten to reveal beneath the surface of repose an older reality of narrative catastrophe" (*Wordsworth* 119). Following Liu, we might argue that by repressing originary narrative the picturesque demonizes and Gothicizes it; when at last it returns as the eruption of

uncanny presences in the picturesque landscape, it imagines cultural origins as violent and ghostly. The most obvious instance of this return of the culturally repressed takes place, of course, in *Salisbury Plain*.

7. The body in pain is of course one of Wordsworth's major concerns in the early stanzas of the poem. The savage is "strong to suffer" (10), whereas the modern poor are "by pain depressed" (26). The implication here is that culture, by partially relieving humanity of physical suffering, makes pain a special condition and thus in effect *creates* the category of pain. To cancel the relief of suffering which culture represents is to return to a condition that did not preexist culture but which it invented as its superseded other.

8. In this stanza Wordsworth, like Milton, associates archaic war and fire in darkness; compare *Paradise Lost* 1.663–69. The links with Pandemonium are reinforced in a later stanza where an old man speaks of "Gigantic beings" who, "throned on that dread circle's summit gray / Of mountains hung in air, their state unfold, / And like a thousand Gods mysterious council hold" (175, 178–80). Cf. *Paradise Lost* 1.792–97.

9. Wordsworth returns to a discussion of Druidism in stanzas 21 and 22, using phrasing from which he draws his account of the hallucinatory vision on Salisbury Plain in *The Prelude* 12.312–53. Although these stanzas are interesting in their own right, they are less directly revealing about the hyperbolic situation of the traveler than stanza 11, which I discuss here.

10. For another reading of Wordsworth's ideas concerning the fragmentation of the body politic, see Henderson 73.

11. A. L. Owen 115 demonstrates that Wordsworth uses Toland's account of Ollamh's wand as Druidic badge in *Prelude* 12: "I saw the bearded Teachers, with white wands / Uplifted" (12.349–50). But Wordsworth was already aware of Toland by 1793: "Long bearded forms with wands uplifted shew / To vast assemblies" (*Salisbury Plain* 191–92). One can trace Toland's attack on priestly superstition in this poem as well; see lines 461 and 548. Although Toland downplayed human sacrifice to emphasize the parallels between the Druids and the Church of England (Owen 117), Wordsworth, moving beyond deism toward a position of more radical dissent, felt that even if he insisted on human sacrifice the parallel still held. For a discussion of Wordsworth, *Salisbury Plain*, Druidism, and Welsh nationalist movements of the 1790s, see Alan Liu, "Wordsworth and Subversion." In his useful analysis of Wordsworth's debts to Welsh politics throughout his career, Liu suggests that Wordsworth largely accepts its terms in the poem of 1793–94, but his own evidence and the largely negative depiction of Druids in the poem suggest that this early in the 1790s Wordsworth has not yet learned to connect the Druids with any radical tradition.

12. Here we might extend our analysis to include the resemblance between Wordsworth's metaphor of slavery in stanzas 50 and 52 and Marx's implicit analogy between slavery and wage labor throughout his work.

13. For a relevant discussion of those passages in which Wordsworth figures the Enlightenment as the sun, see Henderson 81–82.

14. In a reading of *Salisbury Plain* challenged by his essay "Wordsworth and Subversion," Liu argues that the scenes of Druid human sacrifice in the poem refer to the Reign of Terror in France (*Wordsworth* 190–201). But if we accept Mark Reed's suggestion that the poem was composed by September 1793 (145–46), this historical reference

is anachronistic, since the main period of the Terror still lies ahead. A better historical reference for the stanzas on human sacrifice is the war itself, as I have already suggested, which could be discussed in terms of the poetics of violence.

15. See Derrida *Grammatology*. Here I follow Gregory Ulmer, who argues that Derrida's grammatology "is not simply the use of images, but his sustained expansion of images into models. Thus he gives considerable attention in his texts . . . to the description of quotidian objects—an umbrella, a matchbox, an unlaced shoe, a post card—whose functioning he interrogates as modeling the most complex or abstract levels of thought" (xii).

16. Strictly speaking, I should write "both/neither a structure and/nor a houseless waste," but for stylistic simplicity I will use the simpler grammatical form on most occasions below, trusting that the reader will remain aware of the more difficult relation between paired terms.

17. Thus the sailor resembles the personifications of eighteenth-century poetry. According to Steven Knapp, such a personification usually "derives its appearance and behavior from iconographic emblems of its allegorical content"; but this "total dependence *on* its idea is matched by a reflexive consciousness *of* its idea: the personification is self-consciously obsessed with the grounds of its own allegorical being" (3). Such self-obsessed fictional agents abound in the poetry of William Collins, whose "Ode to Fear" Knapp analyzes at some length (87–97). Collins's metrical form and figural concerns influence the young Wordsworth, especially in "The Vale of Esthwaite," in which he repeatedly exposes the uncanny quality of any body that personifies a sheer abstraction. The personification, it appears, resembles a ghost, and both personification and ghost make visible a certain hollow, abstract, inaccessible quality to the self—what Rzepka calls *the self as mind*. By *Adventures*, Wordsworth's experiment with the eighteenth-century tradition produces a sailor whose entranced encounter with a corpse-ghost replicates the fixated self-contemplation of Collins's allegorical figures. The hyperliterary terms of Collins's poems (and of Spenserian allegory as interpreted in the eighteenth century) take on apparently human forms; the sailor seems to be more human than Fear or Despair, yet as we have just seen he is a duplicitous figure, at once a ghost (or figure in a ghost story) and a human form, at once idea and person. If, as I argue elsewhere in this chapter, Wordsworth consciously reworks the archaizing tendencies, the repetitive stanza form, and the formal *tableau* of Spenserian romance, he also reworks the complex figural structure of allegorical personification he inherits from the neo-Spenserian tradition.

18. Although I usually try to keep the gender of the subject neutral, in this sentence and elsewhere I occasionally use the masculine pronoun when referring to the subject, either to be consistent with Lacan's usage or to reflect Wordsworth's presumption that the subject is male.

19. This point about the exchange of women by phallocentric kinship systems has become a commonplace of feminist criticism. For an early and important essay on the subject, see Rubin. At stake in this feminist critique of *Totem and Taboo* is also a critique of the theory of the founding crime in Girard *Violence* 193–222. For a pointed critique along these lines, see Moi "Missing Mother."

20. For a good discussion of the female body in this poem, see Henderson, who points out that the failure of a maternal presence to heal the fragmentation of the body

politic is mirrored in the poem's suggestion that the efforts of Enlightenment are abortive or stillborn (lines 432, 107; Henderson 76–77).

21. Compare Swann on romance as the genre of strange repetition which subverts normative narrative and social control ("Transport" 828–29).

22. This discussion of syntax takes us onto ground explored by de Manian readers of Wordsworth, such as Bahti and Warminski, whose work I will discuss especially in Chapter Five.

23. Compare Christensen's point in his discussion of Weiskel's account of the Wordsworthian sublime: "the more indeterminacy is pursued to its origin, the more the origin begins to appear as indeterminate; it becomes very difficult to specify that first stage of an habitual, determinate relation to the object which is said to precede breakdown and the dialectic of transcendence" ("Sublime" 18).

24. In that case, one could apply Edward Said's theory of beginnings to culture itself. Rather than being a symbolic order founded in a divine origin, culture is perpetually constructed out of contingent, secular acts of inauguration (cf. Said xii–xiii, xvii); it too begins in an act like parricide and continues in repetition (cf. Said 209–10; 12, 377–78).

25. de Lauretis's discussion is directly relevant to *Adventures*, since the latter poem invokes yet subverts the paradigm of male wandering toward female/home which she interrogates at length. For example, "Therefore, to say that narrative is the production of Oedipus is to say that each reader—male or female—is constrained and defined within the two positions of a sexual difference thus conceived: male-hero-human, on the side of the subject; and female-obstacle-boundary-space, on the other" (121). "For the boy has been promised, by the social contract he has entered into at his Oedipal phase, that he will find woman waiting at the end of *his* journey" (133). Wordsworth borrows the terms of this sexual difference while refusing to allow his male hero to arrive at his destination. *Adventures* annuls the social contract of gender, transforming romance from the genre of ocdipal quest into one of generic and gender deviance.

26. Here *Adventures* anticipates the privileged poem of errancy for Bloom and Mileur, Robert Browning's "Childe Roland to the Dark Tower Came" (see Bloom *Map* 106–122 and Mileur *Romance* 32–38). Both poems are instances of texts that repeat themselves endlessly; the final line of "Childe Roland" is the title of the poem, as if the end leads directly to the beginning and so around again. Mileur traces Browning's poem back to Coleridge's "Kubla Khan" and "The Rime of the Ancient Mariner," which we might in turn trace back to *Adventures*, perhaps the fountainhead of this poetic. The vexed problematics of precursor and poet, poet and reader, errancy and self-hatred which structure Browning's poem are already broached in Wordsworth's, which contextualizes all of these issues in terms of cultural dislocation.

Chapter Two: Passing beyond the Visible World

1. As an inquiry and critique of this sort, this play is neither primarily a disguised form of autobiography nor, as David Erdman argues, a combination of autobiography and allegory of events in France. Rather, it interprets both autobiographical self-manipulation and certain French styles of excess as instances of the possible courses of action that follow on the delegitimation of authority. On this point I agree with Jewett, who argues that the play is less an instance of autobiographical self-reflection than an

examination of it: "*The Borderers* is about the failure, even the danger, of painting one's former self" (401). Compare my discussion below of Rivers's manipulation of Mortimer.

2. For another useful analysis of the relation between *The Borderers* and *The Robbers,* see Storch 344–47.

3. I am not interested in arbitrating between these two models of tragedy, which share much more than they might admit, in part because as I argue below *The Borderers* disrupts the classic form of tragedy or ritual. Wordsworth does not say whether the father wounds the son (see the breakfast scene in *Adventures*) or the young man the old (*The Borderers*), nor does he suggest whether it is Herbert or Rivers who must finally be blamed as a scapegoat for the crimes of the play.

4. I use the masculine pronoun here because the members of this audience, like the cultural subjects in Girard and Freud, are gendered masculine.

5. For useful discussions of the familial politics of Burke and Paine, see Blakemore and W. D. Jordan.

6. Discussing the theme of illegitimate birth and lower-class anxiety in the play, Liu argues that its plot "degrades the ethos of classical tragedy from the level of the aristocratic 'house' not just to that of the middle-class family but ultimately to that of the lower-class household. . . . The grandly illegitimate ethos of tragedy (concerned with kingly parricides or incests) thus threatens to degenerate wholly into petty illegitimacies . . ." (*Wordsworth* 277). This degradation of classical tragedy, visible in the great body of the play's material which I do not discuss in this chapter, is one part of a larger process, another part of which is the undoing of classical tragedy on something like its own terms, the aspect of the play I discuss here.

7. In this critique of captivation, Wordsworth both works within (and perhaps helps invent) Romantic theories of drama and resists them. Like De Quincey and Lamb, Wordsworth fears theatrical representations of crime because they seem too real and implicate the spectator in something too much like actual murder (see Jacobus 33–38, 54–68). But here this analysis blossoms into a full-fledged critique of theater; any audience that assembles to watch a tragedy in effect conspires to commit murder. For more on Jacobus and Romantic theater, see the discussion of the September Massacres episode (*Prelude* 10.46–82) in Chapter Eight.

8. This question marks my shift on a familiar reading of the play, perhaps best represented by Thorslev, who asks something of the same question in this way: "The doubt which has occurred to Wordsworth is a Romantic, even an existentialist, doubt: if traditional moral absolutes are gone, what ground or ultimate sanction can there be for any humanly based system of values?" (89). This framing of the play reduces the general dissolution of culture or the symbolic order to a crisis in the grounding of value, dramatically narrowing the play's range of concern to the personal (and existential) confrontation with the meaning of being.

9. The overall context of Rivers's project should clarify his use of philosophy in the play. Rather than representing the essential heartlessness of Godwinian thought, as many critics have argued, Rivers represents what happens when a hyperbolic consciousness manipulates philosophy for alien ends. He is no more interested in philosophical rigor than in political legitimacy, an issue I take up below.

10. Here Erdman's reading of *The Borderers* as a kind of allegory of events in France breaks down. Rivers (or Oswald) is not finally a version of Robespierre, as Erdman argues (23), because in that case he would endorse Lacy's proposal. Rivers repudiates the Jacobin language of civic virtue and social transparency so dear to Robespierre. One can read him as Robespierre only if one argues that through his character Wordsworth interprets Robespierre as someone manipulating Jacobin politics for hyperbolic ends—and in that case, the play once again becomes not an allegory but an interpretation of events in France.

11. I allude to the canceled line of the blind beggar passage of *Prelude* 7, MS. X: "and I thought / That even of the very most of what we know / Both of ourselves and of the universe, / The whole of what is written to our view, / Is but a label on a blind man's chest" (J. Wordsworth, Abrams, and Gill 260). In both *The Borderers* and *The Prelude* Book 7 Wordsworth ultimately conceives of hyperbolic theatricality in the terms of blindness and invisibility.

12. Storch points out the link between the crime and the sense of disembodiment which I attempt to account for in this essay (350–53). Here I describe what Hartman calls the *self-consciousness* of Rivers and Mortimer (*Wordsworth's Poetry* 129) as self-division or self-wounding. Hartman implies that every consciousness must experience such a moment of defining violence to distinguish itself from unindividuated consciousness. But he fails to note that such a break from nature usually leads toward the entry into the symbolic, which has instituted its difference from nature for all of its subjects by means of a sacred violence. When he states that the play "has nothing positive" as an alternative to the intellect as moral ground "except for vestiges of the old 'nature' morality" (129), he neglects the various references in the play, traced above, to symbolic or legal action as privileged forms of cultural construction unavailable on the borders. What Hartman calls *self-consciousness* is the uncanny shape consciousness takes when it has lost a way of representing or naming itself in the terms of the symbolic order.

13. For a study that focuses on the interplay between Rivers and Mortimer and affiliates it with motifs in Shakespeare, Milton, and the later Romantics, see Richardson *Mental Theater* 20–42.

14. Thus one cannot exit this theater any more than one can transcend the horizon of the book in Blake's *The Book of Urizen*. Paul Mann argues that the sons of Urizen who, in the poem's penultimate line, called the earth "Egypt, and left it," repeat the gesture of transcendence which generated the fallen world in the first place; they are caught within the world they wish to escape, much as the critic who reads or interprets this text is caught within the world of writing and of the book depicted within the text itself (64–68). Similarly, the spectator who exits the dungeonlike theater of *The Borderers* or escapes the dark confines of the senses—an attempt that resembles the escape from the confines of the cavernous, Urizenic body—repeats the act that made the theater so confining and dark in the first place. Both of these texts, in turn, resemble Godwin's *Caleb Williams*, where Caleb's final attempt to challenge his persecutor Falkland leads him to condemn himself; it turns out that because of his love for Falkland, Caleb is entirely implicated in the accusation from which he attempts to liberate himself (see Gold). In all three cases—*Caleb Williams* (1794), *The Book of Urizen* (1794), *The Borderers*—the extraordinarily searching critique of law, writing and/or theatricality, the fam-

ily, oedipal relations, and the politics of affection finally extends to the author and reader, who are deprived of any external vantage from which to construct an alternative social order. These texts suggest that in the mid 1790s certain kinds of English radical writing crossed a threshold into a total critique of culture.

Chapter Three: "Oh misery! oh misery!"

1. One result of Wordsworth's conflicted situation is a poetry that at once invokes, sublimates, and criticizes Enlightenment cultural theory. Bewell argues that Wordsworth makes moral philosophy "the silent, informing impulse of a poetry whose systematic preconditions could never be stated" and drives it underground in dozens of shorter poems: "the coherence of *The Recluse* did not lie in its formal structure but instead in the experimental discourse that shaped individual poems" (12–13). But as I will argue below, Wordsworth consistently exceeds such discourses and implicates them in a far less stable literariness. If, as Bewell himself argues, Wordsworth criticizes accounts of encounters with the primitive in "The Discharged Soldier" and *Peter Bell* (90, 100) and parodies the interpretation of the wild child in "The Idiot Boy" (65), then he resists and parodies the very basis of the *Recluse* project. For a relevant discussion, see Nehamas, who argues that Nietzsche writes aphorisms, uses a wide variety of literary styles, and privileges hyperbole to treat philosophy as a form of literature (17–40). By doing this, Nietzsche challenges philosophy's claim to truth and proposes instead a theory of perspectivism which emphasizes the partial and interested nature of every intellectual endeavor (42–73). For Nietzsche and Wordsworth both, to make philosophy literary is fundamentally to change the status of philosophy, not simply to give it a new form of expression.

2. Crime as a figure of hyperbole dominates in Wordsworth's poetry from September 1795 (when he began to revise *Salisbury Plain*) through most of 1797 (including *The Borderers* and "The Somersetshire Tragedy"). On the dating of these poems see M. Reed 25–29. For a description of the contents of "The Somersetshire Tragedy," of which only a few lines survive, see Jonathan Wordsworth, "A Wordsworth Tragedy."

3. For a relevant discussion of secular theodicy, see Mileur *Romance* 21–22 and passim.

4. For "Incipient Madness," see Butler 468–69. Unless otherwise noted, all references to Butler throughout this book are to James Butler's edition of *The Ruined Cottage* and *The Pedlar*.

5. I should reiterate that I use the masculine pronoun to point to the consistent gender bias of Wordsworth, Freud, and Lacan.

6. Henceforth I abbreviate *Concepts* as *C* and *Écrits* as *E*.

7. In the full context of *Concepts*, the gaze is a version of the Lacanian concept of the *real*, discussed earlier in the text, which is the unassimilable or blocking element in the moment of the missed encounter (53, 55), the element that fantasy conceals or veils in a screen (60, 69) or returns to obsessively in repetition (53, 55). As an instance of the split subject (69), this concept of the *real* resembles that of the gaze, which Lacan also describes as unapprehensible (83) or unassimilable. We might argue, then, that the gaze registers the real in the field of vision. One could easily trace a similar analytic through Lacan's later discussions of the concepts drive and transference, both directly relevant

to Wordsworth's understanding of desire and trance. On the link among transference, trance, and transport, see Swann "Transport" 811–15 and 832–33 notes 7 and 13.

8. For Lacan's full discussion of the gaze, see *C* 67–119.

9. Lacan's uncanny presence in the scene of rural labor resembles that of the late eighteenth-century poet, such as the speaker of Gray's "Elegy" or the solitary figure in *Salisbury Plain*, which we discussed in terms borrowed from Rzepka in Chapter One. Lacan's anecdote places his analysis of the gaze in the context of landscape painting and the political configurations of class and labor that it displays. But the anecdote suggests that the laborer in the landscape which the painter (or viewer) tries to appropriate for his own purposes can actively respond to dominance and ridicule its impropriety. A thorough historicizing of Lacan would be able to construct a political genealogy of the gaze.

10. Swann 91 goes on to link her points to Lacan's analysis of the gaze and to historicize it through a discussion of sensationalist literature. For a response to her argument on sensationalism, see below.

11. A point made by Swann: "Yet 'Incipient Madness' also reveals the difficulty of separating, at any moment in this process, captivation from a study of captivation, regulatory law from an economy under regulation, pleasure from the beyond of pleasure. . . . For, at each turn, an apparatus called in to regulate a mesmerizing representational effect itself becomes an object of fascination" ("Suffering" 89). This complicating turn would provide a better starting point for Sitterson's attempt to preserve Wordsworth's texts from reductive psychoanalytic readings. The point is not that the Wordsworthian child is already aware of metaphor, but that Wordsworth transforms the activities of childhood into metaphors of his concerns as a poet.

12. This text also articulates a similar problematics of captivation by sound: within the walls of the ruin the dull clanking of the horse's iron links mix with the "heavy noise / Of falling rain," and as the traveler turns away, he "hear[s] the sound still following in the wind" (24, 32–35). These lines at once recall the archaic ponderousness of Spenserian verse, project the traveler's dislocation onto the noises of another body, and rework the logic of repetition in what Lacan would call the register of the *invocatory drive* (*C* 180, 200). I should emphasize that here and elsewhere Wordsworth is captivated by a powerful disturbance in speech more than a fully self-present, logocentric sound, just as he prefers the play of light and opacity to unmediated vision.

13. See Kristeva and Homans *Bearing* 1–39. For an excellent critique of Kristeva's general privileging of the preoedipal mother, see Judith Butler 79–91. Homans 18–19 distinguishes *literal language* from Kristeva's notion of the semiotic, in part because "Kristeva never wavers in her assumption that the child is male." Following Chodorow, Homans argues that the woman writer need not *return* to the preoedipal, since she did not entirely repress it in the first place. Wordsworth is crucial to Homans's articulation of her stance; she introduces her theory of a literal language in a discussion of the blest babe sequence (*Prelude* [1850] 2.232–81), arguing that the poet conflates his mother's death with his acquisition of language. Building on this passage, she argues that when the young boy enters the symbolic order he is separated from the maternal body; for men, language requires the mother's death because the mother is a pure body prior to language (3–4). In effect, then, Homans uses Wordsworth's own account of the preoedipal stage to contest his androcentric poetics. Yet her dependence on Wordsworth to

establish the terms of her argument suggests that her book is less a critique of Words-worth than an extension of his terms—or, more precisely, an extension of *her reading* of his terms. Wordsworth's account of the blest babe is not nearly as idealizing as Homans assumes; on this point, see three excellent discussions of the passage: Ferguson 131–38; Christensen "The Sublime" 19–20; and Warminski "Facing Language" 21–25. As Chris-tensen argues, for Wordsworth there is no maternal plenitude from which the child is separated because the mother's body is mediated by language from the very start. In effect, Wordsworth strives to return to a maternal presence that he admits never existed. It follows that in seeking a substitute for the maternal body, the poet does not stray from a literal body, as Homans argues (23), but rather learns that desire is necessarily figural and always strays.

14. In his discussion of the famous crossing of the Alps passage in *Prelude* 6, Marlon Ross argues, in a similar vein, that Wordsworth detaches the imagination both from the father (it is an unfathered vapor) and from the mother, whom he does not mention in the passage. But Ross contends that in this moment Wordsworth articulates a heroic, self-originating, solitary masculinity (47). I would argue, however, that the subject of this critique is not the (largely mythical) pompous, macho Romantic poet but rather a radically self-divided, erring, masochistic figure akin to the sailor of *Adventures* or the speaker of "The Thorn." The point is less to demystify a grandiose self-presence than to ask how an entirely ungrounded masculinity, whose desire is *not* some essentialized principle of "pure energy" (9) and is *not* necessarily heterosexual, might nevertheless construct itself at the expense of women.

15. Unless otherwise indicated, all quotations from *The Ruined Cottage* in this chap-ter are from MS. D as printed in Butler 43–75.

16. Manning argues that the poem's thematics ultimately derive from Wordsworth's personal obsession with his mother, who died when he was nearly eight years old. He points out many telling details in these texts, especially in the biography of the pedlar, in support of a rather persuasive genetic reading. But Wordsworth's private obsessions cannot entirely account for these texts, which propose explicit accounts of obsessive repetition which anticipate contemporary psychoanalytic theory on several points. Wordsworth's poetry is less confessional than analytic, less private than cultural in its emphasis.

17. Bersani's account of masochism builds upon that of Jean Laplanche, which fig-ures prominently in Adela Pinch's reading of "Goody Blake and Harry Gill" discussed below. For Laplanche, sexuality and masochism both emerge in the act of representa-tion, when "a nonsexual activity has lost or become detached from its object." "Acts of fantasy or mental representation are themselves, moreover, experiences of psychic pain" (Pinch 843; see Laplanche 85–102). Pinch also argues that masochism structures the subject's relations with others; "the vicissitudes of sadomasochism conspire closely with the vicissitudes of ventriloquism, often involving processes of speaking through or being spoken through an other, under the pressure of suffering" (845). By using Bersani's dis-cussion of the *fort-da* game I hope to extend Pinch's argument, to which I owe this line of investigation. I should also note here that Laplanche, Bersani, and Pinch accept Freud's general theory concerning the mutual derivation of sadism and masochism (see "'A Child is Being Beaten,'" *Papers* 2.172–201; "The Economic Problem in Masochism," 2.255–68; and "Instincts and Their Vicissitudes," 4:60–83); for a dissent, see Deleuze.

18. One confirmation of this reading of Margaret's suffering may be found in a poetic fragment recently entitled "The Baker's Cart," which, together with "Incipient Madness," lies at the genesis of *The Ruined Cottage*. In this fragment the baker's cart, loaded with bread, leaves a poor woman and her five children "as if / [They] were not born to live" (4–5). As the woman watches the cart depart, "in a low and fearful voice / She said, 'That waggon does not care for us'" (Butler 463, lines 15–16). Clearly this is an abandoned woman, and Wordsworth spells out her longing for revenge in lines 17–25, where oral deprivation leads to extravagance, rebellion, and potential violence, working out on the adult level a precise counterpart to infantile revenge.

19. Swann proposes that *The Ruined Cottage*'s "gendered plot is a secondary construction" derived from the primary logic of repetition, such as that in "Incipient Madness," and that its characters personify "the coordinates of his technical apparatus" ("Suffering" 87, 89). Because Swann separates repetition and gender in this way, she must explain the poem's gender concerns by discussing its engagement with the image of the female reader of sensationalist literature. But explaining *The Ruined Cottage* with reference to other sensationalist texts simply displaces the task of interpretation onto them; sensationalism is another aspect of the game of self-division and self-alienation already visible in the rest of the poem. Swann's argument is more convincing when she suggests that the poem, rather than simply reproducing the literature of sensation, is a "self-reflexive study" of that literature's excessive power (93), one that exposes its basis in the pleasures of repetition.

20. By representing his suffering through that of a woman, Wordsworth carries on the discourse that associated acute sensibility with femininity. According to Terry Castle, from the late seventeenth through the eighteenth centuries, femininity was considered the privileged domain of mercuriality, emotional variability, hysteria, and unpredictable temperament and was thus easily associated with certain meteorological instruments such as the barometer or thermometer. The rise of the cult of sensibility in the late eighteenth century, she argues, "pointed to a growing feminization of the male subject," for he began to imitate or absorb "characteristics once seen as belonging only to women" ("Female Thermometer" 13). In contrast to Rousseau and Keats, two examples of such feminization, Wordsworth internalizes feminine sensibility less than he identifies with its embodiment in Margaret or, as we shall see, Martha Ray.

21. On the pedlar's reading, see the discussion in Chapter Four below.

22. When Bersani comments that "[o]ur doubts about the epistemological status of psychoanalysis will be all the more pronounced as we realize the necessity of reading the Freudian text as if it were a work of art" (5), he places Freud on the same perspectival ground occupied by Nehamas's Nietzsche and the Wordsworth who persistently disrupts his own philosophical project.

23. The pedlar's final meditation has remained inexplicable in the terms of humanist interpretation. To accuse the pedlar of indifference to death is to accuse the entire poem, rather than to interpret it, and to defend him as offering a truly reconciled vision of life and death is to miss what is scandalous in his claims. (For examples of engagements with the poem in these terms, see Jonathan Wordsworth *Music of Humanity*, and Philip Cohen, who argues that the addition of the biography of the pedlar/wanderer makes his claims more believable.) Criticism can go beyond the problem of belief or disbelief in the pedlar's final speech only by analyzing the strategy that produces it.

24. The distribution of the *objet a* through a number of images produces the wealth of imagery which Alan Liu finds in the poem (*Wordsworth* 311–25). Slipping into the mode of accusation (against Wordsworth and Cleanth Brooks), Liu argues that "there is also something shockingly dehumanizing about imagery," particularly the imagery of spear-grass (320; italics in the original). Liu fails to ask why Wordsworth depicts a specifically *visual* wealth or why he exposes the dehumanizing effects of imagery in texts directly adjacent to *The Ruined Cottage* ("Incipient Madness" and "The Thorn"). Nor does he ask how the logic of the image may just as easily produce a poetry of radical loss and poverty (in "The Thorn") as of wealth.

25. This trancelike ending is the first instance of a scene Francis King finds in several of Wordsworth's poems to his sister Dorothy Wordsworth. The pedlar's imaginary union with Margaret resembles Wordsworth's trancelike experience of sharing consciousness with (or appropriating the consciousness of) Dorothy in scenes of stillness so great that he almost ceases to breathe. King interprets these moments as Wordsworth's recovery of the prelapsarian unity of being (13) or, one might add, of the fantasy of the mother's presence. King quotes a passage from the "Christabel" MS., associated with "Nutting," which captures most elements of the Dorothy poems: "Come rest on this light bed of purple heath / and let me see thine eye / As at that moment rich with happiness / And still as water when the winds are gone / And no man can tell whither" (14). These lines express almost too directly the fantasy of resting on the maternal body, gazing into the mother's eye, stilling the winds and waters (or the child's tempestuous anxiety), and becoming rich or filled with satisfaction. In a precise counterpart to masochistic fantasy of self-destruction, these scenes depict the wish for death as absolute stillness and repose.

26. Wordsworth rewrites the poetry of errancy and immunity in the so-called "Lucy" poems of late 1798 and early 1799. For example, "Strange fits" depicts the traveler's hyperbolic entrancement by the alien rhythms of the horse's steps and the moon's gradual descent and links the orb's setting to the thought of the woman's death. (For an excellent discussion of "Strange fits" as a poem of "error," see Hartman *Wordsworth's Poetry* xviii–xx.) On the other hand, "A Slumber did my spirit seal" revisits the stance of immunity from death; as Paul H. Fry argues, in this poem death is so effaced it has disappeared: "the conversion we expect between then and now never takes place. Furthermore, there is little or no difference between self and other." Lucy never died because she was never quite alive: "in Wordsworth's shockingly minimal vision, or lack of vision, the spirit is never *un*sealed." Wordsworth achieves "oneness with the other at absolutely any price, including the permanent slumber of spirit" and the effacement of writing (Fry 25–26). Like "Slumber," *The Ruined Cottage* is a kind of antielegy which imagines death not as the loss of life but as being "laid asleep or borne away" (*Ruined Cottage* 371) into a shared, imaginary body.

27. Although as I mentioned above Averill values *The Ruined Cottage* for its departure from sensationalism, he compares it at length with "The Thorn" and concludes that in the latter poem "[t]he premises implicit in the success of *The Ruined Cottage* are laid bare, and they are not so benign and normal as they seem in that poem" (171–80). Yet Wordsworth remains deeply implicated in the obsessions of that poem; as Stephen Parrish argues, "the growth of the poem in the mind of its author almost certainly paral-

lels the growth of the story in the mind of its narrator" (*Art* 106). Parrish's important reading informs that of Christensen, which I discuss below.

Magnuson argues that Coleridge performs a critique of Wordsworth's conception of a natural, inarticulate language (first voiced in *The Ruined Cottage* and its attendant manuscripts) in "Christabel," where Geraldine personifies an irreducible figuration or disturbance in language (Magnuson 120–38). But in contrasting the two poets, Magnuson overlooks Wordsworth's own critique of *The Ruined Cottage* in "The Thorn," which takes over many of the motifs of Coleridge's poem, which in turn were taken from earlier Wordsworth texts. For example, Magnuson rightly traces the question-and-answer format of "Christabel" back to "Goody Blake" (130–32) but neglects to mention its later version in "The Thorn," where (as we will see below) this format is crucial. Although the poets are certainly engaged in a dialogue, one cannot sort it out as a dialogue between partisans of natural language and of figuration; "The Thorn" demonstrates that Wordsworth's position is much more complex than Magnuson suggests.

28. Compare Wordsworth's statement on "Goody Blake and Harry Gill": "I wished to draw attention to the truth, that the power of the human imagination is sufficient to produce such changes even in our physical nature as might almost appear miraculous" (Gill 611–12). Similarly, in a note to "The Three Graves" (1797), one of the texts from which "The Thorn" emerged, Coleridge describes the poem as depicting a "striking proof of the possible effect on the imagination, from an idea violently and suddenly impressed on it" (*Poetical Works* 269).

29. Wordsworth's implicit critique of *The Recluse* in "The Thorn" demonstrates how risky it is for Kenneth Johnston to interpret *The Recluse* entirely on the basis of poems that constitute it (although somewhat unwillingly; he was forced to omit consideration of such poems as "The Thorn" by publishing exigencies; see Johnston xxi). Wordsworth persistently challenges the terms of that large project in his short poems.

30. If Christensen's point is correct, as I think it is, then in "The Thorn" Wordsworth foregrounds and interprets the situation he experienced when he began to draft "Incipient Madness." Raymond Carney, studying the first, obsessive drafts of that poem, argues that "The narration begins with an elementary assertion, an act of mentioning the broken wall; but something strange starts to happen when Wordsworth tries to account for the significance of the wall and the narrator's experience of it. The narrator becomes mesmerized by his own phrases and rhythms, caught in a series of repetitions" (637). Carney goes on to argue that in *The Ruined Cottage* Wordsworth finally does "maintain his composure and powers of movement against all the decompositions of desire that threaten to bewilder and oppress him as much as they do his characters" (641), but he fails to consider "The Thorn."

31. Christensen suggests that this originary disruptiveness of the subject resembles Locke's concept of desire as uneasiness (277–78). This point is especially relevant in the present context because Locke's account of uneasiness in the *Essay* (249–64) inaugurates a line of speculation to which Freud contributes in his discussion of internal excitation as unpleasure in *Beyond the Pleasure Principle*. Excitation, Freud suggests, disturbs a prior, easeful state of things to which all organic life wishes to return (18–37). "The Thorn" has a place in the history that includes Locke and Freud, for as we have seen it links an initial uneasiness or disturbance with a number of issues at stake in Freud's text.

32. This scene demonstrates both that Martha fits Swann's description of Margaret as the personification of a "geometric coordinate" (89) and that this personification is inevitably a suffering woman, a gendered figure in a masochistic fantasy.

33. I should point out in passing that Wordsworth mocks this poem and the entire complex of hyperbolic romance of which it is a part in "The Idiot Boy," portraying a cultural outsider who is neither guilty nor despised but simply an idiot. Taking the logic of "The Old Cumberland Beggar" and similar poems to a comic extreme, he identifies with a wandering horseman who is so simple he can never experience real anxiety. All of the anxiety is given to the mother, who like Martha Ray fears that she has abandoned her child and frantically attempts to rescue him from terrible dangers that, in this re-writing of "The Thorn," never threaten the boy in the first place. Wordsworth even parodies the masochistic chatter of other ballads in the "burr, burr" of the boy's lips, imagining ballad metrics as the expression not of the body's masochistic pleasures but its innocent delight. One can see why Wordsworth declared that this poem was one of his favorites—a choice that seems inexplicable until one recognizes how many intract-able problems it resolves with ease in a manner that he apparently could not use in any other poem. As Mary Jacobus argues (*Tradition* 250–61), "The Idiot Boy" inherits the comic tradition of the late eighteenth century, particularly the burlesque and mock-heroic comedy associated with Don Quixote and the characters in *Tristram Shandy*. This comic mood also informs "The Thorn," where the gossip's superstitious fascina-tion is so overdone that the poem verges on parody, as Wordsworth hints in his Note.

34. In his discussion of the babe's image in the pond, Christensen verges on reading it in the terms of Lacan's theory of the gaze when he argues that the image of the dead child "does not even reflect" the look of the investigator but "on the contrary, seems to make his look the reflection of a gaze already there—as if the fond image of his desire is always already desiring him" (284).

Chapter Four: Ghastly Mildness

1. As Paul Magnuson argues, these new texts participate in a poetic dialogue between Wordsworth and Coleridge: Coleridge replied to *Adventures* in *Ancient Mariner*, to which Wordsworth replied, for example, in "The Discharged Soldier" (Magnuson 68–95). In Coleridge's poem, Wordsworth was confronted with a stunning distillation of the poetics of errancy; no longer faintly resembling a realist story, this poem plunges into an archaic, Gothic mode akin to the Spenserian poetics of *Adventures* and cedes the mariner's will entirely to the caprices of alien, supernatural forces embodied in the celestial bodies and in the weather (cf. the spell of celestial bodies in *Salisbury Plain* and "Incipient Madness"). The mariner strays so far beyond himself that he eventually is "rimed," turned (as Arden Reed argues) into rhyme, into a ghost or personification of a nonsignificative language, and into a rhyme or tale that he must endlessly repeat (155–63). This endless repetition, of course, is linked to the mariner's guilt and thus to a certain psychology of repetition or obsessive return which could be relieved only by a final penance or expiation—a sacred and symbolic violence. But for the mariner, as for the sailor, there is no way back home, and thus he cannot cross the threshold to join in the wedding feast (cf. the sailor's failed reunion with his wife near the end of *Adven-*

tures). On that threshold, he holds the wedding guest spellbound with the power of his eye and the spectacle of his ghostly body (much as the sailor's gibbeted corpse entranced the reader of Adventures and implicated him or her in its series of specular identifications).

2. All citations from the *Pedlar* are taken from Jonathan Wordsworth *Borders* 379–90 and will be cited as "1798 *Pedlar*" in the text.

3. Compare the traveler's entranced movement with the magic progress of the horse's steps in "Strange fits," and his invention of figures in the distance with Margaret's: "On this old Bench / For hours she sate, and evermore her eye / Was busy in the distance, shaping things / Which made her heart beat quick" (454–57). Immediately after these lines Wordsworth describes Margaret's "reeling" with the flax, in effect linking figuration and repetition. For a comparison of Margaret's figuration with the ancient mariner's, see Magnuson 101–3.

4. Wordsworth's careful depiction of the discharged soldier as a figure of figuration carries forward the complex reworking of personification he began in *Adventures*. Now it is clear that the spectral wanderer personifies textuality as such; he embodies no particular mental state (Fear, Despair) as much as the mind's capacity for figuration in general. We might apply this insight retrospectively and argue that the sailor of *Adventures* personifies the Spenserian stanza, complete with its archaizing rhythm and its endless repetition; but it is more likely that Wordsworth carries out this retrospective interpretation himself in "Resolution and Independence," where another uncanny old man, affiliated like the discharged soldier with the deluge (he is, after all, a kind of stone/sea-beast, a fossil [Bewell 266]), is rendered as "a materialized deposit, a kind of personified sediment or precipitate, of the stanzas that serve as the deliberately awkward and alien medium of the speaker's meditation" (Knapp 119). The later poem provides the ground on which Swann's analysis of Spenserian romance and Knapp's analysis of personification may come together. As Knapp writes, in terms that strongly resemble Swann's, the old man's antiquity, his measured speech and labored movement, are nothing other than "the condensed Spenserian stanza (measured, antique, opaque, elusive) whose persistent and finally pointless repetition constitutes this very poem" (119). Moreover, if "The Discharged Soldier" enables Wordsworth to carry out his reworking of Spenser in "Resolution and Independence," it also allows him to affiliate the gradual emergence of personification with the process of maturation in the 1799 *Prelude*, as I will argue in the next chapter.

5. Jonathan Wordsworth, discussing "The Somersetshire Tragedy," argues that "Wordsworth's preoccupation in the spring of 1797 was with neurotic states of mind. The listlessness of Walford's wife, for instance—'Ill fared it now with his poor wife I ween / That in her hut she could no more remain . . .'—finds an echo in the brilliant description of Robert's 'petted mood'" in *The Ruined Cottage*. "A similar preoccupation is found in *The Borderers* and 'Argument for Suicide,' 'The Three Graves,' 'Lines Left on the Seat of a Yew Tree' and 'Incipient Madness.'" This mood may also appear in "the sailor's agitation in the second version of 'Salisbury Plain,'" that is, *Adventures* lines 784–92 ("A Wordsworth Tragedy"). This condition interested Wordsworth in its own right; in a study of the manuscripts of *The Ruined Cottage* which were published in Butler's Cornell edition, Raymond Carney points out how the poet, fascinated by Rob-

ert's mood, expands his description of it until it occupies some thirty lines (639–40). It takes him until "The Thorn," however, to dedicate an entire poem to this particular form of errancy.

6. And, as we will see later in this chapter, is also the pedlar, who becomes a pedler precisely because of this same unease. These demonstrable links between Wordsworth's speakers and anxious, displaced figures like Robert confirm Mileur's argument that the figure of *The Prelude* with which Wordsworth identifies most intensely is the royalist officer described in 9.142–63, a later instance of the anxious man (*Romance* 67–69). For a discussion of the officer, see Chapter Eight.

7. Swann, citing *The Ruined Cottage* 407, points out the link with the "straggling leaves" of Margaret's books (92).

8. See Simpson 179 on the common usage of *relief* as a word "used to describe the general, public enterprise of assisting the poor."

9. The possibility that Wordsworth is rewriting "Animal Tranquillity" in "The Discharged Soldier" is strengthened if we read the final, neglected lines of the earlier poem where the decayed man speaks: "'Sir! I am going many miles to take / A last leave of my son, a mariner, / Who from a sea-fight has been brought to Falmouth, / And there is dying in an hospital'" (17–20). Heather Glen argues that these lines implicitly debunk the speaker's mystification of the old man by showing that he is another human being after all (5–7), much as Bewell argues that the soldier's words debunk the speaker's earlier interpretation of him (see above). But these readings too readily dismiss the content of the decayed man's speech, which includes a number of familiar motifs: a dying mariner, a (ho)spital, and conflicts at sea.

10. Actually, the beggar does see something in that little prospect which should give us pause: "some straw, / Some scattered leaf, or marks which, in one track, / The nails of cart or chariot wheel have left / Impressed on the white road, in the same line, / At distance still the same" (54–58). The old man tracing the random marks on the white road recalls the traveler in the marked, vacant spaces of Salisbury Plain and, more specifically, the old soldier of the early stanzas of *Adventures,* the "helpless friend" whom the sailor cannot abandon "Where thus the bare white roads their dreary line extend" (35–36).

11. In his excellent analysis of the poem in the context of that debate, Gary Harrison demonstrates that Wordsworth, like most of his contemporaries, "reconstructs paternalistic attitudes towards the poor that constitute certain individuals as other in order to legitimate a system of social disequilibrium" (34). Far from binding people together with the bonds of mutual obligation or identification, charity unites the community if at all by marking beggars as socially alien: "the beggar ostensibly returns their favors in an abstract exchange of which he is entirely unaware" (35). No doubt this critique exposes the coercive politics in the contemporary ideology of charity, but it cannot finally account for Wordsworth's poem. Rather than hiding the nonreciprocal nature of charity or pretending that it somehow socializes the beggar, in the poem's core section Wordsworth emphasizes, perhaps even exaggerates, the beggar's alien status, his inhuman indifference to those who help him, as if proleptically reversing the terms of Harrison's critique.

This reading goes awry when it assumes that the poem derives from a position within the contemporary debate on begging. (Simpson also discovers that it is difficult to sort out this poem with a political analysis [162–74]). But in the first stanzas of *Adventures* Wordsworth offers a contrary image of charity, pointing not to the indifference but to the gratitude of the old man, and in "Simon Lee," written soon after this poem, he emphasizes the unsettling implications of excessive gratitude, exploring yet another angle on the question. One suspects that in the poems on old vagrants, as in the Note to "The Thorn," Wordsworth's political and philosophical statements derive from the figural logic of the relevant text, serving as what Freud called *secondary elaboration* of the poem's fantasmatic structure. In the "Beggar," he reverses the figural dynamic of the specular encounters and accordingly alters his political stance, turning against the Godwinian protest of *Adventures* and adopting a particularly conservative line of argument.

12. Wordsworth's reference to the pedlar as a chosen son comes very close to giving him a truly symbolic status. But as always, Wordsworth disrupts this refreshingly straightforward depiction of the pedlar by describing the manner in which he was chosen, inevitably subsuming the process of symbolic initiation into natural, neo-Lockean development. The pedlar is unique, but one can explain his uniqueness in something like sociological or historical, and thus secular, terms. For a useful discussion of the shift from the eighteenth-century notion of an established selfhood to the Romantic idea of selfhood as development, see Siskin 94–124.

13. For examples of texts in which Wordsworth himself seems to envy the indifference and silence of the dead, see "These chairs they have no words to utter" (Gill 255) and the first stanza of a poem known either as "Personal Talk" or "I am not One who much or oft delight" (Gill 269–70).

14. Perhaps in an illegal way; Liu *Wordsworth* 341–47 argues that the pedlar may be an agent of the black market and links his affective wealth with literal riches.

15. For one further link between these two figures, compare lines written for their respective texts: "But deem not this man useless" ("The Old Cumberland Beggar" 67); "Not useless do I deem / These quiet sympathies with things that hold / An inarticulate language . . ." (addition to MS. D; Gill 678; Butler 372).

16. In *The Excursion* itself Wordsworth attempts to correct for the weaknesses of the wanderer's stance by introducing an institutional authority, the Pastor, who by virtue of his vocation stands in for the dead. A hypothesis: with the Pastor, perhaps the least studied of all of Wordsworth's major personae, he finally discovers a mode of poetry which makes peace with the symbolic, and this fact alters his poetic practice in his later years.

Chapter Five: Characters of Danger and Desire

1. All quotations from MS. JJ are taken from the reading text of the manuscript published in Parrish, The Prelude 1798–1799, 123–30, and will be cited by line number as supplied there.

2. Bewell does not always insist that Wordsworth adheres to the traditions of Enlightenment philosophy; at other times he writes that the poet struggles against it (5) or makes it "a silent, informing impulse" of the poetry (12; see below). Here I take issue less with Bewell's larger argument about Wordsworth than with his reading of the 1799 *Prelude* specifically.

3. Wordsworth's engagement with contemporary theories of education is exemplary in this regard. For a discussion of that engagement and Chandler's important analysis of it, see Chapter Seven.

4. Compare Simpson 116-17 on the "tension between inner and outer forms of determination" and between a conception of a typical or unique selfhood. Simpson rightly links these tensions to the evasive politics of the poem.

5. The poem thus escapes both models of identity discussed by Clifford Siskin in his analysis of "the profound shift from the self as static, metaphysical, and inherited to the rounded, psychological subject capable of . . . limitless self-improvement" and indefinite development (95). One could readily use Siskin's account to contextualize the Enlightenment moral philosophy of such importance to Bewell, for that philosophy largely concerned cultural and psychological development. But Wordsworth deviates from old *and* new models of culture and the self.

6. Thus the curiously suspended interrogative-exclamatory rhetoric of MS. JJ is only a small part of the rhetorical and interpretive instability of *The Prelude*, whose longer version Wordsworth hangs, in an even more visible manner, from the failure to begin described in the opening section (1805, 1.1-271). Evidently, having found neither a divine origin nor an authoritative secular discourse on which to base his text, he is fated to begin with the problem of beginning itself and to repeat this gesture throughout his text (Jay 65; cf. Said 12, 255-59, 377-78). Commenting on other lines in this passage, in which Wordsworth writes that "each most obvious and particular thought" of the soul "Hath no beginning" (2.232-37), Paul Jay points out the "serious paradox" that "in the art of composing a poem that seeks to return to the 'beginning,' he has come to realize that there may in fact be none" (58).

7. In a similar vein, Harold Bloom has written of the "baffled residue of the self" in Romantic poetry ("Internalization" 6) and Geoffrey Hartman of the "ravages of self-consciousness" ("'Anti-Self Consciousness'" 47). Jean-Pierre Mileur takes up these accounts in his discussion of the self-vexing properties of Wordsworthian authorship in *The Excursion* and *The Prelude*, a discussion to which this essay owes much (*Romance* 38-72).

8. Wordsworth's positive reading of hyperbole in this text shares many features with the sublime, which I will discuss explicitly in my treatment of the Simplon Pass episode in Chapter Seven. The following discussion takes for granted what many readers of these episodes have demonstrated by now: that they are less recollections of childhood than constructions of childhood by the adult poet (e.g., Weiskel 178; Magnuson 214) and that, as literary constructions, they are organized in an imagistic, thematic, and rhetorical sequence (e.g. Timothy Bahti "Theft"; Manning "Reading" 96: "It is as if the outlines of a plot at first only shadowily glimpsed had been delayed, split off, and had now begun to emerge"). For a strikingly different use of psychoanalysis in this context, see Richard Onorato, who argues that these episodes emerge from Wordsworth's unconscious obsession with the traumatic loss of his mother in childhood (164-219). Mileur's critique of Onorato is relevant for my argument (*Romance* 62-70).

9. My discussion of the theft episodes takes issue with Hartman's reading of "Nutting" as humanized romance in *Wordsworth's Poetry* 73-75.

10. Unless otherwise noted, all references to Bahti in this chapter are to his essay "Wordsworth's Rhetorical Theft." As Bahti points out, in MS. V, the manuscript text

of the 1799 *Prelude,* "Wordsworth is already revising the text toward the 1805 version," adding to these lines the words, *and they troubled me.* He comments, "In other words, the persona's 'troubling' of nature's moon and stars—a representation of his 'own' troubled 'wish' or 'hope & fear'—is immediately met by a corresponding 'troubling' of himself *by* nature. This symmetrical exchange or 'double trouble' between Wordsworth and nature thus introduces the shift in, or exchange of, thefts that closes the passage" (101). The added words already begin to move the sheer disruptiveness of subjectivity toward the masochistic interplay of the theft scenario. The troubling of the lines on *trouble* bears upon any reading of the lines from the blest babe sequence in Part Two—"For now a trouble came into my mind / From obscure causes" (2.321–22)—and suggests that the use of the word *trouble* there introduces into the sequence, however briefly, the masochistic scenario it attempts to repress.

11. The discussion in Chapter One of the imaginary character of rivalry, and its implication in Girard's analysis of the sacrificial crisis, is relevant here and below.

12. The success of this game does not make the boy into a child of nature, a participant in some spontaneous or unself-conscious celebration. Andrzej Warminski argues that the game remains a signifying practice that requires the boy's mimicry of the hooting, his capacity to have "differentiated (marked) the sound of the owls' hooting from all other unarticulated sounds," to have made this mark into a sign of his own voice, and to have "inscribed [nature's] face with his own name" ("Missed Crossing" 996). Like the infant described by Joseph Sitterson, the boy consciously participates in the game of imaginary signification, playing a version of "*fort da* with his own mirror image," an image that "signifies the infant, but is not confused with the infant by the infant" (104).

13. Similarly, the gravestone scene belongs not to the symbolic but to a certain orientation toward the maternal presence. For an excellent analysis along these lines, see Jacobus *Romanticism* 259–66.

14. The initiation into spacing and syntax may have been of special importance to Wordsworth whose "lack of punctiliousness with regard to punctuation in his early verse is notorious" (Bennett 158). He would rather punctuate with interruptions than with marks. In effect, the episode describes the process of being initiated into a language constituted by interruption and periodic silences, a language of the disfiguring or blockage of speech (cf. Bennett 159). On spacing, see Derrida *Grammatology* 68.

15. On Wordsworth's conception of the picturesque as nature's artifice, particularly in the boy of Winander passage, see Spector.

16. The 1798 edition of *The Rime of the Ancient Mariner,* lines 451–56 (Coleridge *Poetical Works* 540).

17. A similar blending of autoeroticism and castration anxiety takes place in the description of the royalist officer in the 1805 *Prelude* 9.143–64, discussed in Mileur *Romance* 67–69 and in Chapter Eight.

18. W. J. T. Mitchell argues that the theft scenes early in *The Prelude* show that the poem was influenced in part by Rousseau's *Confessions,* which also detail the author's childhood thefts (656–57), not to mention the dangerous supplement of masturbation. But Mitchell does not point out that Wordsworth turns the confession of error into a poetics of errancy or deviance.

19. Bewell also misses the psychoanalytic dimensions of the scene, remarking only

that "Death is always already a cultural idea" (215). The link is even closer; it is through the memorialization of the dead that symbolic culture constructs itself.

20. I discuss the 1805 version of this scene further in Chapter Seven.

21. For a discussion of other poems in which Wordsworth refers to "numerous accidents," see Averill *Suffering* 198–222. Emphasizing passages in *The Ruined Cottage* and "Hart-Leap Well," Averill argues that by 1798 Wordsworth deprecates the sensationalist poetry of accident, but we have already seen how sensationalism continues to excite Margaret and the pedlar, and Wordsworth's use of the Shakespearean phrase in Part One suggests that he is embracing what he elsewhere deplores.

22. One need not detour through *The Tempest* to establish the connection; Manning 91–92 argues that *Othello* directly informs *The Borderers*, especially in the scene in which Marmaduke explains how he came to love Herbert while listening to Idonea's stories of her father's adventures (1.1.62–71; 1842 87–98). By emphasizing the motif of narrative seduction in *Othello* and finding it in *The Borderers*, Manning adds to Parker's reading of the play, richly complicates the usual account of its use of *Othello*, and brings to bear upon the spots of time Parker's reading of both *Othello* and *The Tempest*.

23. Reid 547 points out the echo of *The Ruined Cottage* here: "the nightly damps / Did chill her breast, and in the stormy day / Her tattered clothes were ruffled by the wind" (MS. D 483–85). This passage describes Margaret's condition immediately before her death.

24. For useful discussions of the Penrith Beacon, both of which include a reproduction of the chart of the view from the beacon published by James Clarke in *A Survey of the Lakes*, see Kelley *Aesthetics* 120–21 and Liu *Wordsworth* 100–3, who links the beacon with Bentham's panopticon. Liu, using passages in Wordsworth's *Guide to the Lakes*, argues that Wordsworth wished to locate himself in such a panopticon or site of bureaucratic survey and in effect identified himself with local authority. The spots of time, I think, provide a countertext to the *Guide*, disrupting the beacon's gaze and assimilating it to a far less stable economy of sight.

25. Indeed, a grave marked *not* by a stone but *only* by a name is especially suspect in Wordsworth, who argued that epitaphs should, as far as possible, omit the proper name (see Walker).

26. For an excellent analysis of the subtle changes Wordsworth makes in each of these repetitions, see Armstrong 20–23, 30–36.

27. Even the celebration of a maternal presence in the trance passages of *The Ruined Cottage* return in the third repetition of the images, added in the 1805 version, which associates those images with "the blessed time of early love" and "With those two dear Ones, to my heart so dear," Dorothy Wordsworth and Mary Hutchinson (*Prelude* 11.317, 318). See Heffernan 267–68; Armstrong 34–36.

28. This passage thus highlights the brief hint of anality in the first spot of time, where the child stumbles to a "bottom." Adrienne Donald argues that later Romantics, extending the masochistic logic of Wordsworth's texts (especially "Tintern Abbey"), arrive at a masochistic homoeroticism (245), but the various hints in Part One suggest that such homoeroticism is already present and nearly explicit within Wordsworth's texts.

29. This reading may explain why Wordsworth allows such an astonishing admission to appear in the surface of his text. In our post-Freudian age we are too eager, perhaps,

to accept the poet when he makes such an apparent confession, but that confession seduces us away from the more difficult and less oedipal dynamics of the scene: the youth's attempt to master the father's absence by imagining that he killed him and will receive a divine, fatherly punishment in return.

30. For useful discussions of the Gibbet Moss, see J. Wordsworth *Borders* 57; Kelley *Aesthetics* 120; Liu *Wordsworth* 207–10; and Kneale 133–34.

31. Jacobus *Romanticism* 18 argues that the unknown hand is Wordsworth's, but she concludes too quickly that his attempt is to immortalize himself through an epitaphic name: "Wordsworth, in effect, carves his own name in place of the murderer's, so that it may live for ever. But the price of that immortality is empirical death." Such a reading gravitates toward the Lacanian notion of the symbolic, a nonphenomenal and immortal domain founded upon the symbolic death of the subject, but the scene disrupts precisely that conception of the symbolic. In a Wordsworthian move, Jacobus very quickly assimilates the symbolic to the imaginary, complicating and unsettling her initial argument: "it could be said that the murderer whose name is thus kept alive allows the child to find his own face in that of a dead man" (20).

32. I will discuss the relations between cultural dismemberment and autobiography further, especially with reference to Wordsworth's writing of the revolution, in Chapter Eight.

Chapter Six: Unfinished Covenant

1. It would seem to follow that the chief qualification of the idealized poet in the texts of 1800 is the capacity to read the marks on the landscape and know the stories associated with them rather than, as the pedlar, to read nature itself. But actually Wordsworth introduces the poetics of both nature and of local spots in drafts for *The Recluse* in winter, 1798. For a section relevant to "Michael" see the draft "Not useless do I deem," lines 29–43 (Gill 678; Butler 373). The easy juxtaposition of these apparently divergent poetic modes in this draft suggests that Wordsworth does not change his poetics between 1798 and 1800 as much as alter what he emphasizes within an overall philosophical stance. It also suggests that "Michael" and *The Ruined Cottage* bear a similar relation to the draft passages for *The Recluse*, both fleshing out stances only sketched there. Moreover, both poems are presented as tales told near the place with which they are concerned; like Margaret's story, "Michael" is "not unfit" for "the summer shade" (20–21), perhaps that of the oak tree, which still stands at poem's end. However, as I will suggest later in this chapter, such a philosophical continuity probably masks the continuity of Wordsworth's concern with the dismemberment of culture. Where the earlier tale concerns a shelter that decays, the later concerns a shelter that is never completed. See also note 11 below on "Vaudracour and Julia."

2. For useful discussions of "Michael" in the context of the "Poems on the Naming of Places," see R. Parker "Finishing" and Glen 303–38. On the fragility of the shared memories of any small group of people, see Magnuson 266–67.

3. Concerning this claim, Simpson rightly remarks, "what has come down to us of the sources for the poem suggests that the events that went into it might not have happened so very long ago, nor been so remote" (145). The fact that Wordsworth frames recent or contemporary local history in these terms demonstrates all the more that he

is inventing the fiction of an oral tradition, which may have little or no relation to the actualities of rural life, in order to pose or resolve certain problems concerning the formation of culture.

4. To avoid both confusion and unnecessarily long citation forms, I will cite the two Eilenberg essays as follows: "Wordsworth's 'Michael': The Poetry of Property" as "Property," and " 'Michael,' 'Christabel,' and the Poetry of Possession" as "Possession." The latter essay has since been revised into a chapter in Eilenberg's book *Strange Power of Speech*, which does not include a version of the former. Because Eilenberg treats "Michael" much more extensively in the two essays than in the book, I have elected to work with, and cite, the former.

5. Many critics have pointed out the connection with Abraham: Hartman *Wordsworth's Poetry* 265; Manning 41; Bushnell 246–52; and Levinson 68–72. Eilenberg's reading is a useful corrective to that of Levinson, who writes, "The parallel between *The Akedah* and Wordsworth's explicit narrative breaks down in that Michael, by sending Luke to town, substitutes his son for the land, whereas Abraham had substituted the ram (property) for Isaac" (71). Levinson rightly emphasizes the disjunction between these two stories, but in attributing the disjunction to what Michael actually shares with Abraham—his decision to sacrifice his son—she overlooks the *absence* in "Michael" of an animal substitute for the son. Thus Levinson is correct in her conclusion that the "act of substitution . . . forms the vexed nexus between Michael's history and Abraham's," but in a more complex way than she suggests. The crucial point is not that substitution is "an act which, above all others, organizes economic and human relations in developed capitalist societies" (79), but that with the advent of capitalism one form of substitution (symbolic exchange, i.e., sacrifice and/or gift) gives way to another (economic exchange).

Several critics also point out the connections between "Michael" and the story of Jacob and his sons (Manning 51n; Helms; Eilenberg "Property" 20). For an excellent analysis of the interlinked stories of Jacob, Esau, Joseph, and Benjamin in a way that is relevant to my reading, see Goodhart, who argues that together they deconstruct sacrifice.

6. For a useful discussion of the synonymity of these terms, see Christensen *Machine* 138–41 and Eilenberg *Strange* passim. For a discussion of the relations between the proper name, death, and gift exchange, see Derrida *Ear* 3–19.

7. If Michael must ensure the tradition's survival without resorting to ritual, in effect he will force Luke to submit to the tradition's demands without giving him the inheritance in return. Thus the covenant will not be a rite of gift exchange as much as one of enslavement. This line of speculation is confirmed by Baudrillard's theory of the genealogy of servitude: the prisoner of war becomes a slave when the victor, refusing him the honor of putting him to death, keeps him alive as a slave and thus puts him to the "deferred death" of servitude. Even the worker, the slave who is "emancipated" in order that he may work, is subject to this deferred death, whereby the sacrificial gives way to the economic (*L'échange Symbolique* 68; cf. Locke *Treatise* 13–14). Perhaps Michael releases Luke from Isaac's fate only to condemn him to involuntary servitude, substituting economic abjection for human sacrifice.

8. In this he resembles Coleridge's Geraldine, who is, according to Eilenberg, an instance of pure semiotic "displacement," of "the subversion of identity" ("Possession"

219). In effect, Luke subverts Michael's identity in the way that Geraldine subverts Christabel's; the boy is a much darker kind of second self, one that exposes the radical impropriety and self-alienation of the subject.

9. What takes over for the dead father is the objective institution itself. According to Marx, exchange value is the third thing, which makes commodities exchangeable (Goux 34). As one would expect, this third thing takes over some of the aspects of the dead father; Goux argues that exchange value is homologous with the oedipal father, the phallus, and the monarch (9–63), and in a more rigorous argument, André Orléan demonstrates that the market arrives at prices through the Girardian process of unanimous symbolization. In the form of insurance, this anonymous economic domain takes over for kinship as the system that protects against risk and guarantees the payment of debt. As Michael Friedman points out, after the sinking of the *Earl of Abergavenny* on February 5, 1805—the ship captained by John Wordsworth in which William and Dorothy had invested heavily—"[o]nly insurance preserved the surviving Wordsworths directly from a financial loss such as Michael had suffered indirectly" (187). I should add here that this episode demonstrates that Wordsworth was much more implicated in capitalism than he cared to admit and that his is a classic instance of the general pattern described by Raymond Williams whereby members of the country party profited from the system they despised (46–54). For more on Wordsworth as a businessman, see Douglas, who remarks that after 1813 "a surprising amount of [Wordsworth's] time was lavished on getting and spending" (632).

10. John Locke provides one of the clearest statements of this conception of the self in his chapter "Of Slavery" (*Treatise* 13–14). The implications of such a theory of the individual become clear in the chapter "Of Paternal Power," which is especially relevant in this context: "For every man's children being by nature as free as himself, or any of his ancestors ever were, may, whilst they are in that freedom, choose what society they will join themselves to, what commonwealth they will put themselves under. But if they will enjoy the inheritance of their ancestors, they must take it on the same terms their ancestors had it, and submit to all the conditions annexed to such a possession" (36). Here obligation has become a matter of choice; since there is no such thing as an inherent right of fatherhood, familial relations are no more binding than contractual relations between strangers (37).

11. The resemblances between these two texts are telling, for they deal with the undoing of covenants between the generations and between the sexes in similar ways. As a result, Caruth's essay, which fruitfully complicates Austin's account of the performative utterance, is directly relevant to "Michael" and has influenced my line of argument. Wordsworth begins "Vaudracour and Julia" in terms closely associated with "Michael" (see *Prelude* 9.556–57, 560–70), emphasizing once again a premature inheritance, a vow (of love) which in effect formalizes the undoing or failure of a symbolic act (marriage), and a direct association between vow and birthplace. This illicit vow, like the strange rite of farewell in "Michael," follows from the gap between the father's symbolic and economic status, a gap that makes Vaudracour, like Luke, necessarily improper. The link between these texts points to the common status of the illegitimate child and the disinherited son, of improper sexual and social reproduction. For a useful discussion of "Vaudracour and Julia," see Jacobus *Romanticism* 187–205.

12. Wordsworth's deconstruction of gift exchange contrasts sharply with that of

Jacques Derrida, who argues, in his reading of Mauss, that the cycle of gift and counter-ergift cancels temporality in favor of presence and accordingly that a gift is truly a gift only when the giver expects nothing in return (*Given Time* 13). In refusing the logic of reciprocity, Derrida in effect announces a new law of nonreciprocity or nonobligation, repeating the gesture made by Rivers when he vows not to fulfill obligation, to let others die. (See the discussion in Chapter Two.) In contrast, in *The Borderers* and "Michael" Wordsworth suggests that any subject is necessarily implicated in systems of obligation but that such systems, far from confirming self-presence, are economies of accident, cycles of the untimely and hyperbolic. The point is not to remove action from the domain of obligation but to demonstrate that the latter already obeys the logic of noncoincidence, of a genuinely disruptive temporality. Only in this sense can one say that "[t]he truth of the gift is equivalent to the non-gift or to the non-truth of the gift" (27). For a valuable alternative to Derrida's discussion of gift and temporality (e.g. 41), see Dupuy.

13. Of course, as I remarked above, disruption is necessary to set any plot or narrative in motion. Thus Wordsworth does not shatter narrative at the poem's end, but rather allows the earlier disruption to proliferate, to take over the poem, and thus to escape the normative plot resolution. For a relevant reading of Wordsworth's narrative deviance, see Bennett. As Peter Brooks remarks, to read or write a novel is "to be caught up in the seductive coils of a deviance: to seduce, of course, is to lead from the straight path, to create deviance and transgression." But unlike Stendhal, Brooks's example, who "seduces us through Julien's story, then . . . denounces the seduction" (86–87), Wordsworth is caught by deviance and cannot return to the true path. In fact, he has so much difficulty in finishing the poem that "Michael" remains as incomplete as the sheepfold itself (Parker "Finishing" 59–60), as unfinished and improper as "Christabel," the poem it was written to replace.

14. Perhaps the deepest analogue of "Michael" is *The Borderers*. Michael tells the story of the tradition to Luke in much the same way that Herbert speaks to Matilda; each old man attempts to secure his child's life-long devotion by claiming, either through a good story (about a fire in Antioch) or a symbolic act (substitution of ram for child) that he has saved his child's life. Of course, in each case the claim is illegitimate: Herbert indirectly commits matricide to save his daughter, and Michael cannot find a ram. Luke's dissolution and guilty escape overseas, in turn, parallel the rebellion and guilt of a figure such as Mortimer, who also resists the old man's story and abandons him to an unwitnessed death. The lonely shepherd who haunts the desolate sheepfold is thus another captain or Herbert abandoned where no one can give him any aid.

15. For example, Hartman *Wordsworth's Poetry* 265–66; Manning 48–49; Chandler 167; Page 634; cf. Levinson 74–75.

Chapter Seven: Destruction by Deluge

1. Kelley *Aesthetics* 100–1, 105–6, 111, and 117.

2. In certain respects my argument resembles that of Geraldine Friedman, whose most recent essay I read after drafting this book. Friedman reads the Alpine crossing and the spots of time in relation to the September Massacres episode of *The Prelude*, Book 10, concerned "not so much to recover an occulted historical context as to inquire into how history is conceived and reconceived" ("Letter and Spirit" 485). Unlike Fried-

man, I read these *Prelude* passages in conjunction with earlier texts, but like her I focus not on the effacement of historical trauma but on its inscription in different registers.

3. Job 38.8–11; Psalms 104.5–9; *Paradise Lost* 11.893–94; cf. Jacobus *Romanticism* 279.

4. For an account of Wordsworth's plans and drafts toward the five-book *Prelude*, see Jonathan Wordsworth "Five-Book *Prelude*" and Jarvis. On the relations between the "analogy passage," the Arab dream, and the Snowdon episode, see Kishel, Schell, and Bernhardt-Kabisch 461. Moreover, like the analogy passage, which relies heavily upon Wordsworth's reading in travel literature in preparation for writing *The Recluse*, the Arab dream blends together motifs from a wide variety of sources, including Ovid, Josephus, Descartes, and Cervantes (Kelley "Spirit" 566–78; Ragussis 17–34; Smyser; Most).

5. Insofar as the dream takes the reader outside of the self, it is perhaps appropriate that in 1805 Wordsworth has a friend tell the dream, much as he gives the hallucinatory vision of sacrifice to another voice (*Salisbury Plain* 81).

6. Bahti goes on to argue that the both/neither structure "is itself only another version of *the structure of the rhetorical figure as neither/nor*" (620–21), but this actually simplifies the both/neither structure, in effect reducing it to the neither/nor pole at the expense of the both/and.

7. In this reference to the Moebius strip, Bahti follows Lacan, whom he cites (607). See Lacan "Structure" 192–93. The Moebius strip is not foreign to Wordsworth's texts; it is a more sophisticated version of the "naked guide-post's double head" (*Adventures* 170), one produced when the latter is read as an instance of the both/neither rhetorical structure. Like the double head, the strip is a grammatological object (see Ulmer xii), albeit one that a traveler is less likely to encounter in the landscape or to visualize within a dream. (For a discussion of Lacan which bears indirectly upon "Structure," see Ulmer 189–224.) In this context, one could say that the Arab dream is a grammatological fantasia that captures the functioning of ungrounded signification in the duplicitous images of the Bedouin and his stone and shell.

8. Compare Miller 143: "The originating sound from which all words derive is not a single word but a multiplicity of possible words. . . . The original voice is already double, divided against itself. There is no originating unity or simplicity at the source, but an initial equivocity."

9. Warminski "Missed Crossing" 1003–4 reviews the contradictory readings of the flood waters: Bloom "takes the flood as the threat of Nature to Imagination," whereas Hartman takes it more or less as the opposite. Warminski concludes that the flood is "neither *and* both at once."

10. My reading of the dream owes much to the discussion of the absolute object, dream, seduction, appearance, and destiny in Baudrillard *Fatal* 111–79. Many other features of this text follow Baudrillard's paradigm; the stone and shell are instances of the "absolute object," and the entire dream flows from the poet's fascination with and dread of a destiny he cannot evade: "And yet we feel, we cannot chuse but feel, / That these must perish" (5.20–21). Moreover, unlike the Freudian dream, which one can interpret and make significant with reference to unconscious desire, this episode remains in the domain of appearance and of the pure event (cf. *Fatal* 142). A purely deconstructive reading of the dream which is content with tracing the rhetorical structures of its figures or the way in which it foregrounds its status as pure writing (e.g., Bahti, Miller) fails to

explain, as does Baudrillard, why such a self-reflexive text is so fascinating, so seductive.

11. Using the 1850 version, Bahti points to such moments in the text: "an uncouth shape *appeared*"; "He *seemed* an Arab of the Bedouin tribes"; "While this was uttering" (1850 5.75, 77, 110; Bahti 616, 619). The latter formulation, Bahti comments, is "Neither passive . . nor entirely active" (619). Perhaps it is in the middle voice of an entirely self-reflexive and self-referential language.

12. This extravagant logic is so seductive that by the epilogue (5.140–65) the unreasonable or hyperbolic anxieties of the prologue (51–52) appear to be reasonable: "in the blind and awful lair / Of such a madness, reason did lie couched" (5.151–52). Indeed, the reader-dreamer is now willing to give up what he values in order to save it; like another sailor or Robert who is about to abandon his family, he muses that "Enow there are on earth to take in charge / Their Wives, their Children, and their virgin Loves, / Or whatsoever else the heart holds dear" and imagines that he "Could share that Maniac's anxiousness, could go / Upon like errand" (5.153–55, 160–61).

13. Manning argues that Wordsworth attempts to frame the episode not with allusions to Othello's matricidal tales (as in the 1799 version) but rather with references to the *Arabian Nights*, where Scheherezade tells stories to forestall her own threatened death (109–10). But the passages Manning cites undercut his argument; Wordsworth immediately associates the tales of Araby with Othello's storytelling (5.520–24) and, just as dangerously, with the tales told by old warriors such as Herbert (524–25). Moreover, in the important lines added to the drowned man episode in 1816–19, which Manning also cites, Wordsworth reinforces a darker reading: "The succeeding day, / Those unclaimed garments telling a plain tale / Drew to the spot an anxious crowd; some looked / In passive expectation from the shore, / While from a boat others hung o'er the deep" (1850 5.442–46). Manning rightly comments that "the additions . . . introduce the concept of audience," but this audience, like that of *The Borderers*, has gathered to take an anxious pleasure in the sight of one man's death.

14. Here again I follow Baudrillard, who argues that on some level the real frustrates every discourse that would hope to master it by becoming more real than real. The object reverses the usual dynamic, taking revenge upon the subject and canceling its power to know (*Fatal* 7–24, 81–99).

15. This link with *Oedipus Rex* may not be accidental; one could draw an analogy between errancy and the Oedipus complex. Geraldine Friedman, following Derrida *Margins* 242, reads the latter as an instance of catachresis, "a dis-figured analogy missing one of its four members," a "family where a man's wife and mother are the same person" (*History* 138, 147). Similarly, in this instance errancy is a catachresis in which the path and destination are the same. Wordsworth's persistent inscription of oedipal motifs (such as the violence/inheritance of the griding iron, masturbation/castration, the unreadable name of the father, the complex at the gibbet/crossroads, and the conflation of evasion and fulfillment of the oracle's prophecy) in rhetorical or cultural structures closely associated with catachresis suggests that his radically differs from the familiar Freudian version of the Oedipus complex, one that depends much less on the son's rivalry with the father for the mother's love than on the transposition or reversal of terms in a system of differences, or more simply on the disfigurement of a figural structure.

16. Here again is the middle voice of appearance or generalized uttering in which the Arab dream is written; cf. note 10 above.

17. Thus Peter Schwenger is right to interpret this passage as a thinking of disaster and to point out its affinities with the work of Maurice Blanchot and Emmanuel Levinas (118–19).

18. Liu *Wordsworth* 3–31. Wordsworth may be reworking his poetics for the new historical situation of 1804, extending his interpretation of the war's outbreak to its later forms, but the passage's investment in Napoleonic ambition is not nearly as direct as Liu suggests. One should also keep in mind that the imagery of spectral horsemen along a mountain's face appears in early Wordsworth texts, including his brother Christopher's notebook and in "An Evening Walk" (179–90; see Fink *Milieu* 28–34, 89, 135–37). Wordsworth reworks this imagery in the vision of war in *Salisbury Plain* itself, in the "huge and mighty forms" of the stolen boat episode (1799 1.127), possibly in the Cave of Yordas passage, and as Fink points out, in draft lines of *The Prelude* (*Milieu* 54–55). (De Selincourt, whom Fink cites here, associates these draft lines loosely with 1805 4.68–83 and 1850 4.77–92, but in several important ways they anticipate the imagery and phrasing of the imagination passage of Book 6.) Thus the imagination passage mediates the political and martial history of the Alps through several layers of poetic representation: the Gothic rhetoric of the phantasmatic procession and the complex interpretation of culture offered in the Salisbury Plain poems. Its historical reference is less Napoleon's crossing than the cultural dismemberment in which it and the entire enterprise of war from 1793 onward participate.

19. On darkness and light (as well as blindness and insight) in this passage and throughout *The Prelude*, see Jay 83–91.

20. Compare Kelley *Aesthetics* 105–6. Kneale points out that the phrase *Abyssinian clouds* brings together what is below (the mind's abyss) and what is above (nourishing clouds), height and depth (159).

21. In other words, in this passage the core difficulty is not the relation between imagination and nature, for here as elsewhere in Wordsworth's *oeuvre* they are homologous versions of indeterminacy and self-division. The mind's abyss thwarts the mind's progress, much as nature, via the deluge, inundates itself. One cannot finally distinguish, as Hartman attempts to do, between the threatening and threatened forces, since both imagination and nature threaten themselves.

22. The passage also invokes a murderous scenario in its anticipation of the *Macbeth* allusions of the September Massacres passage (10.46–82), discussed in the next chapter. As Keith Hanley points out, it was Macbeth who "murdered 'the innocent sleep' (2.2.33)" (126).

23. Of course, all of these terms share the both/neither structure and thus in this sentence are incompletely formulated. One should speak of readable unreadability, habitable uninhabitability (or the home in homelessness; cf. the home in infinitude of lines 538–39), and unimaginable imagination, and vice versa. But I trust the reader need not be reminded of the complexity of Wordsworthian poetics at every turn.

24. In configuring Snowdon as a kind of Ararat, Wordsworth oddly anticipates the speculations of Edward Davies, who in *Mythology and Rites of the British Druids* (1809), claims that Snowdon was the landing place of those who escaped from the ancient

flood. According to Davies, Snowdon was a center of an ancient "Helio-arkite" Druid-ism, a debased form of the Biblical patriarchal religion (A. L. Owen 210–17). If, as Liu argues, Snowdon is a specifically Welsh mountain, the emblem of a Welsh nationalism that Wordsworth appropriates for an anti-Napoleonic British nationalism in 1804 ("Subversion" 86–87), it is also a Welsh Ararat, the place where the archaic wanderers survive the deluge and create the primitive nation. Here a number of characteristic Wordsworthian concerns meet: the Rousseauist scenario of postdiluvian wanderers; the neoprimitivist myth of the original rustic, patriarchal state; the anointing of the national bard; and the skewing of all these discourses through the privileged breach in the mist.

Chapter Eight: A Mockery of History

1. Hunt's account owes much to that of Furet. On the relation between the rhetoric of the Girondins and the spirit of the Crusades, see Furet 65–69, 71–72; on the rhetoric of plots, see 53–61.

2. For a related discussion of the blending of political and rural festival, see Hunt's discussion of the Festival of Reason (62–64). Wordsworth relies upon this conflation of the Federation Day, May Day, and comic reconciliation in several other texts, especially the sonnet composed on "August 15, 1802" (which begins, "Festivals have I seen that were not names") and the Intimations Ode, whose first stanzas, as Levinson argues, recall the early years of the revolution (80–100).

3. A major portion of the "romance" section of Book 9 is of course the story of Vaudracour and Julia. Taking issue with Liu and Paulson, Jacobus argues that this tale of illegitimate passion unsettles the generic coherence of *The Prelude* and displays the poem's overall impropriety, its unauthored condition (*Romanticism* 188–89, 204–5). In a more rigorously de Manian vein, Caruth demonstrates that this narrative plays out a figural structure of untimeliness and unknowable acts. The episode refigures romance as unreadable illegitimacy, as unresolvable disruption. In a similar way, as I will argue below, the September Massacres passage in Book 10 refigures tragedy as displacement, unreadability, and masochistic fantasy. In effect, then, Wordsworth invokes traditional genres only to disrupt them according to the consistent but difficult figural structure of unreadability—a kind of antigenre of illegitimacy and irresolution.

4. White's work is doubly relevant in this context because he, like Hunt, depends upon Northrop Frye's theory of genre in his analysis of historical writing (White 7–11; Hunt 34–37). In disrupting the familiar generic categories upon which these critics rely, Wordsworth's text exposes the weaknesses of any anatomy of literature. It does so, how-ever, in a different way than that proposed by Fredric Jameson, who criticizes White's typology of historical narrative on the grounds that it omits "the conceptual link be-tween a purely logical play of variables and resultant forms, and the concrete historical situation in which those possibilities flourish or find themselves excluded from the out-set." The revolution books suggest that the attempt to make such a link will always be undercut by what exceeds genre, what is unaccountable in any given system, and what deviates from any proper form. If, as Jameson argues, historical narrative must rely upon a "mechanism of historical selection" which rejects generic possibilities "that cannot empirically come into being in that determinant historical conjuncture" (160), such nar-rative can never finally describe or interpret the very mechanism from which it origi-

nates, especially if the determinate form of that historical conjuncture still remains unclear; as a result, the highly unstable moment that precedes the decision for any particular genre of narrative cannot itself be incorporated into a narrative and remains excessive, unnameable. This excessive moment transforms the typological *combinatoire* of White *and* Jameson into an anxious confrontation with the unreadable combinatory, much as the Gothic repetitions of *Adventures* dissolve a particular symbolic order into the fearful encounter with the violence of sheer figuration.

5. This passage anticipates the first spot of time (1805), in which the scene of violence is also inscribed with an admonitory but incomprehensible monumental writing (11.295).

6. The passage may also hint at this redundant energy in the line "The horse is taught his manage," which John A. Hodgson has linked with several other passages in Wordsworth's texts concerning the quartering or unleashing of horses, colts, heifers, and people (52–54). To extend his analysis: perhaps this line also refers back to the horses of *Adventures* and "Incipient Madness," those embodiments of haunted, obsessive consciousness, thereby bringing the concerns of those texts into the orbit of this passage.

7. This passage is an instance of what Jacobus calls *Romantic theater.* Jacobus argues that *Macbeth* "became the most demonic, inward, and unactable to the Romantic critics of Shakespeare," such as De Quincey and Lamb, in part because the theatrical representation of murder made it all too real (*Romanticism* 37). Regicidal tragedy is dangerous because the spectators (or, more likely, readers) feel a "dangerous pull toward identification which merges audience and actor, making them feel capable of the murderer's forbidden acts as well as longing to prevent them" (62). Like Schiller's *The Robbers*, which I discussed in Chapter Two, it threatens to captivate the audience with the spectacle of violence and make it complicit in crime. In this passage, Wordsworth suggests that his earlier self fell prey to the sort of fascination he exposed and criticized in *The Borderers;* if that young tourist first displaced violence from the scene of historical action onto tragedy, he then identified with the criminal and imagined that he were Macbeth himself.

8. It is typical of *The Prelude,* however, that Wordsworth identifies with Louvet in this episode rather than making the accusation directly, a fact that complicates the Lacanian model of imaginary relations.

9. On Wordsworth's identification with Robespierre, see Hopkins.

10. Like his revolutionary counterparts in France, the young Wordsworth evidently identified with the classical heroes of liberty mentioned in these lines (Harmodius, Aristogiton, and Brutus). (On this point see Hopkins 119.) Moreover, like both Girondins and Jacobins, he hoped that the new government would model its achievements upon those of "ancient Lawgivers" (188)—probably Solon or Lycurgus, the two most frequently mentioned classical founders of the state (H. Parker 146–70).

11. Although Wordsworth's account of his dreams does not match up perfectly with Freud's discussion of traumatic neurosis in *Beyond the Pleasure Principle* (6–8), it is striking that at least indirectly he associates such dreams with children's play, and both dreams and play with a certain trait of desire, albeit less directly than Freud.

12. As Robert Maniquis points out, the 1850 version of this passage raises the issue of sacrifice explicitly: "And innocent victims sinking under fear, / And momentary hope, and worn-out prayer, / Each in his separate cell, or penned in crowds / For sacri-

fice" (10.404–7). He goes on to remark that in these anxiety dreams and in Wordsworth's version of the Reign of Terror generally the "sacrificial hope of finding in a symbolic exchange some sense of life in death is dissolved by indiscriminate massacre" (380). Maniquis and Liu are right to argue that Wordsworth's depiction of the Terror owes much to contemporary (anti-)sacrificial interpretations of the violence in France (Maniquis; Liu *Wordsworth* 148–63), but neither asks whether this interpretation could have become a term within a discourse concerning the loss of efficacy of symbolic gestures generally. The language of sacrifice is much more than a representation of revolution (cf. Paulson), an ideology that justifies both war and violence (Liu *Wordsworth* 155–59), and an inheritance from the Enlightenment critique of religious mystery (Maniquis 375–79); by claiming that the revolution displayed "a de-symbolized violence" (Maniquis 385), its contemporaries also claimed that it threatened certain fundamental cultural institutions. The terms of this discourse thus ramify beyond the question of sacrifice as such and bear upon contemporary conceptions of literary, political, and religious history.

13. For a relevant critique of Freud's theory of the death drive in *Beyond the Pleasure Principle*, see Bersani 54–67.

14. This passage also complicates the apostasy/conversion problematic of 10.275–89. If the vengeful fantasy is indeed a contemporary version of ancient prophecy, then the new religion *is* the old, and apostasy from ancient creed a way of recapturing it. Thus the passage on the ancient prophets as well as the extensive sequence on prophecy and human sacrifice in 12.278–379, which I discuss below, amplify the terms introduced in the passages concerning England's war with France.

15. As Kneale points out, however, in MS. Z (1805), Books 11 and 12 "are already numbered 12 and 13," suggesting that Wordsworth planned to split Book 10 (1805) up into two books from the start (65).

16. Maniquis points out that in the 1850 version of the "ancient prophets" passage Wordsworth "disentangles himself" from an "awkward complicity" in violence (383).

17. Thus Wordsworth's vengeance against Robespierre does not merely reproduce Robespierre's own form of violence, as Hopkins argues (124); Wordsworth relies upon the fundamental distinction between profane and sacred violence, following the ancient logic described by Girard.

18. The chapel is also reminiscent of those buildings that mark a seafaring vessel's safe arrival in harbor. One might think of the *kirk* to which Coleridge's ancient mariner refers after having survived shipwreck (601–9). More likely antecedents appear in Sonnets I, II, and III of William Lisle Bowles's *Sonnets and Other Poems*. According to the notes to these poems, the ruins of Tynemouth monastery (the subject of Sonnet I) "are situated on a high rocky point, on the north side of the entrance into the river Tyne . . . The exalted rock on which the monastery stood, rendered it visible at sea a long way off, in every direction, whence it presented itself as if exhorting the seamen in danger to make their vows, and promise masses and presents to the Virgin Mary and St. Oswin for their deliverance" (159). Similarly, Bamborough Castle (of Sonnet II) was once the resident of Lord Crewe, bishop of Durham, who ministered "instant relief to such shipwrecked mariners as may happen to be cast on this dangerous coast" (160). The echo of these sonnets in Wordsworth's text refigures the survival of the deluge as the voyager's homecoming; perhaps the female vagrant, the sailor, and the discharged soldier, having

come ashore, will finally find a home. Finally, on the banks of the Wensbeck (of Sonnet III) "is situated our Lady's Chapel," immortalized by Akenside as the site where in childhood he spent "many a summer's day" (160–61). Bowles's three sonnets sketch an incipient narrative akin to that in Book 10; the voyager arrives safely on the very shore where he once played as a child, where he and his crew "beat with thundering hoofs the level Sand" (see 10.559–66; 2.143–44).

19. In the final portion of this series he even pauses to meditate on error itself, claiming that when he erred he did so "on the better part / And in the kinder spirit" (741–42), perhaps because he interpreted both tradition and revolution as instances of error (see 743–47).

20. Jonathan Wordsworth argues that the poet never quite admits that anything impaired his imagination and thus does not allow the myth of fall and redemption to become very pronounced in this text (*Borders* 276; compare also Hodgson 45–48). I arrive at a similar argument, albeit via a rather different path and with a much less idealizing interpretation of the poem in view.

Works Cited

Abrams, M. H. "English Romanticism: The Spirit of the Age." In *Romanticism and Consciousness: Essays in Criticism,* edited by Harold Bloom, 91–119. New York: Norton, 1970.

Arac, Jonathan. *Critical Genealogies: Historical Situations for Postmodern Literary Studies.* New York: Columbia UP, 1987.

Armstrong, Isobel. "Wordsworth's Complexity: Repetition and Doubled Syntax in *The Prelude* Book VI." *Oxford Literary Review* 4.3 (1981): 20–42.

Austin, J. L. *How to Do Things with Words.* 2d ed. Cambridge: Harvard UP, 1975.

Averill, James H. "Wordsworth and 'Natural Science': The Poetry of 1798." *JEGP* 77 (1978): 232–46.

———. *Wordsworth and the Poetry of Human Suffering.* Ithaca: Cornell UP, 1980.

Bahti, Timothy. "Figures of Interpretation, The Interpretation of Figures: A Reading of Wordsworth's 'Dream of the Arab.'" *Studies in Romanticism* 18 (1979): 601–27.

———. "Wordsworth's Rhetorical Theft." In *Romanticism and Language,* edited by Arden Reed, 86–124. Ithaca: Cornell UP, 1984.

Bakhtin, Mikhail. *The Dialogic Imagination: Four Essays,* translated by Caryl Emerson and Michael Holquist and edited by Michael Holquist. Austin: U of Texas P, 1981.

Barron, Jonathan, and Kenneth R. Johnston. "The Pedlar's Guilt." In *Romantic Revisions,* edited by Robert Brinkley and Keith Hanley, 64–86. Cambridge: Cambridge UP, 1992.

Bataille, Georges. *Visions of Excess: Selected Writings, 1927–1939,* translated by Alan Stoekl, Carl R. Lovitt, and Donald M. Leslie, Jr. Minneapolis: U of Minnesota P, 1985.

Baudrillard, Jean. *L'échange symbolique et la mort.* Paris: Gallimard, 1976.

———. *Fatal Strategies,* translated by Philip Beitchman and W. G. J. Niesluchowski. New York: Semiotext(e), 1990.

Bennett, Andrew J. "'Devious Feet': Wordsworth and the Scandal of Narrative Form." *ELH* 59 (1992): 145–73.

Bernhardt-Kabisch, Ernest. "The Stone and the Shell: Wordsworth, Cataclysm, and the Myth of Glaucus." *Studies in Romanticism* 24 (1985): 455–90.

Bersani, Leo. *The Freudian Body: Psychoanalysis and Art.* New York: Columbia UP, 1986.

Bettelheim, Bruno. *The Uses of Enchantment: The Meaning and Importance of Fairy Tales.* New York: Knopf, 1976.

Bewell, Alan. *Wordsworth and the Enlightenment: Nature, Man, and Society in the Experimental Poetry.* New Haven: Yale UP, 1989.

Blakemore, Steven. *Burke and the Fall of Language.* Hanover, N.H.: UP of New England, 1988.

Bloom, Harold. *The Anxiety of Influence: A Theory of Poetry.* New York: Oxford UP, 1973.

———. "The Internalization of Quest Romance." In *Romanticism and Consciousness,* edited by Harold Bloom, 3–24. New York: Norton, 1970.

———. *A Map of Misreading.* New York: Oxford UP, 1973.

Bourdieu, Pierre. *Outline of a Theory of Practice,* translated by Richard Nice. Cambridge: Cambridge UP, 1977.

Bowles, William Lisle. *Sonnets and Other Poems* and *The Spirit of Discovery,* edited by Donald H. Reiman. 1800. New York: Garland, 1978.

Brooks, Peter. *Reading for the Plot: Design and Intention in Narrative.* New York: Vintage, 1985.

Burke, Edmund. *Reflections on the Revolution in France.* 1790, edited by Conor Cruise O'Brien. Harmondsworth, England: Penguin, 1982.

Bushnell, John P. "'Where is the Lamb for a Burnt Offering?': Michael's Covenant and Sacrifice." *Wordsworth Circle* 12 (1981): 246–52.

Butler, James, ed. *The Ruined Cottage* and *The Pedlar.* Ithaca: Cornell UP, 1979.

Butler, Judith. *Gender Trouble: Feminism and the Subversion of Identity.* New York: Routledge, 1990.

Carney, Raymond. "Making the Most of a Mess." *Georgia Review* 35 (1981): 631–42.

Caruth, Cathy. "'Unknown Causes': Poetic Effects." *Diacritics* 17 (1987): 78–85.

Castle, Terry. "The Female Thermometer." *Representations* 17 (1987): 1–27.

———. "The Spectralization of the Other in *The Mysteries of Udolpho.*" In *The New Eighteenth Century: Theory, Politics, English Literature,* edited by Felicity Nussbaum and Laura Brown, 231–53. New York: Methuen, 1987.

Chandler, James K. *Wordsworth's Second Nature: A Study of the Poetry and Politics.* Chicago: U of Chicago P, 1984.

Chard, Leslie, II. *Dissenting Republican: Wordsworth's Early Life and Thought in their Political Context.* The Hague: Mouton, 1972.

Chase, Cynthia. *Decomposing Figures: Rhetorical Readings in the Romantic Tradition.* Baltimore: Johns Hopkins UP, 1986.

Chodorow, Nancy. *The Reproduction of Mothering: Psychoanalysis and the Sociology of Gender.* Berkeley: U of California P, 1978.

Christensen, Jerome. *Coleridge's Blessed Machine of Language.* Ithaca: Cornell UP, 1981.

———. "The Sublime and the Romance of the Other." *Diacritics* 8 (1978): 10–23.

———. "Wordsworth's Misery, Coleridge's Woe: Reading 'The Thorn.'" *Papers on Language and Literature* 16 (1980): 268–86.

Cohen, Philip. "Narrative and Persuasion in *The Ruined Cottage.*" *Journal of Narrative Technique* 8 (1978): 185–99.

Coleridge, Samuel Taylor. *Collected Letters of Samuel Taylor Coleridge,* edited by Earl Leslie Griggs. 6 vols. Vol I. New York: Oxford UP, 1956.

―――. *Poetical Works,* edited by Ernest Hartley Coleridge. Oxford: Oxford UP, 1912.

de Lauretis, Teresa. *Alice Doesn't: Feminism, Semiotics, Cinema.* Bloomington: Indiana UP, 1984.

Deleuze, Gilles. *Masochism: Coldness and Cruelty,* translated by Jean McNeil. New York: Zone, 1989.

de Man, Paul. *Allegories of Reading: Figural Language in Rousseau, Nietzsche, Rilke, and Proust.* New Haven: Yale UP, 1979.

―――. *The Rhetoric of Romanticism.* New York: Columbia UP, 1984.

―――. "Time and History in Wordsworth." *Diacritics* 17 (1987): 4–17.

Derrida, Jacques. *Dissemination,* translated by Barbara Johnson. Chicago: U of Chicago P, 1981.

―――. *The Ear of the Other: Otobiography, Transference, Translation,* translated by Peggy Kamuf and edited by Christie McDonald. Lincoln: U of Nebraska P, 1985.

―――. *Given Time: I. Counterfeit Money,* translated by Peggy Kamuf. Chicago: U of Chicago P, 1992.

―――. *Of Grammatology,* translated by Gayatri Chakravorty Spivak. Baltimore: Johns Hopkins UP, 1976.

―――. *Writing and Difference,* translated by Alan Bass. Chicago: U of Chicago P, 1978.

De Selincourt, Ernest, ed. *The Prelude; or, Growth of a Poet's Mind,* revised by Helen Darbishire. Oxford: Clarendon, 1959.

Donald, Adrienne. "Coming out of the Canon: Sadomasochism, Male Homoeroticism, Romanticism." *Yale Journal of Criticism* 3 (1989): 239–52.

Douglas, Wallace W. "Wordsworth as Business Man." *PMLA* 63 (1948): 625–41.

Dumouchel, Paul, ed. *Violence and Truth: On the Work of René Girard.* Stanford: Stanford UP, 1988.

Dupuy, Jean-Pierre. "Totalization and Misrecognition." Dumouchel 75–100.

Eilenberg, Susan. "'Michael,' 'Christabel,' and the Poetry of Possession." *Criticism* 30 (1988): 205–24.

―――. *Strange Power of Speech: Wordsworth, Coleridge, and Literary Possession.* New York: Oxford UP, 1992.

―――. "Wordsworth's 'Michael': The Poetry of Property." *Essays in Literature* 15 (1988): 13–25.

Ellis, David. *Wordsworth, Freud, and the Spots of Time: Interpretation in* The Prelude. Cambridge: Cambridge UP, 1985.

Emsley, Clive. *British Society and the French Wars, 1793–1815.* Totowa, N.J.: Rowman and Littlefield, 1979.

Erdman, David V. "Wordsworth as Heartsworth; or, Was Regicide the Prophetic Ground of Those 'Moral Questions'?" In *The Evidence of the Imagination: Studies of Interactions between Life and Art in English Romantic Literature,* edited by Donald H. Reiman, Michael C. Jaye, and Betty T. Bennett, 12–41. New York: New York UP, 1978.

Ferguson, Frances. *Wordsworth: Language as Counter-Spirit.* New Haven: Yale UP, 1977.

Fink, Z. S. *The Early Wordsworthian Milieu.* Oxford: Clarendon, 1958.

―――. "Wordsworth and the English Republican Tradition." *JEGP* 47 (1948): 107–26.

Freud, Sigmund. *Beyond the Pleasure Principle,* translated by James Strachey. New York: Norton, 1961.

———. *Collected Papers,* translated by Joan Riviere and edited by James Strachey. 5 vols. New York: Basic Books, 1959.

———. *Totem and Taboo: Some Points of Agreement between the Mental Lives of Savages and Neurotics,* translated by James Strachey. New York: Norton, 1950.

Friedman, Geraldine. "History in the Background of Wordsworth's 'Blind Beggar.'" *ELH* 56 (1989): 125–48.

———. "The Letter and the Spirit of the Law: Wordsworth's Restagings of the French Revolution in 'Carrousel Square' and the First 'Spot of Time.'" *Texas Studies in Literature and Language* 34 (1992): 481–507.

Friedman, Michael H. *The Making of a Tory Humanist: William Wordsworth and the Idea of a Community.* New York: Columbia UP, 1979.

Fry, Paul H. "Disposing of the Body: The Romantic Moment of Dying." *Southwest Review* 71 (1986): 8–26.

Galperin, William H. *Revision and Authority in Wordsworth: The Interpretation of a Career.* Philadelphia: U of Pennsylvania P, 1989.

Gill, Stephen C. "'Adventures on Salisbury Plain' and Wordsworth's Poetry of Protest 1795–97." *Studies in Romanticism* 11 (1972): 48–65.

———, ed. *The Salisbury Plain Poems of William Wordsworth.* Ithaca: Cornell UP, 1975.

Girard, René. *The Scapegoat.* Trans. Yvonne Freccero. Baltimore: Johns Hopkins UP, 1986.

———. *Violence and the Sacred,* translated by Patrick Gregory. Baltimore: Johns Hopkins UP, 1977.

Glen, Heather. *Vision and Disenchantment: Blake's Songs and Wordsworth's Lyrical Ballads.* Cambridge: Cambridge UP, 1983.

Godwin, William. *Caleb Williams,* edited by David McCracken. New York: Norton, 1977.

Gold, Alex, Jr. "It's Only Love: The Politics of Passion in Godwin's *Caleb Williams.*" *Texas Studies in Literature and Language* 19 (1977): 135–60.

Goodhart, Sandor. "'I am Joseph': René Girard and the Prophetic Law." Dumouchel 53–74.

Goux, Jean-Joseph. *Symbolic Economies: After Marx and Freud,* translated by Jennifer Curtiss Gage. Ithaca: Cornell UP, 1990.

Greenblatt, Stephen. *Shakespearean Negotiations: The Circulation of Social Energy in Renaissance England.* Berkeley: U of California P, 1988.

Hall, Stuart. "The Toad in the Garden: Thatcherism among the Theorists." In *Marxism and the Interpretation of Culture,* edited by Cary Nelson and Lawrence Grossberg, 35–73. Urbana: U of Illinois P, 1988.

Hanley, Keith. "Crossings Out: The Problem of Textual Passage in *The Prelude.*" In *Romantic Revisions,* edited by Robert Brinkley and Hanley, 103–35. Cambridge: Cambridge UP, 1992.

Harrison, Gary. "Wordsworth's 'The Old Cumberland Beggar': The Economy of Charity in Late Eighteenth-Century Britain." *Criticism* 30 (1988): 23–42.

Hartman, Geoffrey. "Evening Star and Evening Land." In *The Fate of Reading and Other Essays*, 147–78. Chicago: U of Chicago P, 1975.

———. "Romanticism and 'Anti-Self-Consciousness.'" In *Romanticism and Consciousness*, edited by Harold Bloom, 46–56. New York: Norton, 1970.

———. *The Unremarkable Wordsworth*. Minneapolis: U of Minnesota P, 1987.

———. *Wordsworth's Poetry: 1787–1814*. New Haven: Yale UP, 1971.

Heffernan, James A. W. "The Presence of the Absent Mother in Wordsworth's *Prelude*." *Studies in Romanticism* 27 (1988): 253–72.

Heinzelman, Kurt. "The Cult of Domesticity: Dorothy and William Wordsworth at Grasmere." In *Romanticism and Feminism*, edited by Anne K. Mellor, 52–78. Bloomington: Indiana UP, 1988.

Helms, Randel. "On the Genesis of Wordsworth's *Michael*." *English Language Notes* 15 (1977): 38–43.

Henderson, Andrea. "A Tale Told to be Forgotten: Enlightenment, Revolution, and the Poet in 'Salisbury Plain.'" *Studies in Romanticism* 30 (1991): 71–84.

Hobbes, Thomas. *Leviathan*, edited by C. B. Macpherson. Harmondsworth, England: Penguin, 1968.

Hodgson, John A. "Tidings: Revolution in *The Prelude*." *Studies in Romanticism* 31 (1992): 45–70.

Homans, Margaret. *Bearing the Word: Language and Female Experience in Nineteenth-Century Women's Writing*. Chicago: U of Chicago P, 1986.

———. *Women Writers and Poetic Identity: Dorothy Wordsworth, Emily Brontë, and Emily Dickinson*. Princeton: Princeton UP, 1980.

Hopkins, Brooke. "Representing Robespierre." In *History & Myth: Essays on English Romantic Literature*, edited by Stephen C. Behrendt, 116–29. Detroit: Wayne State UP, 1990.

Hunt, Lynn. *Politics, Culture, and Class in the French Revolution*. Berkeley: U of California Press, 1984.

Jacobus, Mary. *Romanticism, Writing, and Sexual Difference: Essays on* The Prelude. Oxford: Clarendon, 1989.

———. *Tradition and Experiment in Wordsworth's* Lyrical Ballads *(1798)*. Oxford: Clarendon, 1976.

Jameson, Fredric. *Situations of Theory*. Vol. 1 of *The Ideologies of Theory: Essays 1971–1986*. 2 vols. Minneapolis: U of Minnesota, 1988.

Jarvis, Robin. "The Five-Book *Prelude*: A Reconsideration." *JEGP* 80 (1981): 528–51.

Jay, Paul. *Being in the Text: Self-Representation from Wordsworth to Roland Barthes*. Ithaca: Cornell UP, 1984.

Jewett, William. "Action in *The Borderers*." *Studies in Romanticism* 27 (1988): 399–410.

Johnson, Barbara. "My Monster/My Self." *Diacritics* 12 (1982): 2–10.

Johnston, Kenneth R. *Wordsworth and* The Recluse. Yale UP, 1984.

Jordan, John E. *Why the* Lyrical Ballads?: *The Background, Writing, and Character of Wordsworth's 1798* Lyrical Ballads. Berkeley: U California P, 1976.

Jordan, Winthrop D. "Familial Politics: Thomas Paine and the Killing of the King, 1776." *Journal of American History* 60 (1973): 294–308.

Kant, Immanuel. *Critique of Judgment*, translated by J. H. Bernard. New York: Hafner, 1951.

Kelley, Theresa M. "Spirit and Geometric Form: The Stone and the Shell in Words-worth's Arab Dream." *Studies in English Literature* 22 (1982): 623–52.

———. *Wordsworth's Revisionary Aesthetics.* Cambridge: Cambridge UP, 1988.

King, Francis. "Love and Landscape in Wordsworth." *The Wordsworth Circle* 18 (1987): 12–18.

Kishel, Joseph F. "The 'Analogy Passage' from Wordsworth's Five-Book *Prelude.*" *Studies in Romanticism* 18 (1979): 271–85.

Klancher, Jon. *The Making of English Reading Audiences, 1790–1832.* Madison: U of Wisconsin P, 1987.

Knapp, Steven. *Personification and the Sublime: Milton to Coleridge.* Cambridge: Harvard UP, 1985.

Kneale, J. Douglas. *Monumental Writing: Aspects of Rhetoric in Wordsworth's Poetry.* Lincoln: U of Nebraska P, 1988.

Kristeva, Julia. *Revolution in Poetic Language,* translated by Margaret Waller. New York: Columbia UP, 1984.

Lacan, Jacques. *Écrits: A Selection,* translated by Alan Sheridan. New York: Norton, 1977.

———. *The Four Fundamental Concepts of Psychoanalysis,* translated by Alan Sheridan and edited by Jacques-Alain Miller. New York: Norton, 1981.

———. "Of Structure as an Inmixing of an Otherness Prerequisite to Any Subject Whatever." In *The Structuralist Controversy: The Languages of Criticism and the Sciences of Man,* edited by Richard Macksey and Eugenio Donato, 186–200. Baltimore: Johns Hopkins UP, 1972.

Laclau, Ernesto. "Metaphor and Social Antagonisms." In *Marxism and the Interpretation of Culture,* edited by Cary Nelson and Lawrence Grossberg, 249–57. Urbana: U of Illinois P, 1988.

Laclau, Ernesto, and Chantal Mouffe. *Hegemony and Socialist Strategy: Towards a Radical Democratic Politics.* New York: Verso, 1985.

Laplanche, Jean. *Life & Death in Psychoanalysis,* translated by Jeffrey Mehlman. Baltimore: Johns Hopkins, 1976.

Lea, Sydney. "Wordsworth and His 'Michael': The Pastor Passes." *ELH* 45 (1978): 55–68.

Leask, Nigel. *The Politics of Imagination in Coleridge's Critical Thought.* New York: St. Martin's, 1988.

Levinson, Marjorie. *Wordsworth's Great Period Poems: Four Essays.* Cambridge: Cambridge UP, 1986.

Litvak, Joseph. "Back to the Future: A Review-Article on the New Historicism, Deconstruction, and Nineteenth-Century Fiction." *Texas Studies in Literature and Language* 30 (1988): 120–49.

Liu, Alan. "Wordsworth and Subversion, 1793–1804: Trying Cultural Criticism." *Yale Journal of Criticism* 2 (1989): 55–100.

———. *Wordsworth: The Sense of History.* Stanford: Stanford UP, 1989.

Locke, John. *An Essay Concerning Human Understanding,* edited by Peter H. Nidditch. Oxford: Clarendon, 1975.

———. *The Second Treatise of Civil Government* and *A Letter Concerning Toleration,* edited by J. W. Gough. Oxford: Basil Blackwell, 1948.

MacLean, Kenneth. *Agrarian Age: A Background for Wordsworth*. New Haven: Yale UP, 1950.

Magnuson, Paul. *Coleridge and Wordsworth: A Lyrical Dialogue*. Princeton: Princeton UP, 1988.

Maniquis, Robert. "Holy Savagery and Wild Justice: English Romanticism and the Terror." *Studies in Romanticism* 28 (1989): 365–95.

Mann, Paul. "*The Book of Urizen* and the Horizon of the Book." In *Unnam'd Forms: Blake and Textuality*, edited by Nelson Hilton and Thomas A. Vogler, 49–68. Berkeley: U of California P, 1986.

Manning, Peter J. *Reading Romantics: Texts and Contexts*. New York: Oxford UP, 1990.

Marshall, David. "The Eye-Witnesses of *The Borderers*." *Studies in Romanticism* 27 (1988): 391–98.

Mauss, Marcel. *The Gift: Forms and Functions of Exchange in Archaic Societies*, translated by Ian Cunnison. New York: Norton, 1967.

Mayo, Robert. "The Contemporaneity of the *Lyrical Ballads*." *PMLA* 69 (1954): 486–522.

McGann, Jerome. *The Romantic Ideology: A Critical Introduction*. Chicago: U of Chicago P, 1983.

Mellor, Anne K. *Romanticism & Gender*. New York: Routledge, 1993.

Mileur, Jean-Pierre. *The Critical Romance: The Critic as Reader, Writer, Hero*. Madison: U of Wisconsin P, 1990.

———. *Literary Revisionism and the Burden of Modernity*. Berkeley: U of California P, 1985.

———. *Vision and Revision: Coleridge's Art of Immanence*. Berkeley: U of California P, 1982.

Miller, J. Hillis. "The Stone and the Shell: The Problem of Poetic Form in Wordsworth's Dream of the Arab." In *Mouvements Premiers: Études critiques offertes à Georges Poulet*, 125–47. Paris: Librairie José Corti, 1972.

Milton, John. *Complete Poems and Major Prose*, edited by Merritt Y. Hughes. Indianapolis: Odyssey P, 1957.

Mink, Louis O. "Narrative Form as a Cognitive Instrument." In *The Writing of History: Literary Form and Historical Understanding*, edited by Robert H. Canary and Henry Kozicki, 129–49. Madison: U of Wisconsin P, 1978.

Mitchell, W. J. T. "Influence, Autobiography, and Literary History: Rousseau's *Confessions* and Wordsworth's *The Prelude*." *ELH* 57 (1990): 643–64.

Moi, Toril. "The Missing Mother: The Oedipal Rivalries of René Girard." *Diacritics* 12 (1982): 21–31.

———. *Sexual/Textual Politics: Feminist Literary Theory*. New York: Methuen, 1985.

Morkan, Joel. "Structure and Meaning in *The Prelude*, Book V." *PMLA* 87 (1972): 246–54.

Most, Glenn W. "Wordsworth's 'Dream of the Arab' and Cervantes." *English Language Notes* 22.3 (1985): 52–58.

Nehamas, Alexander. *Nietzsche: Life as Literature*. Cambridge: Harvard UP, 1985.

Newlyn, Lucy. *Coleridge, Wordsworth, and the Language of Allusion*. Oxford: Clarendon, 1986.

Nietzsche, Friedrich. *On the Genealogy of Morals* and *Ecce Homo*, translated by Walter Kaufmann. New York: Vintage, 1967.

Onorato, Richard J. *The Character of the Poet: Wordsworth in* The Prelude. Princeton: Princeton UP, 1971.

Orléan, André. "Money and Mimetic Speculation." Dumouchel 101–12.

Osborn, Robert, ed. *The Borderers.* Ithaca: Cornell UP, 1982.

Owen, A. L. *The Famous Druids: A Survey of Three Centuries of English Literature on the Druids.* Oxford: Oxford UP, 1962. Rpt. Westport, Conn.: Greenwood, 1979.

Owen, W. J. B., and Jane Worthington Smyser, eds. *The Prose Works of William Wordsworth.* 3 vols. Oxford: Clarendon, 1974.

Page, Judith W. "'A History / Homely and Rude': Genre and Style in Wordsworth's 'Michael.'" *Studies in English Literature* 29 (1989): 621–36.

Paine, Thomas. *Rights of Man.* 1791, 1792. Harmondsworth, England: Penguin, 1984.

Parker, Harold T. *The Cult of Antiquity and the French Revolutionaries: A Study in the Development of the Revolutionary Spirit.* Chicago: U of Chicago P, 1937.

Parker, Reeve. "Finishing off 'Michael': Poetic and Critical Enclosures." *Diacritics* 17 (1987): 53–64.

———. "Reading Wordsworth's Power: Narrative and Usurpation in *The Borderers. ELH* 54 (1987): 299–331.

———. "'In some sort seeing with my proper eyes': Wordsworth and the Spectacles of Paris." *Studies in Romanticism* 27 (1988): 369–90.

Parrish, Stephen Maxfield. *The Art of the* Lyrical Ballads. Cambridge: Harvard UP, 1973.

———, ed. The Prelude, *1798–1799.* Ithaca: Cornell UP, 1977.

Paulson, Ronald. *Representations of Revolution (1789–1820).* New Haven: Yale UP, 1983.

Pinch, Adela. "Female Chatter: Meter, Masochism, and the *Lyrical Ballads." ELH* 55 (1988): 835–52.

Pocock, J. G. A. *Virtue, Commerce, and History: Essays on Political Thought and History, Chiefly in the Eighteenth Century.* Cambridge: Cambridge UP, 1985.

Ragussis, Michael. *The Subterfuge of Art: Language and the Romantic Tradition.* Baltimore: Johns Hopkins UP, 1978.

Reed, Arden. *Romantic Weather: The Climates of Coleridge and Baudelaire.* UP of New England: Hanover, N.H., 1983.

Reed, Mark. *Wordsworth: The Chronology of the Early Years, 1770–1799.* Cambridge: Harvard UP, 1967.

Reid, Ian. "'A Naked Guide-Post's Double Head': The Wordsworthian Sense of Direction." *ELH* 43 (1976): 538–50.

Richardson, Alan. *A Mental Theater: Poetic Drama and Consciousness in the Romantic Age.* University Park: Pennsylvania State UP, 1988.

Rieder, John. "Civic Virtue and Social Class at the Scene of Execution: Wordsworth's Salisbury Plain Poems." *Studies in Romanticism* 30 (1991): 325–43.

Robbins, Caroline. *The Eighteenth-Century Commonwealthman: Studies in the Transmission, Development and Circumstances of English Liberal Thought from the Restoration of Charles II until the War with the Thirteen Colonies.* Cambridge: Harvard UP, 1959.

Roe, Nicolas. *Wordsworth and Coleridge: The Radical Years.* Oxford: Clarendon, 1988.

Ross, Marlon. *The Contours of Masculine Desire: Romanticism and the Rise of Women's Poetry.* New York: Oxford UP, 1989.

Rubin, Gayle. "The Traffic in Women: Notes on the 'Political Economy' of Sex." In *Toward an Anthropology of Women*, edited by Rayna R. Reiter, 157–210. New York: Monthly Review P, 1975.

Rzepka, Charles J. *The Self as Mind: Vision and Identity in Wordsworth, Coleridge, and Keats*. Cambridge: Harvard UP, 1986.

Sahlins, Marshall. *Stone Age Economics*. Chicago: Aldine Atherton, 1972.

Said, Edward. *Beginnings: Intention and Method*. New York: Columbia UP, 1975.

Scarry, Elaine. *The Body in Pain: The Making and Unmaking of the World*. New York: Oxford UP, 1985.

Schama, Simon. *Citizens: A Chronicle of the French Revolution*. New York: Knopf, 1989.

Schell, Richard. "Wordsworth's Revisions of the Ascent of Snowdon." *Philological Quarterly* 54 (1975): 592–603.

Schulman, Samuel. "Wordsworth's Salisbury Plain Poems and their Spenserian Motives." *JEGP* 84 (1985): 221–42.

Schwenger, Peter. *Letter Bomb: Nuclear Holocaust and the Exploding Word*. Baltimore: Johns Hopkins UP, 1992.

Sedgwick, Eve Kosofsky. *Between Men: English Literature and Male Homosocial Desire*. New York: Columbia UP, 1985.

Silverman, Kaja. *Male Subjectivity at the Margins*. New York: Routledge, 1992.

Simpson, David. *Wordsworth's Historical Imagination: The Poetry of Displacement*. New York: Methuen, 1987.

Siskin, Clifford. *The Historicity of Romantic Discourse*. New York: Oxford UP, 1988.

Sitterson, Joseph C., Jr. "Oedipus in the Stolen Boat: Psychoanalysis and Subjectivity in *The Prelude*." *Studies in Philology* 86 (1989): 96–115.

Smyser, Jane Worthington. "Wordsworth's Dream of Poetry and Science: *The Prelude*, V." *PMLA* 71 (1956): 269–75.

Spector, Stephen J. "Wordsworth's Mirror Imagery and the Picturesque Tradition." *ELH* 44 (1977): 85–107.

Springer, Carolyn. "Far From the Madding Crowd: Wordsworth and the News of Robespierre's Death." *Wordsworth Circle* 12 (1981): 243–45.

Storch, R. F. "Wordsworth's *The Borderers*: The Poet as Anthropologist." *ELH* 36 (1969): 340–60.

Swann, Karen. "Public Transport: Adventuring on Wordsworth's Salisbury Plain." *ELH* 55 (1988): 811–34.

———. "Suffering and Sensation in *The Ruined Cottage*." *PMLA* 106 (1991): 83–95.

Thorslev, Peter J. "Wordsworth's *Borderers* and the Romantic Villain-Hero." *Studies in Romanticism* 5 (1966): 84–103.

Ulmer, Gregory. *Applied Grammatology: Post(e)-Pedagogy from Jacques Derrida to Joseph Beuys*. Baltimore: Johns Hopkins UP, 1985.

Walker, Eric C. "Wordsworth as Prose Biographer." *JEGP* 89 (1990): 330–44.

Warminski, Andrzej. "Facing Language: Wordsworth's First Poetic Spirits." *Diacritics* 17 (1987): 18–31.

———. "Missed Crossing: Wordsworth's Apocalypses." *Modern Language Notes* 99 (1984): 983–1006.

Weiskel, Thomas. *The Romantic Sublime: Studies in the Structure and Psychology of Transcendence*. Baltimore: Johns Hopkins UP, 1976.

White, Hayden. *Metahistory: The Historical Imagination in Nineteenth-Century Europe.* Baltimore: Johns Hopkins UP, 1973.

Williams, John. "*Salisbury Plain:* Politics in Wordsworth's Poetry." *Literature and History* 9 (1983): 164–93.

———. *Wordsworth: Romantic Poetry and Revolution Politics.* New York: Manchester UP, 1989.

Williams, Raymond. *The Country and the City.* New York: Oxford UP, 1973.

Wolfson, Susan. *The Questioning Presence: Wordsworth, Keats, and the Interrogative Mode in Romantic Poetry.* Ithaca: Cornell UP, 1986.

Woolford, John. "Wordsworth Agonistes." *Essays in Criticism* 31 (1981): 27–40.

Wordsworth, Dorothy. *Journals of Dorothy Wordsworth,* edited by Mary Moorman. New York: Oxford UP, 1971.

Wordsworth, Jonathan. "The Five-Book *Prelude* of Early Spring 1804." *JEGP* 76 (1977): 1–25.

———. *The Music of Humanity.* New York: Harper, 1969.

———. *William Wordsworth: The Borders of Vision.* Oxford: Clarendon, 1982.

———. "A Wordsworth Tragedy." *Times Literary Supplement* 21 July 1966: 642.

Wordsworth, Jonathan, M. H. Abrams, and Stephen Gill. The Prelude: *1799, 1805, 1850.* New York: Norton, 1979.

Wordsworth, William. *Poetical Works,* edited by Ernest de Selincourt. 5 vols. Oxford: Oxford UP, 1940.

Wordsworth, William and Dorothy. *The Early Letters of William and Dorothy Wordsworth (1787–1805),* edited by Ernest de Selincourt. Oxford: Clarendon, 1935.

Index